Thank you very much for your support during my study in Liverpool.

With best wishes

Zhenquan Wang

FOREIGN INVESTMENT AND ECONOMIC DEVELOPMENT IN HUNGARY AND CHINA

For my mother and my wife

Foreign Investment and Economic Development in Hungary and China

ZHEN QUAN WANG
Centre for Central and Eastern European Studies,
The University of Liverpool, and
Lingnan College, Hong Kong

Avebury

Aldershot • Brookfield USA • Hong Kong • Singapore • Sydney

Published by
Avebury
Ashgate Publishing Limited
Gower House
Croft Road
Aldershot
Hants GU11 3HR
England

Ashgate Publishing Company
Old Post Road
Brookfield
Vermont 05036
USA

A CIP catalogue record for this book is available from the British Library

Library of Congress Catalog Card Number: 95-78518

ISBN 1 85972 245 8

10030912042

Printed and bound in Great Britain by
Ipswich Book Co. Ltd., Ipswich, Suffolk

Contents

Figures and tables

Foreword

It is a formidable task to be invited to write a concise foreword to such a very informative and thought-provoking work.

This book presents the results of a research project supported by the Centre for Central & Eastern European Studies at the University of Liverpool. It investigated the course and the consequences of foreign direct investment (FDI) in the process of economic development and systemic transformation in the economies of Hungary and China from centrally planned to market-oriented systems. The subject is controversial. Viewpoints range from those who believe that foreign investment is the primary engine of economic development, to those who feel that it inhibits or even prevents indigenous industrialisation in developing countries. However, there is no reason to assume a zero sum game. Under a wide range of circumstances, given both clearly specified goals on the part of host countries and an ability to predict the effects of foreign investment on the process of development and transformation, a mutually beneficial outcome should be attainable. There exists a pressing need for an empirical analysis of FDI in the transitional economies. This book is, therefore, timely and especially valuable. It represents the first comparative study of FDI and economic development in Hungary and China during 1979-92.

This book is divided in three main sections. In the first section, the author provides an up-to-date analysis on both FDI policy/regulation, and FDI's extent and trends in two selected transforming economies - Hungary and China during 1978-95. The second section involves an investigation of the determinants of FDI using a simple one-equation model. The third section deals with the economic consequences of foreign investment on the process of economic development and transformation in Hungary and China. It consists of an insightful review of FDI policy, FDI's pattern and trends in Hungary and China, an easy understanding quantitative analysis and supplementing by questionnaire survey of Western investor's experience and prospects.

The author provides a range of interesting results and implications on foreign investment in Hungary and China. An attempt is made to develop and test a one-equation model to specify the determinants of foreign investment in Hungary and China. FDI is treated as a dependent variable and an attempt is made to find the causal relationships between FDI activity and different determinants, as shown in Chapter 4. FDI is then treated as a independent variable in Chapters 7 and 8 in order to determine its impacts on various other economic variables, including economic growth rates and international trade. Empirical tests of this sort reveal that foreign capital inflows play a positive role in the economic development of economies undergoing transformation. The size of the domestic market and relatively cheap labour are generally positively related with FDI inflows in both countries, while the cost-of-capital and political instability are found to be negatively correlated with capital inflows. Though there was a bigger difference between these two sample countries, the role of foreign capital in Hungary and China has grown rapidly and substantially over the past decade, and is found to be positively correlated with economic growth and international trade in both countries. It could be concluded that from an economic perspective the case in favour of a further open policy towards FDI remains strong.

This book is carefully researched and fully documented. It will be of particular interest to specialists and non-specialists in international investment/trade, the economics of Eastern Europe and China, as well as policy makers.

W.Robert Lee, Chaddock Professor
Dr. Nigel J. Swain
Directors
Centre for Central & Eastern European Studies
The University of Liverpool
June 1995

Acknowledgements

This book, a modified version of my PhD dissertation, is a product of research carried out at the Centre for Central & Eastern European Studies, the University of Liverpool. As it has been 'in the mill' for more than three years, I have benefited extensively from suggestions and constructive criticism on the part of many colleagues and conference participants - too large to be adequately summarised in a reasonable preface.

Without naming individuals, I would like to thank many economists and officers of the following institutions: Hungarian Central Statistical Office, Institute for World Economics of Hungarian Academy of Sciences, Agency for International Trade and Investment Promotion, the Hungarian Ministry of International Economic Relations, Kopint-Datorg Economic Research, Marketing and Computing Co. in Budapest. Colleagues in all of these institutions readily and generously provided invaluable and unpublished material, statistics and papers on foreign investment in Hungary.

I am furthermore indebted to those project managers of the western corporations for their helpful collaboration in completing the comprehensive questionnaire on foreign investment in Hungary and China, which was conducted in 1992.

I would like to thank Bob Parry MP, Paul Morris, Bernard J.Foley, Richard J.R. Kirkby, Larry Neil, Andrew Douglas, Panos Michael, Zhu Yiandong, Gill Wilson, Val Dodd, Helen Clarke, Richard Heard, Barbara Schwarz and Mark Pittaway in Liverpool for their constant encouragement and invaluable assistance. I am also grateful to my former tutors, Zhou Zimei, Chen Zhian, Hu Shikai, Zhuang Dejun, Lin Zhirong and Peng Xun for the knowledge and inspiration they gave me during my undergraduate and graduate years at Shandong University; to my former colleagues at Research Centre for Economic Development of the State Council of the People's Republic of China, China International Trust & Investment Corporation

(CITIC) and UNIDO Investment Promotion Service Warsaw Office for their valuable support and encouragement.

Continued academic encouragement, indispensable advice and unswerving support from my supervisors Professor W.Robert Lee and Dr.Nigel J.Swain helped to keep this study alive. I must acknowledge my greatest debt and extend my deepest gratitude. This book would not have been written without the support of the Centre for Central & Eastern European Studies of the University of Liverpool by providing me with such a well structured and supportive research environment. Financial support in the form of the Vice-Chancellor's Scholarship from the University in 1991, and successive Individual Mobility Grants from the EC TEMPUS, a small grant from the Great Britain - China Educational Trust, the Overseas Research Studentship from the Council of Vice-Chancellors and Principles (CVCP) and finally the two-year Research Development Fund Studentship from the University of Liverpool have made possible the study's completion. My debts to Professor W.Robert Lee, Professor Peter N.Davies and Dr.Nigel J.Swain, through whose efforts the preceding grants had been obtained, is greater than simple financial calculations can show.

Further, I wish to thank Anne Keirby and Sarah Markham of the publisher as well as their staff for their helpful assistance in preparing the manuscript and for expediting the publication process.

Finally, I owe a great debt to my wife, my family and one of my best friends Simon Xinming Wu for their tremendous interest in my work, constant support and encouragements over the last few years. Without their constant consideration and moral support, the book would have taken far longer to complete.

The debt which remains unstated, therefore, is a good deal greater than that which can be acknowledged.

All thanks, of course, must be coupled with my own acceptance of full responsibility for the final product, and especially so for the remaining errors, either technical, or conceptual, or interpretative, that remain.

Zhen Quan Wang
Liverpool and Hong Kong
June 1995

Abbreviations

ASEAN:	Association of South-East Asian Nations
BJC:	Beijing Jeep Corporation
BOT:	Build-Operate-Transfer
CCP:	China Communist Party
CEE:	Central and Eastern Europe
CJVs:	Contractual Joint Ventures
CMEA:	Community for Mutual Economic Assistance
COFERT:	Committee of Foreign Economic Relations and Trade
CPEs:	Centrally Planned Economies
DCs:	Developed Countries
EBRD:	European Bank for Reconstruction and Development
EC:	European Community
EEC:	European Economic Community
ECE:	Economic Commission for Europe
EJVL:	Equity Joint Venture Law
EJVs:	Equity Joint Ventures
EOCAs:	Economically Opened Coastal Areas
EPT:	Entrepreneur's Profit Tax
EPZs:	Export Processing Zones
ETDAs:	Economic & Technology Development Areas
FCI:	Foreign Capital Inflows
FDI:	Foreign Direct Investment
FIEs:	Foreign Invested Enterprises
Ft:	Forint (Hungarian local currency)
FTOs:	Foreign Trade Organisations
FWOEs:	Foreign Wholly-owned Enterprises
G-5:	The United States, the United Kingdom, Japan, Germany and France

GATT:	General Agreement on Tariffs and Trade
GDP:	Gross Domestic Products
GI:	Gross Investment
GNP:	Gross National Product
IFC:	International Fund Corporation
IMF:	International Monetary Fund
JVs:	Joint Ventures
KSH:	Hungarian Central Statistic Office
LDCs:	Less Developed Countries
Ltd:	Limited Company
MNCs:	Multinational Corporations
MOFERT:	Ministry of Foreign Economic Relations and Trade in China
MOFTEC:	Ministry of Foreign Trade & Economic Cooperation in China
NBH:	National Bank of Hungary
NEM:	New Economic Mechanism
NICs:	Newly Industrialising Countries
OECD:	Organisation for Economic Cooperation and Development
OCCs:	Open Coastal Cities
OCPs:	Open Coastal Provinces
OLS:	Ordinary Least Squares
PCEs:	Post-Communist Economies
Plcs:	Public Limited Companies
PRC:	The People's Republic of China
R & D:	Research & Development
RMB:	Renminbi, Chinese Yuan
SAIC:	State Administration for Industry & Commerce
SEZs:	Special Economic Zones
SOEs:	State-owned Enterprises
SPA:	State Privatisation Agency
TDZs:	Technological Development Zones
UNCTAD:	United Nations Conference on Trade and Development
UNCTC:	United Nations Council for Transnational Corporations
VAT:	Value Added Tax
WTO:	World Trade Organisation

1 Introduction

Few countries have witnessed such a rapid change in policies and economic performance as Hungary and China in recent decades. Indeed, Hungary and China have both attracted considerable foreign investment throughout the transformation period. There exists, therefore, a pressing need for empirical analysis of the determinants and impacts of foreign capital on economic development and system transformation in these two transforming economies.

In this introductory chapter, we present the structure of the research, examine why it is appropriate to compare Hungary and China, the need for a study of this kind, and the research methods applied.

The importance of FDI and the choice of Hungary and China

Why this study is needed

After 1989, Hungary and China have been considered as the biggest magnets within post-socialist economies in attracting inward foreign capitals. By the end of February 1993, Hungary attracted US$23 billion external foreign loans and US$6 billion foreign direct investment (FDI)[1]. By the end of 1992, China attracted US$100 billion pledged FDI and US$52.34 billion indirect investment. The rapid growth of FDI in Hungary and China reflects its increasing importance for economic policy-making in these countries. There exists, therefore, a pressing need for an empirical analysis of FDI. More interestingly, during the period of 1978-92, Hungary enjoyed a very slow economic growth rate, while China's economy grew on average by 8.8 per cent during 1977-91 and about 13 per cent in 1992.[2] So this raises a problem of whether these foreign capital inflows played a different and yet positive role in the process of economic growth in both Hungary and China during 1978-

1

Many past studies of FDI and joint ventures (JVs) in the Soviet Union and Eastern Europe, as well as in China, have been characterised by a descriptive, practical, institutional and/or legalistic approach, which, with few exceptions, lack a theoretical or analytical framework. Two recent studies have compared FDI in various Eastern European countries[3], but no systematic and empirical comparison has so far been carried out to test the determinants of FDI and to fully assess how FDI has affected economic growth and transformation. This book has been designed to fill this gap and to facilitate a focused consideration of this important topic.

This book will provide a systematic evaluation of the determinants and effects of foreign capital on economic development and system transformation in both Hungary and China during 1978-92, in order to improve our knowledge and understanding of the determinants and the impact of FDI in the economic development process of transforming economies from centrally planning to market systems. More specifically, it presents a theoretical and empirical analysis of FDI in terms of the host country's legislative framework and FDI's pattern, the determinants of FDI, and its contribution to economic development in Hungary and China. By applying new theories of international multinationals (MNCs) and development economics to empirical evidence from Hungary and China, this book attempts to offer a critical analysis of the determinants of foreign capital inflows in both Hungary and China and their impact on economic growth, imports, and exports. It is important to discover whether foreign capital contributes to economic growth rates and exports and is not restricted to import-competing sectors. This is not a simple task. On the one hand, the researcher suffers from the undoubted shortage of data for Hungary and China. On the other, the positive or negative impact of FDI on the development process may depend very much on the economic policy climate within which MNCs operate (Ahiakpor, 1990, p.xi).

The choice of Hungary and China

This book focuses on the subject of FDI in the process of economic development and system transformation of our two sample countries - Hungary and China. Although differences exist in terms of the scale of political change, their inherited economic structure, natural resources, labour supply, foreign trade orientation and integration in the world market, the timing and the implementation of their transformation process, Hungary and China share a similar background of a Centrally Planned Economy (CPE). Hungary and China have been selected for the purpose of this analysis, because they shared the similar starting point of Stalinist Central Planning, the historical process of economic reform has been characterised by important similarities although also noteworthy differences, and their early and gradual move towards economic reform beginning from the 1970s has attracted a large share of FDI. On the one hand, both countries witnessed a drive to achieve high growth rates of industrial output, based on the creation and expansion of industrial capacities in all major branches of production. This was the strategic economic policy aim of socialist countries throughout the post-war period. On the other hand, their different patterns of industrialisation and the specific utilisation and character of foreign investment will illuminate many of the questions considered in this book. Their respective chances of attracting FDI depend on a number of variables: the path and intensity of the implementation of systemic change; location-specific advantages, infrastructure facilities, human capital development (wage costs, managerial, marketing and organisational skills); as well as political and economic stability.

Before 1989, both Hungary and China implemented strategies of gradual economic reforms to transform their CPEs. After the events of Tiananmen Square in June 1989 and the fall of the Berlin Wall in November 1989, Hungary, together with other Eastern European countries and the Soviet Union, rushed toward democracy and liberalisation, and transformed their CPEs into market-oriented systems. China is still trying to maintain a traditional ideology and philosophical allegiance to the Chinese version of Marxist socialist-market principles. Both Hungary and China are facing enormous challenges in managing their respective transition from a CPE to a market-oriented system, and in the process seeking closer integration with the world economy. Nevertheless, both Hungary's continuing privatization and China's assurances, in word and deed, that it will continue to support market-oriented reforms constitute good news for foreign investors seeking access to these domestic markets and labour supply in the 1990s. During the period from 1978 to 1992, both Hungary and China received a lion's share of FDI directed to post-socialist countries.

(1) Hungary and China - two major recipients of foreign capital From 1983 to 1990 FDI grew four times faster than world output and three times faster than world trade. Capital flows, however, became more and more concentrated on the richest parts of the world, and the proportion of FDI flowing to less-developed countries (LDCs) dropped from around 25 per cent of the total in the 1970s to about 20 per cent in the 1980s (Emmott, 1993, p.7). However, inflows of FDI into LDCs surged from US$31 billion in 1990 to US$80 billion in 1993, with almost 60 per cent going to Asia. Geographical proximity still matters - perhaps increasingly so, as there is a cluster of countries where inward flows of FDI are dominated by companies from neighbouring regions.[4]

Whilst the boom faded in the recession-hit industrialised countries, foreign

3

investment has been rushing enthusiastically into those economies that for decades operated under communism: to China and Eastern Europe. Recent rapid economic transformation in Eastern Europe and China has gradually turned the huge potential market into a real market and has thereby provided new opportunities for western firms. Over the last 10 years or so, FDI in these countries has grown dramatically at an unprecedented pace, and the general trend is continuing, despite a marked difference in their two patterns of economic growth and development. By the end of 1993, FDI in Eastern Europe and former Soviet Union amounted to US$18.3 billion, of which Hungary attracted US$6-7 billion, mainly in the fields of car-manufacturing, telecommunications and soft drinks. More and more MNCs are aiming at establishing a much greater manufacturing presence through emerging areas of Asia and Eastern Europe. The rapidly increasing FDI in Eastern Europe and China represents a salient new feature on the international economic scene.

Hungary Hungary is currently seen as the most promising host nation within Eastern Europe in attracting FDI. Since 1989, Hungary has been the biggest recipient of foreign equity capital among Eastern Europe, attracting more than US$7 billion foreign investment, and the number of JVs has increased very rapidly. In 1991 the amount of capital invested in Hungary was US$1.5 billion. By the end of 1992, the number of JVs reached 13,000, with US$3 billion inward direct investment. By the end of 1994, more than half of foreign capital committed to Eastern Europe and the former USSR has been invested in Hungary. More important, Hungary has also welcomed a host of top rank MNCs, including Alcoa, Electrolux, General Electric, General Motors, Ford, Suzuki and Unilever. All are intent on integrating their new Hungarian subsidiaries into their existing global operations and bringing invaluable know-how, technology and managerial expertise in their wake.[5]

One survey conducted by Creditanstalt/EIU shows that 'more than half of foreign investor respondents - 54 per cent - report they are increasing investments in the Eastern European region. However, 17 per cent are lowering their initial investment levels, above all in the former Soviet Union and Yugoslavia. The main reasons for caution are economic and political uncertainties, as well as difficulties surrounding the legal systems in the former communist states'.[6] These risks arise from supply problems, inadequate infrastructure and services, inflation and the threat of devaluation. Western governments can play a vitally important role by insuring against part of the political and economic risk of investing in Eastern Europe. Hungary, in the OECD's view, is an exception, in that its legislation may today be considered to be the most favourable in Eastern Europe.[7] 'A majority of corporations believe Hungary has the easiest investment procedures, because of its longer track record of openness to Western companies'.[8] 'But should this situation (such as rising inflation, and worsening supply labour unrest) persist', the OECD predicted, 'potential investors could be deterred'.[9]

China No other former communist country has acquired as much experience as China in formulating and implementing legislation to attract foreign capital since 1978. China has now become one of the leading host countries among LDCs, in terms of both its accumulated stock and its annual flow of foreign capital. During the first ten years of the open-door policy, China's foreign investment reached about US$20 billion, increasing at an average annual rate of about 30 per cent. By the end of 1992, the number of foreign-invested enterprises (FIEs) rose to 82,300, with US$100 billion contracted foreign capital, of which US$52.34 billion had been utilised. The output of JVs in operation (half of the registered 82,300 were operating at the end of 1992) totalled 4.9 per cent of national industrial production in 1991. In 1992, 40,291 new JVs were approved, with US$58 billion capital contracted and US$16 billion committed, representing significant increases on the 1991 figures. Total income tax submitted by FIEs reached Renminbi (RMB) 10.7 billion (US$2 billion), 52.3 per cent higher than in 1991. FIEs' imports and exports rose to US$43.8 billion, 51 per cent higher than in 1991, and amounted to 25 per cent of national foreign trade. In the first nine months of 1993, China approved 62,000 FIEs, with contracted foreign capital US$81.64 billion, an increase of 120 per cent and 170 per cent respectively over the same period for 1992. In 1993, average investment per project reached US$1.32 million and FIEs' exports accounted for 27.5 per cent of national foreign exports.[10] In 1994, more than US$45.8 billion foreign capital of which US$33.8 billion FDI was utilized, increasing 17.6 per cent and 22.8 per cent over 1993 respectively. By the end of 1994, registered FIEs amounted 206,000, increases 40,000 over 1993. FIEs exports amounted US$34.7 billion, increasing 37.6 per cent over 1993, 28.7 per cent of national total exports.[11]

In the near future, the attractiveness of China as investment location will depend on the domestic as well as the global economic environment, especially on the policy of Western governments towards China, and how much interest (including those passive investors) have in the Chinese market. China will have to compete for reduced global flow of FDI, as major investing countries face weak economic growth, and most FDI in the world economy have been shifting away from developing countries to developed nations.

We believe that in the immediate and long-term future China will continue to evolve in a direction favourable to foreign investors. This will encourage an increasing flow of foreign capital into the country, which will further make China more closely interlocked with Western Europe and the world market.

Comparison In absolute terms, China, Hungary, Czech Republic, the ex-Soviet Union and Poland occupy the leading positions among the CPEs; in relative terms (according to the number of FIEs per million of population in 1992-93), the order is different, with Hungary ranked first, Poland second, Czech Republic third, and China further behind. Compared with these post-socialist countries in Eastern Europe, investment inflows into China were large in absolute terms but remained relatively small in terms of gross domestic product (GDP) and gross investment.

China enjoys several advantages in attracting FDI over Eastern Europe and other East Asian countries, in terms of its domestic markets, abundant natural resources and much lower labour costs. Compared with Hungary, however, many of these advantages might be offset by disincentives prevailing in the Chinese market. These negative factors (including restrictions on capital flows and access by foreign firms to local capital markets; excessive bureaucracy; and, above all, a so-called socialist market system that limits the role of market forces and competition) tend to discourage and limit investment activities by imposing greater uncertainties, and therefore higher risks for foreign firms.

However, both Hungary and China have the potential for rapid economic growth. The opportunities for investment in Hungary and China are enormous, given projected growth rates and the potential of expanding markets. As Emmott (1993) predicts, in the next few years, Central and Eastern Europe will overtake Russia in attracting further FDI. Further liberalization in investment rules may take place in three of the developing world's largest economies: China, India and Brazil. In the latter two of these, however, the main dangers are economic and political instability, and China looks the safest bet (Emmott, 1993, p.27).

(2) The similarity in Hungary's and China's CPE system and reform strategy
Hungary had pioneered its New Economic Mechanism (NEM) in 1968, while China implemented similar political and economic reforms designed to transform its economic system in 1978 (ten years later than Hungary). In this sense, both Hungary and China were characterised by gradual reform.

It was 1948 when the Communist Party fused with the Social Democrats to form the Hungarian Workers' Party and a Soviet-type mechanism for economic planning was introduced,[12] while a similar 'great change' happened in China in 1949. In the late 1970s, however, the inherent weakness of rigid directive planning in socialist countries became obvious. Central planning led to insufficient flexibility, and a lack of adequate incentives to promote quality, innovation and efficiency.[13] Almost all socialist countries found that the model of central planning did not and could not work, and that the 'socialist economy was failing to produce the wealth necessary to support it [public welfare]' (Swain, 1992, p.16).

In 1968 the NEM was introduced in Hungary aiming at creating market socialism - achieving the 'Third Way', in the context of developing a 'mixed economy'. The NEM succeeded in establishing a form of a decentralised planned economy, recognising the multi-sector nature of the economy, and linking domestic markets with foreign markets more closely.[14] But it remained a shortage economy, in which managers had to worry about supplies of inputs and not sales of outputs.[15] Later, Hungary gradually moved further towards a decentralised system of economic management towards maintaining a somewhat precarious macroeconomic equilibrium, while increasingly liberalising prices and access to foreign exchange. Although it suffered from a large foreign debt and stagnant growth, it had a moderately vibrant private economy, a Western-style tax system after the reforms of 1988, and many of the institutional and legal prerequisites of a functioning market economy.[16]

Hungary became less of a shortage economy than was the case before reform[17], but the application of market socialism over a 20-year period demonstrated that, while it was an incomparably superior model to the CPE model, market socialism was not problem-free. 'It failed to provide an environment in which enterprises could produce goods of the quality and technological sophistication required by world markets; and by failing to export successfully... [they] came to believe so wholeheartedly that socialism had failed' (Swain, 1992, pp.1-2). The market was insufficiently diverse to encourage the flow of foreign capital into new, rather than joint, ventures (Swain, 1992, pp.9-10). As a result many people believed that it was impossible to reform a communist economy gradually because of inherited inefficiencies, insufficient mobility of factors of production, real factor-price rigidity and a shock approach to macroeconomic stabilisation. Hungarian economists pointed to the negative experience of reforming countries like Hungary and Yugoslavia, where gradualist efforts in the 1970s and 1980s withered and eventually died.[18] There really were only two alternative development models: capitalism or Soviet communism.

In the case of China, the starting conditions in the mid-1970s differed from those of Eastern Europe in the late 1980s in two major respects: China was a far less developed country, and until the late 1970s, China was largely a closed and centrally planned economy. Moreover, at the start of the reform process in 1978, China had, however, essentially no foreign debt, no budget deficit, and no significant inflationary pressures, and hence met the conditions of macroeconomic stability.[19] In 1975, state-owned enterprises (SOEs) accounted for 97 per cent of fixed assets, 63 per cent of employment and 86 per cent of gross output in industry; more than 92 per cent of retail sales in China were made by SOEs (Howe, 1978, p.31.); the export procurement value in 1978 made up only 2.9 per cent of total gross industrial and

7

agricultural output value. In spite of considerable industrial growth since the foundation of New China in 1949, the level of economic development and living standards were still low. Per capita income in 1978 was only RMB315, equivalent to US$185 at the official exchange rate. The socialist system and the Chinese economy were in crisis, while the economic success of the four Asian newly industrialising countries/regions (Singapore, Hong Kong, Taiwan and South Korea) through promoting exports and inward foreign investment, and the reform experience of some former communist countries in East Europe aroused much interest among the leadership.

Following the experience of the Hungarian NEM, the Chinese government from late 1978 has implemented a reform and open-up strategy of 'crossing the river by feeling the stones', starting with agriculture by 'leaving it up to the market'. The aim was to stimulate every individual, every region and every sector's initiative by redefining the economic relationship - power, responsibility and interest - among the state, localities, enterprises and individuals. Specifically, economic reforms were to encourage the development of other-than state ownership; to increase decision-making power by localities and enterprises; to expand the role of market; to establish a closer link between remuneration and performance; and to reduce the direct involvement of government organs in economic matters. The open-door policy, which was really only part of the wider reform policy, encouraged the expansion of foreign trade, particularly exports, and the introduction of foreign capital, technology and management skills.[20]

The number of directive indicators was reduced and profitability was accepted as an important criterion of enterprise performance. Finally, the domestic market prices were partly aligned with world ones. Since 1990, China has further adopted a so-called 'Socialist market economy' representing a mixed economic system, combining planning and market functions. The Chinese economy has been in a gradual transition from a CPE to a combined planned and market economy, and appears to have been remarkably successful, at least during the initial stage of reform. But the decentralised economic system has not solved the problems of waste, inefficiency and shortage.

Despite similar reform strategies, the development paths of Hungary and China began to diverge after 1989.

The tides of history may have given Eastern Europe no choice but a 'big-bang' transformation, while China was still able to adhere to an traditional ideology, and so far remains steadfast in its philosophical allegiance to the Chinese version of socialist market principles.

While Hungary had to deal with the short-term costs of economic transformation (with a substantial decline in GDP and industrial output between 1989-92) - high inflation and a decline of living standards, China was not plunged into a transformation crisis when it reformed its economy from the late 1970s onwards (see **Figure 1.1**). Instead, China has recorded one of the fastest growth rates of all countries in the world during this period. The average economic growth rate between 1978 and 1992 reached about 9 per cent per annum, while the growth rate in Hungary was only 0.65 per cent during the same period. The more gradual Hungarian transformation process succeeded in stabilising the economy and laying the foundation for further progress towards establishing a free market system.

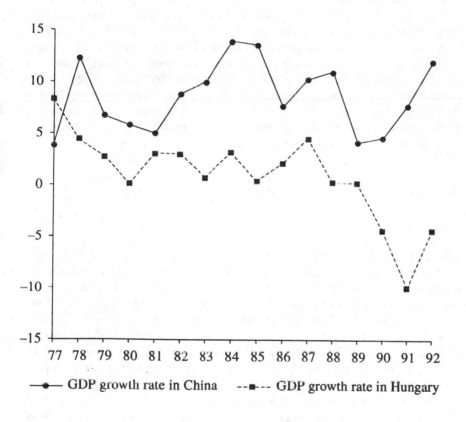

Figure 1.1   **GDP real growth rate in Hungary and China, 1977-92**

Source: China State Statistical Bureau and Hungary Central Statistical Office.

9

China's total foreign trade in 1992 topped US$166 billion, having risen by 27 per cent in comparison with 1991. It exceeded US$200 billion and US$236.7 billion in 1993 and 1994, making it roughly the world's eleventh-biggest trading nation, while its growth rate was the second fastest in the world, only behind Singapore. Its imports grew at 31.9 per cent and exports at 20.9 per cent in 1994. China's GDP in 1994 amounted RMB 4,380 billion, increasing 11.8 per cent over 1993.[21] The successful experiment of China's reform and open-up strategy relies on following four crucial factors: maximizing individual's enthusiasm, maximising to utilize foreign capital, bringing every positive factor into optimizing efficiency, and maximising to develop international markets.[22]

What has made gradualism work in China? Initially, Chinese enterprise reforms did not go much further than the reforms in Poland in 1982 and in Hungary in the 1980s.[23] Competition between SOEs, private firms and FIEs, high saving rates and gradualist approach have been the keys to China's success. 'Unfortunately post-socialist Europe cannot hope to copy these features of the rapid Chinese success..... Even if Eastern Europe had followed the Chinese example of a more evolutionary approach to economic transformation, Eastern Europe would still not have been able to repeat the Chinese success because of the different starting conditions'.[24]

Data sources and research approaches

Data sources

The subject of FDI in economies undergoing transformation is vast, complicated and controversial. It is also a subject that, although evoking much speculation over the years, has received less sustained and systematic attention in terms of data collection and analysis than many other aspects of economic development and transition. It is an extremely difficult task for researchers to build up a good research base and to generate an in-depth study of foreign investment and economic growth in Hungary and China, owing to the complexity of the issue involved, as well as to the difficulties in obtaining proper primary and even secondary data.

Quantifying direct investment presents both methodological and operational problems. Data on FDI in Hungary and China tend to be scarce and far from comparable. It is necessary, at the outset, to emphasise that the data on foreign capital in both countries is rather poor. This limitation is a function both of problems encountered in physical data collection, and in its distortion. Ex-CPEs lack both the trained personnel and Western statistical methods and techniques needed to collect data effectively. The second major problem is data comparability: these transforming economies change their statistical definitions frequently, which obviously cause problems for statistical comparability, and the data that have been collected were assembled by a variety of independent organisations employing varying standards, procedures and definitions. Moreover, unlike international merchandise trade-flows, FDI data are scattered, with different sources frequently providing contradictory information. Uniform definitions of FDI have not been adopted and the deficiencies are particularly severe at a dis-aggregated level, by country or industry. In terms of data analysis, economists in ex-CPEs are much more accustomed to thinking in terms of correlation coefficients, or just quantitative measurements, than in terms of regression coefficients or slopes. Communist countries were excluded from most econometric analyses of LDCs due to 'problems of comparability, both in terms of political and economic structures and the available data'.[25] Thus, while theory-building and empirical validation require the application of quantitative tools, the available data from the ex-CPEs in general presents considerable obstacles to its application.

Because of the absence of any internationally accepted financial or accounting procedures in CPEs, most domestically produced economic statistics have been of dubious value. 'As a rule of thumb, all figures should be treated as approximate'.[26] Nevertheless, a considerable amount of statistical information on FDI in Hungary and China has been published, both by international bodies (several UN agencies, the OECD) and by host countries. The latter are generally of two types: first, approvals data issued by national investment regulatory boards (usually the Ministry of Foreign Economic Relations); and, secondly, production and employment data for the major manufacturing industries from industrial census returns, classified by country of ownership. So an empirical analysis is facilitated by an improvement in the secondary data sources, although considerable deficiencies still exist with official figures too varying from source to source.

In any statistical analysis there is inevitably a gap between the data desired and the data available. So it is in this case, where available information from national and international sources has been assembled and integrated, where applicable, with the theoretical literature and recent empirical research.

The main sources used in this book are as follows:

(1)   Interviews with officials in different agencies of the Hungarian government. From April to May 1993, field work was carried out in Hungary, and the author was able to interview officials in various agencies mentioned in the acknowledgement.

(2)   Documentary materials published by the Hungarian and Chinese authorities, particularly documents, regulations and statistical

11

yearbooks. In recent years FDI has received substantial press coverage. Many reports, articles, and data can be found in various journals, newspapers, books, and official documents. These materials provide information on policy output, original points of view and some important unpublished information concerning FDI policy and development.

(3)   Research papers and publications by Western scholars and correspondents, providing important information about what has happened in the recent past and interpretations of recent FDI development in both countries. These diversified sources have enabled the author to analyze the actual operation of FDI in Hungary and China.

(4)   Questionnaire survey. In order to examine the experience and prospects of foreign investors in Hungary and China, the author conducted a questionnaire survey in the summer of 1992. These survey results supplement our quantitative analysis.

The statistics used in this study, on the whole, have been derived from the publications and press releases of the Central Statistic Offices in both countries. The data for FDI in China seems to be quite reliable, as FDI has more than a 16-year history in this country. Different Chinese state agencies published numerous data on FDI flows. But the data published by the Ministry of Foreign Economic Relations and Trade (MOFERT) differed from those compiled and released by other agencies, both in the total reported amount of FDI and in the specific subitems. The inconsistent data makes empirical analysis particularly uncertain and difficult. Of the several sources, the MOFERT data were probably more reliable, as MOFERT is responsible for approving, regulating and monitoring foreign investment in China. The Hungarian Central Statistical Office (KSH) has collected an admirable amount of data through the use of quarterly questionnaires sent out to newly-formed companies. The data for the 1980s and 1990s, although not perfect, is regarded by the Hungarian economists to be relatively reliable. In synthesising statistical information and recent research, we will address the following questions: what factors influence foreign investors in their decision-making process in investing in Hungary and China? How important is FDI to host countries, in relation to aggregate resource flows and to domestic production?

As we have just discussed above, very few systemic and in-depth empirical and quantitative tests have so far been carried out to test FDI's contribution to economic development and systemic transformation for Hungary and China. This is also because a full evaluation of the contribution of foreign capital is inherently difficult: the period under examination is so recent that many of the long-term effects of FDI may not have clearly developed at this stage; much of the information about the performance of FIEs in China needed for an overall assessment is not available; and there is a 'counter-historical' problem involved in the methodology - since it is almost impossible to say what would have happened without FDI, it is correspondingly difficult to judge what did happen with FDI.

An attempt has been made to identify emerging investment trends but many of the statistics are still too 'raw' to draw final conclusions, as there are some deficiencies in all data and an uncritical use might generate quite misleading results. Most figures generally refer to approved (or intended) investment, as indicated in the firms' applications. Actual investment is a good deal less for several reasons: there is always a lag between approval and implementation; some approved projects never get off the ground; and the actual investments of some firms do not necessarily match their original commitments. Sometimes, the approved data refer to gross investment. They include the equity contribution of both the foreign and domestic capital. Consequently, the data might substantially overstate the equity contribution of foreign investors. The country shares in these data also need to be interpreted carefully. For example, the share of the group 'more than one country' is often large, and no indication is given of its composition in the published data. Moreover, the distinction between foreign and domestic investment is somewhat fuzzy. The official statistics gave the limited sector coverage and the difficulty in interpreting the country shares.

Despite these difficulties and limitations, a preliminary assessment of FDI performance in China is possible. In recent years, the central and local governments have released various information that enable to probe into the initial results of FDI utilisation. Although the information gathered is inevitably limited and 'piece-meal' in nature, it does provide us with many insights into the picture.

However, in the case of Hungary, loans are the major source of foreign capital in Hungary, while FDI plays a similar role in China; and five-sixths of foreign capital present was invested during the last three years. We are not in a position as yet to disaggregate foreign capital into FDI and foreign sovereign loans, and come forward with an in-depth analysis of the effects of foreign investment on output, employment, balance of payment, productivity, technology, training, and market structure at current scale of inward FDI in Hungary. It is only possible to disaggregate FDI and foreign loans in the case of China, while proxying foreign capital inflows (FCI) as FDI in Chapters 4, 7 and 8 in the case of Hungary. This limitation is imposed because:

(1)   The period of FDI history in Hungary is so short that many of the manufacturing FIEs have not put into operation, or many of the long-term effects of FDI may not have clearly developed at this stage.

(2)   Much of the information about the performance of FIEs in Hungary needed for an overall assessment is not available.

(3)   Much of foreign capital inflows in Hungary is taken in the form of foreign governmental or institutional loans. As a consequence, no overall analysis has been carried out on the performance of FIEs. Some support may be provided by inquires and sectoral surveys, but it is likely that they do not tell the whole story.

Research approaches

It should be emphasised that our objective is not to reconstruct the economic history of both countries, but rather to investigate the FDI legal framework and its causal relationship with several macro-economic variables.

The principal method of investigation used is regression analysis of time-series data. The empirical work is conducted in such a way as to establish models for both Hungary and China, with respect to FDI, foreign trade, labour costs and economic growth, including their relationship with each other. One advantage of econometrics is that it permits the processing of a large volume of data and can be used explicitly to test how much growth rates increase or fall as a result of increasing FDI. The regression analysis, however, is only concerned with an historical, average correlation between FDI and other independent explanatory variables.

The period covered by the present study is 1978-92, which is particularly appropriate, both because of the liberalisation of FDI policy and the quality of comparative data. This book will integrate this material within the framework of current theories of direct investment, and in the context of general economic development in both countries since 1978.

FDI is, in fact, not an exogenous factor in the economy, as there are many important factors affecting economic development in both LDCs and the CPEs: labour, domestic savings and investment, foreign capital, and technology. Causal relationships are unclear, partly because direct investments

14

are not the intrinsic cause of economic growth, and partly because these effects also result from other factors partly related to direct investments. FDI and its impact on economic development in these years was so dynamic and complicated, and no existing model can explain FDI throughout the period under consideration. An effort has therefore been made to build an original framework that accommodates multiple dimensions and causal relationships and explains the constant shift of FDI and economic reform in this period.

As the methodology involves empirically testing hypotheses through quantitative analysis, theoretical relationships must be brought into play in a manner that allows for both meaningful measurement and statistical manipulation. However some care needs to be applied when using a theory derived from the behaviour of investors in a capitalist world economy in the very different world of a Soviet-type CPE.

Quantitative research proved to be an effective tool for examining the problem at hand and effectively complementing the qualitative analysis. As discussed at length in Chapters 4, 7 and 8, it provided a means for examining a series of complex relationships over a large number of explanatory variables. Although problems with the data do not allow for a rigorous testing of hypotheses, two country comparative analysis provides the basis for a generalised understanding of phenomena of FDI in these transforming economies. Data presented in this study clarify and confirm many of the predictions of theory. While recognizing its very real limitations, we would hope that quantitative two-country comparison by utilised more frequently in the future to explore problems in international business within the context of ex-CPEs.

Chapters 7 and 8 did provide valuable insights into actual processes of FDI's impact on economic development and external trade in host countries, which lent further credence to quantitative results.

This book attempted to establish a series of relationships as consistent with the data. What is needed for policy determination is a more rigidly specified model that can be utilized for prediction of the magnitude of the relationships involved. This, in turn, requires improvements in both data and methodology.

In the following chapters a body of theory will be proposed and an attempt will be made to validate it empirically. Hopefully, this research will lead to both theoretical and methodological advances, which will serve as a basis for prediction and even for policy-making.

Outlines and structure

Government policies in the host countries play a crucial role in directing foreign capital in order to contribute positively to economic growth and the development process. The analysis of foreign investment, therefore, begins in Chapter 2 with an examination of the policy towards foreign investors in these two countries. The legislative framework in both countries has evolved around a strategy of attempting to attract inward investment whilst not allowing the host countries to be 'exploited' by MNCs policies. This careful balancing act is best seen in the structuring of incentive packages for inward investors.

The overall quantitative trends in foreign investment and its distribution among different regions, economic sectors and source country composition in Hungary and China are explored in Chapter 3. More specifically, it provides a picture of how the pattern of FDI in both countries has changed over the years, both in terms of national origins, aggregate inflows, geographical pattern, and sectoral distribution. MNCs are found to have been more responsive to regional incentives than domestic firms in many cases which have contributed to problems of regional imbalance and over-concentration in specific economic activities.

Hungary and China both won a lion's share of FDI simply because their economies possessed various attributes which made them particularly attractive locations. The determinants of FDI in Hungary and China are examined in Chapter 4. The correlation between FDI and various explanatory variables is examined through an econometric model and by regression analysis. Special emphasis is placed upon macro-economic factors which contribute to the relative attractiveness of Hungary and China as potential host countries for foreign direct investment. The influence of such factors as market-size, growth and cost competitiveness, political stability and capital costs are assumed to have been a major influence on the location decisions taken by foreign firms. These independent variables are correlated with the increasing flow of FDI into these two countries. The choice of host country depends on macro-economic and political considerations, although many of the relevant factors are industry- and company-specific, and others appear to have little or no economic or political basis.

Chapter 5 presents a summary report of a questionnaire survey which was carried out by the author in the summer of 1992 regarding the experience of foreign investors and FDI prospects in Hungary and China. The survey represents a useful supplement and alternative subjective perspective in terms of managerial perceptions to the quantitative method in terms of what factors might be important in investment decision-making process and the performance of FIEs in these two countries.

The potential benefits to both host countries from inward investment are

16

discussed in Chapter 6 which presents a statistical picture of inward investment and its contribution to overall capital formation, its impact on output and trade growth in the local economies. Consideration is given to the macro-economic impact which foreign investment has already made in terms of output, employment, imports and exports, the transfer of technology, the 'demonstration' effect on management methods and industrial relations in local firms. This general assessment in Chapter 6 provides the basic material for the econometric analysis of FDI's contribution towards local economies which appears in Chapters 7 and 8.

Though it is difficult to reach any definite conclusions owing to data limitation and the inherent complexity of FDI, Chapter 9 draws together the conclusions from the study as a whole, and makes several suggestions for future research on inward direct investment in both countries. It also considers the prospects for foreign investment in the subdued economic environment of the late 1990s and beyond in Hungary and China.

Notes

1. FDI can be defined as those investments undertaken abroad involving control of an enterprise (control in the managerial sense of decision making power), and serving as a vehicle for the transfer of needed resources - technology, managerial skills, marketing knowledge, export outlets and capital. See Dunning (1970), p.4; Kindleberger (1969), p.4; Strikker (1968), p.14. In other definition, FDI is an investment which is made to acquire a lasting interest in an enterprise operating in an economy other than that of the investor, the investor's purpose being to have an effective voice in the management of the enterprise. FDI can occur through mergers, acquisitions, minority or majority participation, greenfield investment or joint venture. See IMF (1977), *Balance of Payments Manual*. Excluded in this definition are portfolio investment- which in any case is very small in both countries -and loan capital, which has entered into both countries in large quantities since the 1970s. In this book, I use IMF's definition.

2. *The Economist*, 23 January 1993, pp.17-18 and p.61.

3. Dobosiewicz, Zbigniew (1992), *Foreign Investment in Eastern Europe*, Routledge, London; Artisien, Patrick, Matiga Rojec and Marjan Svetlicic (1993), *Foreign Investment in Central & Eastern Europe*, St. Martin's Press, New York.

4.For American firms, it is Central and South America; for Japanese firms, it is a handful of Asian countries; and for West European firms, it is Eastern Europe, although US is major investor in Eastern Europe.

5.Financial Times (1993), *Eastern Europe: Rejoining the World Economy, A Financial Times Guide,* Financial Times Press, London.

6.Marsh, David (1992), 'Political Worries Fail to Deter Western Investors', which is based on the Creditanstalt/EIU Vienna 1992 East European Investment Survey, *Financial Times,* 12 October 1992, p.3.

7.OECD (1990), *How the OECD Sees JV Financing,* OECD Publications, Paris.

8.Marsh, David (1992), op cit, p.3.

9.OECD (1990), *How the OECD Sees JV Financing,* OECD Publications, Paris.

10.*People's Daily (Overseas Edition),* 7 August 1992, p.1; 23 October 1992, p.1; 24 November 1992, p.4; 9 December 1992, p.4; and 9 February 1993, p.1.

11.China Statistical Office (1995), 'Statistical Report of China's National Economic and Social Development in 1994', *People's Daily,* 2 March 1995.

12.For a detailed discussion of this period, see Swain, Nigel (1992), *The Rising and Falling of Socialism,* Verso, London, pp.38-42.

13.As Norman Scott described that 'In the end, the abandonment of decades of investment rates almost twice as high as those in the industrial market economies was caused by their failure to arrest the deterioration in a whole series of economic performance indicators. Growth rates of net material product continued to decline or stagnate; labour productivity gains continued to slow down; the rate of return on invested capital was falling; the products generated by new or expanded capacities were often of poor quality and rarely competitive on international markets; waste and pollution levels were high; and the scale of the investment effort, combined with lax control of the completion of investment projects once started, resulted in the unproductive immobilisation of construction equipment, materials, and plant, dispersed over a large number of uncompleted projects. A further weakness of investment policy was the limitation, imposed by the scarcity of convertible currency, on imports of capital goods from developed economies. Some of the foreign debt incurred by Poland and Hungary was used to fund or equip factories whose production was destined principally for the 'soft' requirements of CMEA markets... By the same token, there are ample opportunities for foreign investors to participate in upgrading these out-of-date factories to reach internationally competitive standards.' See Scott, Norman (1992), 'The Implications of the Transition for Foreign Trade and Investment', in *'Macroeconomics of Transition in Eastern Europe'*, *Oxford Review of Economic Policy*, Vol.8, No.1, pp.52-53.

14.Sarkozy, Tamas (1993), 'A legal framework for the Hungarian transition, 1989-91', in Szekely, Istvan, P. and Newbery, David M.G. (ed.), *Hungary: An Economy in Transition*, Chapter 13.

15.Schmieding, Holger (1993), 'From Plan to Market: On the Nature of the Transformation Crisis', *Weltwirtschaftliches Archiv*, Vol.129, No.2, pp.217-53.

16.Sarkozy, Tamas (1993), op.cit.

17.Kornai J. *The Hungarian Reform*, pp.72-75, quoted by Swain (1992), op.cit., p.108.

18.*The Economist*, 28 November 1992, p.6

19.It was only until 1991/92 that the outstanding net balance of China's foreign debt increased more than US$60 billion, with debt service obligations (amortisation plus interest payments) reaching a peak of US$7-8 billion per year during 1992-95. This gives an estimated debt service ratio of 9.7 per cent to 10.8 per cent based on total Chinese exports of US$719.1 million in 1991. This is considerably less than the 12-15 per cent, conventionally regarded as the critical debt service ratio, in which situation it threatens to 'crowd out' a country's import capacity to promote economic growth. So China's current debt service ratio is well remain below this critical level, and much less than that of Hungary. See, World Bank (1988), *China's External Trade and Capital*, The World Bank, Washington, D.C. p.28; and Kueh, Y.Y. (1992), 'Foreign Investment and Economic Change in China', *The China Quarterly*, September, Vol.132, p.672.

20.State Economic System Reform Commission (1988), *A Collection of Planning Works on China's Economic System Reform 1979-87*, Beijing: Academy of Central Committee of the China Communist Party Press, p.62.

21.*People's Daily*, 2 March 1995.

22.*People's Daily*, 10 February 1993.

23.Fan, Qimiao and Schaffer, Mark E. (1991), 'Enterprise Reforms in Chinese and Polish State-Owned Industries', The Development Economic Research Programme, STICERD, London School of Economics, China Programme No.13.

24.Schmieding, Holger (1993), op.cit., pp.244-246.

25.Kobrin, Stephen Jay (1977), *Foreign Direct Investment, Industrialisation and Social Changes,* Jai Press, Connecticut, p.56.

26.Hill, Hal (1988), *Foreign Investment and Industrialisation in Indonesia,* Oxford University Press, Singapore, p.29.

2 FDI regulation and policy in Hungary and China

The first step in an analysis of FDI is to ascertain the current FDI levels and the operating environment in the particular country concerned. This requires a review of governmental policies towards foreign investment, as well as current operating and regulatory conditions. This chapter, therefore, discusses and compares the development of FDI policies and regulations that promoted and controlled the inflow of FDI and the management of FIEs in Hungary from the 1970s to 1990s and in China since 1979.

Why Hungary and China adopted FDI policies

The motivation behind Hungarian FDI policies

In the 1970s, it was gradually accepted by the Hungarian government that there might be certain advantages in attracting foreign investment, provided that this would not involve any amendments to existing legal rules or lead to the emergence of a permanent foreign-owned sector. The first step was to allow certain Western service and trade enterprises to set up local offices. The second and much more important development was to allow foreign investors to participate in the hotel, tourism, and other businesses (Dobosiewicz, 1992, pp.21-22).

The most pervading considerations, crucial to the adoption of a FDI policy, were, first of all, the East's need for Western technology in order to improve its economic growth and international exports. It had been argued that the Socialist economies were not able to develop effective methods for the stimulation of technological progress and a fuller utilisation of technology in the interest of a more dynamic economic growth.[1] Fifty years after the 'concessions' of the USSR in the 1920s at the time of the 'New Economic

Policy', Western direct investment was finally regarded as an important part in industrialisation and modernisation. MNCs were increasingly recognised as the most obvious reservoir of Western technology: they provided a short-cut for bridging the embarrassing 'gap' and offered a channel for the transfer of technology that would modernise the structure of industry and promote the internationalisation of technical progress and the division of labour.[2] Such industrial cooperation might also allow the Eastern partners to obtain management 'know-how' and production expertise to ensure maximum efficiency benefits.

Secondly, foreign capital and JVs could minimize the CPEs' direct foreign exchange expenditure by making the West accept return flows of resultant components and finished products. The inflow of foreign capital could also allow the government to maintain the living standards and to pump additional money into the economy. This arrangement permitted balanced financing, easing Socialist foreign exchange problems and facilitating substantial long-term credits. Hungary was, therefore, vulnerable to the jitters of foreign investors because it has relied heavily on foreign capital to modernize its economy, as it has a foreign debt equal to 67 per cent of its GDP - a greater burden than Mexico's 46 per cent.[3]

Above all, the Eastern countries were motivated mainly by the prospect of undertaking large-scale production of previously imported complex products, or of developing new products and industrial sectors while obtaining Western technology and methods. This would enable them to improve their exports without using scarce hard-currency reserves. So with the help of newly established JVs, Hungary could achieve access to advanced technology, production techniques and management know-how, improve its economic and industrial structure, and finally develop advanced industries and improve its export marketing capacity.

At the enterprise level, the primary objectives for Hungarian enterprises entering into JVs included the following: export promotion through the development of new products, the building up of know-how, better utilisation of existing capacity, and cost/availability advantages,[4] or the securing of freely exchangeable currencies to purchase components and technology and to provide capital for construction.[5]

The revolutions in Eastern Europe in 1989 have deeply altered the nature of East-West economic relations. In order to achieve the stated policy aims of economic restructuring, modernisation, the creation of a market-oriented economic system, and re-integration into the world economy, domestic savings cannot be expected to suffice. In the short term, the austerity measures which are part and parcel of stabilisation programmes will add to the downward pressures on capital outlays which are already squeezed because of decades of very high rates of domestic accumulation and a heavy burden of debt-servicing. So the foreign capital requirements of the Eastern European economies in transformation are undoubtedly very large. FDI is regarded by the national authorities as a means of accelerating the achievement of policy goals. Legislation and institutions have been put in place with a view to attracting FDI, and directing it towards what host countries have designated as priority sectors or regions of their economies. Western involvement in this transformation, indeed, has become much greater as it increasingly takes the form of JVs and FDI rather than standard trade-channelled supplies of technology. It was accepted that FDI brought in badly needed capital to a cash-poor economy, as well as modern technology and know-how. Foreign partners were also accepted because they could assist their Hungarian counterparts in marketing products abroad and in training the domestic labour force; new companies from abroad could introduce competition to a market long held in the vice-like grip of state monopolies. As FDI has become an important channel of technology and capital transfer from the West to the East, utilisation of foreign capital, therefore, became an integral part of Hungary's reform and development policy. Inward direct investment was also considered as a form of promoting competition in the home market and an important instrument for Hungary's economic growth and integration into the world economy.[6]

The motivation behind China's open-up policy

After a decade of nationalisation and increased hostility towards foreign investors, one of the first decisions of the post-Mao government was to introduce economic reform and an Open-Door policy, which involved a remarkable change in policy towards foreign investment.

Foreign capital has the central role in the realisation of China's Open-Door Policy. Academic studies of the experiences of other countries in attracting foreign direct investment, articles in the foreign press concerning foreign companies' reactions to the Open Policy as well as investigations by ministerial research departments into the experiences of existing FIEs have all shaped leaders' perception of the needs of foreign investors. For foreign investors, the best means of gaining direct access to a market of 1.2 billion people is to locate production within the country, so bypassing quotas and other protective barriers.

The motives of the Chinese government in attracting FDI through JVs were not dissimilar to those of Eastern European countries. FDI is believed to help relieve domestic capital supply bottlenecks and to promote employment and economic growth. Within the Chinese economic context, even more important is the fact that FDI may increase interactions between the planned domestic economy and the outside world. As Xue Muqiao, one of the leading economists responsible for the new open-policy, declared:

> To be able to repay our debts, we must work out an overall plan for the use of foreign investment... [initially] priority should thus be given to the more profitable light industrial enterprises which need less investment and take a shorter time to build. Their products can soon be exported, enabling us to repay our debts. Big projects constructed with foreign investment, such as oil-mining and coal-mining, should be built on the basis of compensatory trade, that is, repayment for foreign investment in the form of exports. We may also build some badly needed projects, such as iron and steel plants, within the limitations of our resources. Even if they don't produce large quantities of exports, they will help us reduce imports and save foreign exchange. In short, we should balance our foreign exchange payments so as to minimize our foreign debts. .... It is necessary to handle correctly the relationship between self-reliance and the adoption of advanced foreign technology. By bringing in advanced technology, we do not mean depending on foreign aid but improving our own scientific and technological level and our ability to build the country through self-reliance (Xue Muqiao, 1981, p.263).

Sino-foreign JVs were expected to fulfil a number of functions: to provide a powerful supplement to the limited domestic supply of capital; to allow access to Western advanced technology and equipments; to facilitate import substitution or the development of new products or industries; to gain appropriate advanced management know-how and improve exports and increase hard-currency generating capacity; to promote the development of international tourism and create employment opportunities; and to raise the standard of living for local communities. Compared with external borrowing, FDI could be more advantageous to economic development through the infusion of not only capital, but technology, management, and an expansion of the external market.

According to a survey carried out in 1989, the motives for Chinese partners in entering into JV were very diverse and complex. More than three-quarters of the Chinese partners perceived by Western partners were motivated by the acquisition of advanced technology/technical know-how. Slightly more than two-thirds were perceived to be attracted by the gains in foreign exchange and in advanced management techniques and employment creation. The Chinese participants prioritised the promotion of exports, the expansion of domestic market opportunities, diversification into new product activities, preferential treatment by the administration/customs, increased demand for services and increased profitability.[7]

Emerging markets in Hungary and China require Western technology, capital, and access to world markets, which Western companies can provide. Meanwhile, Western firms want new markets, low-cost labour, scare materials, and profitable investment, which those emerging markets aspire to provide.

The framework of FDI in Hungary in the 1980s and 1990s

Hungary was one of the first Eastern European countries to introduce legislation allowing foreign capital inflows in Eastern Europe. The legislation governing JVs in Hungary was enacted in three broad stages: the first law adopted in the 1970s established the legal structure within which JVs between foreign and Hungarian enterprises became possible; subsequent amendments were designed to consolidate the initial legislation by removing some of the formal and practical obstacles in order to make JVs more attractive to potential investors. Secondly, in 1988, two entirely new laws were enacted - Act VI/1988 on Economic Associations (the Company Law) and Act XXIV/1988 on Investments by Foreigners in Hungary (the Foreign Investment Act), which broadened the range of JV activities and facilitated the conditions for profit transfer, capital repatriation, foreign shares. Finally, new regulations came into effect in July 1990 which offered the most attractive tax privileges available within Eastern Europe.

The Decree No.28/1972.X.3. of the Ministry of Finance

On 3 October 1972 the Ministry of Finance published Decree No.28/1972 on Economic Associations with Foreign Participation. This established a series of ground rules for encouraging and controlling inward foreign investment. For the first time it became legally possible for foreign enterprises or legal entities to participate in Hungarian economic associations. This possibility, however, existed only in theory because the competent authority had unlimited discretional power in approving such ventures. As a matter of fact nothing happened for two years. Indeed, for a considerable time after 1972, the Hungarian government simply raised credits from abroad, which were either spent on the purchase of consumer goods for the sake of increasing temporarily the standard of living, or invested in economically non-efficient projects.

Decree No.28/1972 and later amendments stipulated the objectives of Hungary's policy in relation to JVs, their operational sectors, organisation and termination, marketing and financing, foreign currency regulations, tax incentives, investment protection, as well as operational management, in which FDI was to be encouraged in some sectors, whereas in other sectors where JVs were not allowed to operate.[8] Besides sector restrictions, the Decree also set limits on the foreign share of total capital contribution by stipulating that a minimum original capital of Ft50,000. The participation of foreign partner(s) was generally restricted to not more than 49 per cent and could not be transferred to a third party, except with the approval of the company and the permission of the Minister of Finance. Foreign partners could capitalise the value of the asset contribution in the form of cash and contribution in kind and the 1972 law set no fixed time period for the duration of joint associations.

The main provisions operating environment and tax concessions of JVs were as follows:

(1)   JVs operated under the same conditions as local enterprises in terms of domestic purchases. JVs were also entitled to make direct purchases from abroad in convertible currencies, provided they gained a foreign trade permit for this purpose and the convertible currencies used to pay for such imports originated from the JV's own resources.

(2)   Both JV partners were required to agree on the basic principles that would be applied in the marketing of the JV's products, both domestically and abroad, and the extent to which the existing distribution networks of the parties would be used for the marketing and sale of the JV's products.[9]

(3)   The 1972 law stipulated that the JV might raise credits and transact foreign exchange in accordance with regulations applicable to Hungarian economic organisations. All foreign exchange transfers abroad had to be effected through the National Bank of Hungary (NBH). The profits and other sums paid to the Bank would be transferred to the foreign country, and in the event that the foreign party withdrew from the JV, the Bank, having received the share of the capital due to the foreign partner, would transmit that sum abroad in the currency specified in the memorandum of association (Art.11).

(4)   It stipulated that the NBH on application of the foreign partner might guarantee a compensation for loss as a result of nationalisation, expropriation or any other measures having similar effects, up to the amount of that contribution.

(5)   The regulation stipulated that foreign partners's profits when was transferred abroad, would enjoy tax exemption.

26

In addition, JVs were to be subject to the basic income tax at the rate of 40 per cent of the taxable profit not exceeding Ft3 million (Art.7), and 50 per cent on the part exceeding that amount. However, all companies in which the foreign participation reached at least 20 per cent or Ft5 million, were entitled to a 20 per cent reduction in the calculated tax. Further, if the statutory capital of the company exceeded Ft25 million and the foreign share was at least 30 per cent, the company was entitled, if it operated in one of the legally designated priority sectors, to tax reductions of 60 per cent or 100 per cent during the first five years, and of 40 per cent or 60 per cent thereafter. Other incentives were possible over and above these provisions, but were to be applied in each individual case.[10]

This was followed by the Minister of Finance Decree of 1977 amending the Decree of 1972 which regulated the conduct of productive activity. An order issued by the Minister of Finance in June 1979 described the formalities to be observed by the Hungarian party in obtaining permission to participate in a JV.[11] The amendment also committed a JV to establish a risk fund to cover tax and social security fees relating to the wages and salaries (35 per cent at that time and 43 per cent in 1989).

A joint decree of the Minister of Finance and the Minister of Foreign Trade issued in 1982 represented a further step forward. This made it possible to establish JVs in customs-free and free trade zones, where JVs enjoyed more flexible and liberal regulations on company revenue, wages and salaries, prices, investment procedures, government control, the purchase and use of motor vehicles.[12] The requirement for licence application was finally suspended at the end of 1985, and the simplified approval procedure reduced the time needed to set up a JV from 6-12 months to between 2-3 months.[13]

Furthermore, a number of measures had been taken to improve tax concessions if JV activity was deemed to be of particular importance to the Hungarian economy.[14] Special treatment was being given to JVs that contributed to import-substitution or export-oriented, technology innovation, materials saving and energy conservation.[15] FDI in these priority industries, benefited from additional incentives, reflecting Hungary's three-pronged economic policy: to promote export-oriented industries, to reduce dependence on imports, and to attract FDI into heavy industry and traditional industries where Hungary already had a comparative advantage. Another significant measure was the regulation issued by the Minister of Trade in 1987 with regard to foreign trade activities, which became effective on 1 January 1988. This regulation offered JVs national treatment with respect to trade, credit and domestic or international loans. Thereafter, JVs could also sell directly to domestic consumers.

However, despite these measures, from 1972 to the end of 1988, JVs numbered only a few dozen, and the total invested capital was not in excess of US$550 million.

The crucial step towards FDI and JVs, 1988-89

In the late 1980s, Hungary, along with other Eastern European economies, made some major amendments to foreign investment laws. The Company Act VI/1988 and the Act on Foreign Investment at the end of 1988 marked a significant step forward towards a market economy and the creation of an institutional framework for foreign investors. It liberalised the entry conditions and operational environment for FIEs and offered a surprisingly wide range of financial incentives by reducing or eliminating taxes. The most important concessions were a basic tax exemption of three years for all investment in 'priority' areas, and for longer periods in certain circumstances;[16] exemption from the payment of import duties and sales taxes on initial machinery and equipment; and a guarantee that profits and capital could be repatriated.[17] There were initially no restrictions on foreign equity (a foreigner could establish a fully-owned trade company),[18] and very few on the employment of foreign personnel.

Act XXIV/1988 on Foreign Investment[19] reiterated and confirmed existing guarantees and benefits, including a variety of fiscal and financial incentives in the form of 'tax holidays' and grants for investments satisfying specific criteria for foreign investors. The essence of the Act XXIV/1988 was that foreigners in Hungary came under the same terms and enjoyed equal treatment as Hungarian nationals. Under Section 28, foreign companies were able to give special incentives to leading personnel (including Hungarians) by offering part-payment in hard currencies. The companies with foreign participation paid the same entrepreneur's profit tax (EPT) as other Hungarian firms. The rate of the EPT amounted to 40 per cent of the tax base not exceeding Ft3 million and 50 per cent on the part exceeding that amount (Section 14).

The Act reaffirmed tax concessions to foreign investors stipulated in Act IX/1988. It showed that all the regulations concerning the inflow of foreign capital had been liberalised and provided increased opportunities and incentives for foreign investors, which compared favourably with other international arrangements. Hungary, therefore, tried to provide real incentives to foreign investors.

The amendments to the Foreign Investment Law in 1991

The resultant of 1989 political changes and economic transformation represented a turning point in the post-war history of Eastern European countries which had initially demonstrated an open reticence towards Western capital. To this extent, as Gutman indicates, 'the normalisation and expansion

28

of foreign direct investment exemplifies the desire to offer an alternative to the classical forms of technology transfer in East-West industrial cooperation'.[20]

On 1 January 1991, the Hungarian Parliament passed the long-awaited amendments to Law XXIV/1988 assuring foreign investors equal treatment with Hungarian nationals and the elimination of any adverse discrimination. Any Western businesses already involved in or considering a JV with Hungarian enterprises would now benefit immediately from guaranteed state protection and in the event of nationalisation or expropriation an indemnification on their investment in hard currency, estimated at the enterprise's market value. The act also guaranteed that foreign investors' earnings could be converted into hard currency and repatriated in hard currency without any special permits.[21] Capital goods, technology and patents brought into JVs as capitalised assets, as well as those purchased with hard currency from an original cash investment for production or operation of FIEs would enjoy duty-free-entry treatment.

In order to provide additional incentives for foreign investors to enter new markets, Hungary offered the most attractive tax privileges within Eastern Europe. The amendments removed authorization requirements for JVs, even those with a majority foreign stake. The difference was that the tax breaks were of limited duration (they were previously indefinite) and no longer available to JVs engaged solely in trading or most service activities. Existing JVs could continue to enjoy the old tax concessions for a further 5 to 10 years, depending on the type of incentive. In addition, profit reinvested in Hungary was no longer subject to taxation.

Two levels of tax privileges now existed for JVs applying for registration after 31 January 1991. The standard tax concession of a 60 per cent business profit tax break in the first five years of operation and 40 per cent in the second five years was available only for JVs that fulfilled the following criteria: (a) the foundation capital had to exceed Ft50 million (US$714,000); (b) the foreign stake had to be at least 30 per cent; (c) half of the income had to be derived from industrial production, or building or operating hotels.[22]

A full tax holiday for the first five years of JV operation plus a further five years with a 60 per cent tax concession was available to ventures that fulfilled the above criteria and that operated in those priority sectors that remained largely unchanged, although motor-vehicle production and assembly were added to the list, bringing the law into line with reality. Existing JVs or those that applied for registration by 31 January 1991 could maintain the former standard 20 per cent tax concession until the end of 1995. JVs with higher tax concessions would be allowed to maintain them for a period of 10 years from the original start of operations.

The rate of corporation income tax amounted to 35 per cent of the tax base not exceeding Ft3 million and 50 per cent on any part exceeding that amount.

And any means of production, other than in cash, imported by the foreign investors was to be free from customs duty. Further tax allowances were made if a foreign shareholder reinvested his profits to increase the original capital or to acquire further shares, and the investors were to be exempt from pay corporate tax on the proportion of the new investment. In the first year of investment a JV also has the right to deduct VAT.[23] Tax concessions were also available for investments in designated 'underdeveloped' regions, and government grants were available for the development of a company's infrastructure, if a foreign investor was involved and certain requirements were met.[24]

Ventures formed with private and non-state ownership no longer required any formal authorization. But projects involving 10 per cent or more of a state enterprise's assets would still need approval from the State Privatisation Agency (SPA), which oversees the privatisation process.[25] A FIE could acquire land and buildings necessary for the conduct of its business and the law no longer restricted the presidency or directorship of the Board to the Hungarian citizens. The present regulations allow foreign investors to establish or to buy into companies under the same conditions as Hungarian citizens. In fact, there is no need any more for special licenses to start even a 100 per cent foreign-owned venture in Hungary.

These generous provisions were important. The collapse of the socialist systems of Eastern Europe has meant that the former USSR satellite countries were now vying with each other for the good graces of foreign investors. Consequently Hungary's policy towards JVs was both rational and expedient. But this was developed under time pressure and in competition with other Eastern European countries. Nonetheless, over-generous tax breaks, particularly for an indefinite period were a double-edge sword. It can be argued that the real long-term goal must be to encourage foreign and indigenous business people to work under the same conditions in Hungary. The more extensive and various incentives initially are, the more conflict and instability will be generated when they are taken away.

Tax legislation as of 1 January 1992 set a deadline after which tax concessions on foreign investment would no longer be granted. The Law stated that by the end of 1993, foreign investors would not be able to benefit from any outright tax incentives. But concessions prior to this date would remain in effect for the specified period.[26] It was suggested that foreign investors preferred equal treatment with domestic competitors,[27] as they were primarily interested in the maintenance of protected markets, rather than tax relief.[28] But in reality, special treatment for large investment projects was maintained because of the demands of foreign partners. This new incentive scheme which does not discriminate between Hungarian and foreign capital is based on a points system reflecting three criteria: economic performance, sectoral priority and regional priority. An investment that brings in capital in priority sectors and is located in a less developed region, on this basis, will attract a high rating. It is hoped that this step will not lead to a drop in the volume of foreign investments or slow down the growth of the total volume of foreign investment in Hungary.

By virtue of the laws passed to date, compared with other Eastern European countries, Hungary can be classified as a liberal market economy, as it allows currency convertibility, 100 per cent foreign ownership, duty exemptions, and the import of capitalised assets, and there are no restrictions on the employment of foreign nationals in top management positions.

The macro-investment environment in Hungary in the 1990s

International experience indicates the fact that FDI is determined by the totality of economic conditions, including the macro and microeconomic climate, growth potential, and the prospect of long-term social and political stability. The increasing of foreign inward capital on the host country's growth, its technological development and, employment is closely related to the quality of the indigenous environment and its absorptive capacity. The impact of FDI depends on the economic policy of the receiving nation, on the extent which the domestic economy is able to effectively integrate this resource.

In order to attract further FDI, with new technology, management know-how and improved marketing opportunities, the Hungarian government tried to create a rational environment for foreign investment by liberalising its financial and international trade system and accelerating its privatisation process.

The amended Transformation Act in 1991 provided the framework for state-owned companies to be transformed into public limited companies (Plcs) and limited companies (Ltds). This conversion of SOEs into joint-stock companies, as a result of widespread privatisation, offered foreign investors more chances to invest in Hungary. The reasons why Hungary has sought foreign participation in the purchase of SOEs were very similar to those enterprises attracting FDI for creating new enterprises. It was aimed at reducing Hungary's indebtedness by attracting a new inflow of convertible currency with the following objectives: to raise productivity by introducing modern technology, know-how, and management and marketing skills; to bring standards of quality, safety, environmental acceptability, and competitiveness closer to those prevailing on international markets, thereby generating new flows of exports, a larger foreign markets share, and increased convertible currency revenue; and to augment the total amount of capital available to modernise the obsolescent infrastructure and production structures associated with the ageing capital stock. Given the strength of these motives, it is not surprising that Hungary has offered generous legislation designed to attract FDI in its privatisation programme. As a result, half of the inward foreign investment in 1991 had been committed in privatised firms in Hungary.

The development of money and capital markets is also of extreme importance for the investment climate of foreign inward investment. Well-developed financial markets could offer wholly foreign-owned firms and JVs new opportunities employing their cash reserves, and re-investing their profits in securities, if they wish to do so. If it is assumed for some foreign portfolio investors to interest in Hungarian securities, convertibility of the local currency with a relatively stable exchange rate is an important precondition.

From early 1988, a 'stock exchange' was opened in Budapest. At first it opened on a fortnight basing but late in 1988 it became a daily operation.[29] This stock exchange dealt with bonds and treasury bills together with quoting and trading shares. The stock exchange operation made portfolio investment in shares possible for foreigners. However, this possibility was more of a theoretical than practical nature. As long as the Forint remains inconvertible (as convertibility of the local currency with a relatively stable exchange rate is an important precondition for portfolio investment), interest in portfolio investments in Hungary from abroad will remain limited. Indeed, in order to solve this problem, some Hungarian firms have been listed their shares in stock exchanges aboard (such as in Zurich and Frankfurt) and attracted foreign investors to invest in the shares of Hungarian firms.[30] In April 1992, the NBH decided to allow foreigners to purchase state securities indirectly through an investment fund controlled by the government. The Bank's new regulations allowed up to 20 per cent of the fund (some US$37.5 million) to be owned by foreigners. Hungary uses the proceeds from the sale of securities to reduce the budget deficit. Previously, the Bank had barred foreigners from buying Hungarian state securities, fearing that the country would lose money through the transaction as a much higher interest rate has been paid in the securities than that of similar securities in Western Europe. The creation of an investment fund controlling the level of investment made losses less likely.[31]

However, even if it is assumed that no big rush of portfolio investors can be expected in Hungary after the enforcement of the new company law, the Hungarian business environment is moving in the right direction making Hungary more attractive for Western investors than any other Eastern European country.

China's Open-Door policy and FDI regulations

The implementation of the principle of 'self-reliance' between 1965 and 1978 excluded all foreign capital from China. 1978, however, marked an historical turning point for China, as the country announced a dramatic programme for reforming its economic system and opening its economy to the outside world. According to Grub and Lin, 'these policies have differed substantially from the pre-reform stage when external financing was limited, trade highly centralised, and foreign investment prohibited'.[32] Over the past 17 years or so, systematic efforts have been made at central and provincial levels to attract foreign capital from Hong Kong/Macao, Taiwan, and Western countries for various forms of participatory investments in existing Chinese industrial manufacturing enterprises or creating new foreign invested enterprises.

Beginning in early 1979, the government began to adopt an experimental approach, or so-called 'crossing the river by feeling the stones under the water' combining 'activeness' and 'caution'. Reforms have occurred step-by-step, often province by province, with liberalisation occurring first in agriculture and only later in the banking and state enterprise sectors; foreign investors were to be permitted into China in a step-by-step process, initially in a few designated Special Economic Zones (SEZs) regarded as 'experimental labs', where business could be carried out with little state interference and much preferential treatment. If things worked well in these SEZs, the practice could then be extended into other parts of the country.[33] So, from 1979 to 1992, China promulgated over 500 laws and regulations towards FDI dealing not only with taxation and fiscal incentives, but also banking loans, labour relations, trademarks and patents, technology importation and licensing, accountancy practices, arbitration and bankruptcy.[34]

Between 1979 and 1982, China's overall policy towards FDI evolved slowly and foreign capital flows into the country remained limited. From 1983 to 1985, China's efforts to attract FDI were more active. The opening up of 14 coastal cities brought about the first boom in FDI in 1984. However, the over-heated economic problems in 1986-87 led to a policy retrenchment that reversed the trend of FDI growth. The second boom in FDI followed the introduction of the 'Golden Coast' development strategy and increased preferential treatment of foreign investors in 1988. This boom, however, was accompanied by high inflation and other domestic economic problems. The tragic political turmoil in the Spring of 1989 abruptly terminated the boom and curtailed FDI growth. In 1990, the government decided to develop the Pudong New Area as the priority in China's medium-term reform strategy, and this new step led to the third boom in FDI. After 1990, significant structural changes have been undertaken within the Chinese economy.[35] In this section, we will concentrate on the Chinese legal system affecting FDI and JVs during these four stages.

Cautious legalisation relating to FDI, 1979-82

Accepting FDI was an unprecedented course for China after 1949. Efforts in this period were, therefore, concentrated on creating the legislative framework and the SEZs experiment, with FDI deliberately treated as an important capital resource for economic development.

The equity JV Law and other statutory efforts In July 1979, shortly after the 1978 decision on the Open Door policy, the government moved rapidly in taking its first step towards adopting FDI legislation by announcing the Law of the People's Republic of China (hereafter PRC) on Joint Ventures Using Chinese and Foreign Investment (often referred to as the Equity Joint Venture Law, hereafter EJVL).[36] This permitted foreign investors to operate within the territory of the People's Republic of China and highlighted the crucial role of foreign capital in the process of industrialisation. It guaranteed foreign investors property and dividend rights, tax incentives and the entitlement to remit their after-tax profits abroad.[37] It also stipulated the objectives of JVs policy, the approval procedure,[38] JVs' operational sectors, organisation and termination,[39] marketing and financing,[40] foreign currency regulations,[41] investment protection,[42] as well as operational management. One of the most essential government policies towards FDI was that foreign investors were generally expected to furnish their own machinery, equipment and - where possible - raw materials, to be combined with cheap labour to generate an output destined for exports, rather than the domestic market. In other word, FDI ventures were expected to seek to balance their own foreign exchange requirements and help generate extra hard foreign currency to finance the desired import programmes.

The EJVL specified 25 per cent as the minimum share to be held by the foreign partner. Both partners were to share profits, losses and risks according to their respective investment, and shares could not be transferred to a third party except with the approval of the company. Foreign and local partners were allowed to capitalise the value of their asset contribution, which could take the form of cash, contributions in kind, or intangible assets, such as advanced technology.[43]

In a strict legal sense, the EJVL was more a statement of principles than a specific law, as it was a characteristically vague formulation, leaving wide room for discriminatory interpretation. Terms concerning many important aspects, such as taxation, land use, labour management, and input sources, were either omitted or defined only in a very broad way. The absence of a definitive, tried and comprehensive legal framework, especially a tried system

34

of patent protection,[44] created many difficulties.[45] For example, the EJVL usually stipulated that materials and equipment should be supplied from Chinese sources, where and whenever feasible. Yet for investors with even limited knowledge of the Chinese economy, the likelihood of secure and timely supplies was known to be low, in spite of the fact that Chinese 'sales cadres' insisted that once a JV agreement was reached, the necessary Chinese input would be incorporated into the state production and distribution plans.[46] Another problem which arose for foreign investors was the Chinese attempt of combine the earning of hard currency (by selling materials to JVs) with an ambitious, 'leapfrog to export-oriented foreign investment'. It was an approach in sharp contrast with the practice of most industrializing nations in Asia, where foreign investment is part of a policy of import substitution. It was certainly unwelcomed by many Western investors whose purpose in investing is to get a foothold in the vast Chinese market itself, and not to create a Frankenstein of Chinese competition that will undermine them in third country markets.[47]

The weakness of the EJVL was understandable given the lack of relevant experience in China. To some extent, the broadness and even vagueness of the EJVL appeared desirable at this early stage as this allowed both the investors and the hosts more room in negotiating contracts that best fitted specific situations.[48] Moreover, the first law meant to set a general framework within which more specific laws and regulations could be constructed later. As it turned out, the Chinese government continued its statutory efforts in the following three years to fill many of the gaps left by the EJVL. By the end of 1982, there were already about a dozen new laws and regulations concerning FDI activities, covering such aspects as taxation, financing, foreign exchange, labour management.[49]

According to the 'Income Tax Law', the taxable income of a JV was to be the net income in a tax year after deduction of costs, expenses and losses in that year, and the rate of income tax on JVs was to be 30 per cent. In addition, a local surtax of 10 per cent of the assessed tax would be levied. In the case of a foreign participant in a JV remitting its share of profit from China, an income tax of 10 per cent was to be levied on the repatriated amount (Article 1). Certain JVs were entitled to preferential tax treatment: newly established JVs scheduled to operate for a period of 10 years or more with the approval of the tax authorities could be exempted from income tax in the first and second profit-making year, and allowed a 50 per cent reduction between the third and the fifth year of operation. With the approval of the Ministry of Finance, JVs engaged in such low-profit operations as farming and forestry or located in remote, economically underdeveloped outlying areas could be allowed a 15-30 per cent reduction in income tax for a period of 10 additional years. In the case of a JV participant reinvesting his share of profit

35

in China for a period of not less than five years, a refund of 40 per cent of the income tax paid on the reinvested amount could be obtained with the approval of the tax authorities.

'The Individual Income Tax Law' and 'The Regulations on Labour Management in Joint Ventures Using Chinese and Foreign Investment' set a specific stipulation regarding JVs' individual income tax and labour management.[50]

All these important laws and regulations granted to foreign investors significant preferential treatment, that was not enjoyed by domestic enterprises.[51] FIEs were given greater decision-making autonomy in terms of production, raw materials procurement, and marketing than their local counterparts. FIEs were permitted to create and implement its own production plan, provided that it was filed with relevant government authorities in accordance with keeping requirements.

Apart from enjoying favourable tax holidays, deductions, and exemptions, as well as greater decision-making authority in production and marketing, FIEs also enjoyed greater authority than SOEs in hiring and firing employees.

The establishment of four SEZs   A Central Committee meeting on Special Economic Zones held in July 1981 confirmed that 'experiences of many countries in the world have proved that special zones provide a relatively successful form for expanding exports, attracting foreign capital, absorbing technology and developing economies'.[52] The establishment of the four SEZs - Shenzhen, Zhuhai, Shantou in Guangdong Province and Xiamen in Fujian Province in southern China -was another unprecedented step in the overall domestic reform and the development of an Open Door policy. The SEZs were expected to serve as experimental 'laboratories' for new economic policies and were designed to benefit the Chinese economy as a whole.[53]

In July 1979, the central government decided that 'the construction of SEZs should mainly depend on the absorption of foreign capital and funds provided by overseas Chinese',[54] and thereafter granted Guangdong and Fujian Provinces more autonomous power[55] enabling them to find their own solutions to financial bottlenecks for developing the four SEZs' relatively poor infrastructure.[56] So SEZ legislation in 1980 further specified that all construction activities in the zones, such as 'levelling, land preparation, construction work for water supply, drainage, electric power, roads, docks, communications, warehouses and other public facilities', should encourage foreign participation.[57] In addition, foreign companies were encouraged to invest in hotels, tourist development and real estate within the SEZs during this period.[58] Therefore, the 'Market Mechanism' instead of the central planning system played the major role in regulating the economy within the SEZs in order to create an environment similar to that in the West.[59] The central government also granted a large measure of autonomous power to the SEZs, which allowed them to make most of their own decisions without much outside bureaucratic interference.[60]

In order to attract foreign capital into the SEZs, the central and local governments announced a series of preferential measures for investors in these zones, to reduce government intervention and to create an environment in which foreign investors could operate more profitably in a more Western market-oriented context. FIEs in these SEZs enjoyed many liberalised policies and special incentives, including tax holidays and preferential foreign exchange treatment. Tax holidays of up to five years were available to most JVs and tax reductions or exemptions of 20 to 50 per cent were allowed to firms investing more than US$5 million in a single project and introducing advanced technologies that were not available locally. Firms that reinvested their profits in the SEZs were exempted from income tax on the investment amount for up to five years, depending on such factors as the amount of investment, the nature of the technology, and the duration of the project. FIEs within the zones would also enjoy a right to remit profits abroad without remittance tax, an exemption from customs duties on imported machinery, equipment and transportation needed for production, and an exemption from import duties on parts and raw materials used to make export products.[61] FIEs within the SEZs were also allowed to lease land for up to 20 years for commercial purposes, 30 years for manufacturing and tourist purposes, and 50 years for residential purposes. Since their establishment, the SEZs have recorded remarkable achievements in terms of overall economic development, foreign capital and technology utilisation, and export/import growth.

Up to 1982, China's policy towards FDI outside the SEZs remained rather prudent. Foreign ownership was limited to 49 per cent or less in most JVs and restrictions were imposed on domestic sales by FIEs. FDI projects applying for approval during this period often needed to demonstrate a capacity to generate 'products which are mainly for marketing abroad and which can utilize the marketing network of foreign firms to enter the international market and create foreign exchange'.[62]

With the exception of the four SEZs and the two surrounding provinces - Guangdong and Fujian - procedures for project approval were highly centralized and strictly controlled during this period.[63] The decision-making process for FDI projects in China was quite complex, and lengthy. But given the rapid development of FDI and China's contemporary economic system, this complicated structure for FDI decision-making was necessary. As FDI increased, this structure was simplified between 1983 and 1985.

In 1982, one of the Chinese Communist Party's most authoritative journals - Hongqi (Red Flag) - strongly recommended that 'in the near future courting direct investment should become the most important method [of utilizing foreign capital].'[64] And this line had been confirmed by the decision to 'open up' 14 major coastal cities, by conferring on them privileges similar to those enjoyed by the SEZs.

The opening-up of 14 Coastal Cities and new development of FDI regulations, 1983-85

Several important facts increased domestic pressure for a greater emphasis on opening the economy to the outside world in 1983-85. The significant improvement in the macroeconomic situation and the rapid development of rural reform added new pressures for urban industrial change.

The vague legal framework during 1979-82 failed to provide strong incentives as it left potential investors with the impression that the standard tax rates contained a large margin within which the Chinese could discriminate from case to case. It was against this background, and of the disheartening performance of 1980-82, that a new series of tax, tariff and other policy measures were hurriedly introduced between March and May 1983. The measures included:

(1)   Reduction of the tax rate from 20 per cent to 10 per cent on interest income for capital brought into China;

(2)   Complete exemption from import duties and industrial-commercial taxes for machinery and equipment imported for JVs;

(3)   A generous extension of the tax holiday periods for newcomers, especially for investments from Hong Kong, Macao and Overseas Chinese;

(4)   An enhanced (though still vague) prospect of sales to the Chinese domestic market.[65] Especially, in order to encourage wider use of FDI, China announced the 'Implementation of the Regulations of the Joint Venture Law' (hereafter 'Implementation Regulations') in 1983. This contained 118 articles and covered a wide range of legal aspects affecting JVs, such as registration, formation, organisation, operation, taxation, financing, labour termination, and dispute settlement. It was mainly an effort to clarify many issues that had been insufficiently specified or left vague in earlier regulations, and signified the willingness of the government to make new concessions in order to attract the desired FDI.[66]

A more favourable context for FDI growth emerged in the spring of 1984,

38

when Deng Xiaoping remarked that 'we must clarify one guiding principle, which is not to check the opening process, but to open [the door] wide'.[67] Later that year, Deng re-emphasised this principle by saying that:

To realise the goal, China will adhere to the policy of opening to the world both now and in the future. If China closes its doors, it will never succeed in Socialist modernisation.[68]

In October 1984, the Central Committee announced the historic 'Decision on Reform of the Economic Structure', calling for the building of a 'Socialist Commodity Economy' by assigning a larger role to the market in the domestic economic system.[69]

Since then, there appeared to be a special enthusiasm promoting FDI as an important way to aid domestic reform. It soon became necessary to allow FDI to go beyond the limits of the SEZs into China's major industrial cities.

For the first time, China allowed some JVs to sell mainly in the Chinese market, so long as the products were urgently needed or were import substitutes because of the absence of domestic sources of supply. It also stipulated that those imports relating to export-oriented production could be exempted from customs duties ('Implementation Regulations', Art.71). Other preferential treatment included the liberalisation of policies on credit, profits, remittances, and taxes.[70] It reaffirmed that the board of directors was the highest authority of JVs and could decide all important issues ('Implementation Regulations', Art.33, 35 and 36). Though many of the legal rules and definitions were still ambiguous, their standard was considerably improved, providing greater investment incentives for foreign investors.

Based on the successful experience and remarkable performance of the SEZs, the Chinese government took a further step in 1984 to open 14 coastal cities[71] to the outside world. This was designed to attract further foreign capital, technology and management in order to improve overall economic development in these coastal cities, and to develop an export base that would generate foreign currency earnings and meet rapidly growing capital needs.

Following the approach adopted in the SEZs, the 14 cities were given more autonomy in economic decision-making. They could initiate and approve FDI projects up to a stated level of capital investment.[72] They were also given the right to retain and spend foreign exchange generated locally for their own development. This autonomy greatly simplified the approval procedures for foreign invested projects.

Preferential treatment was given to foreign investors establishing JVs in these cities. This included a tax reduction from 30 to 15 per cent for FIEs using high technology or promoting exports, and for long-term investment projects involving more than US$30 million in foreign capital. A JV was normally exempt from income taxes for the first two years after generating an initial profit and paid only half the required taxes between the third and fifth year. A technology-intensive JV was required to pay only half of its income taxes between the sixth and eighth year (Grub and Lin, 1991, p.48). Exemption was also granted from customs duty, and the consolidated industrial and commercial tax for production equipment and building materials imported by FIEs, raw materials, parts and packaging imported for producing export goods, and for private vehicles, office equipment and daily necessities imported for foreign staff. Export products were also to exempt from customs duty and the consolidated industrial and commercial tax.[73] A JV scheduled to operate over a period of 10 years or more could be exempted from income tax in the first and second profit-making years and allowed a 50 per cent reduction in the third to fifth year, as the revised Income Tax Law of PRC on JVs stipulated. Finally, the central government decided that a certain proportion of FIE products could be sold on the domestic market, but permission was mainly given for products using advanced foreign technology that were badly needed by the local economy. However, there was no official ratio was set for domestic and overseas sales of products manufactured with foreign investment.

The period 1983-85 thus saw a rapid process of both vertical decentralisation and horizontal proliferation of FDI decision-making. Local authorities gained more autonomous power in FDI affairs. The opening of these 14 cities reflected, to a large extent, China's determination to pursue an open-door policy in a long term.

Forced retrenchment and improved legislation, 1986-87

In 1986-87, when priority was given to the task of 'improving the domestic investment environment', the central government took several resolute steps towards controlling FDI. An attempt was made to bring foreign trade under better control by imposing stricter regulations on foreign exchange allocation in 1985. In 1986 a more restrictive import and export licensing system, and strict controls on bank credits and loans to FIEs were implemented. Foreign investment projects in hotel construction and other travel services were abandoned or placed under strict control. All these policy adjustment had a very negative impact on FDI growth.

In order to maintain investors' confidence, the government launched a number of efforts to increase FDI by reformulating its policies. Although a FIE was allowed to sell its products in the local market, but if this represented a significant share of its output, the FIEs faced great difficulty in converting profits realised in local currency into hard currency, which was necessary in order to remit profits home. In order to help FIEs to achieve a balance between foreign exchange revenue and expenditure, and to facilitate the remittance of profits abroad, on 15 January 1986 the government promulgated the 'Regulations on Joint Ventures' Balance of Foreign Exchange Revenue and Expenditure'. These encouraged foreign investors to promote international exports and to set up import-substitution firms to produce what China needed by allowing them to sell their products on the domestic markets, thereby reducing imports and saving foreign exchange. FIEs were allowed to use foreign currency in quoting prices and settling accounts when they sold their products to local enterprises, which were able to pay in foreign currency (Art.8). Foreign investors incurring a foreign currency deficit could swap foreign currency among their JVs (Art.9). They could also reinvest their share of Chinese currency profits in other JVs capable of earning more foreign currency, and thereby obtain a repayment of any income tax already paid, as well as additional foreign exchange (Art.10). For import-substitution projects, the government would be responsible for providing foreign exchange assistance in balancing a project's foreign exchange receipts and expenditures. But permission for domestic sales for import substitution became increasingly difficult to obtain and was subject to annual examination.[74] Moreover, JVs were encouraged to use their Chinese currency earnings to purchase local products for export to other countries in order to earn hard currencies.

On 12 April 1986, the government took another step forward by publishing 'The Law of the People's Republic of China on Wholly Foreign-owned Enterprises' (WFOEs) which allowed foreign investors to establish WFOEs while protecting their investment, profits and other lawful rights and interests in China. This law stipulated that all WFOEs were to be free from interference in their operation and management activities, provided they opened account books in China and paid taxes according to the relevant regulations; and would accordingly enjoy preferential treatment concerning taxation exemption and deduction. If a proportion of net profit was reinvested in China, WFOEs might apply for a refund of the income tax paid on the reinvested amount. They were to settle their foreign exchange balance independently, and could remit abroad their legitimate profits, as well as other earnings.

The most important laws during this period were the 'Provisions of the State Council on the Encouragement of Foreign Investment' (hereafter 'the 22 Provisions') promulgated on 11 October 1986, followed by 13 detailed regulations published in the following year or so. 'The 22 Provisions' provided more specific measures for coping with a comprehensive set of problems, such as enterprise autonomy, profit remittances, labour recruitment, and land use.

Most of the provisions simply reemphasized the incentives and regulations already in existence or provided additional investment incentives to foreign investors.[75] The main difference was that special preferences were now granted to the following two categories of FIEs, i.e., export-oriented and

41

technologically advanced enterprises. These were to enjoy several important incentives, such as exemption from paying state subsidies, priority in receiving Bank of China loans, tax exemption for profits remitted abroad, an extended period for income tax reduction, and additional tax benefits for re-invested profits, as well as other privileges in tariffs, land usage, and operational facilities.

At the same time, the government re-affirmed that foreign parent companies would continue to enjoy full participation in all JV decision-making, urged authorities at various levels to 'integrate FDI into the state plan', and specified the price range of major inputs - raw materials, land use fees, and wages - to prevent local abuses. Moreover, considerable efforts were also made to reduce bureaucratic problems.[76]

'Coastal Development Strategy' and two years of retrenchment, 1988-89

During his inspection trips to the coastal provinces in the winter of 1987-88, the ex-Party leader Zhao Ziyang made frank comments on the need to promote a wider economic opening towards the outside world and launched the 'Coastal Development Strategy', based on the theory of 'Great International Circulation'[77]. This strategy declared the entire coastal strip (including the Yangze River Delta around Shanghai, the Pear River Delta near Guangzhou, the Southern Fujian Triangle, and the Liaoning and Shandong Peninsulas) would be opened up to foreign investment. This strategy called for '[placing] two heads outside' - relying on the outside world for both input supplies and market outlet, and declared that China could follow the path of South Korea, Taiwan, Hong Kong and Singapore in order to benefit from the international investment and commodity flows and generate extra foreign earnings for domestic finance, without exposing the centralised industrial core to the outside world. The essential feature of the Chinese approach is that it has simultaneously moved away from 'import substitution' ot 'export-orientated' foreign investment, whilst retaining the basic elements of an inwardly-orientated industrialisation strategy.[78]

The central government also decided to make Hainan - China's second largest and relatively underdeveloped island - the biggest SEZ and a separate province providing an even better investment environment with additional incentives to enhance development. These areas together formed a belt that was the wealthiest in the country and the most attractive to potential foreign investors.[79] As a further effort to lure more FDI into these newly opened areas, the government extended much of the favourable treatment already given to FDI in the SEZs and 'open cities' to these areas by granting generous incentives relating to taxes, customs duties, land use, and local employment. Finally, all areas were given greater autonomy to decide on new FDI projects and were permitted to retain part of locally generated foreign exchange as working funds for their own future development.

The encouragement of WFOEs was clearly related to the severe shortage of capital resulting from two years of a tight domestic monetary policy.

Finally, a key aspect of the 1988 'Coastal Development Strategy' was the call for foreign management. Foreign businessmen had complained so loudly about the difficulties of doing business in China and the logical remedy was to allow them to 'run their businesses according to the international standard'. 'For a while at least', Zhao Ziyang reportedly said, 'the management of Sino-foreign JVs and cooperative enterprises should be left to the foreign side'. This would not lead to the loss of state sovereignty. Instead, it could help China 'shake off the fetters of the old system and promote strict management [at home]'.[80]

The 1988 'Coastal Development Strategy' stirred up some new expectations among foreign investors.[81] Especially small and medium-sized investors willing to exploit the cheap labour resources of the country, responded immediately to this new drive. As a result, FDI flows into China boomed in 1988 and the early of 1989. But it was abruptly interrupted first by the adoption of a rectification and readjustment programme in late 1988 and then by the political upheaval of 'Tiananmen Square Event' on 4 June 1989.

Moreover, since the early 1990s, China has allowed selected provincial governments to establish Economic and Technology Development Areas (ETDAs), offering tax and duty concessions to exporters and foreign investors. 'In a bid to attract more high technology investment, China has set up 27 new high-technology zones across the country, lifting the total to 38. Foreign investors in the zones will pay just 15 per cent income tax - compared with the standard rate of 33 per cent. If they export 70 per cent of their output, tax falls still further to 10 per cent.'[82]

During this period the Chinese government continued to improve the FDI legal framework. The 'Regulation Concerning Charging and Settling in Foreign Currencies within the Territory' promulgated on 1 March 1989 stipulated that a JV could apply to sell its products within China in foreign currencies, as long as its products were a substitute for imports within the state plan, or could be sold to the SEZs, ETDAs and other FIEs, or could be used instead of imported materials and parts for local manufacturing enterprises. 'The Regulation Concerning FIES Opening a Foreign Exchange Account outside China' promulgated on 1 March 1989 allowed FIEs in China to open banking accounts outside China if required by their special business needs. 'The Law of the People's Republic of China on Sino-foreign Contractual Joint Ventures' promulgated on 13 April 1989 encouraged foreign investors to establish export-oriented or technology-advanced manufacturing contractual JVs (CJVs) in China, and could raise funds domestically and internationally, import necessary materials for production and export its products, as long as it could balance its foreign exchange account. It also provided more specific measures for enterprise autonomy, preferential taxation, profit remittance, labour recruitment, land use, and contract termination.

From the outset, China apparently found it necessary to accommodate foreign interests by allowing technologically selected FIEs to target the domestic market. Moreover, the urge to court foreign capital also prompted the Chinese authorities increasingly to compromise their established import-substitution policy, by opening up areas of hitherto strictly-controlled domestic goods and service markets to FDI.

The development of Pudong New Area and China's radical FDI policy, 1990-93

Strengthening FDI regulations: The Chinese government has been keen to attract foreign capital from Hong Kong/Macao, Overseas Chinese and more recently Taiwanese. It has even given greater incentives to these investors. The focus on these regions has been politically informed by the prospect of eventual reunification. The realisation, however, that Hong Kong/Macao and Taiwanese companies have been investing primarily in commercial, non-productive, low-technology projects yielding quick profits, has in turn prompted policy-makers to seek ways to encourage European, American and Japanese investment. The dissatisfaction of the reformist leadership with the pattern of foreign direct investment since 1979 has increased the weight accorded to the interests of foreign investors, particularly from the USA, Japan and Western Europe.

Since the early 1990s, the government has made further special efforts to expand economic and technological cooperation and promote FDI by strengthening FDI regulations. The government, first of all, strengthened FDI regulations by revising 'The Law of the People's Republic of China on Equity Joint Ventures' on 4 April 1990, which redefined the criteria relating to the selection of chairmen of JV boards[83], the period of operation,[84] and non-nationalization.[85]

In December 1990, the central government promulgated another important regulation - 'Detailed Rules and Regulations for the Implementation of the People's Republic of China Concerning Joint Ventures with Chinese and Foreign Investment' which aimed to encourage those JVs that utilised advanced technology or equipment, developed new products, saved energy and materials, up-graded products, and facilitated import substitution; and/or annually exported 50 per cent of total output, maintained balanced foreign exchange accounts or generated on exchange surplus. Like Hungarian legislation, this regulation specified the sectors into which foreign capital would not be allowed or encouraged, such as newspapers and publishing, news broadcasting, TV communications and movies; domestic wholesaling and retailing, foreign trade, insurance. JVs would also only have a restricted role in the following industries: public utilities; transportation; estate; investment or unit trusts; and leasing. Proposals would also be rejected which damaged existing sovereignty or public interests, endangered state safety, or violated China's laws and regulations, produced environmental pollution, and/or failed to meet the requirements of national economic development.

All FIEs would enjoy autonomy in deciding and implementing their production and operation plans, including the purchase of necessary machines, equipment, raw materials, and parts would enjoy the same conditions as local enterprises. They could sell their products on the local market according to an approved sales ratio and obtain permission to exceed this, if required. FIEs could pursue their sales on Chinese and international markets directly or through Chinese agents.

On 1 July 1991, the new merged income tax law - 'China's Income Tax Law for Enterprises with Foreign Investment and Foreign Enterprises' - became effective. This adopted a uniform tax rate identical to that provided under the Equity JV Tax Law, with a substantially lower rate than the maximum 50 per cent imposed under the Foreign Enterprise Income Tax Law. It offered an additional benefit for both JVs and WFOEs in China by exempting profit distributions from taxation. Furthermore, a rate of 15 per cent was applied to FIEs in the SEZs and certain other geographic areas and specific industries.

The basic tax holiday granted by the new law amounted to an exemption from tax for the first two years following the first profitable year of operation and a 50 per cent reduction for the third through to the fifth years. FIEs engaged in agriculture, forestry, and animal husbandry or located in remote or underdeveloped areas may, upon approval, enjoy a reduction of between 15 and 30 per cent in the income tax rate for an additional ten years following the initial period of tax exemptions and reductions.

The strategy of developing the Pudong New Area In April 1990, the Chinese government made a decision of developing and opening up the Pudong New Area - A triangular area lying to the east of the Huangpu River in Shanghai - as the priority in China's economic reform in the 1990s in order to turn Shanghai into an international hub for finance, economy and trade - the New York of New China. 'Pudong will be a place for experimenting in new policies which maybe we can later apply elsewhere in China. ... It will not be capitalism but we will bring market mechanisms into a planned economy, with public ownership remaining the mainstay. With Pudong we can develop the whole of Shanghai and promote development throughout the country'.[86] The government hoped to encourage economic expansion along south-east China's coast and to overcome the concentration of development in the SEZs of the south. Shanghai is the largest city in China, but for nearly 40 years, it languished as an isolated industrial centre forced to remit as much as 90 per cent of its income to the central government. In order to turn to its former glory as the prosperous and cosmopolitan capital of the region, the central government lowered Shanghai's tax burden and allowed it to form its own SEZs and financial markets.

Since then, the central government and Shanghai Municipality have promulgated various regulations relating to Pudong designed to encourage foreign investment, especially those high-tech enterprises, sophisticated manufacturers and financial companies to set up their China operation in Pudong,[87] involving the administration of financial institutions with foreign or Sino-foreign capital, reduction and exemption of income tax and consolidated industrial and commercial tax, customs duties, etc. As a result, the Pudong New Area operates the most open economic policies in China. Apart from implementing various policies enjoyed by SEZs and ETDAs, it also offers additional preferential policies, which include the following:

(1)   Foreign investors are allowed to operate in the tertiary sector developing department stores and supermarkets;

(2)   The Securities Exchange is permitted to issue 'A' Share Stock and 'B' Share Stock for Pudong's development;

(3)   The free trade zone is exempted from duties, licences, and permits relating to the establishment of international trade organisations by foreign or domestic investors and the retention of foreign currency earned, and to circulate foreign currencies are allowed within the free trade zone;

(4)   Foreign investors are allowed to establish financial institutions, such as banks, financial companies and insurance companies, etc.;

(5)   The central government has granted more decision-making power to Shanghai's local government for approving manufacturing and non-manufacturing projects, and for granting import and export rights to enterprises in the Pudong New Area.

In addition, preferential investment policies in Pudong were evident in relation to customs duties, taxation, profit remittance, and the practice of the 'most-favoured system' in the free trade zone (for further details, see **Appendix 2.1**).

FDI policies after Deng's 'Southern Inspection' and radical economic reform
During his inspection trips to the south of China at the beginning of 1992, Deng Xiaoping made frank comments on the need to promote a wider economic opening towards the outside world: 'Opportunities for rapid development had been missed in the past, and we must grasp this opportunity to develop ourselves, develop our economy'. In the Chinese Spring Festival of 1993, Deng re-emphasized that '[I] hope all of you will miss this chance again. It is seldom for China to have such a big opportunity for rapid development'.[88]

Following Deng's speech, China has developed a new framework for opening up the economy to the outside world. Early in 1992, the central government made further efforts to encourage export-oriented and technologically advanced FIEs in China. Foreign investors were to be allowed to operate in specific sectors, such as wholesaling and retailing, accounting and information consultancy, banking and insurance. Beijing, Shanghai, Tianjin, Guangzhou, Shenzhen and Zhuhai were also granted approval rights for FIEs in the tertiary sector. Furthermore, administrative procedures have been simplified and decentralized in order to create a more conduct commercial environment and reduce bureaucratic complexity. Henceforth, many coastal cities are able to offer foreign investors a 'one-stop-service'. Foreign investors, with minor exceptions, are able to deal exclusively with local officials now empowered to act on matters previously dealt with by central and provincial departments. At the same time, the approval period for investment projects was to be reduced from up to three months to a maximum of a few weeks, even a few days.

More recently China has adopted further attractive measures in order to channel foreign investment into non-opened interior areas to assistant the industrialisation of the Chinese hinterland by diverting the major proportion of hard currency returns earned in the coastal region towards the less inhabited interior provinces, to channel foreign capital into areas where technological and infrastructural improvements are necessary, such as power supply, transportation, telecommunications, raw materials, and agriculture, as well as electronics, chemicals, the automobile and construction industries, finance, retailing, tourism and real estate development. The objective is to upgrade existing technology within the next decade. More specifically, China will encourage the following foreign investment projects:

(1)   Projects using advanced technology to improve product quality, save energy and materials, improve enterprise efficiency, or to produce new

47

equipment and materials to meet market demand;

(2)   Export-oriented projects to upgrade product quality and expand exports
        by meeting international market demand, and thereby increasing
        foreign exchange. The Chinese government does not encourage foreign
        investment involving a well-developed technology where capacity
        already exceeds domestic demand, export potential is limited, or where
        exports may need an export quota. Foreign investors are encouraged
        to establish additional large-scale enterprises with advanced technology
        in priority areas, but in other cases small and medium-size projects are
        preferred, where advanced technology can be used to reform existing
        enterprises. Products can be sold at domestic and international
        markets,and China's domestic market is open to FIEs provided they
        can balance their foreign exchange.[89] In order to reduce China's
        infrastructural bottleneck and encourage foreign investment in building
        power stations, highways, railways, bridges, tunnels, docks and
        airports, the government has also adopted and speeded up the build-
        operate-transfer (BOT) formula[90] as an attractive means of attracting
        more foreign capital to large construction projects.

Following the GATT requirements, China is considering giving 'National
Treatment' status to foreign investors, who will enjoy equality with domestic
competitors in all aspects of taxation, sales, transportation, purchase,
distribution, and operation,[91] according to international practice.[92] The
Chinese government is thereby creating a fair competitive environment by
improving the legal framework and the transparency of regulations bringing
Chinese practices closer to international standards.[93]

The Third Plenary Session of the 14th Central Committee of the Communist
Party of China, held in Beijing between 11 and 14 November 1993, published
the 'Decision on Issues Concerning the Establishment of a Socialist Market
Economic Structure'. It clearly declared that the Chinese government 'is
determined to push ahead with further reforms to create a market
economy'.[94] The government is to retain majority ownership of only the
bigger SOEs. Smaller SOEs are candidates for privatisation. Market pricing
is to be extended from product markets (where 90 per cent of prices are now
set by supply and demand) to labour, property and financial markets. The
government is to start asserting control through macroeconomic instruments
instead of administrative orders. Interest rates are to be set by the market. The
People's Bank of China is to become a real central bank. The commercial
banks are to be relieved of making 'policy' loans and will then have to make
their own way without government help. Abolition of the two tier exchange
rate system and the shift to convertibility could happen before the year of

2000 as China is gradually closing the gap between the official and the swap market rates. China is entering a crucial stage of its reform programme: an overhaul of the banking system, far-reaching reforms of the tax regime, further trade liberalisation, and creative approaches to dealing with debt-ridden SOEs.[95] This will require solutions to the problems of growing inequality and macroeconomic instability, if development is to continue at the same pace in double figures.[96] These reforms, especially the unification of the multi-tiered currency at the beginning of 1994 and the establishment of an interbank money market has bolstered China's exports, reserves, and economic growth. More or less, 'a sustainable boom of 10 per cent real GDP growth a year for the rest of the century can be expected'.[97]

The Chinese government realised that in utilising foreign capital, '[we] should implement a strategy of combining import substitution and export promotion. First of all, [we] should make use of foreign capital in order to import advanced technology. As a reward, [we] should open up parts of the domestic market to products for which our country has hitherto relied on imports. The implementation of this strategy will have a positive effect on raising our country's economic capability and technological level, as well as realising [the goal of] industrialisation and building up an independent and integrated industrial system.'[98] Since 1993, the Chinese government has introduced the following preferential policies to encourage MNCs to invest in China: FIEs can regulate foreign exchange freely inside China irrespective of regional location; foreign investors are allowed to operate in the fields of retail sales, finance, insurance, aviation, transportation, and consultancy; MNCs are allowed to set up investment trusts, unit trusts and other portfolio investment corporations in China; investment in high-tech industry will enjoy preferential tax policies and domestic marketing privileges; encouragement has been given to FIEs to list themselves on local stock markets.

More recently, China has become cautious about inward investment since the Mexican crisis in 1994. The government has adopted some tough measures to slow the growth of its foreign debt and is likely to unveil new investment guidelines by the end of 1995 aimed at establishing priorities for investment based on the country's needs, and channelling foreign capital into priority areas such as agriculture, infrastructure (including energy and transportation) and to its disadvantaged hinterland, as well as improving the quality of products, saving energy, cleaning up the environment. It will also seek to distinguish more clearly between various categories of investment that are to be 'encouraged, restrained and prohibited' and phase out tax incentives for certain categories of investment that did not meet the new criteria, such as basic-processing industries that wasted energy. China is going to shifting its method of attracting foreign investment from simply giving favourable conditions to that of mutual benefit and long-term cooperation.[99]

Summary

The rapid introduction of political and social mechanisms in China similar to those in the West will be to the long-term advantage of foreign investors. If and when the government succeeds in overcoming the economic systematic difficulties, it will still need to resolve the major problems that had appeared in the late stage of the development of foreign investments by creating more favourable environment through the introduction and amendments of appropriate laws and regulations: different policies should be applied to different industries and products, to reflect the needs both of exploring China's comparative advantage in the international market and of obtaining advanced technology from the West for domestic development. Yet, after nearly three decades of experiment, many have realised that gradual domestic transformation is indeed the key to the final success of foreign capital in China.

The Chinese leadership is undoubtedly aware that there are limits to the expansion of FDI that is exclusively export-orientated. This is not simply because of Western countries' limited capacity to absorb associated products. Rather, it reflects the fact that the accumulation of any substantial trade surplus, such as China presently enjoys with Western countries, invites political pressures from those countries for a reciprocal opening-up of the domestic market. Against the background of intensified American pressure on China to liberalise imports and the country's own greater readiness to accommodate the GATT/WTO's requirements for membership admission, Chinese authorities do appear to be willing gradually to expose protected domestic industries to competitive international pressures.

FDI's future also depends on China's SOEs privatisation, banking reform and currency convertibility. These reforms are likely to become more difficult in years ahead. China's SOEs (accounting for 43 per cent of China's industrial output, 61 per cent of total fixed investment, and in which 40 per cent are making losses) represent the most serious obstacles to China's integration in the international trading system. If private sector can continue to outgrow SOEs, China can impose further drastic and fundamental reform towards banking and SOEs systems, and make the Renmenbi convertible by the turn of the century, the next half of the 1990s may well see the Chinese economy's integration with the western system of free trade and investment flows accelerate.

Conclusion

An understanding of the policy environment in Hungary and China is an essential prerequisite for a thorough analysis of the pattern, determinants and impact of FDI in the following chapters. Investment policies and incentives in Hungary and China cover a wide range of areas, including the following: the degree of foreign ownership; project duration; choice of investment sectors; size of investment project; choice of investment location; lower corporate tax rates. They also relate to the degree of flexibility in land use policies, management, employment, and wage systems, policies on product pricing structures, and the terms for financing and remitting profits.

Hungary and China attempted to motivate and control the operation of MNCs within their territories. Depending on the type of venture, flexible ownership permits foreign investors to choose between a JV with a local partner and a wholly-owned subsidiary. The foreign investor's ability to obtain majority ownership and management control of the venture ensures sufficient flexibility in production, management, financing, marketing, and other important operational decisions. Aside from the possibility of controlling the degree of foreign ownership, the Hungarian and Chinese governments also regulated the following activities: local input purchases; exports of final products and export market controls; transfer pricing; profit and capital repatriation; royalty payments, management fees, etc; provision of loan capital from local v. foreign sources; local participation in top management; level of employment; obligation to train local labour; forms and degree of competition; establishment of R & D; use of locally owned transportation; and environmental and social protection.

The Hungarian and Chinese legislations do not impose any formal limit on the duration of the investment project, allowing investors to operate either on a short- or long-term basis. This is important for certain large-scale manufacturing and raw material development projects require a substantial outlay in the initial investment stage and have a relatively long payback period.

Both governments encourage foreign investment in most industrial sectors, ranging from high-tech to raw material exploration and extraction, as well as in hotels, consumer goods, construction, and other service-oriented operations. The absence of any restriction on the size of a foreign investment project not only encourages large MNCs to locate their resources in Hungary and China, but enables medium- and even small-sized firms to tap the domestic markets through the form of JVs.

But there has been an over-emphasis on FIEs' export-orientation, which might not only threaten exports of traditional products, but also damage both countries' attractiveness for foreign capital. The local economies see FIEs as a means of attracting foreign capital and modern equipment to produce export goods for sale to the West or for import-substitution, as well as a vehicle for the transfer of technology and managerial expertise. The foreign partner, however, is motivated by better access to local markets, an expanding market share, cheap production sites or plentiful sources of raw materials. Both sets of motives mutually contradict one another. If both countries continue to over-stress an export-orientation strategy, it is likely to cause a great deal of disappointment and operational problems, and will set limit to the advantages of local economies.

From the previous discussion, we can conclude that all former CPEs actively compete with each other by offering attractive incentives to attract MNCs and FDI. However, foreign investment laws creating special 'islands' for foreign capital, including free zones, are not sufficient. These procedures, regulations and conditions should not be unduly cumbersome or complicated. International experience suggests that performance criteria such as minimum local ownership, local employment or export targets, although perceived to be in the national interest, are often counter-productive and either discourage foreign investors or give rise to evasion and corruption. Unrestricted access, save for certain listed investments which would either be prohibited or would need screening and licensing, is commended as a more effective approach. The host country should freely allow the transfer of net revenues realised from the investment.

Reasonable and stable tax rates also provide a better incentive for FDI. Hungary and China offer tax concessions to compensate for their low resource endowment and labour skills, and to offset other disadvantages and risks inherent in investing in both countries, these incentives, though, appear to be of little significance in attracting FDI. Most MNCs regard such incentives to be too volatile and transitory, and tax holidays are viewed as illusory as they are usually given to firms during the early years of their operations, when they are least likely to show profits. Individual foreign investors continue to face considerable uncertainty.

Notes

1. Meisner J.(1973), 'Capitalism and Socialism: The Rival Economic Systems', *Warsaw PWE,* p.129.

2. Michalska, Eva (1973), 'Multinational Corporations and Economic Growth', *Gospodarka Planowa (Planned Economy),* May, Warsaw, p.347.

3. *The New York Times,* 15 February 1995.

4. Hoberg, B. and Wahlbin, C. (1984), 'East-West Industrial Cooperation: the Swedish Case', *Journal of International Business Study*, Spring/Summer, p.66.

5. Becvar O. and Vosicky E. (1991), 'Joint Ventures Are Taking Root in Hungary', in Razvigorova, Evka and Wolf-Laudon, Gottfried (ed.), (1991), *East-West Joint Ventures: the New Business Environment*, Blackwell, London, p.94.

6. See, Young, David G. (1993), 'Foreign Direct Investment in Hungary' and Dunning John D. (1993), 'The Prospects for Foreign Direct Investment in Eastern Europe', in Artisien P.et al (1993) (ed.), *Foreign Investment in Central and Eastern Europe*, St. Martin's Press, London, pp.109-22 and pp.16-33.

7. The Ministry of Foreign Economic Relations and Trade (1989), *Survey of Foreign Invested Enterprises in China*, pp.1-10.

8. JVs in Hungary were to be limited to commercial and service activities, but were not allowed to engage directly in production. While companies might hold some industrial assets, such as specialised machinery and equipment or patent rights, they could not own extensive production facilities. JVs arrangements were to have an export, hard-currency-earning orientation; however, arrangements oriented towards import-saving production for the Hungarian market or other Comecon countries would also be encouraged. See 'Decree No.28/1972 (X.3) PM of the Minister of Finance on Economic Associations with Foreign Participation', in Economic Commission for Europe (ECE) (1988), *East-West Joint Ventures: Economic, Financial and Legal Aspects*, UN Publications, New York, pp.148-153; and McMillan, C. H. and Charles, D. P.St. (1973), *Joint Ventures in Eastern Europe: A Three-country Comparison*, Canadian Economic Policy Committee and Howe Research Institute, Ottawa, pp.61-71.

9. With regard to domestic sales, the 1972 law stipulated that JVs - with the exception of those selling directly to the public at large - had to sell products intended for domestic consumption only to wholesale trade enterprises. Exemption to this rule could be granted at the founding stage of the JV. JVs could export their goods directly, without going through foreign trade organisations, but foreign trade permits or approval was required for this purpose.

10. ECE (1989), *East-West Joint Venture Contracts*, UN, New York, pp.5-35.

11. This procedure involved three phases: (1) declaration of intent to found the company had to be filed with the Ministry of Finance and the Ministry of Foreign Trade prior to preparatory negotiations; (2) upon approval, an application for a permit to commence negotiations had to be filed; (3) finally, application must be made for approval of the agreement. See ECE (1989), *East-West Joint Venture Contracts,* UN Publications, New York, p.34.

12. JVs in customs-free zones were regarded as foreign enterprises from the point of view of customs. Foreign employees' wages and salaries could be freely transferred abroad in convertible currencies (in JVs located in free trade zones only 50% of wages could be transferred), and Hungarian employees could be paid additional remuneration. Goods brought into the country from the free trade zones were considered as goods imported from abroad. See Evka Razvigorova and Gottfried Wolf-Laudon (1991) (ed.), *East-West Joint Ventures: The New Business Environment,* Blackwell, London, p.101; and CEC (1988), op.cit, p.68.

13. See UN (1989), 'Chapter III: Joint venture policies of the socialist countries of Eastern Europe', in *Joint Ventures As A Form of International Economic Cooperation,* Taylor & Francis, New York, pp.34-35.

14. Even though all sectors were open to JV operations, there was a priority list of sectoral preferences in which foreign equity participation was specially encouraged by tax incentives. If the JVs activity was of particular importance to the Hungarian economy, i.e. meeting the priority fields requirements set in the sixth Five-Year Plan (1986-90), such as electronics, agricultural and food-processing machinery and equipment, packaging technologies, pharmaceutical, export-oriented or import-substitution production, advanced technology or material and power saving sectors, tourism, etc, and if the stock capital was over Ft25 million and the foreigner's share over 30 per cent, the corporate tax rate was 20 per cent instead of 40 per cent in the first five years, and became 30 per cent from the sixth year. If the companies were prepared to use their net profit for re-investments and if: (1) the amount of such investment attained 50 per cent of the preceding year(s) (maximum period of five years) but not less than Ft5 million, 50 per cent of the paid-in company tax would be reimbursed upon request; or (2) the investment attained 100 per cent of the tax-net profit of the preceding years but not less than Ft10 million, 75 per cent of the paid-in company tax would be returned upon request. See 'Decree of the Minister of Finance No.45/1984 (XII.21) PM on Corporation Tax and Corporation Super-tax', and 'Joint Bulletin No.8001/1985 (Tg.E.7) OT-PM-KkM on the Scope of Outstandingly Important Activities for the Purposes of the Implementation of Decree No.45/1984 (XII.21) PM on Corporation Tax and Corporation Super-Tax', in ECE (1988), op.cit., pp.154-58.

15.UN (1989), *Joint Ventures as a Form of International Economic Cooperation*, Taylor & Francis, New York, p.34.

16.The Act IX (Section 14) of 1988 defined that the tax privileges to be applied as follows: (1) if the foreign share in the statutory funds attains 20 per cent or Ft5 million, a 20 per cent tax on profits was imposed; (2) if more than half of the price returns arising from the output of products or from operating a company-built hotel exceeded Ft25 million comprising a foreign share of 30 per cent, a 60 per cent tax reduction was granted for the first five years and 40 per cent from the sixth year onwards; (3) finally, if the stipulation under (2) was complied with and the company pursued an activity of particular importance, a 100% tax exemption was granted for the first five years, and from the sixth years a 40 per cent tax reduction would be granted. See *Business Eastern Europe*, 24 October 1988, pp.337-8.

17.A decree issued by the Ministry of Finance concerning modifications in the law regarding foreign exchange policy declared that no permission from the foreign exchange authorities was required for the foreign party to take or send shares out of the country, provided the joint-stock company confirmed that the foreign party obtained such shares in accordance with the pertinent regulations. The company could retain the hard-currency contribution of a foreign participant in the joint-stock company as part of its original foreign exchange held by a Hungarian bank. It could use such funds to procure means of production or permanent stock items without obtaining special permission from the foreign exchange authorities. See, Sarkozy T. (1989) (ed.), *Foreign Investment in Hungary*, Hungarian Chamber of Chambers, Budapest.

18.The primary stock of any limited liability company was not to be less than Ft1 million. Every member entering this form of a company must invest at least Ft100,000 as a primary stake. Upon foundation, at least 30 per cent of the primary stock, and not less than Ft500,000 had to be paid up in cash. For a joint-stock company, the following regulations applied: (a) foundation capital had to be no less than Ft10 million; (b) cash investment had not to be less than 30 per cent of total foundation capital or at least Ft5 million; (c) a share had to have a minimum Ft10,000 value; (d) private shares could be freely bought or sold and be purchased by foreigners; (e) if the joint stock company had more than 200 employees over a given fiscal year, one third of the board was to be selected by the workers; and (f) companies could buy each other's stocks and thus gain majority interests in other enterprises.

19.The English text of this act is provided by Hungary Press, Economic Information, Special Issue, February 1989.

20. Gutman, P.(1993), 'Joint Ventures in Eastern Europe and the Dynamics of Reciprocal Flows in East-West Direct Investments: Some New Perspectives', in Artisien P.(1993), et al (ed.), op.cit., p.61.

21. The only obligation for foreign company to repatriate is to obtain a bank certificate, confirming that it has sufficient funds to cover the amount to be repatriated in hard currency. It's assumed, however, that profit repatriation by a FIEs takes place only at year end, when the company declares its annual profits and/or dividends. See Jermakowicz, W. and Drazek, C. (1993), 'Joint Venture Laws in Eastern Europe: A Comparative Assessment', in Artisien et al (ed.), op.cit., pp.154-5.

22. Hungarian Minister of Finance and the Ministry of International Economic Relations (1991), 'Section 15', in 'Chapter III: Provisions as to the Operation of the Companies', in *Unified Text of Act XXIV of 1988 regarding Investments by Non-residents in Hungary with Subsequent Amendments and Supplements*.

23. See 'The Corporate Law', No.LXXXVI/1991.

24. Young, D.G.(1993), op.cit., p.122.

25. Hungarian Minister of Finance and the Ministry of International Economic Relations (1991), 'Chapter III and V', and *Business Eastern Europe*, 14 January 1991, p.12.

26. *Business Eastern Europe*, 16 March 1992, p.125.

27. Kenneth, Froot A. (1992), 'Foreign Direct Investment in Eastern Europe: Some Economic Considerations', paper prepared for the conference 'Transition in Eastern Europe', 26-29 February 1992, Cambridge, Massachusetts.

28. Hunya, Gabor (1992), 'Foreign Direct Investment and Privatisation in Central & Eastern Europe', paper presented at the 2nd EACES Conference, Groningen, the Netherlands, 24-26 September 1992, p.3.

29. Gerasimov, V.(1988), 'Bond, Shares, Stock Exchange and the Forint', *New Times*, No.51, pp.32-33.

30. See Szekely, I.(1989), 'Reform of the Hungarian Financial System', *European Economy*, No.31, p.115.

31. *RFE/RL Research Report*, Vol.1, No.15, 10 April 1992, p.39.

32.Grub, P.D. and Lin, J.H. (1991), *Foreign Direct Investment in China,* Quorum, New York and London, p.17.

33.Wang Dacheng (1985), 'SEZs: Why An Experiment?', *Beijing Review,* No.39, 30 September, pp.4-5.

34.Faber, M. (1993), 'Governance and the Foreign Direct Investor', *IDS Bulletin,* Vol.24, No.1, p.55.

35.China's economic reforms have mainly included the following: the development of special economic zones and open cities; decentralisation of decision-making at the province and city levels; privatisation, including the breakup of communes and the return of private homes to their owners; the authorization of private ownership of property, along with transfer rights; the development of a flourishing private small business sector; the encouragement of foreign direct investment; the implementation of bankruptcy laws; an enhanced role for managers in state-owned enterprises, with greater authority for decision-making and bottom-line profitability; improved labour laws, especially for foreign-owned enterprises; the development of stock and bond market; and greater emphasis on infrastructural enhancement, and a gradual abolition of state monopolies on foreign trade by permitting more active participation by the private sector in external economic activities to meet four modernisation goals.

36.See Fenwick, Ann (1985), 'Equity Joint Ventures in the People's Republic of China:An Assessment of the First Five Years', *Business Lawyer,* Vol.40, No.3, May, pp.837-54.

37.After submitting corporate income tax, and maintaining a reserve, welfare, and enterprise development fund, net profit were to be distributed among all participants according to contractual stipulations. On the basis of Chinese taxation laws and regulations, the venture was to enjoy preferential treatment, such as tax reductions or exemptions. The foreign investors may be refunded part of the enterprise income tax already paid on profits reinvested in China, according to Art.7.

38.The EJVL stipulated a project screening procedure that required all FDI proposals to be examined and approved by the Chinese authorities concerned with foreign economic relations and trade before any formal application was made. The Chinese authorities were to make final decision as to whether a particular project would be approved within 3 months.

39.Regarding enterprise management, however, the law delegated - at least in theory - an absolute right to the board of the venture, constituted according to the percentage of the partners' shares, to decide all important issues, including development strategy, production organisation, recruitment of top managers and engineering staff, distributing profits and deciding wages for the workers, as well as their recruitment or dismissal within the framework of a signed contract. The president of the board had to be a Chinese, but the positions of vice president(s), however, could be taken up by foreigners. 'On all important issues', the EJVL stipulated, 'all participating sides should consult with each other to find the solutions according to the principles of equality and mutual benefits.' If disputes arose, the venture could turn to the Chinese government or a third party that all sides had agreed upon for arbitration. The EJVL did not set a specified duration period for JVs, but stipulated that this would depend on the specific industry involved. Some JVs in certain sectors were to have a fixed duration, while in other cases no termination date was to be set. If all sides in a JV agreed on extension, an application was to submitted to the appropriate authority concerned for approval six months before expiration. But if a JV became insolvent and liabilities exceeded assets, partners were required to apply for dissolution.

40.As regards domestic purchases, JVs were to give priority to purchasing necessary raw materials and components on local market. But they were entitled to make direct purchases from abroad in convertible currencies, which had to be found from JVs' own resources. In principle, the policy was to encourage FIEs to sell their products on international markets, and greater access to the Chinese market was essentially reserved for JVs that either contributed to import substitution or introduced new technologies.

41.JVs could open a foreign exchange account at various banks or other financial organisations, that were permitted to deal in foreign exchange business by the Chinese foreign exchange administration authority. JVs could also raise credits in the international financial market.

42.The State declared that it would not nationalise or expropriate foreign investment interest. Foreign investors were indemnified for the actual value of any damages that resulted from nationalisation and expropriation in some special cases in accordance with the social public interests.

43.Art.5 stipulated that: 'The technology or equipment contributed by any foreign participants as investment shall be truly advanced and appropriate to China's needs. In case of losses caused by deception through the international provision of outdated equipment or technology, compensation shall be paid for the losses'. Since the terms 'advanced' or 'appropriate' were not clearly defined and thus were subject to interpretation, there was good reason to question how they would be applied.

44. The long-awaited China Patent Law was finally promulgated on 12 March 1984, but did not take effect until 1 April 1985.

45. Masao Sakurai (1982), 'Investing in China: the Legal Framework', *Jetro China Newsletter,* No.37, pp.7-9.

46. *Ta Kung Pao,* 7 April 1982, Hong Kong.

47. Kueh, Y.Y. and Howe, Christopher (1984), 'China's International Trade: Policy and Organisational Change and their Place in the 'Economic Readjustment', *The China Quarterly,* Vol.100, p.836.

48. Ho, Samuel P.S. and Huenemann, Ralph W.(1984), *China's Open Door Policy,* University of British Columbia Press, Vancouver, p.75.

49. The most important laws published in 1980 included the following: 'The Income Tax Law of the People's Republic of China concerning Joint Ventures with Chinese and Foreign Investment' and 'The Individual Income Tax Law of the People's Republic of China' promulgated on 10 September 1980; 'The Detailed Rules and Regulations for the Implementation of the Income Tax Law of the People's Republic of China Concerning Joint Ventures with Chinese and Foreign Investment' and 'The Detailed Rules and Regulations for the Implementation of the Individual Income Tax Law of the People's Republic of China' promulgated on 14 December 1980; and 'The Regulations on Labour Management in Joint Ventures Using Chinese and Foreign Investment' promulgated in July 1980. Since then, a basic FDI legal system thus started to take shape.

50. 'The Individual Income Tax Law' stipulated that 'individual income tax shall be levied on the following categories of income: wages and salaries; compensation for personal services; royalties; interest, dividends and bonuses; income from lease of property; and other kinds of income specified as taxable by the Ministry of Finance'(Art.2). This law further stated that 'income from wages and salaries in excess of specific amounts shall be taxed at progressive rates ranging from 5 to 45 per cent exceeding a certain amount; income from compensation for personal services, royalties, interest, dividends, bonuses and lease of property, and other kinds of income shall be taxed at a flat rate of 20 per cent'(Article.3). Certain individual income, subsidies paid to foreign experts and service personnel working on voluntary foreign assistance projects, and income earned outside of China was to exempt from income tax.

'The Regulations on Labour Management in Joint Ventures Using Chinese and Foreign Investment' dealt with such aspects as the recruitment of additional labour through public selection examination and the labour contract system, the training or retraining of the labour force, the dismissal and compensation of workers and staff members, wages and other benefits, and labour protection.

51. For example, only when a domestic firm had fulfilled its targeted quota would it be permitted to manufacture products in response to market demand (refer to as 'production outside the plan'). However, when a SOE entered into an approved JV agreement with a foreign partner, the SOE assumed an identity that freed it from rigid state planning requirements.

52. SEZ Office of the State Council (1986), *Wen Jian Xuan Bian* (hereafter *WJXB*) *(Selection of Central Documents)*, May, Vol.1, p.36.

53. The government hoped that these zones would provide better investment incentives and the more liberal environment necessary to attract foreign investment more quickly than would be possible in other less accessible areas of the country, and serve as major industrial and export bases. According to Grub and Lin, 'if the SEZs became successful, such experiments would be adopted in other parts of the country. If the SEZs failed, the problems could be identified and avoided elsewhere', see, Grub and Lin (1991), op.cit., p.27.

54. WJXB, Vol.I, p.24.

55. These decisions represented a new policy called 'the overall responsibility system', which allowed Guangdong and Fujian a large measure of freedom in handling their own economic affairs. Accordingly, a moderate revenue contribution to the central government was required from both provinces, but after that was met the two provinces could retain locally generated profits for local development. This new practice was expected to expand the economic incentives and power of the two provinces, and to meet a large part of the capital needs for local infrastructural construction.

56. Zheng, Jianhui (1984), 'The Birth of An Important Decision - A New Step in Opening the Country to the World', *Liaowang*, No.24, 11 June 1984.

57. *XJXB*, Vol.I, p.109.

58. A central document of March 1980 specifically stated that real estate and tourism should be put on priority during this early stage of SEZs construction. See, *WJXB*, Vol.I, p.24.

59. More specifically, prices and wages were allowed to fluctuate along with demand and supply; workers could be hired and fired and were allowed to move from sector to sector.

60. For instance, the SEZs could approve investment projects under RMB50 million for capital goods production and under RMB30 million for consumer goods production. Projects above the limitations but under RMB100 million were subject to provincial approval, surpassing RMB100 million were subject to central approval, see, 'On Several Questions Concerning the SEZs Trial', *WJXB*, p.55.

61. *WJXB*, Vol.I, p.110.

62. Gu, Fuyou and Zhu, Kaiyi (1983), 'An Exploration into Some Issues in Utilizing Foreign Capital for Chinese-Foreign Joint Ventures', *Shanghai Accounting*, reported in *Joint Public Research Service* (hereafter *JPRS*), No.83, p.440.

63. Usually, potential participants would prepare a preliminary proposal based on their initial contacts. This proposal had to be submitted to the local government and the ministries in charge, and through them to the central authority, for approval. If approved, the participants could then start the negotiations. A new proposal based on the negotiated agreement, together with a feasibility study, was again submitted to the local government, the ministries, and the central authority for further approval. If passed, the participants would then start the second round of negotiation on a final contract, which then was directly submitted to the central authority for final approval. Once finally approved, the project contract became valid. For further details, see 'The Provisional Regulation of the Procedure of the Examination and Approval of Sino-foreign Joint Ventures' issued by Foreign Investment Control Commission in 1980, in *WJXB*, Vol.I, pp.325-6.

64. Hongqi Editor (1982), 'Problems Concerning China's Foreign Economic Relations', No.8, p.5.

65. Kueh, Y.Y. and Howe, Christopher (1982), op.cit., p.837.

66. Ranbt, Clark (1983), 'New Joint Venture Implementing Regulations - A Step Forward', *East Asian Executive Report*, November, p.9.

67. Zheng, Jianhui (1984), 'The Birth of an Important Decision - A New Step in Opening the Country to the World', *Liaowang, No.24, 11 June 1984*.

68. 'Chinese Leaders Explain Policy Decisions', *Beijing Review,* No.45, 5 November 1984, p.7.

69. *People's Daily,* 21 October 1984, p.1.

70. 'Implementation Regulations', Art.78, for instance, authorised the Bank of China to accept applications by JVs for foreign exchange loans; Art.79 reassured a 100 per cent remittance of profits and other legally earned income, after being properly taxed; and Art.71 provided tax concessions on the industrial and commercial consolidated tax with permission of the Ministry of Finance.

71. Including Dalian, Qinhuangdao, Tianjing, Yantai, Qingdao, Lianyungang, Nantong, Shanghai, Ningbo, Wenzhou, Fuzhou, Guangzhou, Zhanjiang, and Beihai.

72. Shanghai and Tianjin, for instance, could approve all FDI projects under US$30 million, Dalian under US$10 million, and the other cities under US$5 million, provided project applications did not adversely affect the state plan by requiring for central government capital, materials or other production inputs.

73. 'Special Treatment for Foreign Investors', *Beijing Review,* Vol.27, No.31, 30 July 1984, pp.7-8.

74. 'Mr He Chunlin on Foreign Investment', *China Business Review,* November-December 1987, pp.6-7.

75. These included a further reduction in the income tax rate, easier access to the financial resources available domestically, increased access to the domestic labour market, and more autonomy and flexibility in hiring and firing, as well as other related decisions.

76. Foreign investors would no longer need to go from one government agency to another for project approval or other needs, since a single authorised agency, MOFERT at the central level and the Committee of Foreign Economic Relations and Trade (hereafter COFERT) at the various local levels, were now expected to take full responsibility for dealing with FDI activities.

77. One striking feature of the 'Coastal Strategy' was to promote export-oriented industries by prioritizing labour-intensive, offshore processing activities. The 'appropriate development strategy' emphasized the need to 'put both ends of the production process (the supply of key inputs and the marketing of outputs) on the world market' and mainly required cheap labour,

of which China has plenty. See, 'Premier Zhao on the Coastal Areas' Development Strategy', *Beijing Review,* 8-14 February 1988, pp.18-23.

78. Kueh, Y.Y. (1992), 'Foreign Investment and Economic Change in China', *The China Quarterly,* September, Vol.132, p.638.

79. The Chinese government explained the 1988 'Coastal Strategy' as a natural result of a planned step-by-step process and a logical extension of the Open Door policy. However, a closer look at the main aspects of the new policy, and its motives, suggests that it was basically a response to rising dissatisfaction with the pace of domestic reform and the apparent inability to solve the problems affecting FDI.

80. 'Premier Zhao on the Coastal Areas' Development Strategy', *Beijing Review,* 8-14 February 1988, p.22.

81. Sourtherland, Daniel (1988), 'China Plans Export-led Economy: New Courses Could Expand Foreign Investment Opportunities', *Washington Post,* 24 January 1988, pp.A1, A30.

82. See, Financial Times (1991), *Financial Times Survey: China,* 24 April 1991 and Liu, Yuelun (1993), *China's Policy-Making in the Context of the Reform (1976-90), with a Focus on the Establishment of Economic Development Zones,* unpublished PhD dissertation at the University of Liverpool, p.358.

83. Under the previous provisions of Article 6, the chairman of the board of directors of a JV should be appointed by the Chinese partner regardless of the capital contribution made by the foreign party, which was criticised as unfair, particularly in those cases where the foreign partner contributed the majority capital share to the JV. The amended Article 6 allows a foreign partner to be appointed as chairman of the board of directors as it stipulates that the board chairman can be appointed from either the Chinese or foreign party to a JV, in which case the vice-chairman shall be appointed from the other party.

84. The amendment permits flexibility in the term or duration of the venture and allows the partners to determine whether to establish fixed term for some types of JVs, as the article reads as '... The term of the operations of some types of JVs shall be set, while the term of operations of other types of JVs may be set or may not be set...'. Interestingly, the law does not specify what types of JVs are required to set their duration.

85. The amendments provide that the state could not nationalize or expropriate the assets of FIEs except under certain circumstances related to social and public interests. Even under such circumstances, the state was required to follow legal procedures and to provide appropriate compensation to the affected parties.

86. Financial Times (1991), *Financial Times Survey: China*, 24 April 1991.

87. See, for example, Pudong Development Office of Shanghai Municipality (1990), *Shanghai Pudong New Area - Investment Environment and Development Prospects*, pp.27-31.

88. 'Grasp opportunity for better and rapid development', *People's Daily*, 11 March 1993, p.1.

89. *People's Daily*, 14 October 1993, p.2.

90. BOT is popular around the world as a way of attracting investment to large construction projects. Foreign investors build these large projects, operate/manage them for a stipulated period and then transfer them to the government free of charge.

91. *People's Daily*, 26 April 1993, p.1.

92. The new incentive scheme, which does not discriminate between domestic and foreign capital, is based on a points system derived from three criteria: economic performance, sectoral priority and regional priority. High points would thus be allocated to an investment which brings in capital in priority sectors and is located in a less developed region. See, *People's Daily*, 26 April 1993, p.1.

93. Financial Times (1993), *Financial Times Survey: China*, 18 November 1993, p.6.

94. 'China Speeds on to Market', *The Economist*, 20 November 1993, p.85.

95. Many large SOEs are still soaking up subsidies to cover losses. About 31 per cent of SOEs reported losses in the first half of 1993, but the actual figure is probably far higher. For example, in Shenyang, the northern heart of Chinese heavy industry, the municipal government estimated that 38 per cent of factories in its care are losing money. Chinese government attempted to shift some responsibility for loss-making companies away from the state by turning SOEs into corporate entities, similar in responsibility, if not ownership structure, to a Western company. See Financial Times (1993), *Financial Times*

Survey: China, 18 November 1993, p.8.

96. Financial Times (1993), *Financial Times China Survey,* 18 November 1993, p.3.

97. 'China Speeds on to Market', *The Economist,* 20 November 1993, p.86.

98. Wu Zhenkun and Song Zihe (1991), *Development Strategies of Opening up the Economy,* Academy of Central Committee of the China Communist Party Press, Beijing, pp.45-46.

99. *People's Daily,* 24 April 1995, p.1.

3 Patterns of FDI and JVs in Hungary and China

This chapter examines the overall quantitative trends in foreign investment and its distribution among different areas and economic sectors in Hungary and China between 1978 and 1992 by using available official data and computations. The analysis of the macro-picture of FDI is a necessary precondition for the quantitative analysis of the determinants and contribution of foreign investment on economic development and systematic transformation in Hungary and China in the following chapters.

Introduction

FDI has emerged as a major phenomenon in the world economy since the 1950s. Throughout the 1960s FDI grew at twice the rate of GNP in the OECD countries. Thereafter, the amount of FDI has increased rapidly, with the growth rate more than four times that of GNP growth (7.8 per cent), and three times the growth rate of world exports by volume (9.4 per cent) during the 1970s. The second half of the 1980s witnessed a marked growth in FDI from approximately US$47 billion in 1985 to US$132 billion in 1989, increasing at the annual rate of 29 per cent. By the end of 1989, the accumulated FDI around the world was US$1,500 billion (Emmott, 1993, pp.7-9).

Capital flows, however, became more and more concentrated on the richest parts of the world, as their share as hosts of total FDI increased from 73 per cent on average between 1981-83 to 80 per cent in 1984-88, and the proportion of FDI flowing to LDCs dropped from around 25 per cent of the total in the 1970s to about 20 per cent in the 1980s as their external indebtedness increased. But capital flows to LDCs in Pacific Asia and Latin America, including Singapore (12 per cent), Brazil (12 per cent), Mexico (11 per cent), China (10 per cent), Hong Kong (7 per cent), Malaysia (6 per cent), Egypt (6 per cent), Argentina (4 per cent), Thailand (3 per cent) and Colombia (3 per cent)[1] increased at a faster rate than those to developed countries. Now, although the boom has faded in the recession-hit industrial countries, foreign investment has been rushing enthusiastically into those countries that for decades were blighted by communism: to China and Eastern Europe.

The rapidly increasing FDI in Eastern Europe and China represents a salient new feature on the international economic scene. In Eastern Europe, the countries in transition from CPEs to the market are faced with three challenges. First, they want to become a part of the world economy, i.e. redirect their economic relations towards the West. Second, they are eager to overcome their development lag and to implement a re-construction policy, which implies the increasing involvement of Western capital. Third, the transition to the market encompasses the foreign trade sector as well. The opening up to the world requires liberalising foreign trade, introducing convertibility, transforming property structures, all of which is part of the domestic reform programme.

By the end of 1991, Eastern European economies had only attracted US$9.6 billion FDI in stock, which accounted for 0.2 per cent of world FDI, although these countries might become large potential FDI recipients in the near future. Hungary is currently seen as the most promising host nation within Eastern Europe in attracting FDI. More than half of the committed foreign capital in Eastern Europe and the former USSR has been invested in Hungary.

China is growing so fast in last two decades, achieving a typical growth rate of nearly 10 per cent per annum, where a return to free markets has brought an influx of private foreign capital. The transition that China has made to rapid growth from poor undercapitalised stagnation has been closely associated with the adoption of capitalism and of property rights for foreign investors, since China liberalised its policy towards private economic activity and opened the economies to market forces in 1978. It has now become one of the leading host countries within LDCs in terms of both its accumulated stock and annual flow of foreign capital.

Given the prospect of faster growth in the transforming economies, China and Eastern European countries have become a focal point for direct investment. Investing in Eastern Europe and China might become one of the world's most profitable investment opportunity for the next 10 years.

Joint ventures and foreign investment in Hungary

This section provides a general overview of FDI in Hungary over the past 15 years or so by using available statistics to examine the level of investment, origin of capital, and its sectoral and geographical distribution. An attempt has been made to identify emerging investment trends but many of the statistics are still too 'raw' to draw final conclusions, as there are some deficiencies in all data and an uncritical use might generate quite misleading results.

FDI and JVs: general trends

After the nationalization of foreign ownership in 1948-49, no foreign property existed in Hungary through the 1950s and 1960s. In the early 1970s, the Hungarian government realised that foreign investment could shorten the technical gap between the West and East, and decided to change the regulations to allow FDI in some areas of the economy. Indeed, 'Hungary had been successfully raising many hundreds of millions of dollars from consortia of European and Japanese banks over the 1970s. Suddenly, with the declaration of martial law in Poland and the prospects of a Reagan presidency in the USA, Eastern Europe became an unattractive investment' (Swain, 1992, p.132).

Due to internal economic conditions, the inflexible regulation, and conflicting goals, it is no surprising that only a few JVs established between 1972 and 1979. **Table 3.1** suggests that the growth of JVs and FDI in Hungary was a gradual phenomenon, as foreign investment in Hungary was still very modest in the first half of the 1980s. Hungary recorded a mere 50 JVs between 1972-83, accounting for US$5 million in foreign capital.[2] By 1985, about 50 JVs had been established, with a capital of US$50 million, predominantly in the service sector and mainly in tourism. By December 1986, 70 JV agreements had been signed, with more than half in manufacturing (predominated by less technology-intensive), whereas those established during the 1970s had mostly been located in the service sector. The sum of foreign capital committed was only about US$80 million, of which US$20 million was accounted for by one single banking venture - the Central European Investment Bank. From the end of 1986 to the end of 1988, another 230 JVs were founded with an additional US$250 million foreign inward investment. Western European countries were the leading investors, with Germany (27 per cent), Austria (22 per cent) and Switzerland (9 per cent) accounting for a large proportion of the registered JVs and committed capital. The United States represented a major source of FDI, but concentrated its investment in a few, large undertakings during this period.[3]

Table 3.1

JV and estimated foreign investment in Hungary between 1974-92

Year	Number of JVs	Accumulative FDI (in million US dollar)
1974	2	na
1980	6	na
1981	7	na
1982	12	na
1983	32	na
1984	61	na
1987	107	na
1988	282	289.00
1989	1,400	384.00
1990	5,146	1200.90
1991	10,788	2800.00
1992	14,889	4900.00

Sources: Data on JVs before 1987 came from Economic Commission for Europe (1988), *East-West Joint Ventures: Economic, Business, Financial and Legal Aspects,* United Nations, New York, p.73; Data on JVs between 1988-91 is from 'Investing in Hungary: the State of Play', Royal Institute of International Affairs, London, Discussion Paper No.34, 1992.

It can be concluded that Hungary has been able to attract FDI with accelerating speed during the second half of the 1980s, but foreign equity is still relatively insignificant in relation to Hungary's foreign debt in convertible currency and its relative needs and absorptive potential.

In 1988, FIEs increased to 282 with total capital US$1,148 million in which foreign capital shared 46 per cent, amounting US$523 million. The average capital per JV was approximately US$2.293 million[4] (see **Table 3.2**).

Among the total equity capital US$523 million of 282 JVs in 1988, 32 per cent (around US$167 million) were invested in joint financial institutions, 25 per cent (around US$130 million) in the capital-intensive hotel business, and 43 per cent (about US$226 million) in other business sectors (See **Table 3.3**).

Among the 282 JVs in Hungary in 1988, 120 firms were active in manufacturing sector, with construction material production the most popular investment, accounting for 24 cases (24 per cent). There were 17 JVs in the chemical industry, food processing, and engineering & equipment respectively (14.2 per cent each), 13 in the electro-technical and electronics sector, 11 in textiles & clothes (9.2 per cent), and 21 other JVs (17.4 per cent), which included book printing and bicycle assembling (See **Table 3.4**).

Table 3.2
Distribution of capital of JVs in 1988

Number of JVs	Amount of capital
15	> US$8.5 million
41	US$1.6 - 8.49 million
36	US$850,000 - 1.59 million
91	US$333,000 - 849,000
23	US$160,000 - 332,999
71	< US$160,000
5	unknown

Source: Benedek, T. (1991), 'Hungary: Pioneer in Joint Ventures', in Evka Razvigorova and Gottfried Wolf-Laudon (ed.), *East-West Joint Ventures: The New Business Environment*, Blackwell, London, p.108.

Table 3.3
Capital distribution of 282 JVs in 1988

Branches	Number of JVs	Committed capital	Percentage (%)
Finance	5	US$167 million	32
Hotel	3	US$130 million	25
Others	274	US$226 million	43
Total	**282**	**US$523 million**	**100**

Source: Own calculations based on Hungarian 282 JVs in 1988.

Table 3.4
Sectoral distribution of manufacturing JVs in Hungary in 1988
(total 120 firms)

Sector	Number of JVs	Percentage of JVs (%)
Construction materials	24	20.0
Argo & food-processing	17	14.2
Machine-building & equipment	17	14.2
Chemical industry	17	14.2
Electro-technic & electronics	13	10.8
Textiles & clothes	11	9.2
Non-classified	21	17.4
Total	**120**	**100.0**

Source: Own calculations based on Hungarian 282 JVs in 1988.

Up to 1988 Western investors were relatively interested in the agricultural & food processing sector, but the chemical industry, especially light chemicals and pharmaceutical attracted most of foreign capital committed. The machine

71

and equipment sector had more JVs than textiles and clothing, indicating that it was not easy to attract FDI into labour-intensive areas, although labour costs were relatively low in Hungary.

Table 3.5 shows that 73 per cent of foreign investors in Hungary in 1988 came from Western Europe. Companies from Scandinavia had not shown any great interest in investing in Hungary, only representing 8.2 per cent. The North America and Asian remained very small share (7.8 per cent and 2.1 per cent respectively).

Table 3.6 shows that neighbouring Austria and Germany were the most dominant Western investors in Hungary, accounting 27 per cent and 21 per cent of the total 282 JVs respectively, followed by Switzerland (26 JVs, 9.2 per cent), USA (20 JVs, 7.1 per cent), and Sweden (15 JVs, 5.3 per cent). Excluding the figure of banking sector, by the end of 1988, Austria had invested a total of US$27 million into the Hungarian economy, although the average Austrian capital share per JV was less than half a million US dollar. Only in three cases did the Austrian capital contribution in Hungarian JVs exceed Ft100 million (US$1.7 million).[5]

Table 3.5
National origins of foreign partners of 282 JVs in 1988

Areas	Number of JVs	Percentage (%)
Western Europe	206	73.0
Scandinavia	23	8.2
North America	22	7.8
Asia	6	2.1
Mixed	17	6.0
Others	8	2.8
Total	**282**	**100.0**

Source: Benedek, T. (1991), op.cit., p.107.

Table 3.6
Countries with JVs in Hungary in 1988

Country	No of JVs	Country	No of JVs
Austria	77	Greece	2
Germany	62	Japan	2
Switzerland	26	France	2
USA	20	Canada	2
Sweden	15	Norway	2
Holland	11	Portugal	1
Italy	10	India	1
Britain	10	Belgium	1
USSR	4	Cyprus	1
Finland	3	Spain	1
Denmark	3	Australia	1
South Korea	2	Liechtenstein	2
Anonymous	2	Luxembourg	2
Mixed	17		
Total			**282**

Source: Benedek, T. (1991), op. cit. p.107.

German companies had invested a total amount of Ft1,073 million (US$17.9 million) in Hungary by the end of 1988, exclusive the banking sector. This represented a capital contribution of only Ft25.5 million (US$0.43 million) per JV, which was even less than the Austrian case. There were three JVs, in which German capital share exceeded Ft100 million.[6]

The United States involved in 20 JVs in Hungary in 1988. The most important American investment was Citibank Budapest which Citibank owned 80 per cent of the Ft1.0 billion capital (US$17 million). Outside the banking sector, the US firms invested a total sum of Ft285 million (US$4.75 million). The average US capital contribution in Hungarian JVs was only Ft24 million (US$0.4 million) per JV. This figure was even lower than the average Austrian and German ones.

Japanese companies were reluctant to invest in Hungary as they only involved in five JVs, two of which were in the banking sector, and three in production. The Japanese contribution in these three non-banking JVs was Ft300 million (US$5 million). The average contribution of Japanese companies per JV was therefore much higher (Ft100 million or US$1.67 million per JV) than that of Austrian, German or US.

Many well-known international companies could be found among Western JV partners in Hungary, including Siemens, Volvo, Nokia, Mcdonald, Levi-Strauss, Adidas, McCann-Erichson Advertising, Voest, IKEA, Citibank, Henkel, and Schwarzkopf.

JVs in Hungary were highly concentrated in the capital city - Budapest: almost 118 FIEs (64 per cent of the total JVs) operated in Budapest. Eleven of the remaining 66 JVs had an office in Budapest, while their main activities were elsewhere.

Foreign-invested enterprises, 1989-91

When Western business interest in Central and Eastern Europe was stimulated by the collapse of communism in 1989 and the rise of democracy in 1990, Hungary was better prepared to attract FDI than its former socialist allies (Young, D.G., 1993, pp.109-110).

The most dramatic liberalisation, together with the market-oriented political and economic transformation after 1989, resulted in an impressive increase in the annual number of registered JVs and the value of FDI. Hungary was the first choice or regarding as the 'port of entry' for investment with the idea of serving the whole Eastern European markets. Since then Hungary was regarded as an attractive, but still not fully reliable investment area.

Foreign investment grew very rapidly during the period 1989-91, increasing four times between 1989 and 1990 (from US$250 million to US$1.0 billion) and almost doubling again between 1990 and 1991 (to US$1.7 billion). As **Table 3.7** illustrates, in 1989 the presence of foreign capital in Hungary increased significantly. By the end of 1989, the total value of foreign capital investment reached US$300 million, and the overall number of JVs grew to 2,000.[7] They became increasingly concentrated in retailing, foreign trade, and other services,[8] with only a few major investments oriented towards manufacturing.

Since the implementation of 'spontaneous' privatisation, the acquisition of well-established SOEs, cooperatives and private firms became favoured over establishing JVs. The number of JVs rose to 5,693 by the end of 1990 (Young, D.G., 1993, p.110), the total amount of capital invested in FIEs was Ft274.1 billion (US$4.3 billion), of which Ft93.2 billion (US$1.5 billion) was contributed by the foreign partner in cash or kind, about the same as the FDI stock in Pakistan, Uruguay or Cameroon.[9]

Table 3.7
Percentage of foreign ownership in JVs 1989-91

Percentage of foreign ownership	Number of JVs		
	31 Dec 1989	31 Dec 1990	1 Jan - 30 Jun 1991
0-20	195	793	502
21-30	176	798	352
31-50	817	3,279	1,287
51-60	118	433	306
81-90	17	146	115
100	27	244	515
TOTAL	**1,350**	**5,693**	**3,077**

Source: *The Hungarian Observer,* Vol.1, 1992, p.16.

The above picture had changed rapidly after 1991. While the first peak (US$1.46 billion in working capital was invested in this country, 4 per cent of GDP) was reached in 1991, when the amount contributed by foreign investors had doubled to US$3.2 billion and the number of registered JVs in Hungary reached to approximately 11,000. The value of foreign investment per JV increased to US$330,000. The average share of the foreign contribution to the start-up capital in 1989 was 24 per cent, 34 per cent in 1990, and 37 per cent in 1991. **Table 3.7** reveals that while the majority of investors in 1991 still preferred taking shares in the region of 30-50 per cent, an increasing number were taking a controlling share (above 50 per cent). In addition, the number of WFOEs grew rapidly over 1989-91. This tendency reflected increasing confidence of Western investors in investing in Hungary.

By the end of 1991, the stock of foreign investment was about US$3.0 billion, which amounted 6.9 per cent of GNP in 1991, and represented over half of US$5.0 billion total capital stock committed by Western investors to Eastern Europe. This may be modest when compared to investment levels in southeast Asia or Southern Europe, but was high when compared to the records in Central and Eastern Europe. Notwithstanding these sharp increases, the absolute importance of FDI in Hungary remained modest.

JVs distribution by country origin EC-based firms accounted for 36.3 per cent of the JVs in January 1990.[10] UP to the end of 1990 Austrian firms had contributed 23.5 per cent and German firms 22 per cent of foreign capital invested in Hungary. Austrian firms, however, were the leading investors (by number of JVs). Austria had contributed roughly US$300 million in about 1,000 JVs. In January 1991 there were 1,400 German JVs in Hungary, which amounted to 36 per cent of the total number of JVs, and 30 per cent of the influx capital. German investment was worth between US$300 million and US$400 million. The greatest number of JVs had been formed by German and Austrian firms, which, with few exceptions, had entered into small ventures targeted at weak spots in the domestic market. Since 1990 there came a substantial upswing in British investment in Hungary, but it still trailed far behind that of the leading competitors. Other major investments were made by companies originating from France, Switzerland, Italy and Sweden.

The largest amount of foreign capital (35 per cent) had been brought into the country by US firms, which concentrated on strategic investments, often aimed at markets outside Hungary. US companies, such as Ford, GE, GM, Guardian Glass and Sara Lee, were looking to markets in Western Europe, Eastern Europe, as well as in Hungary, to justify their investments. With the finalisation of the Y10 billion Japanese Yuan Suzuki JV for the manufacturing of passenger cars in early May 1991, Hungary saw a sizeable increase of Japanese investments over the last few years.

On a currency basis, the foreign contribution to newly registered JVs during 1990 and 1991 was 26.9 per cent in US dollars, 23.7 per cent in Austrian Schillings, 16.2 per cent in German Marks, 7.6 per cent in Dutch Guilders, and 25.6 per cent in other currencies.[11]

JVs distribution by industry sectors Foreign investment diversified widely among different sectors and industries across the economy. **Table 3.8** and **Table 3.9** show sectoral distribution of FIEs and FDI, revealing that FDI projects tended to cover a greater range of activities.

There were also a marked switch in foreign investments towards manufacturing industry and away from services (including finance, hotels and restaurants) since the end of 1989. According to Young's (1993) study, about half of foreign capital invested in Hungary in 1990 went into manufacturing industries, in which engineering and light industries led the way, followed by building materials, chemicals and food processing. With tremendous demand for improved services and initial start-up costs relatively low, it was not surprising that service sector received 20.6 per cent of total investments in 1990. Retail trade also received a significant share of foreign investment (13.6 per cent) in 1990. The largest number of JVs - 1661 -was formed in this sector (Young, D.G., 1993, pp.112-3). Another survey conducted by the

Hungarian Ministry of Industry & Trade in May 1991 revealed that 21.8 per cent of foreign capital was invested in manufacturing industry, 11.4 per cent in construction and 26.7 per cent in tourism and domestic trade and retailing.[12] Manufacturing industries, such as food industry, construction, machines and light industry received more and more attraction from foreign investors. Foreign investment in manufacturing and some exported-oriented sectors, such as automobiles and electrical goods production, accounted for 22 per cent of JVs registered at the end of 1991, but 57 per cent of total foreign capital was invested mainly in the form of purchase of equity (sometimes a majority holding) in existing enterprises.[13] By the end of 1991, the share of manufacturing in total foreign investment had risen from less than 50 per cent in 1990 to almost 64 per cent, while that of services had fallen from 22 per cent to less than 13 per cent.[14]

Table 3.8
Distribution of FDI invested by sector (%)

Industrial sectors	1989*	1991**
Manufacturing	35.0	58.0
Transport & communication	3.0	0.9
Health services	4.0	0.3
Hotels & restaurants	18.0	8.2
Trade	4.0	11.9
Finance	30.0	8.7
Others	6.0	11.7

Notes: * End of March 1989. ** End of December 1991.
Source: Economic Intelligence Unit (1992), *EIU Country Report: Hungary*, No.3, p.24.

Table 3.9
Cumulative JVs by sector at the end of 1991

Industrial sectors	No. of JVs	Foreign Capital (in million Ft)	Total Capital (in million Ft)
Food	225	15932.8	49,744.5
Textiles	71	2,679.6	7,693.6
Wearing apparel	178	1,243.1	2,790.8
Leather	73	528.9	2,801.2
Wood & wood products	114	846.5	2,314.5
Paper & paper products	28	1,771.9	5,652.9
Publishing & printing	209	969.9	2,383.2
Chemicals	104	4,826.1	9,182.6
Rubber & plastics	153	3,241.0	24,794.3
Non-metallic products	118	4,612.5	14,794.3
Basic metals	34	1,848.1	7,711.9
Metal products	168	2,752.9	5,732.7
Machinery & equipment	450	4,145.3	9,786.0
Electrical equipment	69	2,449.5	4,805.3
Communication equipment	71	5,157.9	10.992.8
Precision instruments/office equipment/computers	153	2,739.5	9,229.4
Transport equipment	142	7,880.4	19,177.6
Furniture	37	292.4	1,054.8
Total Manufacturing	**2,397**	**63,918.3**	**190,191.4**
Transport & communication	230	962.4	7,955.5
Health services	77	364.4	708.6
Hotels & restaurants	432	9,113.4	19,823.7
Trade	4,970	13,186.4	50,834.5
Finance	52	9,630.8	18,783.0
Other	2,630	12,920.2	42,876.6
Total	**10,788**	**110,095.9**	**331,173.3**

Source: Economic Intelligence Unit (1992), *EIU Country Report: Hungary*, No.3, p.25. It was based on the data from Hungarian Central Statistical Office.

The figures for mining, electricity, agriculture, and community services were, however, much less impressive. Agriculture was one potentially attractive sector which was neglected by foreign investors. Given the sector's importance to the economy as a whole, at first glance it appeared surprising that only 78 JVs were formed with a foreign capital contribution of US$7.8 million.[15]

The majority of FIEs in Hungary was established with a small amount of initial capital. The average amount of starting capital decreased from about Ft48.2 million at the end of 1990 to only Ft27.8 million at the end of 1991, which revealed the absence of medium-sized foreign investments in Hungary.

The Hungarian car industry, however, attracted medium-size foreign investment. In early November 1991, General Motors' (hereafter GM) 67 per cent stake in the vehicle producer, Raba Railway Carriage & Machine Factory, enabled this JV to become one of the Europe's most advanced automobile production facilities.[16] The Hungarian-assembled Astras, GM Europe's most up-to-date model, enjoyed a 22.5 per cent local price advantage over imports of the same model from other European GM plants because of tax exemptions, customs waivers, and low labour costs.[17]

In April 1991, another car JV - Magyar Suzuki Co., in which Japanese partner holds 40 per cent - was established to provide the Hungarian market with a second plant for the local assembly of passenger cars. Although its annual capacity of 60,000 cars had been fully reached by 1994,[18] the success of the Magyar Suzuki will come only if the Hungarian-made parts measure up to world standards, local work habits come to match those in Western countries, and Hungarian managers meet international standards.[19] United Technologies' US$10 million investment in manufacturing electrical distribution systems in December 1991 in Godollo further demonstrated that Hungary had been rapidly becoming an area of particular interest for automobile components manufacture. Indeed, never before or since had Hungary experienced such fast-moving development in the areas of privatisation and FDI in automobile industry as it did between November 1989 and 1991.

General Electric's purchase of the light bulb manufacturer Tungsgram - Eastern Europe's leading light bulb manufacturer - marked Hungary's third-largest deal with Western investors.

The tobacco industry represented another interesting picture of FDI. In November 1991, Philip Morris (hereafter PM) and Austrian Tabak Werke signed an agreement to purchase the Eger Tobacco Factory, with the former taking 80 per cent and the latter a 20 per cent stake. Eger had already been producing Marlboro cigarettes under licence from PM, which amounted 80 per cent of the Hungarian market for internationally recognise cigarette brands. In December 1991, BAT Industries from the UK purchased the Pecs

Tobacco Factory, investing about £20 million in the venture.

The banking and insurance industries also saw an inflow of foreign capital. A number of banks, such as Creditanstalt, Credit Bank, Leumi Bank, Kulturbank and Normura Investment Bank Hungary went into mixed ownership. Hungarian branches of foreign banks grew at an extremely dynamic rate since 1990. The 13 fully or partly foreign-owned banks operating in Hungary accounted for 12 per cent of the basic capital of financial institutions, their profit tripled in 1990 compared with 1989, reaching Ft6.5 billion (US$81.2 million), 4.5 per cent of their balance main sum, more profitable than fully Hungarian financial institutions as their services were much more competitive than local banks. Privatisation of the insurance industry also created opportunities for Western firms, such as Aegon of the Netherlands, SA Allianz of Germany, to enter into partnerships with large insurance institutions on a broader scale.

A swiftly growing branch of services was trade sector, especially retailing and related production. Puma, Kodak and McDonald's service and distribution network developed very rapidly. More and more foreign investors became interested in acquiring controlling stakes in privatised department stores, hotels and other tourist enterprises, and even privatised foreign trade organisations (FTOs) in Hungary.[20]

Top JVs in Hungary in 1991 As **Tables 3.10** and **3.11** show that an increasing number of famous international MNCs were found to be very active among Western JV partners in Hungarian market.

We can see that the largest 20 FDI projects, in terms of invested foreign capital, were dominated by US firms and concentrated in manufacturing industries, such as motor, oil, and electronic industries. All these top rank MNCs were intent on integrating their new Hungarian subsidiaries into their existing global operations and bringing invaluable know-how, technology and managerial expertise in their wake.

A significant proportion of foreign investment has been attracted by two regions: Budapest and the northwestern counties (see **Figures 3.1** and **3.2**). Because of its advantages in political, economic and infrastructure, Budapest area attracted over 50 per cent of FDI in 1990-92. The northwest region near the borders with Austria and Slovakia attracted about 7.4 per cent of total FDI (including Purina in Gyor and Suzuki in Esztergom) in 1990. These two regions not only offered better business prospects and a higher level of infrastructural development, but also benefited from its close proximity to Austria and the rest of Western Europe.

Table 3.10
Top 11 JVs in Hungary in 1991

Investor	Nationality	Share (%)	Deal (£m)	JV & Sector
Sanofi	French	40	75	Chioin - pharmaceuticals
General Electric	American	50	150	GE Tungsram - lighting
Guardian Glass	American	80	115	Hunguard - glass
Ford	American	100	83	Ford Hungarian - vehicles
Prinahorn Group	Austrian	40	82	Dunapack - paper
General Motors	American	67	66	GM Hungary - vehicles
Electrolux	Swedish	100	65	Lehel - refrigerators
Sara Lee	American	51	60	Compack - food
Nestle	Swiss	97	38	Nestle Intercsocolade - food
Agrana	Austrian	49	35	Szabadegyhazi Szeszipari - food
Susuki	Japanese	40	30	Magyar Suzuki - vehicles

Source: Denton N. (1991), 'Hungary Takes the Lead on Foreign Investment', *Financial Times,* 14 May 1991, p.2.

We can see that most of foreign investment in Hungary were concentrated in those most developed and favourably situated areas with a better infrastructure, all the advantages of the presence of other industries, and a relatively more efficient administration. This could result to widen the economic disequilibrium between different regions. The government should learn how to persuade investors to take a greater interest in underdeveloped regions, and how to use efficient regulatory measures to avoid foreign investors only influx into those sectors with low investment requirements, high profit rates, and labour-intensive, and concentrated in certain specific locations.

Table 3.11
The list of the 20 biggest investors in Hungary

Company	Country	Industry
1. General Motors	USA	motor
2. Royal Dutch/Shell Group	Great Britain/the Netherlands	oil
3. Exxon	USA	oil
4. Ford	USA	motor
5. IBM	USA	computer
6. Suzuki	Japan	motor
7. BP	Great Britain	oil
8. Mobil	USA	oil
9. General Electric	USA	electronics
10. Daimler Benz	Germany	motor
11. Fiat	Italy	motor
12. Samsung	South Korea	electronics
13. Philip Morris	USA	cigarette
14. Matsushita Electronic	Japan	electronics
15. ENI	Italy	oil
16. Unilever	Great Britain	food
17. E.I. Du Pont de Nemours	USA	chemical
18. Siemens	Germany	electronics
19. Nestle	Switzerland	food
20. Renault	France	motor

Source: *The Hungarian Observer,* Vol. 2, 1992, p.10.

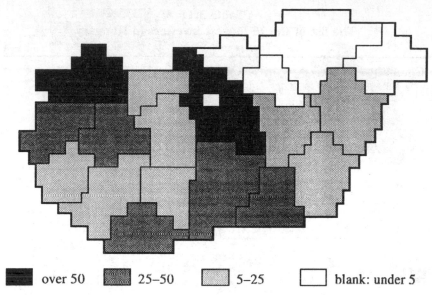

| over 50 | 25–50 | 5–25 | blank: under 5 |

Source: Central Statistical Office

Key to counties

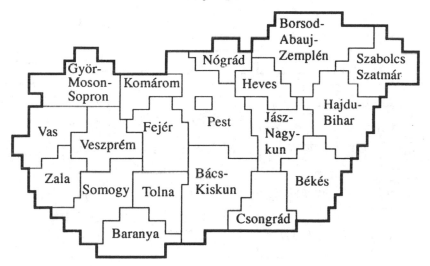

Note: In addition to 412 foreign-owned undertakings in the countryside there were 778 in Budapest.

Figure 3.1   Geographical distribution of FDI by 31 December 1991

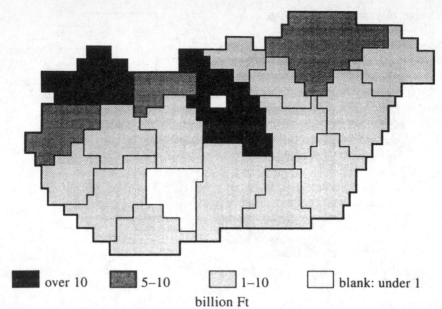

 over 10   5–10   1–10   blank: under 1

billion Ft

Source: Central Statistical Office

Key to counties

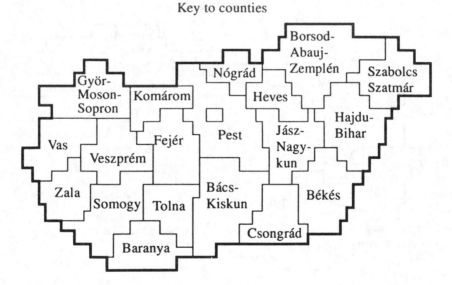

Note: Foreign investment in Budapest was of 124 billion Ft.

Figure 3.2 Geographical distribution of foreign-owned undertakings

According to the Hungarian National Bank, the rapid influx of foreign working capital continued in 1992, with about US$10 million in cash being invested monthly. In the first five months of 1992 foreign investment totalled US$60 million. By the late June 1992, an additional 3,000 JVs were formed, foreign capital inflows accounted as much as that during the entire year of 1991, rising to more than US$70 million. 'Up to now, Hungary has relied the most on foreign investment to flesh out the private sector, attracting more than US$5.5 billion since 1988, over half the total for Central and Eastern Europe'.[21]

Hungary continued to attract considerable interests from foreign investors in 1993. The first two months of 1993 saw about US$200 million in FDI had flowed into the country, consisting of US$170 million in cash and US$30 million in equipment, bringing the total FDI in Hungary to over US$5 billion. By the middle of 1993, the biggest investors in Hungary were Germany (18.4 per cent), Austria (18 per cent), Belgium (16 per cent), and the US (5 per cent).[22] About 77 per cent of foreign investment came from Western Europe. In 1993, about US$1.7 billion foreign capital was invested in Hungary, in which 65 per cent invested in industry, 10 per cent each in trade and finance (only Hungary in Eastern Europe has managed to attract substantial foreign investment into the important financial service sector), 6 per cent each in hotels and property, and 3 per cent in transport. Within industry, 27 per cent went into engineering and machinery, 19 per cent to food and agricultural products, 5.5 per cent each to light industry and building materials, 3.5 per cent to chemicals, 2 per cent to energy and 1.5 per cent into construction.[23] Foreign investors also bought about US$4 billion government bonds in 1993 alone.

The share of foreign partners in the non-agricultural business assets grew steadily from 6-7 per cent in 1992 to 25-30 per cent by the end of 1994. This figure was comparable to the current situation in Austria, but was far away from the government's target: private sector would be control over 50 per cent of the economy by the end of 1994, and foreign investments would grow rapidly in the coming years by reaching US$10 billion by the end of 1995, which amounts to a 15-16 per cent ownership share and could substantially accelerate economic growth.

Table 3.12 shows the top 50 FIEs in Hungary by the end of 1993 were dominated by the US and German firms and concentrated on manufacturing industries, such as motor, oil, telecommunications, food & soft drinks, cigarettes, banking and other services. It can be concluded that international MNCs have moved parts of their activities into Hungary in such a manner as to allow the Hungarian companies to become an integral part of MNCs' global

Table 3.12
Top 50 foreign investment commitments in Hungary

Rank	Investor	Nationality	Hungarian partner or venture
1	General Electric	US	Tungsram
2	Volkswagen-Audi	Germany	Audi Hungaria Motor
3	US West International	US	Westel, Westel 900
4	General Motors	US-Germany	GM Hungary
5	Suzuki, C Itoh, International Finance Corporation	Japan, International	Magyar Suzuki
6	PTT Netherlands, Telecom Denmark and other Scandinavian operators	Various	Pannon GSM
7	Allianz	Germany	Hungaria Biztosito
8	Transroute International, Banque Nationale de Paris, Caisse des Depots, Strabag	France, Austria	Hungarian Euro-Expressway
9	Alcoa	US	Kofem (Hungalu subsidiary)
10	Ferruzzi, Unilever	Italy, Netherlands-UK	NMV
11	Prinzhorn Group	Austria	Dunapack, Halaspack, Szolnok Paper Mill
12	Ansaldo, subsidiary of IRI	Italy	Ganz-Ansaldo
13	PepsiCo International	US	FAU
14	Guardian Glass	US	Hunguard
15	Alitalia, Simest	Italy	Malev Hungarian Airlines
16	Hungarian Investment Company	UK	Nikex, others
17	Sanofi	France	Chinoin
18	Ford	US	Ford Hungaria
19	Sara Lee – Douwe Egberts	US	Compack
20	Coca-Cola Amatil	Australia	Budapest Likoripari V, others
21	Kempinski, Dresdner Bank	Germany	Grand Hotel Corvinus Kempinski
22	Nestle	Switzerland	Nestle Intercsokolade
23	Siemens	Germany	Telefongyar, others
24	Banca Commerciale Italiana, Bayerische Vereinsbank The Long-Term Credit Bank of Japan, The Sakura Bank, Societe Generale	Italy, Germany, Japan, France	Central European International Bank Group
25	First Hungary Fund	US	Various
26	Stollwerck	Germany	Budapest Confectionery Company
27	Marriott, GiroCredit, others	US, Austria	Duna Intercontinental
28	Agrana	Austria	Hungrana
29	Hoechst – Messer Griesheim	Germany	Oxygen and Dissolved Acetylene Co
30	Voest-Alpine	Austria	Dunai Vasmu
31	Ferruzzi – Beghin-Say	Italy (France)	Matravidek, Szerencs, Szolnok sugar factories
32	Reemtsma	Germany	Debreceni Dohanygyar
33	Electrolux	Sweden	Lehel
34	Total	France	
35	British-American Tobacco	UK	Pecsi Dohangyar
36	Hungarian-American Enterprise Fund	US	
37	Sarp Industries	France	Dorog Refuse Incinerator
38	Philip Morris	US	Egri Dohangyar
39	Amylum	Belgium	Szabadegyhazi Distilling Company
40	Julius Meinl	Austria	Csemege-Meinl
41	Aral	France	
42	Skanska	Sweden	East-West Business Centre
43	European Bank for Reconstruction and Development*	Financial institution	Various
44	Columbian Chemicals	US	TVK
45	Institutional investors	US	Fotex
46	Accor	France	Pannonia Hotels
47	Tengelmann	Germany	Skala-Coop, Kozert
48	Primagaz, Calor Gas (in JV Pamgas)	France, UK	Primagaz Rt
49	Tetra-Pak	Sweden	Tetra-Pak Hungary
50	Atex	CIS	Ikarus

* Updated EBRD figure show commitments of $616m at end-October 1993, of which $124m disbursed.

Sector	Type	Year	Size of major shareholding	Investment in dollars
Lighting	Privatisation	1990	100%	$550m
Car engines	Greenfield	1993	100%	$420m
Cellular telephony	Joint venture greenfield	1990	49%	$330m
		1993	51%	
Cars and components	Joint venture greenfield	1990	67%	$300m
Cars	Joint venture greenfield	1991	60%	$250m
Mobile telecoms	Joint venture greenfield	1993		$250m
Insurance	Joint venture	1990	67%	$220m
Motorway construction and operation	Concession	1993		$200m
Aluminium	Joint venture	1992	51%	$165m
Food and detergents	Privatisation	1992	90%	$160m
Paper	Joint venture	1990	40%	$160m
Electrical engineering	Privatisation	1990	75%	$130m
Soft drinks	Privatisation	1993	79%	$115m
Glass	Joint venture	1989	100%	$110m
Airline	Privatisation	1992	35%	$100m
Various	Portfolio investments	1990		$100m
Pharmaceuticals	Privatisation	1990	51%	$100m
Car components	Greenfield	1991	100%	$100m
Coffee	Privatisation	1991	100%	$100m
Soft drinks	Privatisation	1991	100%	$100m
Hotel	Greenfield	1987	85%	$95m
Confectionery	Privatisation	1991	97%	$94m
Telecoms equipment	Privatisation	1991	100%	$94m
Banking	Joint venture	1979	64%	$87m
Various	Portfolio investments	1990		$80m
Confectionery	Privatisation		70%	$80m
Hotel	Privatisation	1992	90%	$77m
Sugar, starch	Privatisation	1990	53%	$70m
Industrial gases	Privatisation	1991	97%	$70m
Steelmaking	Privatisation	1992	50%	$70m
Sugar	Privatisation	1991	40%	$70m
Cigarettes	Privatisation	1992	85%	$68m
Fridges	Privatisation	1991	100%	$65m
Petrol stations, propane-butane gas distribution	Greenfield, Privatisation			$65m
Cigarettes	Privatisation	1991	51%	$60m
Various	US govt-supported equity investment fund	1990		$60m
Pharmaceutical waste treatment	Privatisation	1993	52%	$60m
Cigarettes	Privatisation	1991	80%	$60m
Distilling	Privatisation	1991	99%	$60m
Retail	Privatisation	1991	51%	$59m
Petrol stations	Greenfield			$57m
Office development	Greenfield			$56m
Telecoms, various		1992		$55m
Carbon black	Joint venture	1993	60%	$55m
Retail	Share placement	1991	32%	$54m
Hotels	Privatisation	1993	51%	$52m
Retail	Privatisation	1989–92		$50m
Bottled propane-butane gas	Privatisation	1992	51%	$50m
Packaging	Greenfield	1992	100%	$50m
Buses	Privatisation	1991	30%	$50m

Source: FT statistics

strategy producing certain products or components on a large scale for the world market.

Although FDI has increased rapidly, especially over the past four years, Western firms have been slow to commit the large investment sums originally anticipated. Moreover, it was reported that progress in attracting foreign investment for infrastructural projects in Hungary had been painfully slow even in 1994 as the government failed to develop adequate regulatory and tariff structures to cope with the privatisation of vital services, which made it very difficult to attract foreign investment.[24] The rate of FDI has been rather lower than expectation of Hungarian government, which needs more foreign capital in every branch of the economy. Even compared with Greece or Portugal, the capital inflow was insignificant. If Hungary really wants to privatise rapidly, in a few years the share of foreign investment in industrial fixed assets must exceed the level of 30 per cent.

The resolution of these problems and the success of JVs in Hungary would depend very much on the success of economic transformation. An increasing inflow of foreign capital into Hungary would, in turn, help accelerate Hungary's transformation process, economic development, and integration with Western Europe and the world market.

Summary and prospects

Despite a dearth of reliable statistics, the following patterns in foreign investment in Hungary can be discerned.

First, while most interests were directed towards tourism and services, particularly in the fields of consultancy and marketing, where the initial capital outlays are small, there were great interests in manufacturing production, such as metallurgy, engineering, and chemicals. Although there were a number of JVs in which Western capital share exceed Ft100 million, much of this inward investment was small-scale. A significant proportion of foreign capital was concentrated in material production. We also observed that an increase in the absolute numbers of new JVs was accompanied by a lowering of the average foreign investment, which implied a rapid fall in the size of new FIEs and most foreign investors restricted their financial commitments to the minimum amount required by foreign investment law. So far, foreign investment in Hungary performed quite well, but below expectations and requirements. Judged by the yardstick of the rapidly increasing number of FIEs, the results were so far reasonably satisfactory. Judged by the amount of capital invested by foreigners, the picture was less encouraging.

Second, investment geared to import substitution and with a broad diversification of activities predominate; conversely, export-oriented projects were modest, and contradict Hungary's objective of strengthening its involvement in the international division of labour; Up to 1990, FDI in Hungary was of the import-substitution type: the MNCs' objective was to service the growing domestic market. Since 1992, foreign investment tends to become more export-oriented as a result of Hungary's specific factor endowment and small market size. Although Hungarian needs for major inflows of FDI are high, the foreign investors' response seems unlikely to match them in the medium term.

Third, FDI is frequently regarded by both foreign and domestic partners as a means of avoiding the foreign exchange and foreign trade restrictions by the host country. In this respect it is merely a substitute for foreign trade transactions.

Fourth, the so-called gold rush into Hungary - led by automobile, lighting and glass companies - yielded significant gains for the state treasury. Since 1989, Hungary has attracted more than US$6 billion foreign investment, smaller by the standards of emerging Asian economies, but by far the largest amount of any country in Eastern Europe. The distribution of foreign investors by national origins remained more or less unchanged over the past years, by far most foreign investment originate from America and neighbouring Western Europe (as American investors accounted for more than US$3 billion of total FDI and Western Europe accounted for 33 per cent of the total value of foreign capital in Hungary),[25] which traditionally enjoyed strong trading links with Hungary that made it easier to upgrade their cooperation to direct investment. So far, Japanese investors have not shown a significant interest in investing in Hungary.

The rate of foreign capital inflows will greatly depend on Hungary's economic reforms and political stability.[26] The greater possibility of Forint convertibility in next few years will facilitate the inflow of increased foreign resources into Hungary; continued political stability will generate strong confidence among foreign investors who under the current political situation in Eastern Europe and the former Soviet Union would switch their investments from less stable states, such as the former Yugoslav Republics, into more stable countries in this area, such as the most advanced reformers - Hungary, Poland, Czech-land, and Slovakia.

Foreign investment and joint ventures in China, 1979-94

Despite frequent shifts in policy, China managed to maintain the Open Door policy throughout last decades and succeeded in attracting a large amount of foreign investment in a limited period.

Relying on the MOFERT data, this section will provide a comprehensive picture of the quantity and pattern of capital inflow, major forms of investment, investors origins, and the geographic and sectoral distribution of investing activities over the last 16 years.

FDI in 1979-82: the first wave

China's efforts to encourage foreign investment inflows started in 1979, however, large FDI inflows did not occur until 1984. The 1979-82 efforts, with active experiments within the SEZs and cautious implementation outside these zones, started to yield mixed results - averaged only US$440 million during the first four years.

At the end of 1980, China only signed 20 EJVs contracts with foreign investors, with US$0.17 billion accumulated inward foreign capital. In 1981, China utilised about US$8.781 billion foreign capital, with foreign loans US$2.461 billion and FDI US$2.077 billion, in which 20 EJVs contracts was US$20 million foreign capital and 169 CJVs with US$1.435 billion foreign investment. **Table 3.13** revealed that more than 46 per cent and 40 per cent of foreign capital came from Hong Kong and the USA.

Table 3.13
EJVs by major source countries in China in 1981

Country/ Region	No. of Contracts	Total Investment (10,000)	Foreign Direct Investment	
			Value ($10,000)	Percentage (%)
Hong Kong	10	2,242.0	928.0	46.44
USA	5	1,616.5	803.5	40.21
Japan	2	388.0	202.8	10.15
West Germany	1	69.0	34.5	1.73
Australia	1	46.0	23.0	1.15
Philippines	1	12.5	6.3	0.32
Total	20	4,374.0	1,998.1	100.00

Source: Liang, Xi (1981), 'New Development of Utilisation of Foreign Capital in China', *Almanac of China's Foreign Trade (1981)*, p. V-286.

Table 3.14 shows that most foreign invested projects concentrated on small-scale labour-intensive industries, including light industry, foodstuff processing and electronic assembly, which involved very limited capital commitment and unsophisticated assembly/processing technology.

Table 3.14
EJVs by industry in China in 1981

Industry	No. of EJVs	Total Investment (US$10,000)	Foreign Capital	
			Value (US$10,000)	Percentage (%)
Light industry	4	735.0	346.5	17.34
Foodstuff	3	1,058.5	529.3	26.49
Electron	3	1,190.0	493.0	24.67
Machinery	3	474.2	235.3	11.78
Textile	2	612.5	246.2	12.32
Tourism	2	26.4	12.8	0.64
Petroleum	1	200.0	100.0	5.05
Commerce	1	40.0	20.0	1.00
Communic-ation	1	37.5	15.0	0.71
Total	20	4,374.1	1,998.1	100.00

Sources: Long, Chucai (1982), 'China's Utilisation of Foreign Capital', *Almanac of China's Economy (1982)*, pp.IV-130-131.

Although the Chinese government often insisted on acquiring advanced technology through JVs, their absorptive capacity needed to be considered. Evidence shows that problems frequently occurred in JVs involving high technology, as the Chinese industry was not able to supply the reliable components and parts required to implement the technology, many needed to be imported. Foreign investors found it advantageous to provide unsophisticated technology for which components and parts could be supplied in China. Few cases of JVs with foreign partners supplying a high level of technology had proved to be successful. The Chinese government's requirement of acquiring 'the most advanced technology' through JVs appeared to be too ambitious, given the relatively low ability of the Chinese partners to absorb imported technology during the early stage of open-up.[27]

In 1982, the Chinese government signed US$1.8 billion contracted foreign loan. The central government approved 20 newly EJVs with US$242 million, and CJVs 110 with foreign capital US$0.3 billion in 1982. By the end of 1982, China reached over 949 arrangements with foreign investors, with US$20.5 billion committed foreign capital, of which over half was flowed into the four SEZs and the two surrounding provinces - Guangdong and Fujian. Foreign loans dominated the scene, with US$13.55 billion amount of capital by 27 contracts. FDI amounted US$6.01 billion with 922 arrangements, of which compensation trade and CJVs dominated 36 per cent and 57 per cent of the total number of FDI contracts signed. **Table 3.15** suggests that EJVs yielded only limited success during this period, only with US$0.14 billion and 83 EJVs.

From 1979 to 1982, FDI inflows were relatively small, amounting to approximately US$1.2 billion. In particular, equity investment was insignificant, accounting for less than 10 per cent of total FDI inflows. Direct investment concentrated largely on CJVs and oil exploration activities (46 and 42 per cent, respectively). For other investments, the bulk of inflows occurred in the form of compensation trade, which accounted for about 95 per cent of total investment activities. During this period, China failed to attract the desired level, scale and type of FDI. This fact pushed China to open up more favourable to the foreign investors.

Both **Tables 3.13** and **3.15** indicate that the largest foreign investors in China were firms from Hong Kong and Macao since 1978. The popularity of China as an investment location for investors from Hong Kong could be explained by the following factors: geographical proximity, cultural affinity, the Chinese connection, and gateway function of Hong Kong (Chen, Jinghan, 1993, p.182). Among the millions of emigrants or their descendants from China living in North America, Western Europe, Hong Kong/Macao, and Taiwan, there are some who have amassed considerable fortunes and are prepared to look for investment opportunities and put some of their funds in the 'old country' for profits. Following the liberalisation of foreign investments, they started to acquire the equity in numerous state-owned industrial establishments, office buildings, and service enterprises, or create new enterprises in China by taking advantage of ethnic connections in order to make a contribution to the prosperity and stability of China. More important, Hong Kong companies are keen to transfer the labour-intensive processes of their textile and electronic production to mainland China so as to

Table 3.15
Joint ventures by country/region at the end of 1982

Country/Region	Accumulated EJVs at end of 1982		New approved EJVs in 1982	
	No.of EJVs	Foreign capital ($10,000)	No. of EJVs	Foreign capital ($10,000)
Hong Kong	55	6,233	14	841
USA	11	5,196	4	853
Japan	5	753	-	-
Philippines	4	396	-	-
France	1	20	-	-
West Germany	1	35	-	
Switzerland	1	400	-	-
Denmark	1	251	-	-
Australia	1	23	-	-
Thailand	1	27	-	-
Norway	1	125	1	125
Sweden	1	600	1	600
Total	83	14,059	20	2,419

Sources: Long, Chucai (1982), 'China's Utilisation of Foreign Capital', *Almanac of China's Economy (1982)*, pp.IV-130-131.

move further up the product cycle into more sophisticated production as well as to bypass quotas. Moreover, there was evidence that Western MNCs used Hong Kong firms as conduits, or their Hong Kong offices as gateways to enter into the Chinese market owing to Hong Kong's geographical and ethic advantages. A Western company with unique technology and skills may wish to enter the Chinese market, but may lack managerial resources and cultural sensitivity required to do so quickly. It can, however, provide the technology to a Hong Kong firm, which, in turn, can establish a JV in China, or establish a Hong Kong office first, and then use the Hong Kong base to invest in

China.

During the first four years (1979-82), China's actively promotion for attracting foreign capital yielded a moderate success. Although the basic JVs law on equity investment was promulgated in 1979, detailed investment regulations regarding the implementation of the law were not available, or were not yet well defined, the market mechanism had not worked properly, and the Chinese had little experience in equity investment, so foreign investors perceived the market risk as high due to the newly opened market and economy. Therefore, many foreign investors still adopted a 'wait-and-see' attitude - waiting for the market conditions to become more certain before making investments, or to make non-equity investment in the form of compensation trade and CJVs in order to secure a positive return on investment. Moreover, CJVs were more suitable as a means of market entry because CJVs were more flexible in operation and management. Finally, oil exploration was considered extremely promising and potentially profitable as a vast offshore area was opened to foreign oil companies.

The second wave: 1983-85

In 1983-85, the inflow of foreign capital was a rather substantial achievement, as FDI growth appeared promising. An improved domestic environment, an enlarged geographic opening,[28] and the decentralised decision-making contributed to the increase enthusiasm for foreign investment development in the country. Throughout this period, local authorities, especially those of the 14 'open cities', were moving fast in initiating FDI projects, sending delegations abroad to search for potential partners, and formulating local laws and regulations attractive to foreign companies. Foreign investors responded positively and promptly.

As a result, FDI inflow increased significantly in this period. The total number of FDI contracts signed doubled every year between 1983-85. **Table 3.16** shows that the number of external loans and direct investment contracts increased from 690 in 1983 to 2,204 in 1984 and 3,145 in 1985, while the amount of foreign capital grew rapidly from US$3.43 billion to US$4.79 billion and US$9.87 billion, in which the agreements of FDI increased from 638 to 2,166 and 3,073, with pledged foreign capital from US$1.92 billion to US$2.88 billion and US$6.33 billion respectively.

By the end of 1983, the total number of contracts for foreign loans was 79, with pledged foreign capital US$14 billion, utilized capital US$11.9 billion, the total number of contracts for FDI was 2,452, with pledged FDI US$7.5 billion and utilised FDI US$2.68 billion. By the end of 1984, China reached 4,000 agreements of utilisation of foreign investment, with US$25.3 billion pledged foreign investment, in which FDI was US$10.35 billion, indirect

Table 3.16
Statement of China's pledged foreign capital, 1983-85

Project	No. of Contract			Amount of Foreign Capital (US$10,000)		
	1983	1984	1985	1983	1984	1985
1. External Loans	52	38	72	151,331	191,642	353,421
Loans from Foreign Governments	47	29	59	90,178	50,465	102,053
Loans from International Financial Institutions	5	9	13	43,840	96,950	113,151
Other	-	-	-	17,313	44,227	138,217
2. FDI	638	2,166	3,073	191,690	287,494	633,321
EJVs	107	741	1,412	18,837	106,655	202,970
CJVs	330	1,089	1,611	50,270	148,402	349,615
Joint Exploration	18	-	4	100,087	-	35,959
WFOEs	15	26	46	3,950	9,991	4,566
Compensation Trade	168	310	-	10,199	16,167	26,034
Other	-	-	-	8,347	6,279	14,177
Total	690	2,204	3,145	343,021	479,136	986,742

Sources: *Almanac of China's Foreign Trade,* 1983, p.1096; 1984, p.1069; 1985, p.1213, MOFERT, Beijing.

foreign investment (external loans) US$14.9 billion. The amount of utilised foreign capital totalled US$17.2 billion, which was about 10 per cent of domestic total investment in the same period.[29] According to one official estimate, about one third of the total FIEs run smoothly, one third did well but experienced foreign exchange problems, and the remainder lose money.

In 1985, foreign investment enjoyed continued rapid growth. The new approved FDI projects were 3,073, with pledged FDI US$5.93 billion, increases of 65.6 per cent and 130 per cent over 1984 respectively. In which, EJVs were 1,412 with pledged foreign investment US$2.03 billion, increase of 90.6 per cent and 90.3 per cent over 1984 respectively; CJVs were 1,611 with pledged FDI US$3.5 billion, increase of 47.1 per cent and 130 per cent over 1984 respectively; joint exploitation contracted amounted 4 with pledged FDI US$0.36 billion; WFOEs amounted 46 with pledged FDI US$0.45 billion. By the end of 1985, the total number of contracts for FDI was 6,300, of which EJVs 2,300, CJVs 3,800, joint exploration 35, and WFOEs 120. The total pledged FDI was US$16 billion, of which EJVs US$3 billion (20 per cent), CJVs US$9 billion (60 per cent), joint exploration US$2.7 billion (17 per cent), and WFOEs US$0.5 billion (3 per cent). The committed FDI totalled US$6 billion, 36.4 per cent of the pledged FDI in the same period, a evident fact that the contractual foreign investment was much more than the investment that was actually utilised. Foreign investors were still not confidence in China's investment environment. Meanwhile, China borrowed US$3.53 billion foreign loans, including US$1 billion from foreign government, US$1.13 billion from international financial institutions, and US$0.6 billion from buyers credit and/or foreign banks. By the end of 1985, the pledged external loans over the past 7 years totalled US$20.3 billion, with capital commitment totalling over US$15.6 billion invested into 150 key construction projects.[30]

The sources of foreign investment were also diversified during this period. While Hong Kong and Macao firms were dominant and kept increasing their involvement on the mainland, foreign firms from other developed countries caught up fast. Investment by firms from the United States, Singapore and Japan, in particular, increased significantly. Those of Western Europe also rose rapidly.[31]

Foreign investment also extended into a wide range of economic sectors in this period. However, the tourism-related industry attracted the lion's share of the foreign capital actually used. By the end of 1985, over 50 per cent of the total FDI was invested in real estate sector, mainly as the construction of luxurious hotels. Other sectors, including manufacturing, made less impressive progress but were nevertheless moving ahead as well (Pearson, 1991, pp.69-72).

The third wave: 1986-89

Table 3.17 suggests that FDI in 1986-87 did not enjoy the continued rapid growth due to the strong negative impact of the policy retrenchment. While the external loans in 1986 amounted US$8.4 billion pledged capital (increased 137.9 per cent over 1985) with 53 contracts and with capital commitment of US$5.01 billion (increased 100.1 per cent over 1985), FDI contracts signed dropped by almost 50 per cent compared with 1985, pledged FDI (US$2.83 billion) dropped 52.2 per cent over 1985, while the actually utilized FDI (US$1.87 billion) grew at a rate of only 13 per cent, compared to the 35 per cent in 1985. Moreover, fourteen months after the issue of 'the 22 Provision' in October 1986, statistics still failed to show much positive response from foreign firms. In 1987, pledged external loans amounted US$7.82 billion, a drop of 7 per cent over 1986, while actually utilised loans amounted US$5.8 billion, an increase of 15.76 per cent over 1986. Newly approved FIEs were 2,230 in all (of which EJVs amounted 1,395, CJVs 789, WFOEs 46, joint exploration 3), totalling pledged foreign capital US$3.71 billion, an increase of 30.85 per cent over 1986, while actually committed capital was US$2.3 billion, an increase of 23.39 per cent over 1986. More important, as a result of the policy regarding favoured sectors, more FDI was attracted into the fields that the country found desirable. FDI in the manufacturing activities increased noticeably from 76 per cent in 1986 to 85 per cent in 1987, while foreign investment in service industries (such as hotels, real estate) was slowing down.

As poor management, inefficiency, excessive bureaucracy, complicated legislation and lack of an essential market system still existed during 1979-87, many foreign investors, therefore, still adopted a 'wait-and-see' attitude. The phenomenon could be seen from the fact that the contractual foreign investment was much more than the investment that was actually utilised. From 1979 to 1987 only 39 per cent of contracts actually committed (Chen, Jinghan, 1993, p.170).

The 1988 'golden coast' and further expansion of 'open cities' drove a large number of foreign companies into China in the hope of establishing a market share in this huge market and as a result, foreign capital flow into China boomed. The number of external loans' contracts increased from 56 in 1987 to 118, with pledged foreign capital US$9.81 billion and committed capital US$6.49 billion, increases of 25.54 per cent and 11.74 per cent respectively over 1987. The number of FDI contracts amounted to 5,945 (in which, EJVs 3,909, CJVs 1,621, WFOEs 410, joint exploration 5), increases of 166 per cent over 1987, nearly half of the accumulated projects in 1978-87, with pledged foreign capital US$5.29 billion, 42 per cent more than 1987. The actually utilised foreign capital was US$3.19 billion, an increase of 40 per cent over 1987. Moreover, pledged foreign investment in tourism-related sector dropped from 33 per cent in 1985 to 6.7 per cent in 1988, while it increased rapidly to 90 per cent in manufacturing sector.

Table 3.17

Foreign capital inflows, 1979-89 (in million US$)

Types	1979-82	1983	1984	1985	1986	1987	1988	1989	1979-89
Direct Investment	1160	635	1258	1659	1875	2314	3194	3393	15486
EJVs	103	74	255	580	805	1486	1975	1610	6887
CJVs	530	227	465	585	794	620	780	600	4601
Oil Exploration	487	292	523	481	260	183	212	200	2637
WFOEs	40	43	15	13	16	25	226	280	658
Other Investments	760	281	161	298	369	333	546	381	3129
International Leasing*	--	--	--	--	48	20	161	--	--
Compensation Trade	725	197	99	169	181	222	317	--	--
Processing & Assembling	35	84	63	129	140	91	69	--	--
Total	1920	916	1419	1956	2243	2647	3740	3774	18615

Source: MOFERT: *Almanac of China's Foreign Economic Relations and Trade*, various issues.

* Data for early years are not available.

By the end of 1988, foreign invested projects totalled 15,997, with pledged FDI US$28.2 billion and committed FDI US$12.1 billion, of which JVs accounted for 96 per cent of the total contracts signed, 84 per cent of the total committed FDI and 76 per cent of the total utilised FDI. Even in the year of 1988, the US$2.3 billion of FDI utilised in JVs which accounted for 86 per cent of the total amount of utilised FDI in that year was much higher than the US$142 million of FDI utilised in WFOEs which accounted for only 5 per cent of the total amount of utilised FDI (Chen, Jinghan, 1993, pp.176). JVs were the major form of industrial cooperation in China. Ours survey in Chapter 5 will show that the popularity of JVs was due to the Chinese partners' ability to provide foreign investors with significant information and knowledge of the Chinese economy which was unfamiliar to them.

Among the 47 FDI source countries/regions, investors from Hong Kong were still dominant, followed by USA, Japan and EEC. The popularity of Hong Kong as a source of investment was mainly because of its adjacent location, cultural affinity and the Chinese connection. Many Western MNCs used Hong Kong as the gateway to access the huge Chinese domestic market.[32] Those of Taiwan rose rapidly (partly as a result of promulgation of the 'Provisions for Encouraging Investment from Taiwan Compatriots' in July 1988). Most of foreign investment dominated in coastal cities, while Guangdong Province was the biggest host province of FDI over 1978-88. Foreign investment was diversified into various economic sectors, mainly in energy, transportation, communication, chemistry, machinery, electron, building materials, light industry, foodstuffs, textile, clothing, farming and fishing, and tourism.[33] China has been recognized as a competitive investment alternative in the competition with its Asian neighbours for attracting FDI.

In 1989, China signed 130 external loan contracts with pledged foreign capital US$5.19 billion and committed loans of US$6.29 billion, reduction of about 47.17 per cent and 3.1 per cent respectively compared with 1988 due to the 'Tiananmen Square Event' on 4 June 1989. China also signed 5,779 new contracts (in which EJVs were 3,659, CJVs 1,179, WFOEs 931, joint exploration 10) with foreign investors, with pledged FDI US$5.6 billion and committed FDI US$3.39 billion, increase of 5.84 per cent and 6.33 per cent respectively over 1988. Pledged and committed foreign investment in China in this year still totalled US$11.48 billion and US$10.06 billion, drops of 28.28 per cent and 1.64 per cent respectively compared with 1988. Inward investment from Hong Kong dominated 57.9 per cent of the total FDI in 1989, followed by USA (11.4 per cent) and Japan (7.8 per cent). FDI projects were diversified according to the following economic sectors, manufacturing (83 per cent), commerce and catering (9 per cent), agriculture & forestry & husbandry & fishing (2 per cent), building (1 per cent) and other (5 per cent).

Guangdong Province dominated 59 per cent of the pledged total FDI in 1989, followed by Fujian Province (16 per cent), Liaoning Province (9 per cent) and Shanghai (6 per cent). By the end of 1989, China had approved 21,776 foreign invested projects from 47 foreign countries/regions, with pledged FDI US$33.76 billion and committed FDI US$15.49 billion.[34]

Table 3.17 indicates that by the end of 1989, total foreign capital inflows reached about US$18.6 billion. Direct investment, including equity and CJVs, oil exploration and, WFOEs, accounted for over 80 per cent of these inflows (reaching US$15.5 billion), while other investments such as leasing, compensation trade, and processing and assembling accounted for the remaining 20 per cent. WFOEs remained weak until the mid-1980s, but gained a substantial growth in 1988-89. Two major factors contributed to the large increase in equity investment during this period. One was the increased specification of the laws governing both JVs and WFOEs, as well as the laws concerning the protection of copyrights and patents. The other factor was the significant improvement in market conditions.

Most foreign investment in China came from other Asian countries and economies, especially Hong Kong and Japan, which accounted for 60 and 13 per cent respectively (See **Table 3.18**). With the exception of the United Sates and more recently Taiwan, other countries played a minor role.

This pattern of FDI inflows was consistent with the pattern of trade flows between China and other countries. Between 1984 and 1989, most of China's trade took place with other Asian countries and accounted for over 60 per cent of the total trade with the rest of world. Again, Hong Kong and Japan were the largest trading partners, followed, albeit distantly, by the United States. The United States was strong during the early period from 1979 to 1986, but weakened substantially after 1986, and particularly in 1988-89. As a result it was surpassed by Japan, dropping to become only the third largest investor. 'Although the absolute level of investment did not decline, the U.S. share in total investment inflows decreased substantially from about 20 per cent in 1984 to only 8 per cent in 1989' (Grub and Lin, 1991, p.84). The Japanese approach to investment in China was almost entirely different from that of the United States. During the early period, Japanese firms were extremely cautious and because of the uncertainty associated with the newly opened market, they believed that exporting, rather than investment, was a better approach to penetrate the Chinese market. This was followed by establishing lucrative JVs in the service sector and gradual investment in the manufacturing sector. By 1988, Japanese investment had more than doubled that of the United States and Japan became the second largest investor. Taiwan and South Korea had emerged as the major sources of FDI inflows to China since 1988. Higher costs of production at home, particular labour costs, have forced firms from Hong Kong, Japan, Taiwan and South Korea to shift labour-intensive production to lower-cost countries in the region. Geographical and cultural factors have also been important in the growth of their investment patterns.

Table 3.18
FDI inflows by country of origin, 1984-89 (in million US$)

Country	1984	1985	1986	1987	1988	1989	1984-89
Hong Kong & Macao	748	956	1132	1588	2068	2037	8528
Japan	225	315	201	220	515	356	1832
U.S.A.	256	357	315	263	236	284	1712
Britain	98	71	27	5	34	29	263
Singapore	1	10	13	22	28	84	158
Italy	18	19	23	16	31	30	138
Australia	0	14	60	5	4	44	129
Germany	8	24	19	3	15	81	151
France	20	33	42	16	23	5	138
Other	45	456	42	177	241	442	1103
Total*	1419	1956	1875	2314	3194	3393	14150

Source: MOFERT, *Almanac of China's Foreign Economic Relations and Trade,* various issues.
* Including other investment inflows.

The geographical distribution of foreign investment inflows indicated that foreign investment activities had been concentrated in coastal provinces and cities (See **Table 3.19**). During 1979-84, investment in Guangdong Province alone accounted for over 40 per cent of total inflows. Together with Shanghai and Fujian Province, investment in these three areas accounted for about 60 per cent of the total foreign investment in China.

The strong investment inflows to the coastal areas occurred for several reasons, such as better developed production facilities, close links with overseas Chinese, and well-educated labour. The share of investment in the coastal areas declined somewhat during 1984-89, however, owing to the opening up of other areas and to the strong promotion by other local provincial governments to attract foreign investment.

Table 3.19
Foreign capital inflows by province, 1984-89 (in million US$)

Province	1984	1985	1986	1987	1988	1984-89
Beijing	119	379	420	624	143	1684
Tianjin	106	69	94	14	110	392
Liaoning	44	254	75	106	192	672
Shanghai	431	771	303	338	333	2176
Fujian	236	377	65	118	463	1258
Shandong	105	100	49	39	260	553
Guangdong	1409	2199	869	1258	2242	7977
Other	425	1221	668	757	1321	4392
Total	**2875**	**5369**	**2542**	**3254**	**5064**	**19103**

Source: MOFERT, *Almanac of China's Foreign Economic Relations and Trade,* various issues.

Since 1988, the pattern of sectoral distribution of investment inflows also changed substantially, shifting from real estate activities to manufacturing, in which FDI was heavily concentrated on machinery and equipment, with a small portion going to the food-processing industry. Altogether, foreign investment made important contribution to the sectoral development of service, export manufacturing, and oil exploitation. Hong Kong/Macao investments had been concentrated heavily in light industry, textiles, electronics, chemicals, and heavy industry. American investment tended to be more widely distributed according to economic sector.

Fourth wave: 1990-94

In 1990, foreign investment enjoyed stable growth in China. The committed external loans amounted US$6.53 billion, an increase of 3.96 per cent over 1989, while pledged external loans was US$5.1 billion, a decrease of 1.65 per cent over 1989. In terms of FDI, 7,273 new FDI projects were approved, with pledged foreign capital US$6.596 billion and committed FDI US$3.49 billion, increases of 25.85 per cent, 17.81 and 2.80 per cent over 1989 respectively (see **Table 3.20**).

Manufacturing projects dominated 93.7 per cent of the total 7,273 new projects, and 86.3 per cent of the committed foreign capital. WFOEs raised rapidly to 1,860, with pledged FDI US$2.44 billion, increased 99.79 per cent and 47.78 per cent than 1989. Its proportion amounted to 37.1 per cent of the total pledged FDI in the same year. By the end of 1990, WFOEs totalled 3,385, most of them were export-oriented enterprises. In 1991, the average foreign investment in newly approved FIEs was about US$1 million. Only 2 per cent projects were above US$10 million, while 52 per cent were under US$0.5 million.[35]

At the first stage of investment, foreign investors were reluctant to invest in infrastructural and agricultural projects because the return on investment was longer term and less secure. However, in China, as in all developing countries, improvement and development of infrastructure and agricultural advancement are the keys to the long range success of national economic policy. Statistically, between 1979 to 1988, foreign investment in the transportation and communication industries constituted only 1.4 per cent of the total amount of foreign investment; 3.2 per cent in agriculture, fisheries and forestry; but 28 per cent in estate investment. Real estate in combination with foreign investment in the processing industries accounted for in excess of 50 per cent of the total foreign investment in China. According to one estimate, compiled by Crosby Securities, a Hong Kong stock brokerage, the share of foreign investment in China's expenditure on infrastructure development rose to 13 per cent in 1990 from 2 per cent in 1982. The trend was expected to continue.

Investment from Hong Kong and Macao was still dominant in the total pledged FDI in 1990, followed by Japan (6.9 per cent) and USA (5.4 per cent). It should be noted, however, that investment from Taiwan grew rapidly in 1989 and 1990 (roughly US$1 billion each year), and was expected to grow more rapidly. Taiwanese investments may exceed those of U.S. firms since it was impossible to determine the amount of Taiwanese investment that was disguised through their subsidiary operations in Hong Kong, the United States, Canada, and Singapore.[36] The same was true for South Korean investments, estimated to be US$1.5 billion as of December 1990. It was estimated that about 5 per cent of FDI in China was, directly or indirectly of 'Mainland origin' - from the foreign subsidiaries of Chinese companies.

Interestingly, the number of WFOEs in 1990 exceeded that of the CJVs for the first time. There were 1,861 WFOEs recorded in 1990 with US$2.44 billion contracted investment, compared with 1,778 and US$1.26 billion respectively for CJVs. This trend was followed by a further increase in 1991, in which 2,795 WFOEs established with US$3.67 billion contracted capital (US$1.44 billion been utilized), compared with 1,779 newly approved

103

Table 3.20
Statement of China's utilized amount of foreign capital, 1990

Forms	Approved Agreements			Utilized Amount	
	Number	Amount (US$ bn)	% Change over 1989	Amount	% Change over 1989
1.External Loans	**98**	**5.09937**	**-1.65**	**6.53452**	**3.96**
Loans from Foreign Governments	82	0.72	-51.10	2.52357	17.43
Loans from International Financial Institutions	16	1.893	121.10	1.066	-1.73
Buyer's Credit	-	0.8312	-16.16	0.898	39.99
Loans from Foreign Banks	-	1.653	-4.19	2.044	-9.94
Issue Bands and Share to Foreign Countries	-	0.00297	-97.89	0.00297	-97.89
2.Foreign Direct Investment	**7,237**	**6.59611**	**17.79**	**3.48711**	**2.79**
EJVs	4,091	2.70395	1.69	1.886	-7.42
CJVs	1,317	1.25410	15.78	0.674	-10.41
WFOEs	1,860	2.44381	47.77	0.683	83.92
Joint Exploration	5	0.194	-4.66	0.24431	5.22
3.Other Foreign Investment	**-**	**0.39021**	**-43.80**	**0.26776**	**-29.70**
International Leasing	-	0.05108	-29.04	0.03045	-52.31
Compensation Trade	-	0.20265	-57.31	0.15874	-39.25
Processing Assembly	-	0.13648	-7.53	0.00786	40.96
Total	**7,371**	**12.0857**	**5.29**	**10.29**	**2.29**

Source: MOFERT (1990), *Almanac of China's Foreign Trade,* p.580.

projects, US$2.14 billion and US$764 million respectively for CJVs. This development seems to be an indicator of strong confidence by foreign firms and a pointer to the improvement of the investment climate in China. WFOEs will be dominant by the end of this century.

Starting from the opening-up and development of Pudong New Area, foreign investment in China boomed in 1991. China signed 12,978 FDI projects, with pledged foreign capital US$11.98 billion, increases of 78.4 and 81.6 per cent over 1990 respectively. By the end of 1991, China had utilized US$52.34 billion FDI, with 42,701 approved FIEs, in which more than 20,000 had put into operation and FIEs' output in 1991 amounted 4.9 per cent of the total industrial production in the same year.

The data contained in **Table 3.21** provide measure of China's absorption (realised) of foreign capital between 1979 and 1991. They suggest a number of important findings. First, the provincial absorption of FDI had been consistently higher than that of the various central ministries in both absolute and relative terms. This trend reflected the deregulation of decision-making powers relating to FDI accommodation down to the provincial level. Secondly, similar changes favouring the provinces occurred in the absorption of foreign loans, even though during 1985-90 the ministries consistently enjoyed a substantially higher share of borrowing. It should of course be borne in mind that the ministries are representative of the state and are therefore likely to have better access to foreign government loans. Third, if FDI and foreign borrowing were taken together, it is clear that China's provinces (whose share rose from 36 per cent to 53 per cent between 1985 and 1990) gained significantly at the expense of the ministries (64 and 47 per cent respectively). Even so, the central government continued to exert important leverage in the allocation of foreign loans, with the amount under its control in 1990 (US$4,477 million) far exceeding that within the purview of the provinces (US$2,058 million). Fourthly, within the total FDI intake, EJVs gained - at an accelerating pace - at the expense of CJVs to become the most important form of FIEs in China. This development underlined the increasing confidence felt by foreign partners seeking to make long-term commitments, in the wake of improvements in China's legal framework and investment environment.[37] Finally, the dramatic increases in FDI in the form of WFOEs particularly reflected added confidence by foreign investors, as did the declining important of compensation trade.

The national FDI rate of growth was overwhelmingly dominated by the performance of the 11 Open Coastal Provinces (OCPs), which absorbed the lion's share of the national total. The data in **Table 3.22** do indeed show that almost all the later-established OCPs and Open Coastal Cities (OCCs) experienced much higher rates of growth of FDI, in particular Liaoning, Hebei, Shandong, Shanghai, Jiangsu and Hainan. The outcome was that after

Table 3.21

Chinese intake of foreign capital, 1979-91 (US$ m)

(a) Realised loans and FDI by provincial and ministerial borrowers (percentage shares in brackets)

	Loans		FDI		Total		
	Provincial (1)	Ministerial (2)	Provincial (3)	Ministerial (4)	Provincial (1) + (3) (5)	Ministerial (2) + (4) (6)	PRC Total (5) + (6) (7)
1979-84 average	-	-	476.50 (69.70)	207.16 (30.30)	-	-	-
1983	-	-	-	-	-	-	1,980.64
1984	-	-	-	-	-	-	2,704,52
1985	281.09 (11.22)	2,224.87 (88.78)	1,318.04 (67.38)	638.11 (32.62)	1,599.13 (35.84)	2,862.98 (64.16)	4,462.11 (100.00)
1986	1,033.66 (20.61)	3980.91 (79.39)	1,741.65 (77.62)	502.08 (22.38)	2,775.31 (38.24)	4,482.99 (61.76)	7,258.30 (100.00)
1987	1,428.42 (24.61)	4,376.53 (75.39)	1,782.73 (67.36)	863.88 (32.64)	3,211.15 (37.99)	5,240.41 (62.01)	8,451.56 (100.00)
1988	2,460.20 (37.93)	4,026.53 (62.07)	3,149.69 (84.22)	589.93 (15.78)	5,609.89 (54.86)	4,616.46 (45.14)	10,226.38 (100.00)
1989	2,410.88 (38.35)	3,874.82 (61.65)	3,437.37 (91.09)	336.12 (8.91)	5,848.21 (58.14)	4,210.94 (41.86)	10,059.15 (100.00)
1990	2,057.63 (31.49)	4,476.89 (68.51)	3,436.15 (91.51)	318.79 (8.49)	5,493.78 (53.39)	4,795.61 (46.61)	10,289.39 (100.00)
1991	-	-	-	-	-	-	11,137.98

(b) Realised FDI by types of JVs (percentage shares in brackets)

	FDI total	EJVs	CJVs	Joint exploration	WFOEs	Compensation trade	Others
1979-81 average	373.56 (100.00)	21.77 (5.83)	117.77 (31.53)	106.04 (28.39)	0.33 (0.09)	94.08 (25.18)	33.57 (8.99)
1982	649.27 (100.00)	34.29 (5.28)	177.77 (27.38)	178.52 (27.50)	39.31 (6.05)	122.40 (18.85)	96.98 (14.94)
1983	915.96 (100.00)	73.57 (8.03)	227.38 (24.82)	291.50 (31.82)	42.76 (4.67)	197.28 (21,54)	83.47 (9.11)
1984	1,418.85 (100.00)	254.73 (17.95)	465.02 (32.77)	522.92 (36.86)	14.94 (1.05)	98.45 (6.94)	62.79 (4.43)
1985	1,956.15 (100.00)	579.88 (29.64)	585.04 (29.91)	480.61 (24.57)	12.95 (0.66)	168.59 (8.62)	129.08 (6.60)
1986	2,243.73 (100.00)	804.47 (35.85)	793.79 (35.38)	260.33 (11.60)	16.30 (0.73)	181.10 (8.07)	187.74 (8.37)
1987	2,646.61 (100.00)	1,485.82 (56.14)	619.96 (23.42)	183.20 (6.92)	24.55 (0.93)	222.26 (8.40)	110.82 (4.19)
1988	3,739.66 (100.00)	1,975.40 (52.82)	779.93 (20.86)	212.19 (5.67)	226.16 (6.05)	316.59 (8.47)	229.39 (6.13)
1989	3,773.45 (100.00)	2,037.16 (53.99)	751.79 (19.92)	232.20 (6.15)	371.42 (9.84)	261.29 (6.92)	119.19 (3.16)
1990	3,754.87 (100.00)	1,886.07 (50.23)	673.56 (17.94)	244.31 (6.51)	683.17 (18.19)	158.74 (4.23)	109.02 (2.90)
1991	4,370.00	-	-	-	-	-	-

Notes: The residual category of 'others' in section (b) of the table represents the settlement value of equipment provided by foreign partrers for purpose of 'processing/asembling', and that of equipment leased. 'Compensafion trade' is valued similarly.

Sources: Kueh, Y.Y. (1992), op.cit., pp.644-645, 'Table 2'.

Table 3.22

FDI growth rates in the Coastal Areas in China, 1979-90 (accumulative total in US$ m)

	1979-84	1985	1986	1987	1988	1989	1990	Annual growth rate (%) 1985-90
SEZs	895.87	1,230.64	1,711.43	2,078.89	2,520.86	3,134.05	3,789.68	25.23
Shenzhen	589.05	782.45	1,163.18	1,443.31	1,743.30	2,045.30	2,435.70	25.50
Zhuhai	246.24	299.69	344.87	378.69	426.09	479.37	548.47	12.85
Shantou	9.41	24.05	45.00	80.98	127.60	175.25	299.11	65.56
Xiamen	51.17	124.45	158.38	175.91	223.87	433.67	506.40	32.40
OCCs	472.59 (472.59)	747.71 (774.24)	1,082.06 (1,148.45)	1,559.73 (1,665.45)	2,097.10 (2,346.31)	2,823.53 (3,254.93)	3,465.69 (4,116.32)	35.90 (39.68)
Dalian	-	14.32	44.81	94.71	169.59	250.16	451.45	99.40
Tianjin	12.87	45.38	88.19	221.32	282.47	313.89	350.82	50.54
Qingdao	-	2.30	13.03	27.03	39.36	97.37	143.25	128.49
Shanghai	123.00	230.54	379.44	593.45	826.62	1,248.74	1,425.93	43.97
Guangzhou	336.72	455.17	556.59	623.32	779.06	913.37	1,094.24	19.18
OCPs	2,120.18 (2,256.05)	3,050.12 (3,326.04)	4,161.07 (4,628.70)	5,290.07 (6,104.84)	7,221.62 (8,330.71)	9,555.15 (11,117.78)	12,266.59 (14,043.34)	32.09 (33.39)
Liaoning	33.11	57.69	105.87	196.71	327.26	453.40	710.71	65.24

Hebei	4.95	13.19	24.46	34.80	53.90	97.63	142.10	60.87
Shandong	16.42	50.62	115.64	180.51	292.06	455.39	641.09	66.16
Jiangsu	-	33.47	67.23	153.58	279.09	406.22	540.19	74.41
Zhejiang	33.62	60.25	85.02	121.32	165.11	219.07	268.21	34.80
Fujian	69.83	188.43	250.93	306.28	451.75	799.78	1,119.67	42.82
Guangdong	1,862.27	2,491.77	3,275.39	4,006.18	5,218.44	6,541.68	8,123.99	26.66
Hainan	19.11	43.10	75.69	84.80	207.25	302.22	405.24	56.55
Guangxi	80.87	111.60	160.84	205.89	226.76	279.76	315.39	23.09
Beijing	350.00	438.82	588.53	694.32	1,197.50	1,517.66	1,796.61	32.57
Provincial total	2,859.02	4,177.06	5,918.71	7,701.44	10,851.17	14,288.50	17,724.65	33.52
PRC total	4,102.00	6,071.00	8,315.00	10,962.00	14,701.00	18,475.00	22,230.00	29.64

Notes: Figures in brackets for OCCs refer respectively to the sum total for all the 15 OCCs and the 11 OCPs (including Tianjin and Shanghai). The PRC total covers FDI sponsored by the various central branch ministries (including notably offshore oil exploration), in addition to the provincial total.

Source: Kueh, Y.Y. (1992), op.cit., p.649, 'Table 3'.

mid-1980s, there was a definite trend towards the equalisation of relative FDI shares between such pioneer areas as Shenzhen, and advanced municipalities such as Shanghai and Beijing whose developed economic base initially made them the most obvious destinations for foreign capital.

In terms of FDI stock accumulated since 1979, the U.S.dollar figures presented in **Table 3.22** generate the following regional percentage shares (see **Table 3.23**) in the national FDI total (FDI sponsored by the central ministries is excluded): These figures highlighted the importance of the 11 OCPs, but also showed the special role of Guangdong and its three SEZs recipients of FDI. It is true that the percentage share for Guangdong during 1979-84 may contain an upward bias, but there was no doubt that the provincial share declined steadily since the mid-1980s. Even so, Guangdong and its SEZs still accounted for the largest share of accumulated FDI stock.

The regional distribution of FDI also reveals that the relative share of the 11 OCPs in the national stock total remained constant (around 80 per cent) during 1979-90. This suggests that observed regional redistribution of FDI reflected a shift from the south along the coast to new northern frontiers, rather than from coastal to interior provinces.

Accelerated increases in foreign investment and changes in its regional allocation were also accompanied by significant changes in its industrial distribution. Foreign investment had been heavily skewed towards industry and services, whereas agriculture received a minimum share. There had, however, been a pronounced shift from services to industry since 1985 in terms of realised FDI. This development no doubt reflected investors' improved confidence in China as an investment outlet. But notwithstanding the marked shift in favour of manufacturing, at the beginning of the 1990s the service sector continued to be a substantial recipient of foreign investment. This is particularly the case with 'late-comers', such as Shanghai, Hainan and even Guangxi. If the current frenzy with which Hong Kong capital is being poured into real estate in South China is any indication, the 1990s may well witness a further rise in the service sector's share of foreign capital (Kueh, 1992, pp.653-5).

Following the booms in 1984, 1988 and 1991, FDI in China reached its fourth boom in 1992. In this year, the newly approved FDI projects amounted to 40,291, with US$45.89 billion pledged FDI and US$16 billion committed FDI, increases of 2.6, 3.8 and 1.5 times respectively on 1991 figures. It is interesting to mention that Shanghai Pudong New Area, where 2,012 projects were set up with US$3,357 million of contracted foreign capital in 1992, which exceeded the totals of the previous 12 years in number and value.[38] The scale of investment also expanded rapidly.[39] By the end of 1992, the accumulated FIEs had risen to 82,300, with US$100 billion pledged FDI and US$52.34 billion committed FDI. About half of the approved JVs had been put into operation. Total tax revenue submitted by the operating JVs recorded RMB10.7 billion (US$2 billion), 52.3 per cent higher than 1991. FIEs' import and export volume rose to US$43.8 billion, 51 per cent higher than 1991 and amounted about 25 per cent of national foreign trade volume in 1992.

Table 3.23
FDI regional distribution, 1979-90 (%)

	1979-84	1985	1986	1987	1988	1989	1990
11 OCPs of which:	79	80	78	79	77	78	79
Guangdong	66	60	55	52	49	46	46
3 SEZs of Guangdong	29	26	26	25	22	19	18
Shenzhen	21	19	20	19	16	14	14

Investment from Hong Kong and Macao still ranked first in terms of FDI in 1992 (so far some US$21 billion was pumped into the mainland, about 50 per cent of total FDI in China), followed by USA (more than US$6.3 billion by the end of 1992), Japan (8,700 Japanese funded enterprises contracted US$6 billion Japanese capital, of which US$3.88 billion was utilized)[40] and Taiwan. The official stock of Taiwanese investment in mainland China jumped from US$3.4 billion at the end of 1991 to US$9 billion at the end of 1992, unofficial estimate even higher, at between US$15 to US$25 billion.[41] By the end of 1992, companies from South Korea had initialled direct investment agreements worth US$616 million in China.[42] We can see that changes in investment policies and environment had affected not only the total level of foreign investment, but also the choice between equity and loan capital.

Foreign investors were pouring their capital into this rapidly growing market in 1993. China approved 83,000 new FIEs with US$111.4 billion contracted foreign capital, in which US$27.5 billion had been utilized, increases of 71.1 per cent, 91.72 per cent and 149.95 per cent compared with the figure by the end of 1992. Only in the first nine months of 1993, an influx of US$15 billion of foreign investment had been utilised (1.5 times more than the same period of 1992). The average contracted FDI per project increased to US$133,000, 12.9 per cent more than that of 1992 (US$117,800 per project). With regard to the origin of home countries/regions, 63 per cent of those new registered FIEs in the first 9 months of 1993 from Hong Kong, 13 per cent from Taiwan, and 7.3 per cent from the USA. Apart from a trend towards larger projects, foreign investment also became more widely distributed with inland provinces showing a bigger percentage jump (from a low base) in new investment than coastal regions. Inland provinces such as Guizhou, Hubei and Gansu doubled numbers of FIEs in 1993, although there remains a vast development gulf between the coast and the hinterland. The OCCs and OCPs were still enjoying rapidly growth of foreign capital inflows. For example, from January to September 1993, Jiangsu Province had newly approved 7,476 FIEs, with contracted investment US$7.74 billion (the average contracted FDI per project increased to US$1,030,000, 40 per cent more than that of the same period of 1992) and utilized capital US$1.7 billion, increasing 190, 260 and 360 per cent over the same period of 1992, respectively. By the end of September 1993, Jiangsu Province had approved 17,600 FIEs, with contracted FDI US$16.68 billion and utilized capital US$3.699 billion,[43] only less than that of Guangdong Province, where the number of approved FIEs was 40,000.[44] In the first ten months of 1993, Guangdong Province approved 15,977 FIEs projects, with US$29.43 billion contracted foreign capital in which US$6.8 billion has been utilized, increasing 60 per cent, 114 per cent and 87 per cent on the figures at the same period of 1992.[45] In the first ten months of 1993, Shanghai approved 3031 FIEs, with US$6.12 billion contracted foreign investment, 1.9 and 2.3 times on the figures of the same period of 1992. Accumulatively Shanghai has approved 6,320 FIEs, with US$12.8 billion contracted foreign capital. China had successfully attracted 10 per cent of US$152 billion international capital flows in 1993 all over the world.

By the end of 1993, total contracted and actual foreign investment since 1979 was US$216.91 billion and US$56.48 billion, and more than 186,580 individual projects had been approved and 50,000 FIEs were operating, and 41 per cent of them were well-run and make a profit.[46] The countries/regions of origin of foreign capital increased from 80 in 1991, to 122 in 1992, and to 146 in 1993, led by Hong Kong/Macao, Taiwan, the United States, Japan, Singapore, the United Kingdom, Thailand, Canada, Germany and Australia (See **Table 3.24a**). It is clear that Hong Kong's share in China's total realised FDI was constantly closer to two-thirds. Japan's share has, however, never been substantial, it reached 11 per cent and 13 per cent in 1989 and 1990. By the end of 1993 Taiwan overtook the USA and Japan and become the second largest investor in mainland China. Taiwan appears to be poised to emulate Hong Kong in relocating its labour-intensive export production to the mainland prior to technological upgrading as well as seeking investment outlet overseas for its highest level of foreign exchange reserves in the world.[47]

The contracted foreign investment was down 26 per cent in 1994 to US$82.6 billion after the boom of the previous years. But the actual utilised

Table 3.24

(a) Top ten investors in China: 1979-93

Country/Region	Number of projects	Pledged investment (US$ bn)
1. Hong Kong/Macao	114,147	150.90
2. Taiwan	20,982	18.46
3. United States	12,019	14.60
4. Japan	7,812	8.90
5. Singapore	3,122	4.80
6. United Kingdom	616	3.30
7. Thailand	1,399	2.10
8. Canada	1,540	1.80
9. Germany	569	1.40
10. Australia	1,309	1.20

Sources: Ministry for Forcign Trade and Economic Cooperation (MOFTEC).

(b) Top ten foreign investors in China in 1994

Country/Region	Pledged direct investment (US$ bn)
1. Hong Kong/Macao	20.20
2. Taiwan	3.29
3. United States	2.49
4. Japan	2.08
5. Singapore	1.18
6. South Korea	0.72
7. United Kingdom	0.69
8. Germany	0.26
9. Thailand	0.23
10. Canada	0.22

Sources: MOFTEC, reported by *People's Daily (Overseas Edition)*, 7 April 1995, p.1.

FDI in the first nine months in 1994 rose to US$22.72 billion, up 27 per cent on the corresponding period in 1993, and more important, the figure as a whole in 1994 was a record US$33.8 billion compared with US$27.5 billion in 1993 reflecting the surge in commitments made in 1992-93. This represented about half of all FDI to LDCs worldwide in 1994. Investment from Hong Kong, Macao and Taiwan was well down in 1994 on the year before, but still led the field. Foreign investors from Hong Kong and Macao poured US$20.2 billion into mainland China, followed by Taiwan with investment of US$3.39 billion, America US$2.49 billion and Japan US$2.08 billion (See **Table 3.24b**). The government's credit squeeze imposed in mid-1993 severely affected real estate projects and contributed to the slowdown of foreign investment. The average investment in a single project was US$1.7 million compared with US$1.3 million in the same period in 1993. By the end of September 1994, more than 210,000 FIEs were approved with pledged investment of US$275 billion and US$85.1 billion actual utilised capital.[48] But newly contracted foreign investment dropped sharply in 1994 after the hectic pace of the two preceding boom years: foreign investors pledged new investment of US$82.6 billion in 1994, a drop of 25.8 per cent over 1993; the numbers of new projects were down by 43 per cent to 47,549. Utilised investment reached US$33.5 billion compared with US$25.8 billion in 1993, a 30 per cent increase. The size of projects were also up from an average US$1.3 million to US$1.7 million. Foreign investment noticeably shifted towards infrastructure, as telecommunications was up by more than 30 per cent over 1993, while it was sharply down in real estate sector from 39.3 per cent of the total in 1993 to 28.9 per cent in 1994. Moreover, more foreign investment was markedly being directed to inland areas and to central and western parts of the country. By the end of 1995, FDI in China is expected to reach US$100 billion.[49]

In the next decade, China will rely much more on FDI and, increasingly, on portfolio investment. The inflow of portfolio investment in 1992 was just US$393 million, or a mere 3.5 per cent of the level of FDI. But in 1993 portfolio investment reached US$5 billion, or 24 per cent of FDI. It is estimated that between 1994 and 2000 portfolio investment in shares, bonds, and other instruments issued by Chinese firms will reach US$133 billion, or almost half the projected FDI level. Many investment banks believe that China's equity and bond markets will dominate the emerging Asian financial markets within a decade or so. If the past decade has been the era of FDI in China, the next looks like being the age of the portfolio investor. Though China's foreign debt reached US$83.5 billion and US$100 billion at the end of 1993 and 1994 respectively, its increased foreign currency reserves (US$31.8 billion in June 1994), potential growth and huge domestic market will still enable China to borrow from the international capital market in the future.

Summary

China utilized US$1.98 billion foreign capital in 1983, US$4.65 billion in 1984, US$10.29 billion in 1990, US$11.55 billion in 1991, US$19.2 billion in 1992 (12.5 per cent of total FDI US$400 billion destined into LDCs in 1992), US$25.8 billion in 1993 (10 per cent of total FDI flows in the world in 1993), and US$33.5 billion in 1994.
Foreign investment in China since 1990 has revealed five new trends:

(1) By far the majority of the existing FIEs has been small-size business, as most foreign capital has been channelled into labour-intensive low-wage industries such as clothing, textiles, foodstuffs processing and the production of electrical and mechanical components, rather than into industrial sectors with a potential for long term international market growth. Except a number of cases, foreign investment has failed to bring about the expected levels of technological autonomy and international competitiveness among Chinese firms: foreign investors have restricted the flow of information and R&D to their Chinese subsidiaries to the bare minimum;

(2) However, since 1992, this picture has been changing rapidly. Many world-famous MNCs, such as America's Motorola, Dupont, IBM; Japan's Mitsubish, Matsushita; and Holland's Phillips, started to invest in large-scale projects in China. More and more famous Western MNCs have started to redirect their international investment strategies, switch their focus towards China's large potential market and made their medium- and long-term investment plans in China. As a result, more and more high value-added and large-size projects with advanced technology have been initiated. If the 1980s was the age for Hong Kong and Taiwanese companies involving in small-scale processing activities such as textiles, the 1990s could be considered as the golden years for MNCs to move into China in a big way;[50]

(3) Since the late of 1980s, foreign investors started to shift into infrastructural sector, such as power generation, highway, railways, bridges, harbours and ports. Such are the needs for increased capacity that China has been forced to allow direct foreign ownership of roads, local railways and power stations. Foreign investors in Zhejiang and Fujian owned equity in the lines and are able to develop land adjacent to the railways;[51]

115

(4)   Foreign investment are spreading into inland areas of China: its share among this country increased from 7.8 per cent to 20 per cent and FDI utilizing growth rates in inland areas were much higher than that of costal areas;

(5)   Foreign capital channelled into real estate increased very rapidly in the last two years, 25 per cent of contracted FDI in 1992 was pledged into real estate area;

(6)   China was also opening new fields on a 'trial basis' to foreign investors, including finance, insurance, retail businesses and construction, which attracts a large interest for MNCs.[52]

'Foreign investors are more enthusiastic about China than about any other emerging market'.[53] China has not only become the first alternative FDI destination for foreign investors among LDCs, but also become one of the main foreign capital recipients all over the world, only behind the United State in 1993-94.

Conclusion

In this chapter, an in-depth analysis has been provided of inward investment activity in Hungary and China. The scale and pace of foreign investment in both countries is exciting and dramatic. It has been demonstrated that FDI has been increasing substantially in 1980s and produces a net addition to capital formation in the host countries, although it accounts for a small but increasing proportion of total capital formation.

The deregulation and privatisation in both countries in the 1980s and 1990s have presented increased opportunities for investment and engendered greater competition in many formerly monopolised or heavily regulated industries. To date, Hungary has attracted FDI stocks comparable with those of Ireland, Portugal and Spain, while China has become one of the leading host LDCs for FDI in terms of annual inflow and stock of FDI. The huge potential market, stable political situation, 35 per cent annual saving rates, the self-confident China and its self-promoting regional politicians suck in foreign investment. In addition, the immense financial and managerial resources of overseas Chinese businessmen - in Hong Kong, Taiwan, South-East Asia and even North America, play significant role in promoting FDI and economic growth in China.

There are certain common features for foreign capital in both countries:

(1)   Foreign investment in manufacturing in Hungary and China has been largely of two types: those that produce for local markets, frequently with government encouragement and protection, that is, 'import substitution'; and those that supply home markets from so-called export platforms. The latter were usually labour-intensive, relying upon the availability of substantially cheaper suppliers of unskilled, but trainable, labour in the host countries. The average investment-scale is relatively small, with low technologies, contrary to the host countries' desires.

(2)   A large proportion of machinery and equipment contributed as part of equity from foreign investors were of moderate technology (in the 1960s or 1970s), or reconditioned equipments or obsolete technology in the international market. Furthermore, most of FIEs were allocated in labour-intensive sectors, such as low-tec service industries, construction, hotel and catering, food processing (which has clearly limited the hoped for technology transfer) rather than technology intensive. Only 3 per cent of FIEs were technological advanced projects in China during the period under study.

(3)   About one-third of foreign capital was channelled into energy, real estate, light industry, and basic processing industry, while foreign investment in those priority industries, such as electronics, chemical and machinery manufacturing was limited. As a result, FIEs competed with local enterprises for materials, quota, and international markets, further intensifying the contradiction between material demand and supply, and reduced government revenues and foreign exchanges.

Evidences revealed that more and more foreign firms were financing some of their JV activities through local resources (banking loans), as MNCs enjoy some advantages in borrowing local funds, given a strong home currency. In addition, it has been estimated that US$100 foreign investment needs US$900 coordinating domestic investment. So there is a strong criticism: China/Hungary encouraged and operated JVs, but is China/Hungary utilising foreign capital, or foreign capital is utilising local capital? Moreover, most of domestic coordinating capital has been allocated to new FIEs or expansion projects, to the detriment of the technological upgrade for existing SOEs. Nearly two-thirds of SOEs in both countries are equipped with out-of-date technology and equipment, which is responsible for low levels of efficiency and profitability. So while most of foreign investment was channelled into newly established projects or expansion programmes, domestic enterprises had to use their own development funds to set up new JVs with foreign partner, leaving its own machinery and equipments far lagged behind reasonable technological standards due to shortage of development funds. It is essential for both countries to attract foreign investment into technological reform and up-grade, and based on these reform to further increase its manufacturing technological level.

Notes

1.IMF (1992), 'Recent Trends in FDI for the Developing World', *Finance & Development,* Vol.29, No.1, March, pp.50-51.

2.Istvan Toldy-Osz (1989), *The Hungarian Trade Journal,* February, Vol.39, No.2, p.6.

3.Ibid., p.6.

4.Istvan Toldy-Osz (1989), *The Hungarian Trade Journal,* February, Vol.39, No.2, p.6.

5.The highest Austrian investment had been made in VEAV-Bramac Co. Ltd., in which the Austrian partner Bramac Dachsteinwerk owned 49 per cent of the total capital of US$4.99 million. The second most important Austrian investment was in the hotel sector. Stuag Bau-AG from Austria owned 40 per cent (US$1.96 million) of Hotel Liget Public Co. Ltd., which had a total capital of Ft295 million (US$4.9 million). The third largest Austro-Hungarian JV was Metritechnic Commercial & Servicing for Automation Co. Ltd., in which the Austrian Festo Maschinenfabrik owned 55 per cent (US$1.93 million) of Ft211 million (US$3.52 million) capital. This JV was established in 1982 representing Festo's products in Hungary, and designing and producing electronic system.

6.The biggest German-Hungarian JV - a textile printing factory had a total capital of Ft568 million, of which the German KBL Manufaktur Koechlin owned 50 per cent, Ft284 million or US$4.7 million. In the second largest German-Hungarian JV - Sopilen Chemical Fibre Work Ltd, the German company - Geco owned 52 per cent of Ft310 million (US$5.2 million) capital. Two German companies S. E. S. and Deuma together own 49 per cent of a capital Ft22.6 million (US$3.7 million) in the JV - MD Engineering and Commercial Ltd, which produced dividing doors, designed and constructed building and structural engineering.

7.Benedek, T. (1991), 'Hungary: Pioneer in Joint Ventures', in Razvigorova, Evka and Wolf-Laudon, Gottfried (1991), (ed.), *East-West Joint Ventures: The New Business Environment*, Blackwell, London, p.106.

8.In order to test the 'water', FDI likes to inflow into those trade and services activities where a minimum investment can produce huge and fast returns rather than those modest, large-scale and long-term manufacturing sectors.

9.Dunning J.H. (1993), 'The Prospects for Foreign Direct Investment in Eastern Europe', in Artisien, P., et al (1993) (ed.), *Foreign Investment in Central and Eastern Europe*, St.Martin's Press, p.17.

10.Gutman P.(1990), 'From Joint Ventures to Foreign Direct Investment, New Perspectives in Eastern Europe and the Soviet Union', paper presented at the international conference on 'Opportunities and Contracts for East-West Soviet Ventures', Moscow, 7-16 December 1990.

11.Available statistics on foreign investment were based on the 'currency of contribution' as recorded in JV agreements and not on the basis of the investors' country of origin. See Michael Marrese (1992), 'Hungary Emphasiscs Forcign Partners', *RFE/RL Research Report*, Vol.1, No.17, 24 April 1992, p.30, 'Table 3' and p.32; and the Economist Intelligence Unit *EIU Country Report: Hungary*, No.3, 1992, p.26.

12.Business Eastern Europe, 10 June 1991, p.178, and *RFE/RL Research Report*, 19 June 1992, Vol.1, No.25, p.65.

13.Foreign investors normally purchased share of equity in existing enterprises, followed by modernising some branches of the manufacturing sector, where accorded with their long-term business strategy aimed at yielding exceptionally high returns, or meeting certain market shortages, such as soft drinks, computer hard- and soft-wares, textiles and footwear, and chemical & electrical industry.

14.Scott, Norman (1992), 'Economic Transformation in Hungary', *European Economy*, Vol.3, p.56.

15.Economic Intelligence Unit (1992), *EIU Country Report: Hungary*, No.3, pp.25-28.

16.*Magyar Hirlap and The New York Times*, 14 March 1992, *Weekly Bulletin (MTI)*, 20 March 1992.

17.*Heti Vilaggazdasag*, 29 February 1992.

18.*Heti Vilaggazdasag*, 20 April 1991.

19.*RFE/RL Correspondent's Report*, Budapest, 23 April 1991.

20.'Franchising in Eastern Europe', *The Economist*, 6 April 1991, pp.66-67.

21.*Financial Times*, 1 November 1993, p.17.

22.*Financial Times*, 23 November 1993, p.6.

23.The Economist Intelligence Unit (1993), *EIU Report: Hungary*, p.22.

24.Marsh, Virgina (1994), 'Privatisation Angers Foreign Investors', *Financial Times*, 23 December 1994.

25.*The New York Times*, 15 February 1995.

26.Mihaly, Simai (1990), *Foreign Direct Investment and Joint Ventures in Hungary: Experience and Prospects*, Hungarian Scientific Council for World Economy, Budapest, p.8.

27.Chen, Jinghan (1993), 'The Environment for Foreign Direct Investment and the Characteristics of Joint Ventures in China', *Development Policy Review*, Vol.11, No.2, pp.180-81.

28.The open-up of 14 coastal cities in April 1984, followed with establishment of 3 coastal triangular economic zones - Yangtze River Delta, the Pearl River Delta and a triangular area in southern Fujian Province in February 1985.

29.Xiao, Yuzhou (1984), 'Rapid Development of China's Utilization of Foreign Investment', *Almanac of China's Foreign Trade (1984)*, p.43.

30.Zhang, Zi (1985), 'Continued Development of Utilisation of Foreign Capital', *Almanac of China's Foreign Trade (1985)*, MOFERT, Beijing, pp.39-40.

31.Pearson, Margaret M. (1991), *Joint Ventures in the People's Republic of China: the Control of Foreign Direct Investment under Socialism*, Princeton University Press, Princeton, pp.66-67.

32.Grub P.D. and Lin, J.H. (1991), *Foreign Direct Investment in China*, Quorum, New York and London, pp.77-89; and Chen, Jinghan (1993), op.cit., p.182.

33.Liu, Yiming (1988), 'Rapidly Development of Foreign Investment in China in 1988', *Almanac of China Foreign Trade (1988)*, MOFERT, Beijing, p.46.

34.Yu, Xiaoxong (1989), 'Continuous Development of FDI in China in 1989', *Almanac of China's Foreign Trade (1989)*, MOFERT, Beijing, p.45.

35.Wu, Zhao (1991), *Survey of Foreign Direct Investment in China*, Press of Finance and Economics of China, Beijing.

36.Yu, Xiaosong (1990), 'Stable Development of FDI in China in 1990', *Almanac of China's Foreign Trade (1990)*, MOFERT, Beijing, p.49.

37.Kueh, Y.Y. (1992), 'Foreign Investment and Economic Change in China', *The China Quarterly (Special Issue: The Chinese Economy in the 1990s)*, September, Vol.132, p.647.

38.*People's Daily*, 31 May 1993.

39.For instance, the averaged contracted foreign capital per project in Fujian Province increased from US$730,000 prior to 1989 to US$1 million in 1989, and US$1.38 million in 1992. Those projects over US$10 million also rose from 17 in 1991 to 112 in 1992. See *People's Daily*, 25 September 1993, p.2.

40.The ratio of Japanese investment in China among Japan's total outward investment increased from 2.8 per cent in 1990 to 14.1 per cent in 1992, while the same ratio of USA dropped from 26.9 per cent in 1991 to 14.9 per cent in 1992.

41.*People's Daily (Overseas Edition)*, 7 August 1992, p.1; 22 October 1992, p.1; 24 November 1992, p.4; 9 December 1992, p.4; and 9 February 1993, p.1.

42.*Financial Times*, 14 June 1993.

43.*Peoples' Daily*, 2 November 1993, p.2.

44.*People's Daily*, 30 October 1993, p.1.

45.*People's Daily*, 25 November 1993, p.2.

46.According to an official survey conducted by the State Administration for Industry & Commerce (SAIC) in 1993, about 41 per cent (27,658 FIEs) of 67,458 FIEs in operation made a profit, totalled US$8.15 billion; 51 per cent (34,150 FIEs) made a loss, amounted US$13.75 billion; the remaining 8 per cent FIEs were just break-even. See, *People's Daily (Overseas Edition)*, 19 September 1994.

47. Compared with Hong Kong, Taiwan certainly has a stronger industrial base and demand for technological upgrading of its industrial structure. See Kueh, Y.Y. (1992), op.cit., p.676.

48. *People's Daily*, 28 October 1993, p.2; *Financial Times China Survey*, 7 November 1994, p.6.

49. The State Statistical Bureau of China (1995), *Annual Report on China's Economic and Social Development in 1994*, The State Statistical Bureau of China, Beijing, p.3.

50. Lardy, Nicholas R. (1988), *China's Entry into the World Economy: Implications for Northeast Asia and the United States*, University Press of America, New York and London, pp.35-38.

51. *Financial Times Survey: China*, 18 November 1993, p.12.

52. *People's Daily*, 25 August 1993; and Walker, Tony (1993), 'Investment in China Set to Top US$100 billion', *Financial Times*, 8 November 1993, p.5.

53. 'China Speeds on to Market', *The Economist*, 20 November 1993, p.85.

4 Determinants of foreign capital in Hungary and China

Since very little systematic and in-depth empirical quantitative research[1] has so far been carried out to test the determinants of foreign capital in those countries making the difficult transformation from CPE to a market economy, the objective of this chapter is to shed light onto these issues by exploring and analyzing what factors best explain foreign capital inflow into Hungary and China during the period of 1978-92. More specifically, the chapter will test the relative importance of independent variables, including market size, cost-of-capital, labour costs, tariff barriers, exchange rates, import volumes and economic growth in OECD countries as well as political stability within the framework of one-equation model.

Introduction

Hypotheses of determinants of foreign capital inflows

This survey of hypotheses is selective in focusing on the main current of thought rather than on coverage of all the publications.

Theoretical studies of foreign investment include the differential rates of return theory, the market-size hypothesis, the product cycle theory, the industrial organisation theory, the internalization theory, the currency area hypothesis, the customs area hypothesis, and an eclectic approach.[2] They might be classified in four groups: hypotheses assuming perfect markets (including differential rate of return hypothesis, portfolio hypothesis, output and market-size hypotheses), hypothesises based on market imperfections (including behaviourial hypothesis, Vernon's production cycle hypothesis, oligopolistic reactions hypothesis, international hypothesis), hypotheses on the propensity to invest (including liquidity hypothesis, currency area hypothesis) and determinants of the inflow of FDI - the propensities of countries to attract these FDI (including political instability, incentives, and cheap labour).[3] These studies have identified many important factors that a firm should consider when making investments in foreign countries, which could be conveniently classified into micro-, macro- and strategic-determinants as shown below.

The microdeterminants of FDI, following industrial organisation theory or the so-called Hymer-Kindleberger (HK) theory,[4] are concerned with those firms and industry characteristics and numerous ownership-specific advantages, which have been found to confer certain advantages on MNCs compared with most of their local rivals, such as product differentiation; technological and advertising effects; product cycle as well as the size of firm; oligopolistic market structure and behaviour; excess managerial capacity; financial and monetary factors (including access to cheap capital and diversification of investment); and access to raw materials.[5] But the possession of ownership-specific advantages alone represents only a necessary and not a sufficient condition for FDI, this would not explain why a firm should engage in foreign production. To explain the preference for investment abroad over exporting from the home country, theorists have turned to another group of location-specific factors, including trade barriers, host government policies, relative labour costs, and market size and growth. The influence of these factors may depend upon the stage of the product's life cycle, as between a new, mature or standardised commodity. One or a combination of these factors may tip the balance and encourage the firm to locate production facilities abroad.[6]

The discussion of the macrodeterminants of FDI follows closely the theories of corporate investment behaviour and emphasizes the importance of the size and growth of the host market, the factor prices, exchange rates, profitability, and the tariffs protection. The empirical studies suggest that one of the most important macrodeterminants is the size of the host country's market as given by the level of gross domestic product (GDP). This is particularly true in the case of import-substituting FDI. The growth-of-size hypothesis postulates a positive relation between changes in the host country's GDP and the inflow of FDI. The growth of the market is measured by either the percentage change or the change in levels of GDP, and these changes are expected to be directly related to the inflow of FDI.[7] We can conclude that

> characteristics of host countries such as market size, market growth, stage of development and the presence of local competition, will influence decisions on direct investment. Particularly if trade barriers exist in the host country, factors such as size of market are clearly relevant to the possibility of exploiting economies of scale in

production and marketing (Hood and Young, 1979, p.59).

Other 'macro effects include changes in tariffs and taxes, political risk, variations in wages and interest rates due to differential inflation rates or other factors, and son on' (Rugman, 1982, p.23).

The price-determinant hypothesis postulated that FDI is inversely related to the exchange rates, wage rates and the cost of capital (Kwak, 1972, pp.376-83). The differential rates of return theory argues that if expected marginal revenues are higher abroad than at home, given the same marginal cost of capital for investment at home and abroad, there is an incentive to invest abroad.

Turning to the influence of various obstacles to trade, such as transportation costs, tariff and quotas on FDI, the literature suggests that a tariff imposed by a nation to support its domestic industry will attract foreign investors, since they can avoid the customs duty by replacing exports with host-country production (Dunning, 1973, pp.289-336; Rugman, 1980, p.367). The higher these obstacles are, the greater are the incentives of foreign investors to establish a plant locally and thus service the market into which it is difficult to export. High tariff barriers are associated with high inflows of FDI, whereas trade liberation tends to reduce these inflows (Aliber, 1970, pp.17-34).

The literature on strategic determinants of FDI refers to various long-term factors: the desire to defend existing foreign markets, the desire to diversify the firm's activities horizontally, vertically or conglomerately, to gain/maintain a foothold in a protected market or to gain/maintain a source of supply that may prove useful in the long run; the desire to induce the host country into a long term commitment to a particular type of technology and know-how; and the desire to gain the advantage of complementing another type of investment. These factors have mainly indirect effects on the decision to invest abroad, but are directly relevant to the profitability of JVs (Reuber et al., 1973). The profit maximisation theory of the firm has also found to effect the location decision behaviour of MNCs (Stevens, 1974).

It is clear that a generalized theory of FDI must integrate both macro and micro variables, as is achieved explicitly in Dunning's eclectic theory and implicitly in internalization theory. Following Ronald Coase's concept of transaction costs (it is more efficient for a firm to create and use an internal market, rather than incur the prohibitive transaction costs of an outside market), Buckley and Casson (1976) argued that the growth of FDI is governed basically by the costs and benefits of internalising markets. Internalisation is regarded as an alternative to domestic diversification in two ways - first, by marketing its product internationally and second, by international portfolio diversification, making profits in a variety of currencies, it will be financially diversified, earning its returns in a variety of currencies. Rugman (1975, 1976, 1977a,b, 1981) argued that the advantages given by international financial diversification have led to superior stock market performance by MNCs over purely domestic firms, even after allowing for size and industry influences. He further claims that internalisation in itself represents a general theory of the multinational enterprise, which demonstrates that the multinational is an organisation using its internal market to produce and distribute products in an efficient manner in situations in which a regular market fails to operate (Rugman, 1982, p.11).

Dunning's eclectic theory (1977, 1979) hypothesises that investment value is not solely a function of political risk, but is a function of the combined consideration of ownership, internalisation and location-specific advantages. He puts these variables in the form of three conditions which a firm has to satisfy in order to undertake a particular FDI: first, it must possess exclusively some comparative advantages over other firms in the host country; second, the benefit of internalising the above advantages through FDI must be viewed by firms to be greater than other means of their penetration, e.g. licensing or outright sale of a patent; and, third, the host country must have some location advantages over the home country of the firm, e.g. lower wage costs, cheaper energy or materials, and investment incentives. The greater the ownership advantages that firms of one nationality possess over firms of another nationality, the greater the propensity of the firm to internalize rather than externalize these advantages; and the more it pays a firm to exploit these advantages by using country-specific endowments of a foreign rather than a domestic location, the more firms engage in international production.

Following the Heckscher-Ohlin model and MacDougall theory of capital movements, Casson (1979, 1985) further developed Dunning's eclectic theory of internalisation by integrating the theory of international capital markets, the theory of the firm and the theory of trade to explain how market imperfections create an incentive for international control of production and FDI.

> When factor prices differ between locations and barriers to trade are low there is normally an incentive to base different stages of production at different locations, so as to match factor intensity at each stage to factor abundance... Locational factors also influence the incentive to internalise (Casson, 1979, p.61).

Empirical studies of determinants of the inflow of FDI

The number of independent variables examined in many theoretical and empirical studies is very large, and they include not only economic but also social, cultural and political aspects.[8] Our discussion of empirical studies will focus on the following determinants of inflows of FDI hypothesis: market size or potential market, political instability, supply of cheap labour and the cost of capital. Our empirical survey is selective and only focus on economic variables and political stability.

Market-size hypotheses Many inductive experiments have been carried out to identify the variables which may be particularly relevant to a country's propensity to attract FDI in LDCs, and produced conclusive evidence to support this theory in terms of significance of correlation between FDI and market size.

Bandera and White (1968) found a statistically significant correlation between the U.S. FDI in European Economic Community (EEC) countries and EEC incomes, and concluded that various motives for foreign investments can be adequately summarised as a desire to penetrate the growing market defined in terms of level and growth of GDP of host countries. Stevens (1969) demonstrated a statistically significant relation between the flow of FDI from the U.S.A. into Argentina, Brazil and Venezuela and the sales of the U.S. companies in the manufacturing sector of these countries during 1957-65.

Scaperlanda and Mauer (1969) examined the same hypothesis using the U.S. data on FDI in the EEC for the period 1952-66 and came to the conclusion that market size hypothesis is supported statistically. Goldberg (1972) maintained that these investments can be explained not by the size of the EEC market but by the growth of the market (Goldberg, 1972, pp.692-99). Reuber et al (1973) found that the flow of FDI (on per capita basis) into LDCs was correlated with their GDP but not with the change in GDP or value added in manufacturing industries and the growth of their GDP, a point emphasised by Bandera and White (1968). Takahashi's (1975) regression estimates proved that the GNP of the host nations (as proxy for the market size), but not the difference between the growth rates of GNP of the host country and investing countries, is a significant determinant of U.S. FDI. Schwartz (1976) concluded that after an initial investment has been undertaken in a country on the basis of its size or growth, sales and profits of the affiliates are better determinants of further investments.

Majumdar (1980) finds that the market size or market potential is the most important factor in influencing the electronic calculator companies' decision to undertake foreign production (pp.360-361). Schollhammer and Nigh (1984) and Nigh (1985) found that German/USA FDI in LDCs was affected positively by market size of the host country. Recent studies (OECD, 1983; Petrochilos, 1989; Moore, 1993) show that FDI is sensitive to the size of the host country market, as measured by the level of the GDP or economic growth rates. Other important studies bearing directly or indirectly on this hypothesis are by Basi (1963), Polk et al (1966), Morley (1966), Moose (1968), Severn (1972), Ahmed (1975) and Sabirn (1977). A number of survey studies further confirmed this finding that size or growth of market is one of the most important determinants of FDI.[9]

In spite of their differences with regard to the assumptions, data, methodology and specification of the variables, most studies have come out in support of the dependent relation of FDI to the size or growth of the markets in host countries (see, for example, Dunning, 1979).

Labour costs The supply of cheap labour in LCDs has always been regarded as one of their comparative advantages in attracting foreign capital. Whereas the evidence from survey reports (e.g.Forsyth, 1972) in support of cheap labour has been rather weak, the results of some of time-series and cross-country analyses have been strongly in its favour. For example, Riedel's (1975), Young (1978), Majudar (1980) and Tsai (1991) concluded that relatively lower wage is one of the most important factors of absorbing FDI in the case of South-East Asian economies. Agarwal (1978) found a significant positive correlation between German FDI and relative lower wage costs in Brazil, India, Iran, Israel, Mexico and Nigeria. Juhl (1979) obtained similar results at the sectoral level of German FDI in Colombia, Ecuador, El Salvbador and Mexico. Huang (1992) suggests that labour costs of US affiliates abroad play a significant role only when profitability is taken into account. Jeon (1992) and Moore (1993) find that both Korean and German outflow FDI is influenced by the factor of exploitation of the cheap labour in LDCs. O'Sullivan (1993) found that the slower real wage growth rate (compared with the U.S.A. and major EEC countries) and exchange rate changes were strongly correlated with FDI in Ireland during 1960-70.

> The cost factor was clearly the primary consideration behind the plants set up in the developing countries..., the large wage rate differentials between the United States and the developing countries still provided some cost advantage to locating production plants in the latter group of countries (Majudar, 1980, p.362).

It is also found that the influence of differences in wage levels between investing and host countries is obviously greater in the case of FDI in industries producing labour intensive products and components than in other industries.

Political instability Political instability in a host country is likely to discourage the inflow of FDI, i.e. to be negatively correlated. However, whereas the majority of survey reports have concluded that political instability has a negative effect on the inflow of FDI, the empirical evidence produced by survey and cross-section studies can be judged only as mixed, some in favour and others against this hypothesis. U.S. Department of Commerce (1954), Robinson (1961), Basi (1963)[10], Aharoni (1966), U.S. National Industrial Conference Board (1969), Swansbrough (1972), Root (1978) and Petrochilos (1989) supported a negative correlation between the inflow of FDI and political instability. Piper (1971) and Reuber et al.(1973) concluded that political variables are of minimal concern to investors and are generally given the same treatment in the FDI decisions by them as in the domestic investment decisions. Levis (1979) found that economic considerations were the prime determinant of the flow of foreign investment, whereas political factors were the second order determinants. Bennett and Green (1972), Green and Cunningham (1975), and Kobrin (1976) found that there was no significant relation between the flow of US direct investment and political instability abroad, while emphasising the role of economic variables in the decision to invest abroad - allocation of US direct investment is closely related to market potentials proxied by GNP and population. In a very detailed analysis of ASEAN countries, Situmeang (1978) concluded that political instability was statistically unrelated to the flow of FDI in all industrial sectors.

The conflict between the results of these studies is quite apparent. Apart from the fact that these studies have used varying kinds of data and analytical methods, a very important source of this conflict is the definition of political instability. Political instability does not always enhance political risk for FDI. *Other relevant variables:* Petrochilos (1989) followed Jorgenson's (1963, 1965, 1967) hypothesis (i.e. FDI is determined by the cost of capital), and found that the Greek central bank's discount rate was one of the main determinants of FDI in Greece during the period of 1955-78. Huang's (1992) study finds that cost of capital and exchange rates have no significant impact on US outward investment, while US GDP and the sales of US affiliates abroad have strong positive influence. In the case of Japanese overseas direct investment, cost of capital and exchange rates, as well as the change of Japanese GDP and the sales of Japanese affiliates abroad are found to have significant positive impact on Japanese capital outflows. High unit labour cost in Japan also pushes Japanese FDI abroad.

Empirical studies in currency area hypothesis are primarily focused on the relation between FDI and exchange rate changes (Aliber, 1970,1978[11]; Cushman, 1985, 1988; and Klein and Rosengren, 1991). While a few studies have shown that devaluation of the currency of a country discourages the inflow of FDI in that country (for example, Scaperlanda, 1974), most found that devaluation encouraged inflow of FDI and discouraged outflow of direct investment (see, Alexander and Murphy, 1975). Kohlhagen (1977) analyzed major exchange rate realignments of the currencies of the U.K., France and

Germany during the 1960s showed that currency devaluations increased the relative profitability of domestic production vis-a-vis foreign production and thus induced the inflow of FDI into the devaluing countries. Using the U.S.-Canadian time series data, Sachchamarga (1978) further supported the hypothesis that the depreciation of the foreign exchange value of a country's currency encouraged FDI into that country and discouraged its capital outflows. The effect of a currency devaluation on the FDI of any particular industry will be determined by whether it is relatively more dependent on the foreign market for the export of its output or for the import of its input. Cushman (1988) found that the effects of expected appreciation of real foreign currency and of real exchange rate risk were ambiguous: the expected appreciation of the dollar was associated at significant levels with reductions in U.S. FDI inflows from the five other countries during 1963-86; and increases in foreign exchange risk were significantly associated with increases in these inflows (p.334). Moore (1993) and O'Sullivan (1993) find that exchange rate changes/risks are strongly correlated with FDI. These studies have shown that the exchange rate is only one of many factors influencing FDI decisions.

Horst (1972) found investing countries' export and FDI may be substitutes for one another, and suggested that nominal tariff rates may be a satisfactory explanatory variable. When Orr (1975) disaggregated Horst's 18-industry sample to a 70-industry 3-digit level, he failed to replicate the latter's result, concluding that 'higher tariffs discourage imports but there is no evidence that U.S. controlled production in Canada is substituted for these imports' (p.233). Majumdar (1980), Petrochilos (1989) and Moore (1993) found that FDI is sensitive to host-country tariff rate, while Baldwin (1979), however, found the tariff variable to be insignificant.

Conclusion

The proceeding theoretical and empirical studies have employed varying methods which have differed not only as regards their theoretical basis, but also in terms of whether the analysis was short-term or long-term, and whether the determinants were studies from the point of view of the home company undertaking the investment or from the point of view of the attractiveness of host country. Moreover, most of the proceeding hypothesises and empirical studies took into account only some FDI determinants, sometimes constrained by the availability of data or unsatisfactory analysis methodology.

To explain the choice of FDI, it is necessary therefore to take into consideration location-specific factors in either home or host countries.

These include variables such as trade barriers and other government policies, market characteristics, costs and productivity. Where such factors favour a foreign rather than a domestic location, then the FDI route will be chosen in place of export. So limited progress can be made by applying geographical location theory, tax and tariff theory and the theory of imperfect competition to modify or replace the orthodox theories (Giddy and Young, 1982, p.58).

The proceeding discussion has presented a number of factors as being likely to play a significant role in the foreign investment decision. Most empirical studies and surveys indicated that size of market, political stability and labour cost were the most important determinants of investment abroad. 'Defensive' reasons come next in importance, particularly fears of losing existing markets and barriers to trade. Other 'investment climate' variables associated with exchange rate stability and tax structures have also been found to be significant (Hood and Young, 1979, p.79).

Variable specification and one-equation model

This section attempts to undertake an econometric analysis, which involves the building of a one-equation model, and the specification and the test of a number of alternative hypotheses.

Variable specification

An important aspect of any quantitative work is the proper specification of the model. The choice of variables here was dictated by the earlier discussion on the determinants of FDI constrained in some instances by the availability of data. With two exceptions - the US long-term bond yield and the average growth rate in OECD countries - the independent variables were chosen to reflect the attractiveness of the Hungarian and Chinese markets as the potential locations for foreign capital.

According to the preceding analysis, foreign capital in any period is assumed to be a function of the size of the host country's market, which is given by the level of GDP. The use of level of output as an explanatory variable is consistent not only with received theory regarding the determinants of corporate investment in general but also with the determinants of FDI and has been used in other studies mentioned above.

While the size of the domestic market is an important factor, its growth rate is also thought to influence foreign capital inflows. Therefore, another two variables are incorporated into our determinant analysis: the percentage rate of growth of the GDP and the change of GDP in absolute terms. The former has been used in a number of studies (Edwards, 1964; Brash, 1968; Goldberg, 1972; Petrochilos, 1989). The later can be found in theory of investment behaviour.

Foreign investment can be viewed as an attempt by profit-maximizing firms to minimize their costs of production or marketing. A firm might undertake foreign investment because of manufacturing cost advantages (low labour costs or proximity to natural resources) in the host country. The neo-classical hypothesis suggests that low labour cost plays an important positive role in decisions to invest overseas, and that low-wage countries expect a higher inflow of foreign capital than high-wage ones. In considering the advantages of the low labour cost and the extent to which cheap labour has affected foreign capital inflow in both Hungary and China, a ratio of wage rates between Hungary/China and the USA (see **Appendix 4.1** and **Appendix 4.2**) has been employed.

An alternative incentive for FDI arises out of a desire to lower marketing costs in a country where the firm is already exporting. The firm might set up production facilities in that market rather than exporting to it in order to obtain marketing cost saving (providing that production cost disadvantage do not overwhelm the marketing savings). Savings obtained by producing locally might include avoiding protectionist barriers or reducing transportation costs. 'A growing host-country market might encourage local investment, especially if export costs are high' (Moore, 1993, p.125) when foreign exporters find it more profitable to establish production facilities inside a country's tariff wall rather than to write off their investment in the local market or continue to serve it from lower-cost locations abroad through exports (Jeon, 1992, p.529). So our discussion relies on international trade hypothesis - the higher the tariff barriers, the higher the flow of investment is likely to be.[12] In this study we include TARIFF, representing the averaged trade-weighted ad valorem tariff rates for all import products in Hungary and China over the period covered, to explain why FDI is chosen to replace exporting to these two countries.

In order to test the hypothesis that FDI is determined by the cost of capital, two variables have been used: the first is the U.S. government long-term bond yield, a summary measure of the long-term market opportunities available to foreign investors in their home markets, as the United States is one of the top four investing countries and accounts for almost one third of the total foreign capital invested in both Hungary and China;[13] the second is the Hungarian/Chinese discount rate, a measure of the opportunity cost of borrowing in the host country, as most foreign invested enterprises in Hungary and China can, and do, finance some of their JV activities through local resources.[14] The discount rate is preferred to any Hungarian and Chinese long-term rate since local capital resources are likely to be tapped by foreign firms for working rather than long-term capital.

In considering the role of the political 'climate' and the extent to which political instability in Hungary and China affected FDI, particularly in the light of the CPE before 1989 compared with political and economic transformation after 1989 in the case of Hungary, and the political instability during 1986-87 and 1989 in China, a dummy variable has been employed to capture such effects. In the case of Hungary, political stability is expressed as a shift of political power from an extreme Socialist rightist to a more democratic and free-elected government, while political instability in China is defined as leadership changes from leftist to rightist and social upheaval. Given the presumption that foreign investors are generally not sympathetic to post-Socialist regimes in Hungary and the political instability in 1986-87 and the 'Tiananmen Square Event' in 1989 in the case of China, it has been decided to let the dummy variable (D) take a value of $D=1$ for the period of 1978-88 and $D=0$ for the period of 1989-92 in the case of Hungary, while $D=1$ for 1986-87 and 1989, and $D=0$ for all other periods in China.

Other factors which do not strictly relate to the general attractiveness or production advantages in the host country may affect foreign investors' decisions on setting up production facilities in one specific host country rather than exporting to it. Foreign companies might find advantages in building a production factory rather than exporting to a country with a depreciating currency. Though a few studies have shown that devaluation of the currency of a country discourages the inflow of FDI in that country, the majority of economists who have tested this hypothesis statistically have come to the conclusion that devaluation encourages inflow of FDI and discourages outflow of direct investment. The exchange rate variable (EXRT) is therefore employed to designate the exchange rate risk.

Some studies argue that the rapidly growing imports and import liberation in a host country tend to reduce entry barriers and lead to temporary decline of FDI, as direct investment and exports could be substituted for one another (Horst, 1972; Jeon, 1992). But contrary arguments have been advanced that increased imports may cause FDI to rise. Thus, the imports variable (IMP) is used to evaluate the correlation between FDI and the host country's imports, i.e. to test whether FDI is export-generating or whether it curtails their exports from home or other bases. That is, whether FDI is a complement to or a substitute for exports becomes a matter of concern.

OECD growth rates over 1978-92 was added to capture whether economic growth in main capital-exporting countries affects the inflow of foreign capital in Hungary and China. It is presumed that economic prosperity in the home market indirectly assists parent firms' expansion and accumulation of assets for both export, licensing and direct investment. However, a parent company may exploit business opportunities in the domestic market, at least in the short

133

term, if the real growth rate of the home economy is relatively higher or vice versa.

> The optimistic case for cross-border investment depends on economic growth in these emerging regions and in the industrial countries, as well as, most of all, on a continued propensity to dismantle barriers (Emmott, 1993, p.27).

Though the bigger the wage differences between home and host country are, the more the former invest in the latter, nominal wage differences may not induce direct investment if labour productivity is very low. Countries with low labour productivity may create less incentive for foreign investors to establish a production facility to use cheap labour than those with high labour productivity together with relatively cheap labour. Unfortunately, time-series data about the labour productivity in Hungary is not easily available. So a productivity variable (PRDTVY) has only been introduced in the case of China.

In this chapter, FDI is treated as an endogenous variable of the system, being determined within the general framework of the system by various independent variables: the size of market, protective tariff rates, two cost-of-capital variables (i.e. host country's central bank's discount rate and the U.S. government long-term bond yield), wage rates, exchange rates risk, imports, political climate, and the average growth rates in OECD countries.

One-equation linear model

In the case of Hungary, time series data for the period 1977-92 were fitted into the following basic form of function - linear formulation:

$$FDI = a_0 + a_1 GDP + a_2 GDPA + a_3 GR + a_4 TARIFF + a_5 WAGE +$$
$$a_6 BOND + a_7 DISCOUNT + a_8 EXRT + a_9 IMP +$$
$$a_{10} GROECD + D + U_t$$

where

> FDI = Real annual change in foreign direct investment in period t (US$ bn in current prices) in Hungary;
> GDP = Real Gross Domestic Product (GDP) (US$ bn in current prices);
> GDPA = Absolute real change in GDP (US$ bn in current prices);
> GR = Real GDP growth rate (%);

TARIFF = Average tariff rate facing with foreign exporters into Hungary, proxy for tariff protection as defined in text;

WAGE = Ratio of Hungary's average wage/US average wage (%);

BOND = US government long-term bond yield (%);

DISCOUNT = Hungarian central bank's discount rate (%);

EXRT = Exchange rate between US dollar and Hungarian Forint;

IMP = Changes in Hungarian imports (US$ bn);

GROECD = Average growth rate in OECD countries;

D = Dummy to capture political effects, for years 1978-89 D = 1, and all other years D =0;

U_t = Stochastic error terms, i.e. is assumed to be independently and normally distributed with zero means and constant variance.

In the case of China, time series data for the period 1977-92 were fitted into the following form of formulation:

$$FDI = a_0 + a_1 GDP_{t-1} + a_2 GR_{t-1} + a_3 TARIFF + a_4 WAGE +$$

$$a_5 BOND + a_6 DISCOUNT + a_7 EXRT + a_8 IMP +$$

$$a_9 GROECD + a_{10} PRDTVY + D + U_t$$

where

FDI = Real annual change in foreign direct investment in period t (RMB bn in current prices) in China;

GDP = Real Gross Domestic Product (GDP), lagged by one period (RMB bn in current prices);

GR = Real GDP growth rate (%), lagged by one period;

TARIFF = Average tariff rate facing with foreign exporters into China, proxy for tariff protection as defined in text;

WAGE = Ratio of China's average wage/US average wage (%);

BOND = US government long-term bond yield (%);

DISCOUNT = China central bank's discount rate (%);

EXRT = Exchange rate between US dollar and Chinese RMB;

IMP = Changes in Chinese imports (RMB bn);

GROECD = Average growth rate in OECD countries (%);

PRDTVY = Real change in national productivity growth rates (%);

D = Dummy to capture political effects, for years 1986-87 and 1989 D = 1, and all other years D =0;

U_t = Stochastic error terms, i.e. is assumed to be independently and normally distributed with zero means and constant variance.

Expected sign of explanatory variables

The first question to address is whether the signs of the individual coefficients conform to theoretical expectations.

FDI is assumed to be expressible as a linear function of economic and political variables. On a priori grounds one would expect the sign of the size-of-market (GDP) coefficient to be positive. Similarly, the growth hypothesis would indicate that the relation between FDI and the change in GDP in absolute terms as well as the real percentage growth of the GDP should be positive.

The coefficient for the tariff-protection variable is expected to be positive if foreign export firms decide to locate production facilities in the importing country in order to avoid tariff barriers.

The WAGE variable is designed to control for production cost advantages in the host country. WAGE is the ratio of real wage between host country and the United States. The lower the host country wage, the larger should be the flow of foreign capital. We could expect the low labour cost on foreign inward capital to be positive, given the preference of foreign investors to host countries with cheap labour.

The two cost of capital variables control for factors that would induce foreign firms either to invest in their home markets rather than set up production facilities in a host country or to finance their investment projects through local resources (i.e. local banking loans). These two variables, representing opportunity costs, would be expected to be negative.

A nominal devaluation of domestic currency results in increases in exports and decreases in imports, which in turn lead to increases in FDI. But recent studies show that exchange rate has a contradictory effect on FDI in the short term and differ between various groups of LDCs. So the impact of exchange rates on FDI remains ambiguous and uncertain.

Direct investment and exports could be substituted for one another, so the effect of host country's imports (home country's exports) on FDI is expected to be negative. But recent empirical studies indicate that increasing imports in a host country may cause foreign capital to rise. Hence, the overall expectation of the effect of imports on foreign investment is uncertain.

Generally, economic prosperity at home country may cause MNCs to tend to locate production facilities in those rapidly emerging markets, so we would expect that the real growth rate in the OECD countries would cause foreign investors to exploit business opportunities in manufacturing industries in these two host countries.

In the case of China where productivity data is available, lower growth rate of productivity may be negatively related to FDI.

Finally, the coefficient of political dummy (D= 1,instability) would be expected to be negative, as foreign investors prefer political stability which a CPE or hardliner countries with dictatorships cannot always ensure.

Empirical results and interpretation

Time-series data between 1978 and 1992 for Hungary and China (see **Appendix 4.3** and **4.4**) were fitted into our one-equation models and were estimated by ordinary least squares (OLS) regression. The use of OLS, enabling the estimation of over-identified equations, purges the endogenous explanatory variables and minimizes the problem of multi-linearity, while the standard errors are corrected for heteroscedasticity. It was used to derive estimates of the coefficients of various independent variables described as above, and their effects to the dependent variable FDI.

An assessment of the usual tests of significance reveals that the D-W (Durbin-Watson) statistic is of a magnitude which manifests an absence of positive first-order serial correlation at the 1 per cent level, which the F-statistic values permit rejection of the null hypothesis that all estimated coefficients are not significantly different from zero. The coefficients of determination adjusted for degrees of freedom (R square) denote the explanatory power of the equations in the model.

The regression results presented in **Table 4.1** and **Table 4.2** contain the estimated equations and customary tests of significance. Overall, the linear formulation of the model is appropriate, as a large number of coefficients of determination, adjusted for degrees of freedom are quite high and all estimated equations perform significantly since their estimated F-statistics are well above tabulated F values. Given the satisfactory results of the linear regression analysis and the considerable movements in the levels of the variables, the linear formulation of the model seems to be applicable to both cases.

Empirical results for Hungary

The coefficients of the estimated least-squares regression function applied to the case of Hungary are displayed in **Table 4.1**.

The sign of the regression coefficients for the size-of-market variables (GDP, GDPA -change in absolute terms), TARIFF, WAGE, GROECD, and the two cost-of-capital variables agree with underlying economic theory for all the estimated equations. With regard to the political dummy to capture the effects of the previous Communist regimes in Hungary before 1989, its

137

Table 4.1
Empirical results of the determinants of foreign direct investment in Hungary, 1978-92

Variable	1.1	1.2	1.3	1.4	1.5	1.6	1.7	1.8	1.9	1.10	1.11
Constant	3.43 (0.26)	5.05 (0.51)	9.65** (2.59)	10.85* (3.31)	9.50* (6.25)	9.66** (2.27)	5.44 (0.47)	4.64 (1.41)	7.07*** (1.76)	9.27* (5.12)	13.07** (2.85)
GDP	0.72* (5.53)	0.73* (7.36)	0.72* (8.13)	0.77* (11.88)	0.74* (20.36)	0.72* (6.14)	0.77* (9.54)	0.72* (7.03)	0.73* (7.34)	0.71* (17.75)	0.54* (3.42)
GDPA	0.58* (6.49)	0.59* (8.53)	0.60* (9.61)	0.61* (10.30)	0.62* (11.74)	0.60* (8.07)	0.60* (7.70)	0.58* (7.94)	0.59* (7.73)	0.63* (10.04)	0.41* (3.63)
GR	-0.02 (-0.24)	--	--	--	--	0.01 (0.01)	0.01 (0.02)	-0.01 (-0.26)	-0.01 (-0.10)	--	-0.05 (-0.56)
TARIFF	0.07 (0.51)	0.05 (0.51)	--	--	--	--	0.06 (0.49)	0.06 (1.04)	0.04 (0.52)	--	0.001 (0.001)
WAGE	0.12 (0.61)	0.10 (0.64)	0.11 (0.77)	--	--	0.11 (0.62)	--	0.11 (0.70)	0.10 (0.62)	--	0.34 (1.22)
BOND	-0.15 (-1.22)	-0.15 (-1.39)	-0.14 (-1.43)	-0.16*** (-1.73)	-0.13*** (-1.81)	-0.14 (-1.27)	-0.17*** (-1.54)	-0.15 (-1.42)	-0.15 (-1.45)	-0.09 (-1.05)	-0.30*** (-1.62)
DISCOUNT	-0.45* (-5.17)	-0.45* (-5.95)	-0.46* (-6.82)	-0.46* (-7.02)	-0.45* (-7.70)	-0.46* (-6.08)	-0.45* (-5.60)	-0.45* (-6.09)	-0.46* (-6.42)	-0.52* (-9.03)	-0.52* (-4.51)
EXRT	0.01 (0.10)	-0.01 (-0.05)	-0.03 (-0.98)	-0.04*** (-1.54)	-0.03** (-2.10)	-0.03 (-0.83)	-0.01 (-0.12)	--	-0.02 (-0.62)	--	--
IMP	0.20 (0.30)	0.11 (0.22)	-0.07 (-0.25)	-0.14 (-0.47)	--	-0.08 (-0.21)	0.08 (0.13)	0.14 (0.71)	--	--	--

GROECD	0.49** (3.29)	0.51** (4.50)	0.54* (5.21)	0.53* (5.51)	0.51* (3.84)	0.53* (4.26)	0.50* (4.11)	0.51* (4.06)	0.48* (4.32)	--
DUMMY	-3.95* (-5.28)	-4.10* (-7.72)	-4.22* (-8.52)	-4.29* (-9.53)	-4.11* (-6.68)	-4.11* (-6.39)	-3.97* (-6.57)	-4.01* (-6.38)	-4.33* (-8.09)	-3.72* (-3.34)
R^2	0.84	0.92	0.83	0.81	0.91	0.93	0.92	0.94	0.92	0.95
$\bar{R}^2$	0.81	0.89	0.79	0.77	0.86	0.89	0.90	0.93	0.90	0.92
D-W	3.24	3.18	2.90	2.61	3.18	3.1	3.25	3.33	3.29	2.64
S.E.	0.40	0.32	0.31	0.29	0.36	0.3	0.35	0.35	0.35	0.65
F	130.83*	245.37*	295.69*	380.1*	176.67*	170.84*	191.29*	186.46*	310.33*	67.46*

Note: Number of observations = 15, t-statistics in parentheses

* Significance at the 1 per cent level of confidence
** Significance at the 5 per cent level of confidence
*** Significance at the 10 per cent level of confidence.

Source: For critical values of the t-distribution and F-distribution, see Cassidy (1981), pp.279-84.

coefficient is negative in all equations, a result which is consistent with the interpretation that foreign investors prefer political stability and a free market system. No clear pattern emerges with regard to the sign of the coefficients for GR, EXRT and IMP variables.

Regarding the significance of these coefficients, the evidence supports the size-of-market hypothesis, as the respective coefficients of GDP and GDPA are significantly different from zero at the 1 per cent level of confidence. But not only does the real growth rate of GDP - GR - having an ambiguous sign, it is also never significant at the 10 per cent level of confidence. The significant positive coefficients on GDP and GDPA suggest foreign capital inflow towards Hungary during the period under consideration was affected positively by the market size of the host country. We can conclude that FDI in Hungary is correlated with the size of Hungarian market and the change of GDP but not with the growth of its GDP, which agrees with some of the earlier empirical studies (Stevens, 1969; Scaperlanda and Mauer, 1969; Reuber et al, 1973).

Similarly, the evidence supports one of the two cost-of-capital variables hypotheses, since the coefficient for the Hungarian discount rate is significant at the 1 per cent level of confidence in all equations. This result suggests that foreign investors can finance some of their projects through the local financial market due to the high local central bank's discount rate. However, the other cost-of-capital variable, i.e. the U.S. long-term bond yield, does not seem to have influenced the inflow of FDI in Hungary. Although the sign of its coefficient agrees with a priori expectations in all equations, it is hard to estimate its significance, since the respective coefficient in equation 1.4, 1.5, 1.7 and 1.11 (Table 4.1) is significantly different from zero at the 10 per cent confidence level, but not significant in the other seven equations. This finding seems to be supportive of Petrochilos's study, which examines the same hypothesis using the Greek data on FDI for the period of 1954-77 and comes to the conclusion that foreign investment is correlated with the Greek discount rate but not with the U.S. long-term bond yield (Petrochilos, 1989, p.89).

Furthermore, the labour cost and the tariff-protection hypotheses are supported by the empirical evidence, but neither WAGE nor TARIFF is statistically significant at the 10 per cent level of confidence in those equations in which they appear. Though Hungarian wages per worker still average just US$2,000 per year compared to some US$20,000 in Western Europe, taking advantage of the low-cost labour is not a secret in their decision-making process of investing in Hungary. Moreover, as foreign investment decisions in a CPE are taken on quite different criteria, tariff rates variable is only one of those factors influencing investment decision-making process.

Our analysis also shows that both EXRT and IMP have a mixed sign and are not statistically significant at the 10 per cent level, although they maypartly support their hypotheses.

The real average growth rates in OECD countries (GROECD) has a positive and significant influence on FDI in Hungary throughout, as this variable is statistically different from zero at the 5 per cent level of confidence and for most of these it is also significant at the 1 per cent level in most equations. This seems to indicate that the real growth rate of the OECD economies is one of the significant determinants of FDI in Hungary.

Finally, with regards to the effects of the Communist regime before 1989 on FDI, the statistical evidence indicates that the previous CPE had a strong inverse relation with foreign capital. In all estimated equations the coefficient of the political dummy is negative and significantly different than zero at the 1 per cent level of confidence. Moreover, the introduction of the political dummy has a strong impact on increasing the overall fit of the model and improving the confidence level of the coefficients of other explanatory variables. The evidence, therefore, supports the hypothesis that foreign investors tend to prefer political stability, which in this case can be interpreted as preferring a free market system to a CPE.

The results of the foregone quantitative analysis seem to indicate that the main determinants of FDI in Hungary during the period of 1978-1992 were the size of the market (as measured by the level of GDP and the change of GDP in absolute terms), the average OECD growth rates, the Hungarian discount rates, and the degree of political stability. The first two variables stimulated foreign investors to explore the Hungarian market by investing there, but the last two variables discouraged prospective investors, causing them to invest at home or in other countries rather than in Hungary.

The findings regarding the size-of-market variables, the central bank's discount rates as well as political stability and the home country's real growth rates tend to conform to the earlier similar works which suggested that the size of the local market and the political situation are the most important factors when a foreign firm is considering outward investment. Our questionnaire survey in 1992 also revealed that as soon as a local market is open to foreign investors and the market size has grown to a level warranting the exploitation of economies of scale, it becomes one of the targets for MNCs and the inflow of FDI. As a matter of fact, most Western investors moving into Hungary are motivated, above all, by the desire to establish market share and gain a foothold in the host market (Wang, 1993, pp.245-247).

In the light of the limitation, the quality of data and the consequent restriction on the possibilities for the analysis, the empirical results are broadly consistent with expectations.

The multiple regression results for the coefficients of the estimated least-squares for various explanatory variables and their contribution to the dependent variable in China are shown in **Table 4.2**.

It can be observed that all explanatory variables are fitted much better to the model for China than that for Hungary, as the coefficients of determination and adjusted for degrees of freedom are quite high, their estimated F-statistics for the whole regression is highly significant and much higher than the tabulated F statistics. All the equations in Table 4.2 explain nearly 95 per cent of the variation in FDI during 1978-92. To summarize the results for the model, these fairly simple and entirely linear equations provide convincing evidence that these tested dimensions of all explanatory variables (except for TARIFF rate) do, indeed, affect foreign capital in China in the predicted fashion.

The table shows that all explanatory variables (except TARIFF) have the predicted signs. The sign of the regression coefficients for the size-of-market variables (level of GDP and real GDP growth rate), and the two cost-of-capital variables agree with underlying economic theory for all of the estimated equations in which the variables appear. The sign of the size-of-market coefficient (GDP and real GDP growth rate) is positive, while the sign of both cost-of-capital coefficients are negative. With regard to the low cost labour in China, the quantitative analysis provides evidence to support the hypothesis that there is a significant positive correlation between FDI and relatively cheap labour costs, since its coefficient is positive throughout all equations. The relation between FDI and TARIFF, the tariff protection variable, is expected to be positive, but the quantitative analysis of this variable seems to be inconsistent with the hypotheses and expectations that high tariff barriers against foreign exports will encourage investment in local production facilities, since it shows a negative coefficient in equations 2.1 to 2.5.

The estimated coefficients of other control variables in Table 4.2 generally exhibit the expected signs. The positive coefficients of EXRT suggest that the change of exchange rates made foreign investors switch exports away instead of a more permanent presence through direct investment when the devaluation of Chinese currency moved favourably for FDI rather than exports. The negative coefficients on China's imports further confirm previous studies that capital outflow and good exports could be substituted for one another. These two results are quite different from the findings in Hungary, where these variables carried uncertain signs. The average growth rates of OECD countries carry positive coefficients in all equations in which they appear. The productivity variable PRDTVY was a negative coefficient, suggesting that

Table 4.2
Empirical results of the determinants of foreign direct investment in China, 1978-92

Variable	2.1	2.2	2.3	2.4	2.5
Constant	109.34* (5.03)	109.69* (5.72)	95.44* (3.80)	91.10* (4.11)	90.02* (4.05)
GDP (t-1)	0.018 (1.07)	0.013*** (1.73)	0.017*** (1.79)	0.022** (2.83)	0.021** (2.70)
GR (t-1)	0.18 (0.34)	--	--	--	--
TARIFF	-3.29* (-4.61)	-3.11* (-7.29)	-2.62* (-5.11)	-2.75* (-5.41)	-2.57* (-5.57
WAGE	4.78 (1.19)	3.55** (2.29)	3.20*** (1.51)	4.35** (2.23)	3.71** (2.00)
BOND	-2.06** (-3.53)	-1.93* (-4.95)	-2.05* (-3.85)	-1.80* (-3.60)	-1.95* (-4.07)
DISCOUNT	-4.53** (-2.93)	-4.18* (-4.14)	-3.19** (-2.53)	-3.74** (-2.92)	-3.24** (-2.72)
EXRT	19.09** (2.51)	16.83* (4.98)	12.85** (3.19)	13.81* (3.47)	12.44* (3.31)
IMP	-0.16 (-1.15)	-0.12** (-2.42)	-0.09 (-1.40)	-0.11*** (-1.76)	-0.09*** (-1.55)
GROECD	1.03 (1.25)	1.22** (2.35)	--	0.55 (1.02)	--
PRDTVY	-0.50 (-1.09)	-0.61*** (-2.11)	-0.19 (-0.61)	--	--
DUMMY	-5.57*** (-2.13)	-4.97** (-2.86)	-3.56*** (-1.58)	-2.91*** (-1.56)	-2.91*** (-1.55)
R^2	0.98	0.99	0.96	0.94	0.97
$\bar{R}^2$	0.94	0.95	0.94	0.91	0.94
D-W	2.47	2.33	2.00	2.33	2.24
S.E.	1.60	1.41	1.94	1.84	1.84
F	318.33*	449.23*	262.04*	295.06*	329.18*

Note: Number of observations = 15, t-statistics in parentheses
         *   Significance at the 1 per cent level of confidence
         **   Significance at the 5 per cent level of confidence
         *** Significance at the 10 per cent level of confidence.

Source: For critical values of the t-distribution and F-distribution, see Cassidy (1981), pp.279-84.

there is a negative correlation between the level of productivity in China and the degree of foreign investment flows. This interesting result confirms that the productivity in Chinese manufacturing enterprises has seriously dampened the inflow of foreign capital, from the quantitative point of view. Finally, the political dummy shows a negative sign in all equations throughout. These two results closely parallel the findings in Hungary.

As far as the significance of these coefficients is concerned, we can see that the size-of-market hypothesis is strongly supported by our empirical evidence since the coefficient of GDP is significantly different from zero at the 10 per cent confidence level in most equations, with the exception of equation 2.1 (and in 2 out of 5 equations it is also significant at the 5 per cent confidence level), though the absolute size of the coefficient is smaller than that in the Hungarian regression due to a 1-year lag in the case of China which made them incomparable. Although the GR parameter is positive (compared with the uncertain sign in the case of Hungary), it is not statistically significant at the 10 per cent level of confidence. GR explains little and is unhelpful in strengthening the influence of other variables or improving the fit. This finding suggests that the flow of FDI into China is correlated with the host country's GDP but not with the growth rates of GDP, a point emphasized by Bandera and White (1968) and Reuber et al (1973).

The evidence also supports the cost-of-capital hypotheses since the coefficient of the U.S. long-term bond yield is significantly different from zero at the 5 per cent confidence level (and in 4 out of the 5 equations it is also significant at the 1 per cent level), and the coefficient of the central bank's discount rate is consistently significant at the 5 per cent level of confidence. Both variables have influenced the inflow of foreign capitals in China to a great extent.

Unlike the situation in the case of Hungary, with exception of equation 2.1, the right-sign coefficients of WAGE variable appear significantly different from zero at the 10 per cent level of confidence (2 out of the five are also significant at the 5 per cent level). This suggests that low cost labour makes a significant contribution to encouraging foreign firms to invest in China between 1978 and 1992. The variable approximating protectionist barriers in the host country, average TARIFF, though statistically significant at the 1 per cent level of confidence in all equations, carries an unexpected negative sign, indicating that it did not cause foreign export firms to locate production facilities in China in order to avoid tariff barriers. Thus the tariff-protection hypotheses are not supported by the empirical evidence. This finding parallels the finding in Hungary.

With regard to exchange rates and imports used as independent variables, the results show that most EXRT coefficients are statistically significant at the 1 per cent level, which indicates that this parameter seems to be necessary for the proper specification of the equation, while the IMP variable partly supports its hypotheses, as its coefficient is nearly or weakly significant (only 3 of the 5 equations are statistically significant at the 10 per cent level). These two results are the reverse of those in Hungary.

While the GROECD has a positive and significant influence on foreign investment in Hungary, it is not statistically different from zero at the 10 per cent confidence level in most of the equations in which this variable appears. This finding seems to suggest that the real average growth rates in OECD countries is a very weak explanatory variable for the determinants of FDI in China. This may partly be explained by the fact that 60 per cent of the total inward investment into China was from Hong Kong and Taiwan. Though the PRDTVY variable is always negative, it is barely significant.

In all estimated equations, the coefficient of the political dummy is negative and significantly different than zero at the 10 per cent confidence level, though not as strong as the regression results for Hungary where it shows at the 1 per cent level of significance. This statistical evidence provides strong and clear support for the expectation that there is a negative correlation between the flow of foreign capital and political instability. It further supports the hypothesis that foreign investors tend to prefer political stability, which in this case can be interpreted as preferring stable environment or reform-minded leadership.

In most equations, the market size parameter (GDP) is shown to have a significant and positive effect on FDI, while GR is uniformly positive, but never quit significant. The variables representing the cost-of-capital, BOND and DISCOUNT, and political dummy, D, consistently have a significant and negative effect on FDI, while the variables designed to measure production cost advantage in the host country and the exchange rate risk, WAGE and EXRT are always consistent with expectations. Of the other control variables, IMP and PRDTVY, always have a negative effect on FDI. Their significance varies somewhat, however, with the choice of independent variables. The real GDP growth rates in OECD countries (GROECD) is uniformly positive, but is significant only when regressed in omitting the GR variable.

The results of the foregone quantitative analysis seem to indicate that the main determinants of foreign inflow capital in China during the period of 1978-92 were the size of the market (as measured by the level of GDP), the low-cost of labour, favourable exchange rates as well as the two variables of cost-of-capital, and the degree of political stability. The first three variables stimulated foreign investors to explore the Chinese market by investing there, while the last three variables discouraged prospective investors,causing them to invest at home, or in other countries rather than in China.

These findings also conform to earlier similar empirical studies, which generally consider the size of local market, political stability and labour costs are the most important questions and the predominant determinants when a foreign firm is considering an outward investment in China. More and more foreign firms are attracted by the rapid growing market and the low-cost advantages, which stimulate them to move their establishments into this relatively cheap-labour country to gain a competitive edge. Favourable exchange rates also induce foreign firms to locate production facilities in the importing country in order to gain a more permanent presence and avoid tariff barriers.

The significant coefficient of the political dummy has a negative sign, indicating political instability had a strong inverse correlation with foreign capital inflows. The significant coefficient of the Chinese discount rate and U.S. government long-term bond yield variables suggest that foreign investors can finance some of their projects through the local financial market owing to the high local central bank's discount rate, or invest at home to gain risk-free returns of investment. All these variables dampen the interest of prospective foreign investors for ventures in China.

Conclusion and suggestions

Conclusion

This chapter was designed to identify political and economic factors that would best explain the pattern and determinants of FDI in Hungary and China during 1978-92.

The high adjusted R square value, indicating that the variables in the model can explain most of the variation in the dependent variable, suggests that most of the explanatory variables are the proper major determinants of FDI in these two countries.

The results generally support the hypotheses that FDI is determined by the size of the host country market, cost-of-capital, and political stability. We also find that foreign capital seems to be sensitive to exchange rates and labour costs in the case of China, while averaged real growth rates in OECD countries are found to be an important factor in determining investment flows in Hungary. There is little evidence that real GDP growth and productivity affect FDI in China in an important way. No convincing evidence was found to support the idea that imports will systematically and significantly replace capital inflows. Other variables may partly support their hypotheses but are not statistically significant.

In both Hungary and China, the level of real GDP agrees with underlying economic theory and empirical studies, which appears to be consistent with the often made argument that economies of scale in marketing and production

146

make a growing domestic market an attractive target for FDI. It should be very well understood that, while the changes in the legal framework are necessary for further progress, the economic environment and especially the market size and conditions play a decisive role in attracting foreign capital. It also implies that larger economies are much more likely to receive investment than small ones.

The importance of tariff rates is ambiguous. The sign of all estimated coefficients in the case of Hungary, as expected, are positive but none of these coefficients are significantly different from zero at the 10 per cent level.[15] This seems to indicate that tariff rates are meaningless in a CPE where foreign investors' decisions are taken on quite different criteria.

The cost-of-capital hypothesis is supported by our evidence as most of the coefficients on the Hungarian/Chinese discount rate and the U.S. government long-term bond yield show significant inverse relations with the inward flow of foreign capital into Hungary and China, which indicates these variables discouraged prospective foreign investors from establishing JVs in Hungary and China during the period of 1978-92.

The estimated coefficient on WAGE is positive in both cases, which conform with expectations and earlier findings, but can only be accepted as significantly different from zero in the case of China. It is insignificant in Hungary, which supports those findings that relatively cheap labour is weakly correlated with investment inflows. This can partly explain the fact that the former attraction of the cheap labour offered by LDCs decreased. Those factors such as widening selling possibilities, the economic atmosphere, technical development and high-skilled labour, attracted foreign investors more than cheap labour or raw materials.

Considerable evidence has been found that investment into China has been importantly affected by the change in value of the Chinese currency, while it played a relatively small but ambiguous role in FDI in Hungary. While IMP is positive and sometimes significant at the 10 per cent level for the regressions in the case of China, it shows uncertain signs, none of which is significantly different from zero, in the case of Hungary.

The OECD real growth rates seem to play a relative minor role in foreign capital inflows in China but it plays a prominent role in the case of Hungary. This may reflect the fact that the majority of FDI accumulated in China came from Hong Kong and Taiwan, rather than from OECD countries, as was the case in Hungary. The conclusions above may imply that the nearness of the former socialist economies in Eastern Europe to OECD countries might work to encourage FDI. However, the clear importance of market size in the regression estimates signals a long-term disadvantage for the relatively small economies of Eastern Europe, including Hungary.

Labour-cost advantages might also be critical for China and Hungary.

Recent evidence suggests that labour costs is becoming a relatively minor part of total production costs (for example, direct labour cost in standardized automotive components are only 10-15 per cent of total manufacturing costs). Thus, the relative advantage that LDCs can offer through low-cost labour has become much less important in recent years, a trend that surely will continue (Miller, 1993, p.17). LDCs that have more highly skilled labour available at relatively low wages can favourably influence plant location decisions. The hope for poorer LDCs may be not in attracting mature major corporations which will continue to concentrate on richer markets, but rather on locating newer MNCs from other developing countries.

The results above indicate that China's low wage, especially in comparison to Hungary and other Eastern European post-socialist countries, might gain comparative advantages in attracting FDI,[16] but the benefits of low wages might be seriously eroded because of low productivity and political instability. This provides some justification that incomes programmes should keep real wage increases tied to productivity improvements, economic development should keep pace with political stability.

The evidence further implies that the rapid exchange rate fluctuation and over-devaluation of local currency together with subsequent rapid imports liberalisation may indeed seriously reduce foreign capital inflows in the long term, because these two variables carry an uncertain coefficient in the case of Hungary. A gradual approach towards exchange rates and imports liberalisation, as China's evidence suggests, may favour foreign capital inflow into the host country.

Suggestions for further research

It seems appropriate to emphasize several limitations of studies such as the present one, in the hope that further research will be encouraged. While this research provides some clues concerning FDI in Hungary and China, much work clearly remains. For example, other factors, such as special privileges and concessions, which may overcome some disadvantages and have played important roles in attracting and motivating FDI, have not been incorporated into our quantitative model. It is likely that an important firm-level database is needed to fully understand investment flows.

Instead of relying on single equation techniques, a high priority is to develop complete simultaneous equation models of foreign investment behaviour. Such models avoid a major deficiency of previous studies by more clearly distinguishing exogenous from endogenous variables. An obvious supplement or alternative to the quantitative method is using case studies and surveys to ascertain what other factors might be important. For example, a county dummy as proxy for geographical proximity might be an important factor determining foreign investment inflows, as proximity may reflect low transportation costs for intermediate inputs and easier monitoring of projects. Again, without further study, one can only speculate what factors a foreign investor will consider when making direct investments. Finally, our quantitative analysis could not monitor the effects of the 'pull' of investment opportunities in these emerging markets themselves. The wide ranging economic reforms in China and economic transformation to free market economy in Hungary have generated greater investor confidence in the growth and creditworthiness prospects for these transforming economies. The decline in interest rates in most Western economies certainly provided an added impetus to investors searching for high-return instruments to look at the very attractive yields available in both fixed-return and equity investments in these emerging markets. These variables and methods may provide essential clues for comprehension of foreign investment in transforming economies.

Notes

1. Most literature published in both the West and the East on the determinants of FDI and JVs in Eastern Europe and China is of rather general nature and based on its authors' own experiences and newspaper clippings.

2. For a comprehensive survey of theories of FDI, see Lizondo (1991), 'Foreign Direct Investment', in *Determinants and Systemic Consequences of International Capital Flows, IMF Occasional Papers,* No.77, IMF, Washington, D.C. pp.68-82.

3. Agarwal, J. P. (1980), 'Determinants of Foreign Direct Investment: A Survey', *Weltwirtschaftliches Archiv,* Vol.116, pp.739-44.

4. The HK theory is addressed to the question of why a foreign-owned firm is able to compete with indigenous firms in the host economy, given the innate advantages of an indigenous firm.

5. See, Caves (1971), pp.1-27; Horst (1972), pp.258-66; Hymer (1976).

6. Hood and Young (1979), *The Economies of Multinational Enterprises,* Longman, London and New York, p.44.

7. Scaperlanda and Mauer (1969), pp.558-68.

8. Those factors include political and economic stability, stable labour force, the importance of the real rates of return in the recipient country; ready availability of foreign exchange; access to local finance; existence of a good

JV partner; taxation incentives; and duty-free imports, as well as size of market, raw materials and low cost labour, and so on.

9.See U.S. Department of Commerce (1954); Robinson (1961); Basi (1963); Brash (1966); Kolde (1968); Deane (1970); Andrews (1972); Forsyth (1972); Reuber et al (1973).

10.Basi (1963) included in his survey both developed as well as LDCs as host nations. His interview data indicated that political consideration play a greater role in investment decisions related to LDCs.

11.The author introducing foreign exchange risk into the theory of FDI, found that MNCs has a lower cost of capital due to its lower perceived foreign exchange risk, MNCs enjoy some advantages in borrowing local funds in the host-country, given a strong home nation currency.

12.See, Horst (1972); Young (1978); Majumdar (1980); Petrochilos (1989); Moore (1993).

13.Some economists explained the sharp growth of foreign investment inflows in these transforming and other LDCs primarily in terms of the 'push' effect of the unusually low interest rates and bond yield prevailing in the United States, arguing that the boom in flows coincided with a sharp decline in US interest rates and the drying up of the so-called junk bond market, which offered investors a domestic alternative in the high risk/high return areas. See, Ahmed and Gooptu (1993), p.11.

14.Aliber (1978), introducing foreign exchange risk into the theory of FDI, found that MNCs had a lower cost of capital due to its lower perceived foreign exchange risk, MNCs enjoy some advantages in borrowing local funds in the host-country, given a strong home nation currency.

15.This finding doesn't agree with the majority of empirical studies, but does confirm Baldwin's (1979) conclusion where tariff variable is found to be insignificant.

16.It implies that China will enjoy a bigger cost advantage in low-skill labour-intensive industries than in others.

5 Survey of foreign investment in Hungary and China

As discussed in Chapter 4, an obvious supplement or alternative to the quantitative analysis is to use questionnaire survey or case study to ascertain the objectives and performance of foreign investors in both Hungary and China. This chapter presents the results of a survey of Western investors in both Hungary and China conducted in 1992. It investigates why Western firms decided to invest in Hungary and China rather than at home, why they chose Hungary/China rather than other Eastern European countries as their investment destinations, why they preferred JVs to other forms of industrial cooperation, how they chose their local partners, and how they considered their experience and prospects of making direct investment and establishing JVs in Hungary and China. Questionnaires were sent to three hundreds Western firms involved in manufacturing or service activities in Hungary and six hundreds Western firms involved in JV operation in China. The valid responses numbered 90 Western firms for Hungary and one hundred twenty firms for China. Respondents varied from chief executives to project managers responsible for Eastern European/Chinese affairs or public relations.

Most firms in our present study established their JVs in Hungary between 1988-90. The 90 JVs varied in terms of absolute amounts and percentage participation in the risk capital, ranging from US$50,000 to US$1 billion, and from 35 per cent to 75 per cent respectively. The number of employees varied from 10 to 1,500. The sample firms produced a wide variety of goods in Hungary, mainly concentrated in the chemicals, engineering, metal and electric manufacturing, and food industries. The number of companies with investments in China fully participating in our survey totalled one hundred twenty, comprising forty British firms, twenty German firms, thirty from Hong Kong, 8 from the Netherlands, 4 from Austria, 2 from Finland, 2 from Italy, 6 from Japan, and 2 from Singapore. They distributed in manufacturing industries such as automobiles, pharmaceuticials, engineering, electronics and

151

food-processing. The following report describes the overall conclusions of the survey as a whole.

A survey of foreign investment in Hungary

Reasons for investment in Hungary

Our survey showed that past contacts with Hungarian firms had affected the surveyed firms' investment decision-making in Hungary: 62.5 per cent of the respondent firms already had a previous association with Hungarian firms, mainly through exports & imports and followed the full route, including exports/imports - licensing - long-term cooperation in production. Only 37.5 per cent of the respondents followed the direct route, moving straight from home operation to establishing a JV in Hungary. Prior to entering into a JV agreement in Hungary, 56.2 per cent were involved in industrial cooperation with firms in other Eastern European countries and/or China, mainly in the forms of imports/exports and JVs.

Half of the surveyed firms started their production with local partners by acquisition (buying or taking-over local existing factories) because they wanted to tap existing distribution channels or to purchase market share, 25 per cent by replacing or renewing technology and equipment in existing factories, 12.5 per cent started their operation by constructing new factories (greenfield) owing to the absence of a suitable partner, or unclear ownership and high liabilities.

The respondents regarded their JVs in Hungary either as a bridge-head/foothold for other Eastern European markets (stated by 31 per cent of the surveyed firms), import-substitution (25 per cent), a test-ground for future (25 per cent), or competing with rivals in the local market (12.5 per cent).

Why Western investors chose Hungary as a host country When planning an overseas venture (regardless of location), prospective investors generally seek to exploit existing or potential advantages in the host country, whilst maximizing their own competitive superiority in technology, know-how and marketing. In the case of Hungary, these company-specific advantages are combined with: a relatively inexpensive and qualified labour force, including a high percentage of well-trained specialists; and in some cases, a significant pool of locally developed technology and domestic capital which could only be commercialised through foreign capitalization.

Our survey found that one of the main motives of Western firms deciding to invest in Hungary was to establish market share in this country. Of particular attraction to foreign investors were a high level of domestic demand for some raw materials and manufactured products, as well as a wide range of business and personal services which were either unavailable in the local

Table 5.1
Motives for investing in Hungary

Responses	% of the respondents		
	Major importance	Some importance	Less important
Better access to the Hungarian market	68.8	25.0	6.2
Expanding exports/opening up new markets by investing there	56.3	25.0	18.7
Maintaining a foothold/test-ground in Eastern Europe	50.0	37.5	12.5
More opportunities provided by economic transformation	37.5	30.0	32.5
Expected higher profits in Hungary	25.0	31.1	43.9
Successful experience of previous industrial cooperation	18.6	25.0	56.4
Use of relative low-cost labour	18.8	43.8	37.4
Investment incentives in Hungary	12.5	43.8	43.7
Competing with existing rivals in the local market	12.5	31.3	56.2
Diversification into new production lines in potential market	12.5	12.5	75.0

market or greatly depended on imports. In the medium term, JVs were predominantly oriented towards the domestic market. **Table 5.1** shows that most of the respondent firms regarded better access to the Hungarian and other Eastern European markets as the most important motive in investing in

Hungary. Expanding exports or opening up new markets by investing there was stated to be of major importance by 56.3 per cent of the surveyed firms, and maintenance of a foothold/test-ground in the Hungarian market was thought of major importance by 50 per cent of the respondents. The opportunities provided by the current economic transformation and future potential also played a major important role in their investment decision-making in Hungary. Expectations of higher profits in Hungary, successful experience of previous industrial cooperation, competing with existing rivals in the Hungarian market, use of relative low-cost labour ('the key attraction for foreign capital will be the high-quality work-force available at low wages'[1]), and the local investment incentives were also considered as important motives behind the decision of investing in Hungary.

As far as the investment incentives in Hungary are concerned, 50 per cent of the respondents regarded the government's tax incentives on re-investment of profits in the JV as attractive, 31.3 per cent described them as insufficient, 12.5 per cent said they were very attractive, and 6.2 per cent totally inadequate. This fact seems to suggest that foreign investors in different sectors had a different view on Hungary's tax incentives. Nevertheless, the tax and other incentives in Hungary had some influence on foreign partners' policy on re-investing parts of their profits in JVs according to the response of 44 per cent firms.

Locational choice - Hungary versus Eastern Europe/China In reply to the question: 'Did your firm make any comparison before investing in Hungary in relation to alternative investment sites in other Eastern European economies or China?' 56.3 per cent of the surveyed firms did not compare Hungary to other Eastern European countries for a particular JV. The remaining 43.7 per cent stated that they did compare the markets in other Eastern European countries when they answered the question: 'Why did your firm chose Hungary but not other Eastern European countries as a host country?'

Some 75 per cent of the respondents (29 firms), which chose Hungary but not other Eastern European countries as their investment destination, considered Hungary a more attractive proposition for investment than other Eastern European countries; 62.5 per cent of the surveyed firms (24 firms) said the political and economic situation in Hungary was more stable than other Eastern European countries. Hungary offered greater trading/investment freedom and allowed greater participation in JV operational management. Of the 39 respondents which made a comparison, 50 per cent regarded this as one of the major factors in their locational decision.

Other factors, such as previous successful sales and industrial cooperation (regarded by 50 per cent of the respondents which made a comparison as of major importance) and establishing a share of the Hungarian market (regarded by 37.5 per cent as of major importance), also played an important role in their locational decision-making.

In the case of comparison carried out before investing in Hungary in relation to an alternative investment site in China, the smaller cultural, legal and infrastructural gap with Western Europe, considerable knowledge and experience about the Hungarian market, and geographical proximity were stated by 62.5 per cent, 50 per cent and 43.8 per cent of the 39 surveyed firms respectively as reasons of major importance why they chose Hungary rather than China as a host country for direct investment. That investing in Hungary should help them to penetrate other Eastern European markets was also regarded as of major importance by 50 per cent, of some importance by 25 per cent, as less important by 25 per cent of the 39 firms.

The choice of JV and local partner

Compared with other forms of technology transfer such as licensing or equipment purchasing, technology transfer through JVs appeared to be the most effective in Hungary. With credit financing becoming more difficult for Hungary, JVs become the most popular form of East-West cooperation to help raise economic growth rate, efficiency, and living standards in the 1990s.

Our survey showed that for 68.8 per cent of the respondents, the chance of increasing sales in Hungary played a role of major importance in their preference for JVs to other forms of industrial cooperation, while another 31.2 per cent thought this of some importance. Achieving further exploitation in the Hungarian market was also reported by 62.5 per cent firms in our present survey as a factor of major importance. The successful economic transformation in Hungary (mentioned as of major importance by 50 per cent of the firms, and of some importance by a further 25 per cent) provided more opportunities for Western investors to increase sales and exploit the Hungarian market.

Western investors preferring JVs to other forms of industrial cooperation were also attracted by the prospects of greater profits, greater participation in decision-making, as JVs allowed foreign investors reducing or sharing investment risk with local partners, improving their working relationship with local partners, facilitating technology transfer, and, overcoming the local firm's hard currency shortage. As the OECD reported: 'this form of activity is currently considered in the West to be much more effective than granting new loans which would only add to the debt burden and whose use donor countries would not be able to control'.[2]

As far as partner selection is concerned, our survey showed that 62.5 per cent of the respondents regarded that the local partner's strengths met the primary needs of the JV as of major importance. The partner's particular knowledge of local political, economic and market environment (mentioned as of major importance by 56.3 per cent, some importance by 25 per cent and less important by 18.7 per cent), the local partner's status (mentioned as of major importance by 50 per cent, some importance by 31.3 per cent and less important by 18.5 per cent), and past business relationship (regarded as of major importance by 50 per cent, of some importance by 18.8 per cent, and less important by 31.2 per cent) were also the most predominant factors which affected the selection of local partners for JVs.

The availability of a suitable facility as a going concern, access to partner's marketing network, materials and capital, and the partner's favourable offer or strategic location, were also thought to be of some importance in the choice of a particular local partner in Hungary.

Management decisions

JV's operational decision-making   In order to assess the extent of control exercised, the respondents were asked to indicate who (the foreign partner, the Hungarian partner, or both) made operational decisions in nine commonly recognized decision areas. We found that most of the decisions relating to price setting, management recruitment, marketing and long-term production planning were made jointly by both partners. Wage setting, local labour training, raw materials purchases, and local employee recruitment were normally done by the Hungarian partner, who had better knowledge of local market. Foreign partners were overwhelmingly responsible for setting of product range, quality, and technical standards.

Only a very small number of foreign managers and technicians were working in the surveyed JVs in Hungary. Western firms increasingly hired local executives, but weaker business and technical qualifications often required additional training at a cost (our survey shows that 62.5 per cent of the firms had Hungarian employees who went abroad for training purposes over the past three years, for a period of normally less than 6 months). Although foreign investors were faced with various difficulties, it became clear that foreign partners had been gaining more and more say in management of JVs in the 1990s. Some of the tougher business decisions were implemented more easily than anticipated in Hungary.

Decision-making on production and product choice   Sample firms were asked 'Which factors influenced your firm's choice of product(s) currently manufactured by the JV?'

The responses indicated that the most common procedure (cited by 37.5 per cent of the firms in our present survey) was to look for gaps by analyzing the structure of the Hungarian market and its suitability for a given product, then carried out activities that had not been pursued, or manufacture those products that had not been produced domestically before, or relied heavily on imports. A product suitable to both partners was mentioned by 18.8 per cent of the firms in our present survey, a product with highest labour content and nature of existing sales in Hungary was cited by 12.5 per cent of firms respectively.

To the question 'Was your home product suitable for the Hungarian market, or did it require modifications?' 68.8 per cent of the respondents indicated that their product was suitable in its original form; only in 31.2 per cent cases were minor modifications required.

Surveyed firms were asked how would they compare the quality of JV's product relative to that of similar products made at home: 50 per cent of the respondents stated it was of the same quality, 25 per cent said of slightly lower quality, and the remaining 25 per cent cited of higher quality or of much lower quality.

Differences in business approaches between partners Some 68.8 per cent of the surveyed firms stated that there were some differences in business approaches between each partner. Examples were that collective decision-making in Hungary was slow and bureaucratic (quoted by 52 per cent of the firms), differences in financial analysis (50 per cent of the firms), the Hungarian partners lacked business alertness (37.5 per cent), and finally, Hungarian firms' long-term planning lacked flexibility to adjust to short-term market changes (18.8 per cent of the surveyed firms).[3]

It appeared that the main differences in business approach had a 'moderately restrictive' effect on the JVs (68.8 per cent of the respondents said this), while the other 31.2 per cent of firms assessed the effects either as severely restrictive or alternatively as negligible.

The performance of JVs in Hungary

Our survey showed that foreign investors' predominant objectives were profitability (56.3 per cent of the surveyed firms), growth (56.3 per cent of the firms), quality of product (43.8 per cent of the firms), increasing sales in Hungary (25 per cent of the respondents), and export (18.8 per cent of the respondent firms).[4]

Performance The respondents were asked to compare their profitability in Hungary with that at home. **Table 5.2** shows that 43.8 per cent of the firms described their operations in Hungary as less profitable than those at home, whilst 37.6 per cent thought that their operations in Hungary were either more profitable than, or as profitable as, the home-based operations.

Comparing their profitability in Hungary with that in other developing

157

countries, we found that 56.3 per cent of the respondents thought their operations in Hungary were either more profitable than, or as profitable as, the operations in other developing countries, while the remaining 31.3 per cent perceived their operations in Hungary as less profitable than in other developing countries.

Table 5.2
Profitability at home and in Hungary

Response	% of the firms
Operations in Hungary were less profitable than those of home	43.8
Operations in Hungary were as profitable as those at home	18.8
Operations in Hungary were more profitable than home-based operation	18.8
Too early to comment	18.6
	100.0

Table 5.3
Expected and actual return on investment

Response	% of the surveyed firms
Returns on investment had reached expectation	50.0
Returns on investment had not reached expectation	25.0
Too early to comment	18.8
Information withheld on confidential ground	6.2
	100.0

We can conclude from our 1992 survey that on the whole foreign investment in Hungary was slightly less profitable than home-based investment, but more or as profitable as investment in other developing countries.

The respondents were then asked whether, on the whole, their projects' returns on investment had reached expectations. **Table 5.3** reveals that 50 per cent of the firms were satisfied with the rate of return on capital employed. Only 31.3 per cent considered that their total profits remitted abroad to date had exceeded their initial investment in the JV.

Sample firms were asked: 'Since the JV started operation in Hungary, how do you evaluate your exports to Hungary?' **Table 5.4** shows that 56.3 per cent of the respondents increased their exports to Hungary, and another 31.3 per cent maintained the value. Only 6.4 per cent of the firms said exports had declined because the JV merely replaced home-based production.

Our survey showed that 75 per cent of the respondents either met or exceeded their objectives, while in the remaining 25 per cent of firms the actual outcome fell short of objectives.

Table 5.4
Exports to Hungary after setting up of JVs

Responses	% of the respondents
Exports to Hungary had increased	56.3
Exports to Hungary remained the same	31.3
Exports to Hungary had decreased	6.4
	100.0

Based on the measures of success in terms of profitability, exports to Hungary following the establishment of the JV, and the firms' own perception of success, the respondents were further asked to state 'On balance, how do you rate the performance of your JV activities in Hungary to date?' The responses are shown in **Table 5.5**.

All these findings strongly suggest that foreign firms followed a multiple - rather than single -objective strategy of investing in Hungary. Foreign firms, on the whole, were prepared to accept a lower rate of profit in order to pursue their global investment strategy in Eastern Europe aimed at longer-term prospects of enlarged markets. Some evidence showed that lower profitability in Hungary than on similar home-based investments did not imply that Western firms were dissatisfied with the rate of returns on capital invested in their JVs.

Table 5.5
Overall level of success of JV in Hungary

Responses	No. of firms	% of the respondents
Totally successful	5	5.6
Very successful	38	42.3
Average successful	36	42.0
Not successful	11	12.1

In their multiple-objective strategy, the firms' projected financial results were supported by other targets: most of the firms in the study reported that the establishment of JVs led to an increase or at least maintenance in their exports to that country. The general conclusion was that the respondent firms were tilted towards success rather than failure, as 87.9 per cent of the firms regarded their JVs as successful.

Prospects for JVs and foreign investment in Hungary

Hungary has been by far the largest recipient of FDI among Eastern European countries. Can Hungary remain one of the leading host countries within Eastern Europe and former Soviet Union in attracting foreign investment in the future? What kinds of problems Western investors were faced with investing in Hungary? Were there any lessons to be learnt for those who are investing in the market now? This section focuses on political risk and operational problems of investing in Hungary.

Problems encountered by Western firms in Hungary We found many of the obstacles confronting foreign investors in Hungary were common to some other Eastern European economies undergoing transformation from central planning to market system. Understandably, the scope and repercussions of these problems varied from industry to industry and differed between individual firms. The experience of Western investors to date revealed a variety of operational difficulties.

The major concern facing investors and potential investors, not surprisingly, was the political and economic environment of the host country. *The Business International and Creditanstalt 1992 East European Investment Survey* found that the economic factors were the primary determinants as far as FDI in Eastern Europe was concerning, followed closely by the political environment (except for the Yugoslav successor states).[5]

The respondents were asked to select according to the question 'Which factors were the prime determinant in your decision-making concerning direct investment in Hungary?' Our survey showed that only 37.5 per cent out of the 90 firms thought political variable played the most important role in their investment decision-making in Hungary, while the remaining 62.5 per cent considered that economic factors (such as local market potential and expected investment returns) constituted the prime determinant. Our conclusion further confirmed the findings of the *Business International and Creditanstalt 1992 East European Investment Survey* shown as above.

The firms in our present survey were then asked 'How do you evaluate current and future risk in Hungary and China?' **Table 5.6** reveals that 42.9 per cent of the respondents believed that there was some risk in investing in Hungary, while 35.7 per cent thought there was 'no risk' for investment in Hungary.

In contrast, 9.5 per cent of the 90 surveyed firms regarded it as 'very risky' to invest in China, and 53 per cent thought there was 'some risk'. These responses seemed to suggest that foreign investors were more confident of Hungary's political stability than China's.

Table 5.6
Comparison of political risk investing in Hungary and China (%)

	Very risky	Some risk	Hard to predict	No risk
Hungary	--	42.9	21.4	35.7
China	9.5	53.0	33.0	4.5

One of the biggest headaches Western firms complained of investing in Hungary was the negotiation process, which took months longer than expected, and three to four times as long as expected for a similar deals in the West. The respondents were asked about how long the negotiation process to enter into a JV agreement in Hungary took. 37.5 per cent out of the 90 firms replied that it took less than half a year, 44 per cent between half a year to 2 years, 12.5 per cent spent more than two years reaching a JV agreement with the Hungarian partner.

The surveyed firms were further asked to indicate major problems their JVs faced during implementation stage in Hungary in terms of frequency (see **Table 5.7**).

Inconsistent rules governing FDI, poor infrastructure (i.e. transport, electricity, water supply, telecommunications and transport, inadequate information, and data facilities),[6] shortage of hard currency, and the

161

Table 5.7
Frequency of major problems encountered by foreign firms

Responses	% of the surveyed firms		
	More frequent	Some frequency	Less frequent
Inconsistent rules	42	17	41
Poor infrastructure	42	25	33
Short of hard currency	25	8.3	66.7
Unconvertible of Forint	25	8.3	66.7
High inflation and rising costs	17	67	16
Can't achieve full production capacity	17	3	80
Poor profitability	17	25	58
Economic environment too uncertain	17	17	66
Negotiation with local partner too difficult	17	17	66
Restructuring costs too high	5	17	78
Difficult to recruit/fire staff	16	33	51
Political environment too volatile	10	17	73
Personal dispute among host and foreign executives	5	17	78
Inadequate incentives to employees	5	8	87
Lack of suitable local partners	8	9	82

nonconvertibility of the Hungarian currency (Forint) were reported as the more frequent problems encountered by Western investors, which not only caused a great deal of anxiety/disappointment among foreign investors and rendered difficult operation of undertaking, but also set limits to the advantages the Hungarian hoped for from the inflow of foreign capital in terms of the expansion of exports and adoption of new products and

162

manufacturing processes on an increasing scale.

Low productivity and rising costs, especially high restructuring costs, were also frequently involved in some JVs. Owing to inadequate incentives to motivate employees working hard and increasing productivity, the Hungarian was 50 per cent less productive than Western expatriate for the same job in one JV. Another manager reported that Hungarian workers were four times less productive than Western colleagues for the same job. As one Western executive observed, 'firms should elucidate early on short-term incentives to create long-term devotion', but unfortunately 'most firms fail to motivate new local staff adequately',[7] which was a further cause of low efficiency, poor quality and low profitability. In the case of taking-over an existing firm, the foreign investor must invest at least twice, first when taking-over the enterprise, and again when reconstructing it. There were quite a few examples in Hungary, such as Ford, Suzuki, General Electric,[8] where the expenditure of the foreign firms on takeover had to be repeated or doubled in order to restructure the enterprises. This caused some foreign partners to curb their initial investment, or pull out from the Hungarian market entirely.

'Finding a suitable partner ... moves up in the rankings as the most problematic issue facing Western investors in Hungary'.[9] Some firms had to purchase a whole plant site in Hungary due to lack of suitable partner. But bad debt, environmental damage of sites, worker's health and product liability all became inheritable, which led many Western companies shy away from high risk investments in such sectors as chemicals or pharmaceutical industries.

Other problems, such as inability to achieve stipulated production capacity, uncertain economic environment, difficulties in negotiating with local partners, and in reconciling local and Western systems of accounting, and problems relating to labour motivation and industrial relations practices were also reported by some firms in the survey.

Other companies considered that unavailability and/or inadequate quality of local supplies of raw materials and components for production,[10] difficulties in raising finance and obtaining financial guarantees from local banks as quite frequent obstacles of operational practices.

Overstaffing was reported to be worse than expected in Hungary. *The Business International and Creditanstalt 1992 East European Investment Survey* reported that 16 per cent of its respondents found overstaffing a big problem faced with foreign investors.

Changes of investment environment and future investment climate Table 5.8 shows foreign investors' views of how the conditions had been changed over 1989-92 in Hungary.

Table 5.8
Foreign investor's opinions of changes in Hungary over 1989-92

Responses	Improved		Unchanged		Worsened	
	No. of firms	% of respondents	No. of firms	% of respondents	No. of firms	% of respondents
Market growth potential	26	28.6	32	35.7	32	35.7
Political stability	51	57.1	26	28.6	13	14.3
Local economic growth	19	21.4	26	28.6	45	50.0
Profit remittance policies	13	14.3	71	78.6	6	7.1
Import restriction	51	57.1	26	28.6	13	14.3
Local finance possibilities	38	41.7	37	41.6	15	16.7
Profit expectation	35	38.5	33	37.2	22	24.3
Labour costs	7	7.6	21	23.0	62	69.4
Prices of raw materials	8	8.4	37	41.6	45	50.0

Our survey showed that 50 per cent out of the 90 firms thought the investment climate in Hungary in the next five years (1992-97) would become more attractive, and 43 per cent thought it would remain the same, while only 7 per cent thought it would be still subject to uncertainty. Some 71 per cent of the 90 surveyed firms believed that their JVs would perform satisfactorily in the next five years.

The survey further revealed that a majority of the respondent foreign firms (71.4 per cent) had plans for further investment expansion in Hungary; 14.3 per cent had decided against further investment. For the remaining 14.3 per cent, further expansion would depend on Hungary's transformation process, economic growth and political stability.

A survey of foreign investment and joint venture in China

This section presents the results of our survey of Western investors in China by focusing on the choice of China as an investment host country, the method of entry into the Chinese market, and how they chose their local partners, and how they evaluated the experience and prospects of making direct investment in China.

Reasons for investment in China

Why Western investors chose China as an host country The main motives Western firms decided to establish JVs in China in the 1980s were to create market presence in this particular huge market, to secure an image, and to get acquainted with Chinese business practice and the country's economic climate. They were also occasionally to attain monopoly positions and to pursue long-term strategies by virtue of having been the first to appear locally and/or increase profits (in some cases it included the short-term repatriation of dividends and profits) by means of capturing market share. For the Hong Kong and Taiwanese investors, the huge mainland market, the relatively low-cost labour, and the securing of an economic investment in a possibly reunified China, are of particular interest. These motives have not changed even in the 1990s - Western investors saw establishing market share in the huge Chinese market as the primary reason to invest in China, even though China failed to open its domestic market sufficiently to foreign investors, especially in the early stages, when the government encouraged foreign investors to sell their products abroad rather than in the domestic market.[11] The collapse of the Soviet Union and East European socialist states has deflected the attention of European companies in particular away from China towards markets nearer home where cultural differences are also less apparent.

In order to test our hypotheses and findings in Chapter 4, the respondents in our present survey were asked about their major motives for investing in China.

Table 5.9 shows that nearly 81 per cent of the respondents regarded better access to the Chinese market for growth of sales, market share, and profit as one of the most important motives for investing in China. This finding confirmed the MOFERT 1986 survey, in which 63 per cent of the 81 JVs regarded gaining access to the huge potential Chinese market and using China as a production base to serve other Asian countries in the long term.[12]

Maintaining a foothold/test-ground in the Chinese market was thought of major importance by 47.6 per cent, and expanding exports or opening up new markets by investing there was stated to be of major importance by 42.3 per cent of the surveyed firms. One third of firms stated that greater potential opportunities provided by the current economic transformation also motivated them to invest in this potential market.

Table 5.9
Motives for investing in China

Responses	Percentage of the surveyed firms		
	Major importance	Some importance	Less important
Better access to the Chinese market	80.9	19.1	-
Maintaining a foothold/test-ground in the Chinese market	47.6	28.6	23.8
Expanding exports or opening up new markets by investing there	42.3	14.3	43.4
More opportunities provided by economic transformation	33.3	38.1	28.6
Competing with existing rivals in the Chinese market	28.6	38.1	33.3
Diversification into new production lines in potential rapid growth area	19.0	19.0	62.0
Expected higher profits	14.3	52.4	33.3
The desire to induce China into a long-term commitment to a particular type of technology	9.5	33.3	57.2
Investment incentives in China	9.5	47.6	42.9
Use of relatively low-cost labour	9.5	23.8	66.7
Establishment of an export base	9.5	9.5	81.0
Successful experience of previous industrial cooperation	9.5	23.8	66.7
Access to local natural resources	-	14.3	85.7
The advantage of complementing another type of investment	-	19.0	81.0

Our survey revealed that expansion of their sphere of operations through JVs was regarded by many leading Western companies as a key aspect of strategy, sometimes even more important than the immediate returns on capital. A production site in China provided an easy way to realise an alternative to

166

domestic production with lower production costs for the Far East markets. It also showed that short-term profit maximisation was only a secondary consideration for large MNCs with a view of long-term strategies for future expansion - competing with rival companies, strengthening a larger share of Far East and world production, gaining technical advantage, enabling stood-down models to be transferred at low cost, and a more rational division of labour.[13] It should be noted that 66.7 per cent of the 120 respondent firms stated that use of relatively low-cost labour played a less important role in their decision-making concerning investing in China, compared with the factor of targeting the 1.2 billion consumer market.

Competing with existing rivals in the Chinese market (28.6 per cent thought to be of major importance, 38.3 per cent some importance, 33.3 per cent less important), diversification into new production lines in China (19 per cent considered this of major importance, 19 per cent some importance, 62 per cent less important), and expected higher profits (14.3 per cent of major importance, 52.3 per cent of some importance, 33.3 per cent less important) were also considered as important motives behind their decisions to invest in China.

Other motives, such as successful experience of previous industrial cooperation, investment incentives, and the desire to induce China into a long-term commitment to a particular technology and then monopolise the local market, also played an important role in their investment decision-making in China.

These findings were further confirmed by a random-sample survey of 1,066 FIEs carried out by State Statistical Bureau of China in March 1994, in which the bureau found that the main factors attracting FDI were: a potential market of the 1.2 billion consumers, abundant human resources, and tax privileges and other incentives. About 92 per cent of the 1,066 FIEs cited the huge Chinese market; 56 per cent believed that China's abundant human resources was another important factor drawing them to China. A further 56 per cent stated that tax privileges and other incentives were also important.[14]

We can therefore conclude that most of Western investors moving into the Chinese market in the period was motivated above all by desire to establish market share and strengthen their market presence in the local market, which is still relatively unexplored. Investment would be intended either to produce for the local market (market-based) or to serve as an export-platform for markets elsewhere (factor-based). Although exports were the priority, future sales in the domestic market were possible as long as the foreign exchange account of the venture was balanced. Moreover, in a few cases where the technologies or products involved were urgently needed by the local authorities, this precondition was sometimes waived, and this lured a large number of foreign companies, mostly in manufacturing activities, into China in the hope of establishing a foothold in the domestic market. These findings further confirm the results of the quantitative analysis in Chapter 4 -the main objectives of foreign investors were to gain access to the potential huge Chinese market, and to use China as a production base by taking advantage of its cheap labour to serve other Asian countries in the long term.

Both Chapters 4 and 5 firmly confirmed that foreign investors seem to have been strongly attracted by the size of the Chinese market. The cheapness of the labour force was of secondary significance. Labour costs were one of the most important questions when a foreign company was considering an outward investment. Although China has abundant cheap labour, which naturally increases the profitability of investment and leads a growing number of Western firms to move labour-intensive branches of production to China, labour quality is poor. Many foreign investors complained about the shortage of skilled workers. It was reported that many workers had insufficient skills and required at least four to six months training; the quality of the administration staff was even worse: they needed at least one year's training. The payment of high salaries to attract skilled workers, and expenditure on staff training meant higher production costs for foreign investors. Even though taking advantages of low-cost labour was one of main initial reasons for investors in their investment decision-making in China, productivity in China was much lower than that of some other Asian countries.

Locational choice - China versus Eastern Europe The next step of the inquiry was to investigate the choice of China in relation to alternative investment sites in Eastern Europe. In reply to the question in our questionnaire: 'Did your firm make any comparison before investing in China in relation to alternative investment sites in Eastern European economies?' 12 firms did not compare China to other Eastern European countries for a particular investment venture, while 10 firms established JVs both in China and Eastern European countries. The remaining 98 firms said that they did compare China with Eastern European markets.

In terms of locational strategy, two trends were therefore discernible: first, the choice of China was not part of a rigorous search for alternative locations, as the decision behaviour of MNCs was characterised by non-comparative go/not-go situations.[15] Nevertheless, some firms established JVs in both China and Eastern European countries. Most firms thought China's huge market, cheap labour, possible penetration into other Far East markets by investing in China, and thus generating higher expected profits were playing an important role in their decision-making to invest in China rather than in Eastern European countries.

Some 85 per cent of the respondents which chose China but not Eastern European countries as a host country for a JV showed the desire to establish a share of the huge Chinese market. Another 56 per cent of firms considered China a more attractive proposition for investment than Eastern European countries; 44 per cent of the respondent firms declared the political and economic situation in China was more stable than Eastern European countries. Other firms declared that China possessed an abundant and relatively cheap labour pool, offered greater trading and investment freedom, and allowed greater participation in JVs' management.

In this section, we have investigated why China was selected as an investment destination vis-a-vis Eastern Europe. The empirical evidence suggests that the principal motives of foreign investment in China were the maintenance of a foothold/test-ground in this huge market. The ongoing economic transformation provided a solid incentive to invest. The impression gained from these respondents was that China's successful and gradualist reform, and the potential market had favourably influenced Western firms' decision to establish JVs in China.

The choice of JVs and local partners

Since China opened its economy to foreign investment in 1979, an increasing number of foreign companies have entered into JV investment in China, whether or not they had experienced other forms of trade and industrial cooperation with Chinese enterprises prior to establishing JVs. A number of options are available: an acquisition, JV, JV-acquisition or greenfield, each of which has its own advantages and disadvantages. Which is the most appropriate? Why JV has become the predominant form of FDI in China? As the OECD reported in 1990, as far as China and Eastern European countries were concerned, JVs represented the most developed form and longer term reciprocal activities. With the JV option now available in all Eastern European countries and China, JV investment took on even more interest for Western companies.[16] The decision, to a large degree, depends on the investor's reasons for coming to China (market share versus low-cost resources) and the industry in which the investment was being made.

Our survey showed that the chance of exploiting the Chinese market played a major importance role in their preference for JVs to other forms of industrial cooperation, stated by 71 per cent of the respondents. The desire to achieve greater participation in decision-making was also stated by 47.6 per cent of firms as a factor of major importance. The successful economic transformation in China (mentioned as of major importance by 33.3 per cent of the firms) provided more opportunities for Western investors to increase sales in the Chinese market.

Reducing/sharing investment risk with local partners was also regarded to be of major /some importance respectively by 26.3 per cent of the surveyed

169

firms. Other motives for Western investors preferring a JV agreement to other forms of industrial cooperation included the prospects of greater profit, improving working relationship with local partner, facilitating technology transfer, and overcoming the local firm's hard currency shortage.

In a country like China in the 1980s where retail and distribution networks were grossly underdeveloped, it often made sense for a company looking to establish share to acquire an existing enterprise that had a distribution network in place and/or a strong local brand. But many of the disadvantages or risks of an acquisition could be overcome by going the JV route, including leaving behind debt and other potential liabilities. Tapping the knowledge of the local business environment and taking advantage of distribution networks were the primary reasons for entering into JVs rather than acquisition or greenfield. Our survey showed that the main reason for the popularity of JVs, as opposed to other forms of industrial cooperation, was the foreign partners expected their Chinese partners to help them overcome specific obstacles to operating within the country, where the business environment was not only different from that in developed countries but also from that in many LDCs. This included the political and economic structure in a CPE, cultural and language differences, current business practices, management systems, and knowledge of government procedures in both local and central governments. Foreign investors preferred to form JVs with local firms as a method of establishing themselves in the unfamiliar Chinese economy. While foreign partners believed that the Chinese partners possessed important specialised local market information which they needed, and their ability to form true 'strategic alliances' was crucial for long-term access to the Chinese market, the Chinese considered JVs as a good method of attracting FDI to China because they could share control over the operation with foreigners.

The primary reason behind those firms who chose the greenfield route was that no suitable partner existed, rather than because they wanted to avoid the potential liabilities and long negotiating process involved with an acquisition. As one respondent stated that 'no unit existed that met our technological standard'. Other reasons that our respondents gave for going-it-alone from scratch was the desire to avoid the difficulties with local partners, the greenfield route was thought to be the quickest way to establish its own presence in the Chinese market.

Foreign firms, which wish to establish a JV and achieve further exploitation in the local market, usually meet a great challenge - the selection of local partner, whose strengths should meet the primary needs of the venture. Partner selection requires extensive consideration of the fit between the JV's needs and the partner's strengths.

Other features of potential local partners, such as the size and stability of local firm, the status of a potential partner, past association and certain resources, also played very important roles in decision-making of partner selection. For the Chinese partners in establishing JVs, the primary objectives are the introduction of foreign technology and management expertise, increase in foreign exchange through export earnings and a supplementary source of capital.

Table 5.10 shows foreign investors' views of what factors influenced their selection of local partners. It shows that availability of a suitable facility as a going concern, partner's particular knowledge of local political, economic, and commercial environment, and the local partner's strategic location, were the most predominant factors.

Table 5.10
Partner's selection for JVs in China

Responses	Percentage of the 120 surveyed firms		
	Major importance	Some importance	Less important
Availability of a suitable facility as a going concern	47.6	19.0	33.4
Partner's particular knowledge of local political, economic environment,etc.	47.6	28.6	23.8
Partner's strategic location	47.6	14.3	38.1
Partner's strengths meet the primary needs of the JV	33.3	28.6	38.1
Past business relation	28.6	14.3	57.1
Status of local partner	28.6	52.4	19.0
Access to partner's marketing network, local materials and capital	9.5	42.3	48.2
Local government's recommendation	9.5	14.3	76.2
Partner's favourable offer	--	33.3	66.7

The partner's strengths which met the primary needs of the JV, past business relationship and connection, and finally the status of local partner were also thought as some importance in their decision-making process in choosing particular local partner in China. We should note that the factors, such as local government's recommendation and the partner's favourable offer were perceived as less importance in partner's selection. But two sample firms did emphasize that they had little possibility of choosing their partners in the middle of 1980s.

These findings bear some differences with those in the case of Hungary. It also differs with Artisien's study on joint ventures in Yugoslav industry. Artisien found that 64 per cent of the 42 cases selecting their partners was based on previous association, 21 per cent was approached by Eastern European enterprises and another 12 per cent was due to a combination of the above two factors. Thus previous association stood out as one of the most predominant factors in the selection of Eastern European partner.[17]

Management decisions

In order to assess the division of managerial control among partners and the extent of control exercised, the respondents were asked to indicate who (the foreign partner, the Chinese partner, or both) made operational decisions in nine commonly recognized decision areas. Our survey revealed that wage setting, local labour training, raw materials purchases were normally made by the Chinese partner, who had better knowledge of local market. Foreign partners were overwhelmingly responsible for setting product quality and technical standards. Areas where joint decision-making was prevalent included setting prices, management recruitment, long-term production planning, and marketing. The foreign partner's insistence on joint decision-making in marketing highlighted the difficulties inherent in reconciling two major objectives: increasing JV's exports to generate foreign currency upon which its share of profits may depend; and protecting its home market from potential Chinese competitors. Thus, the findings included: first, the foreign firm retained virtually full control over quality and technical standards, which by implication illustrated the Chinese enterprise's priorities to compensate for a lag in technology and improved distribution channels in the West; second, joint managerial control appeared to be favoured wherever the Chinese firm's operational control could benefit from the foreign partner's greater industrial maturity; finally, the Chinese partner's managerial influence was mostly felt in areas where its better knowledge of indigenous market conditions placed it in a stronger position to assess the viability of a project.

Our survey revealed that some foreign firms resolved the above dilemma by entering into an agreement for producing new or complementary products, and by assuming full responsibility for the sale of the JV's output in the Western markets. The foreign partner's preference for joint responsibility in the choice of product range stemmed from the Chinese firm's restricted distribution network and comparatively poor selling record in the competitive Western markets. Product range was closely related to quality standards, which were dictated by the foreign partner with minor joint consultation; here, the foreign partner's predominance reflected its greater managerial and technical expertise.

Most studies of decision-making structures within JVs concluded that local partners played a limited role - foreign partners controlled production, finance and management, while the local partners were responsible for public relations, labour relations and (sometimes nominally) domestic distribution. This may be true in the earlier stages of China's Open-up Policy. In the late 1980s and the first half of 1990s, Chinese partners were increasingly involved in JVs' management. We could argue that the majority of JVs were in the hands of local partners. Some foreign partners reported that it was very difficult to appoint a local national as the real top man, because the latter were unable to participate fully in the Western system of decision-making. However, some foreign investors appointed top managers from local Chinese.

A key consideration for firms setting up a JV in China was the choice of product to be manufactured there: the firm's choice seemed to rest between manufacturing the full range of products of its home-based operations, a selected part of that range, a product of that range, or a new product not manufactured at home. Against this background of alternative product strategies, sample firms were asked: 'Which factors influenced your firm's choice of the product(s) currently manufactured in China?'

The responses in **Table 5.11** indicated that the most common procedure (cited by 71.4 per cent of the surveyed firms) was to look for gaps in the economy by analyzing the structure of the Chinese market and its suitability for a given product, then carry out activities that had not previously been pursued in the country, or manufacture products that had not been produced domestically before, or relied heavily on imports.

Amongst other factors influencing the choice of product, a product suitable to both partners was mentioned by 33.3 per cent of the respondents, a product with high profits and a new product in the Chinese market were cited by 14.3 per cent of the surveyed firms respectively. Others replied that the choice of product was based on the nature of existing sales in China, its highest labour content, and sole product in the Chinese market.

To the question 'Was your home product suitable for the Chinese market, or did it require modifications?' Some 23.8 per cent of the respondents indicated that their product was suitable in its original form; only in 8.6 per cent cases minor modifications were required.

Our results suggest that foreign investors normally looked for new market opportunities and targeted those sectors, such as car manufacturing, hotels, trade, finance, health care, cultural service, consulting, computerised data processing, telecommunications, and infrastructure, where SOEs did not exist or were not sufficiently active.

Table 5.11
Factors influencing the firm's choice of product

Responses	Percentage of the surveyed firms
The Chinese market	71.4
Product suitable to both partner	33.3
Product with high profit	14.3
New product in the Chinese market	14.3
Nature of existing sale to China	9.5
Product with highest labour content	9.5
Sole product in China	4.7
Non-applicable	14.3

The performance of JVs in China

Our survey showed that JVs' predominant objectives for investing in China were profitability (86 firms), growth (79 firms), increasing sales in China (62 firms), export (40 firms) and quality of product (34 firms).[18]

Profitability The firms in our present survey were asked to compare the profitability of their operations in China with that at home. Table 5.12 shows that 40 per cent of the respondents described their operations in China as less profitable than those at home, whilst 30 per cent of them thought that their operations in China were considerably either more profitable than, or as profitable as, the home-based operations.

Comparing the profitability in China with that in other developing countries, we found that 30 per cent of the respondents perceived their operations in China as less profitable than in other developing countries, 40 per cent of the surveyed firms thought their operations in China were either more profitable than, or as profitable as, the operations in other developing countries, though most of JVs began to realise profits during the third year of their operation. This fact goes a long way towards explaining China's relative attractiveness as a host country.

We can conclude that foreign investment in China was on the whole slightly less profitable than home-based investments, but more or as profitable as investments in other developing countries.

Table 5.12
Profitability at home and in China

Response	Percentage of the respondents
Operation in China is less profitable than those at home	40
Operation in China is as profitable as those at home	15
Operation in China is more profitable than home-based operation	15
Too early to comment	30
	100

Why did foreign investors accept lower profitability in China than on similar home-based investment? This can be explained partly by the Western companies' strategy of entering the Chinese market with a long-term perspective. Their global investment policy in relation to China had the multiple objectives of profitability, growth and exports. Profit is not an immediate goal of the Western firms in many cases. Most of the foreign firms did not wish to forego benefits of an enlarged market in the medium- and long-terms solely for the purpose of superior profits in the short term.

The respondents were then asked whether, on the whole, their projects' returns on investment reached expectations (see **Table 5.13**): 25 per cent of the respondents were satisfied with the rate of returns on capital employed, whilst 40 per cent considered that the returns on investment was below expectations. The remaining 35 per cent stated that it too early to comment.

Exports Export performance is commonly regarded as one of the important objectives for JVs in China. The Chinese authorities and its foreign exchange regulations increasingly required JVs to stipulate an export target in order to balance their foreign-exchange accounts. In the 1980s, most JVs in China were asked to set an export target as a percentage of total output which was gradually increased to a fairly high level over the first three years of operations. An average target of 70 per cent by the end of the third year of operation was typical.

Table 5.13
Project's return on investment with expectation

Response	Percentage of the respondents (%)
Return on investment has reached expectation	25
Return on investment has not reached expectation	40
Too early to comment	32
Information withheld on confidential grounds	3
	100

As discussed earlier, many JVs had to use hard currency to import raw materials and components to meet their production demands, as well as to repatriate capital and profits, while the Chinese currency (Renminbi) is non-convertible. Although it was stipulated in the Chinese JV regulations that, in a few cases (most in the cases of import-substitution JVs), those with a foreign-exchange imbalance could receive help from the Chinese government, no specific guarantee was provided. Getting permission to convert Renminbi into hard currency was exceedingly difficult in practice. So, it was crucial for JVs and FIEs to export their products or other related semi-finished products to their home countries or other markets in order to balance their hard-currency accounts, otherwise, they would run at foreign exchange deficits. This further highlights the conflicting objectives of each partner: the main objective of the foreign partner was to gain access to the Chinese market, while the Chinese partner emphasised exports. For foreign investors, it is significant to evaluate whether FDI is export-generating or whether it curtails their exports from home or other bases. That is, whether FDI is a complement to or a substitute for exports becomes a matter of concern.

With this in mind, the respondent firms were asked: 'Since the JV started operation in China, how do you evaluate your exports to China?' **Table 5.14** shows that 40 per cent of the respondents increased their exports to China, thus confirming that the establishment of an overseas production subsidiary results in a higher company profile, the consequence being an increased volume of purchasing from the overseas subsidiary and also from the parent company. This has been noted by Newbould, Buckley and Thurwell.[19] Another 30 per cent of the surveyed firms maintained the value of their exports to China. Only in 30 per cent cases had exports declined because the establishment of JVs in China was merely a substitute for home-based production.

Table 5.14
Exports to China after setting up of JVs

Response	Percentage of sample firms (%)
Exports to China have increased	40
Exports to China have remained the same	30
Exports to China have decreased	28
Information withheld	2
	100

We further asked about the firms' own perception of overall success in China. Our survey showed that 47.6 per cent of the respondents considered they had either met or exceeded their objectives.

In terms of profitability and exports following the establishment of the JVs, the sample firms were asked to state 'On balance, how do you rate the performance of your joint venture activities in China to date?' The responses are shown in **Table 5.15**.

Table 5.15
Overall level of success of JV in China

Responses	Percentage of respondents (%)
Totally successful	4.7
Very successful	23.8
Averagely successful	52.4
Not successful	19.0

Our survey broadly confirmed those findings of both foreign and Chinese institutions: despite all the difficulties and costs that pioneering investors encountered, most FIEs had yielded satisfactory results. An official Chinese survey of 4,000 FIEs in operation in 1987 shows that 37.3 per cent of FIEs had exceeded their original expectations, 48.2 per cent had 'met their objectives', and only 14.5 per cent were facing serious difficulties in realising their original plans.[20] A large number of FIEs increased their registered capital, shares or investment in other FIEs. Another survey of 10,000 FIEs in operation conducted in 1990 revealed that 85 per cent of FIEs performed satisfactory. The success rate of FIEs in Shanghai was as high as 98 per cent.[21] Studies conducted by Western institutions reached similar conclusions. A.T.Kearney, Inc., a Chicago-based international management consulting firm, found in a 1987 survey that most foreign companies investing in China were satisfied with their investment results. When asked to assess their own results against corporate criteria for targeted returns on investment, 28 per cent of the executives interviewed said they greatly exceeded their targets, 22 per cent exceeded their targets, and 44 per cent met their targets. In addition, 90 per cent of the chief executives indicated that they would still have invested in China with their present knowledge.[22] One survey conducted by MOFERT for the period between 1991 and 1993 revealed that more than 90 per cent FIEs ended up producing deficits and started to produce profits since 1991. Moreover, FIEs performance was significantly related with their investing areas, investing forms, investment scale, sales direction and management capacity. Those FIEs investing in priority areas such as export-oriented, high-technology or import-substitution industries, which have been highly encouraged and supported by the Chinese government, were normally performing more successfully than others. Export-oriented FIEs and those having a large investment scale and advanced technologies normally enjoyed more success and large profits.[23] The success of FIEs was also evident by the fact that 92 per cent of those 544 FIEs in operation made a profit totalling RMB0.32 billion with revenue RBM0.13 billion in 1992.[24]

All these findings strongly suggest that firms followed a multiple - rather than single - objective strategy. Foreign firms, on the whole, were prepared to accept a lower rate of profit in order to pursue their global investment strategy in China aimed at long-term prospects of enlarged markets. Our survey together with others showed that lower profitability in China than on similar home-based investments did not imply that firms were dissatisfied with the rate of return on capital invested in the JVs, as the firms' projected financial results were supported by other targets: in at least 67 per cent of the 120 respondents in this study reported that the establishment of the JV led to an increase in or maintenance of their export levels to China.

Investing in China - the political risk Before 1989, most foreign investors regarded the political situation in China as stable, and awarded it a relatively high score of satisfaction. However, the 1989 'Tiananmen Square Events' had an adverse impact on foreign investors, as far as perceptions of political stability were concerned. However, the adverse effect of the Tiananmen Square episode appeared to last for only a short period, as the total amount of utilised FDI from the beginning of 1989 to July 1991 was US$8.5 billion, 76 per cent of the total FDI during 1979-88.[25]

In order to test foreign investor's perceptions of China's political stability after the 'Tiananmen Square' in June 1989, the respondents were, therefore, asked to select according to the question: 'Which factor is the prime determinants in your decision-making concerning direct investment in China?' It shows that only 29 per cent of the surveyed firms thought that political variables played the most important role in their investment decision-making in China, while the remaining 71 per cent considered that economic factors (such as local market potential, and expected investment return) constituted the prime determinant in their decision-making concerning direct investment in the Chinese market. So as far as political and economic factors are concerned, we found that economic variables generally appeared to be more significant and consistent determinants of FDI than political variable in China. This finding suggested that foreign investors were confident about China's political stability, but more confident about China's economic situation.

The respondent firms were then asked 'How do you evaluate current and future risk in China and Hungary?' **Table 5.16** reveals that 33.3 per cent of the surveyed firms reported that it was 'hard to predict' China's current and future political risk, 52.4 per cent thought there were 'some risks' in China for the current and future foreign investment, while 9.5 per cent and 4.7 per cent of 21 firms said respectively 'very risky' and 'no risk' investing in China. Some 17 per cent of the respondents reported that it was 'hard to predict' current and future political risk in Hungary, 33 per cent stated no risk at all, and 50 per cent thought there were 'some political risk' in Hungary for the current and future foreign investment.

Problems encountered by foreign firms operating in China Our survey found that the most acute problems faced by foreign firms in operating in China were constant changes of government policy and the increasing threat of labour disputes over pay and living conditions.

Table 5.16
Comparison of political risk investing in China and Hungary
(Percentage of the surveyed firms)

	Very risky	Some risk	Hard to predict	No risk
Hungary	--	33	17	50
China	9.5	53	33	4.7

The frequent criticism of foreign firms could be listed as follows: an erosion in the favourable treatment of foreign investors; steep rises in the costs of business due both to inflation and arbitrary increases in business charges (The problem of 'hidden costs' of doing business in China was a great concern for foreign investors. Labour costs which included insurance, accommodation, virtually mandatory bonuses and other charges were much higher than anticipated. Inflation was also darkening the mood among investors); labour disputes; policies that contradict international business practices, such as retrospective charges for infrastructure facilities; an unresponsive legal system for dispute settlement; the rapacious levying of fees and charges by local officials; and inadequate infrastructure facilities.

Our survey suggests that potential investors should be aware of the following additional operational problems while considering committing investment in China. These include: the parlous state of much of the country's infrastructure; difficulties of arranging distribution and supply due to a crumbling transport system; bureaucratic strictures that complicate personnel management; opaque rules and regulations; and an unreliable legal system whose dispute-settling mechanisms are loaded heavily against the foreign partners.

Our survey generally supports the following claims: the shortages of energy, raw materials, and components has often forced many FIEs to purchase them at high prices or import to meet their production demands; the low quality and unexpected high cost of labour, the ambiguous and vague laws and regulations, as well as the imperfect financial markets and the shortage of foreign exchange were most serious constraints on the operations of FIEs.

Changes of macroeconomic environment for JVs in China Exchange-rate stability, political stability and an efficient labour force were the key factors for Hong Kong, Singapore, Korea and Taiwan in attracting a substantial amount of FDI in the 1970s and 1980s. Although China's investment environment has improved substantially since the early 1980s, it is not yet up to considerable standards required by foreign investors. **Table 5.17** shows the

Table 5.17
Foreign investors' opinions concerning changes in China over 1990-92

Responses	Improved		Unchanged		Worsened	
	No. of firms	% of the respondents	No. of firms	% of the respondents	No. of firms	% of the respondents
Market growth potential	104	81.0	17	14.0	6	5.0
Political stability	74	61.9	34	28.6	11	9.5
Local economic growth	74	61.9	28	23.8	17	14.3
Profit remittance policies	40	33.3	57	47.6	23	19.1
Import restriction	40	33.3	51	42.9	28	23.8
Local finance possibilities	40	33.3	40	33.3	40	33.3
Profit expectation	51	42.8	34	28.6	34	28.6
Labour costs	-	-	57	47.6	63	52.4
Prices of raw materials	6	4.8	23	19.0	91	76.0

results of foreign investors' view of how macroeconomic and political conditions had changed between 1990-92 in China.

Future investment climate and investment plans in China   Over the past 17 years, China appeared to have overestimated the attraction of preferential tax treatment for foreign investors. The inflow of foreign capital, however, highly depends on the prospects of 'soft' investment environment. Foreign investors regard the host country's growth potential, the availability of infrastructure facilities and political stability as much more important in their investment decisions than tax concessions.

In order to further test the respondents' evaluation of the investment environment in China in the next five years from 1992-97, they were asked to indicate 'Over the next five years, how do you evaluate the investment climate in China?' Our survey showed that 66.7 per cent of the 120 firms in the survey considered that the investment climate in China over the next five years would become more attractive, while only 9.5 per cent and 14.3 per cent respectively stated it would worsen and remain the same. Some firms indicated that 'if you have a short-term perspective, you will become very hesitant'; but 'we are very optimistic about the liberalisation trend. Phases of uncertainty, even a leadership change, will not affect the move towards market opening'. This findings reveals that foreign investors felt confidence about investment climate in China over the next five years.

The respondents were further asked 'Over the next three years, how about your plans concerning investing in China'. Our survey revealed that a majority of the firms (52.4 per cent) had plans for further investment expansion in China, while 23.8 per cent had decided against investing or planned to decrease their pledged investment. Further expansion would depend on China's transformation process, economic growth and political stability (as 23.8 per cent of the surveyed firms stated).

Conclusion and implications

Despite the constraints imposed upon such survey by low respondent and data deficiencies, it has been possible to derive substantial conclusions from this chapter.

The survey revealed that former knowledge of and business relations of partners provided a reference of decisive significance for the establishment of JVs. The majority of successful JVs had 'grown out' of already existing business relations. It also revealed that foreign firms which took a step-by-step approach including intermediate stages, such as exporting/importing, licensing, industrial cooperation, were more successful than those which followed a more direct route.

Local partners were motivated by additional capital for modernisation, restructuring, survival and creation of export capacities; the acquisition of advanced technology; saving hard-currency outlay by import substitution, creation of new, well-paid jobs; favourable fiscal and tax treatment; and improvement of technical, managerial, organisational and marketing knowledge.

The potential domestic markets, advanced economic reforms, and other comparative advantages made Hungary and China as preferred investment locations for foreign capital. Foreign partners were motivated by capturing of emerging markets in Hungary and China, taking advantage of less strict environmental regulations and competitive labour costs, and establishing possible bridge-heads towards other Eastern European and Pacific Asian countries (but the difficulties and/or impossibilities to make supplies to these markets is regarded a negative trait).

In their perception of advantages associated with JVs as a form, foreign firms listed most frequently the sharing of risk and better local knowledge of the domestic partner. With regard to JVs' management and decision-making, foreign firms did not hesitate to spell out in detail the rights and responsibilities of the respective partners within JVs. It seemed that this gave rise to no practical problems, as the majority partners always involved the other in all important decisions, if for no other reason than sharing risks. The division of managerial responsibilities between partners was complementary rather than competitive: the foreign partner generally determined quality and technical standards, the local partner's influence was felt mostly in areas where his knowledge of local market conditions could benefit the JVs, such as recruitment of staff and purchasing of raw materials in the local market, joint managerial control was typical centred on domestic and international marketing of the JV's products. At the same time, Western partners realised that there were some differences between local partner and foreign side in some aspects of JV's management, especially considered slow decision-making process and lack of flexibility to adjust short-term goals to changed market as greatly cumbersome.

The identification by sample firms of several performance objectives (profitability, growth and exports) demonstrated that foreign investors in Hungary and China followed a multiple - rather than single - objective strategy. The acceptance of lower profitability in Hungary and China than similar home-based investment was compensated by the increase in exports to and enlarged markets in both Hungary and China.

Our survey also suggested that foreign investment in Hungary and China resulted in closer integration between foreign firms and the domestic economy: unless they were unavailable or below world market quality standards, JVs inputs were mainly purchased locally, while outputs were oriented principally towards the domestic markets. Local partners were satisfied with improved balance and profits; increased exports and labour productivity; and acquisition of new technologies and know-how.

A firm's success depended on the choice and quality of the JV product. Foreign investors normally based their market decisions through pre-investment study of the host country's market structure, and directed their product towards the top end of the local markets.

Conflicting interests and confrontations because of different strategic goals resulted in some foreign withdrawals from the local markets. Uncertain economic prospects, the slowness of privatisation, inflation and devaluation, and bureaucratic administration, underdeveloped infrastructure, inconvertibility of local currency jeopardized potential foreign investment in both countries.

This survey also highlighted the problems at the negotiation and operation stages of JV agreements. Difficult and time-consumed negotiation was reported as a rather serious problem by foreign partners, resulting in 100 per cent ownership acquisition in some cases. The major problems during operation could be divided into fields, such as conflicting goals, human resources management, marketing, 'hard' and 'soft' investment climate, and financial constraints.

This chapter strongly supports Chapter 4 that the market size, political stability, and other factors can explain why Hungary and China have attracted a lion's share of foreign direct investment within the post-socialist countries, but the clear importance of market size signals a long-term disadvantage for that the relatively small economies of Eastern Europe (including Hungary) in attracting foreign capital. So, we may partly answer the question - why China is more successful than Hungary in terms of accumulated stock of FDI:

(1) Apart from the political instability in 1986-87 and 1989, China offered more stable political situation than many Eastern European countries. Moreover, political upheaval in South-east Asia may cause a reassessment of regional investment risks which favours China.

(2) China total volume of imports and exports is projected to rise to amount US$400 billion by the year 2000, and aggregate imports between 1995-2000 are estimated at US$1,000 billion. Total GNP will be the same as America's but smaller than that of the 13-member European Community,[26] though its GNP per capita will only amount to about 20 per cent that of America and 13 per cent of Japan by 2025.[27] The 1.2 billion consumer market will motivate more and more foreign investors to establish production facilities in China in order to get better access to this huge potential market for growth of sales, market share and profits.

(3) China's economy grew on average by 9-10 per cent during 1979-94, much more favourable than the OECD average growth rate by 2.8 per cent during 1977-92 and Hungary's 0.8 per cent over 1979-92. Even though the potential political shake-ups will slow down China's current 9 per cent growth to 6 per cent by the late 1990s, China will continue to be one of the major forces of world economic growth in the future.[28]

(4) The supply of cheap labour in China offers foreign investors considerable incentives to establish JVs in China. The bigger wage differentials between developed and also many developing countries and China have provided some cost advantages to locating production plants inside China. This has offered investors from Hong Kong/Macao, and Taiwan opportunities to transfer their labour-intensive production processes to mainland China so as to move further up the product cycle into more sophisticated production as well as to bypass import quotas by selling in the Chinese market. Furthermore, China's Eastern Coastal cities, with their relatively good industrial and commercial infrastructures, cheap but well trained labour, essential source of raw materials, and easy geographic access, also offered a potential processing base which could substitute for those in other East Asian countries/regions such as Hong Kong, Singapore, Malaysia, and

Taiwan, where wages are rapidly rising.

(5) Our survey suggest that foreign investment in China are on the whole slightly less profitable than home-based investments, but more or as profitable as investments in other developing countries. At least two thirds of foreign invested enterprises exceeded their original expectation or met their strategic objectives. The likely rate of return on investment in China is, therefore, regarded as higher than, or as equal to, that available elsewhere.

Notes

1.Rollo, J.M.C. et al., (1990), *The New Eastern Europe: Western Responses,* Pinter, London, pp.107-8.

2.*Business Eastern Europe,* 5 February 1990, p.43.

3.Total percentage is larger than 100 duc to multiple responses.

4.The percentage of sample firms is larger than 100 due to multiple responses.

5.Business International & Creditanstalt (1992), *1992 East European Investment Survey,* October 1992, Vienna, p.3.

6.Underdeveloped business infrastructure in Hungary and the other Eastern Europe suggests that enormous investment opportunities exists in the field of infrastructure. Foreign investors has been active in this sector, and is likely to make a growing contribution in shaping the future business environment.

7.*Business Eastern Europe,* 8 July 1991, p.212.

8.General Electric bought its share in Tungsram for US$150 million and invested US$300 million into reconstruction.

9.Business International & Creditanstalt (1992), *1992 East European Investment Survey,* October, Vienna, p.3.

10.It was exacerbated by the legacy of a centralised system of material supplies and the monopoly of state-owned enterprises, which often operated obsolete production facilities. Linked to this problem is the absence of incentives for subcontractors to supply parts according to internationally recognised quality standards. Moreover, the government encouraged FIEs to subcontract components and parts to local firms, rather than import. So some foreign investors have to invest in the JVs' supply lines and build up vertically-integrated production networks.

11.Chen, Jinghan (1993), 'The Environment for Foreign Direct Investment and the Characteristics of Joint Ventures in China', *Development Policy Review*, Vol.11, No.2, p.171.

12.Chen, Jinghan (1993), op.cit., p.177.

13.Short-term profit maximisation might be the primary motive of small- and medium-size foreign firms, normally from Hong Kong, which concentrated on small-scale labour-intensive industries.

14.*People's Daily (Overseas Edition)*, 28 March 1994, p.1.

15.Kelly, M. W.(1981), *Foreign Investment Evaluation Practice of U. S. Multinational Corporations*, UMI Research Press, Ann Arbor.

16.OECD (1990), *Investing In Post-Socialist Countries*, Paris: OECD Publication, pp.23-24.

17.Artisien, Patrick (1985), *Joint Ventures in Yugoslav Industry*, Gower Publishing Co. Ltd, Hants, pp.99-100.

18.Total greater than sample total of 120 because of multiple responses.

19.Newbould, G. D., Buckley, P. J. and Thurwell, J. (1978), *Going International: The Experience of Smaller Companies Overseas*, Associated Business Press, London, pp.26-29.

20.Zhang Haoruo's Closing Speech at the Central Committee's Foreign Investment Meeting in October 1987.

21.*People's Daily*, 21 November 1990.

22.A.T.Kearney (1987), *Manufacturing Equity Joint Ventures in China*, A.T. Kearney, Chicago.

23.*People's Daily*, 10 February 1993.

24.Ibid., 30 October 1993.

25.*People's Daily*, 19 September 1991.

26. Many economists predict that China will exceed America in total GNP by 2010, not as late as 2025 as most of those forecasts are based on straight-line projections of growth at 8-9 per cent a year. But with China's huge, unwieldy bureaucracy, weak constitutions, poor infrastructure, lower education levels and huge non-mechanised agricultural sector, growth of 5-6 per cent a year over the next 30 years will be quite an achievement. See 'World Politic and Current Affairs', *The Economist*, 12-19 September 1993, pp.15-21.

27. *The Economist*, 12-19 September 1993, p.15.

28. *People's Daily*, 17 November 1993, p.5.

6 Foreign capital and economic development in Hungary and China

Any assessment of the impact of foreign capital inflows needs to investigate their contribution to local economies in terms of capital provision, output and productivity, employment, the balance of trade, the transfer of technology, training and management, as well as their impact on the market structure in the host country. This chapter, therefore, analyses FDI's contributions to economic development and transformation in Hungary and China during 1978-92, based on review of literature, secondary data and results of my personal visits to Hungary and China.

Theoretical evaluation of the impact of FDI

In the period following World War II, foreign investment was frequently accused of having adverse effects on growth resulting in a net capital drain from LDCs, a deterioration in the balance of payments, and a slowdown in economic growth.[1] It was also criticised for introducing inappropriate products or production technology in LDCs and imposing unreasonable prices and conditions on technology transfer;[2] creating an enclave-type growth, with few linkages backward or forward to the local economy.[3] Critics drew attention to the import of raw materials, parts, components, and sub-assemblies. They also questioned the extent of technology transfer on the grounds that it was usually the production of more standardised products which was transferred abroad, and suggested that a large part of the overseas production was undertaken simply as a means to circumvent trade barriers.[4] It was argued foreign investment induced host governments to relax their tax efforts, increase their consumption expenditure, liberalize imports, and crowd out domestic investment, and caused domestic savings to fall.[5]

'After two decades of sometimes emotionally loaded discussions and controversial host country policies towards FDI, its contribution to growth, employment, structural changes, technological modernisation, exports and general economic performance has been widely acknowledged. The overwhelmingly positive attitude of a number of national economies vis-a-vis FDI is a convincing proof of the fundamental changes taken place in the assessment of this vital factor of production.'[6] Experience throughout the world since the 1970s shows that foreign investment can play an important positive role in any country's economy. FDI has been seen as an important resource to supplement local financial sources and increase output, employment and exports by bridging the savings-investment gap, giving LDCs access to productive capacity technologies and management resources, and contributing to local economic growth and development[7] through the supply of capital, technology and management with high levels of productivity, efficiency and profitability. The foreign exchange earned and the taxes derived from foreign investment can play an important part in increasing domestic savings and reducing a country's debt burden.

The effects of FDI on the receiving countries can be classified as economic, social and political. While the political and social aspects of FDI are no doubt very important, such an analysis lies outside the scope of this study. The economic consequences of FDI can be divided into macro and micro components. Macro-effects can further be divided into primary and secondary linkages. Primary linkages are associated with growth, output, employment, balance of payments, productivity, technological know-how, and training of labour and management. Secondary linkages are essentially inter-industry linkages and are related to the way in which FDI integrates or not with the local economy, through, for example, local markets, to locally produced materials and components, as well as by attracting new industries. The micro-influences of FDI are related to structural changes in economic and industrial organisation - the creation of a more competitive environment or conversely with the worsening of monopolistic and/or oligopolistic elements in the host economy.

Provision of capital

Since the 1970s, FDI has been seen as a source of funds which might bridge the gap in the host economies between desired investment and indigenous resources by supplementing domestic savings and relieving foreign exchange shortages. Though MNCs have increasingly generated a large proportion of their capital requirement locally, they have indirectly mobilised local savings by offering attractive investment opportunities in domestic capital markets.

However, these potential benefits provided by MNCs may be reduced by various offsetting influences: the actual inflow of capital is often fairly small, with most finance coming from reinvested profits and local savings; and MNCs borrow locally and divert domestic savings from other productive uses. In fact the contribution of foreign capital to world-wide capital formation has been small (Petrochilos, 1989, pp.28-29).

Effects on output and economic growth

One of the most significant effects of FDI is on the output and, consequently, on the growth of host nations. The argument is more forceful in the case of LDCs, where inward investment is looked upon as a means of fostering economic development by either increasing the capital stock of the host nation following FDI, or by providing for the more efficient utilisation of existing resources in cases where foreign investors take-over domestic firms.

The extent to which FDI can affect the level and composition of national output and its growth can be gauged by reference to alternative assumptions regarding macro economic policy pursued by the host nation. If the host government could always achieve full employment of resources then inward investment would not affect the size of the national product, compared with any alternative pattern of resource utilisation. But if it is likely that inward investment absorbs resources which would otherwise have remained unemployed, then the net output generated by FDI represents an increase in real output for the host nation.[8] Similarly, if inward investment could improve the efficiency of domestic resources, either by shifting them from less efficient to more productive sectors of the economy or by raising their existing sectoral productivity, then again domestic output would grow. This suggests that FDI can exert a pronounced influence where it is possible to absorb surplus resources and/or improve their efficiency through alternative allocations.

Effects on employment

Capital means investment and investment often means employment. All nations are seeking new investment and want to create more jobs. Any direct relationship between investment and employment depends on the assumption of 'fixed' technical coefficients of production that link investment with enhanced possibilities for additional labour absorption. However, the assumption of fixed technical coefficients overlooks the importance of technical progress. If technical coefficients are 'fixed', then is possible for investment and employment to be positively related to one another. However, by contrast, if investment implies a change in the coefficients, investment and employment may also vary in opposite directions, or investment may tend to remain constant while employment falls.[9] In the face of 'varying' technical coefficients, investment can be inversely related to employment.[10]

It can be argued that FDI does not simply substitute new employment opportunities for old ones, but helps to create new employment. However, the available evidence suggests that the effect of FDI on employment is low. Its effects depend on the specific conditions of host countries, the sectoral location of investment and the types of activities undertaken, and reflect not only the degree of substitutability between new and old employment opportunities and possible inter-industry linkages, but also the capital/labour ratio associated with FDI.[11] The impact of FDI on employment creation in LDCs has been disappointing. Yet, by virtue of their very existence in host nations, MNCs clearly make some contribution to increasing the aggregate level of employment.

Both theory and empirical evidence suggest that the aggregate employment effects of FDI are minor, although there may be larger sectoral or regional impacts. It is very difficult to establish with any accuracy the probable net effect of foreign investment on employment since the impact of FDI on local employment is a complex matter and relevant information is often not available.

The balance-of-payments effects of FDI

Foreign exchange is regarded by the 'double-gap' (savings and foreign exchange) theory[12] as a scarce resource and a constraint affecting growth in just the same way that a deficiency of savings does. Increased foreign aid, import substitution policies and greater FDI have all been seen as means by which the foreign exchange bottleneck in LDCs could be relieved.

The evaluation of the effects of FDI on the balance of payments of the host country takes the form of examining the physical and financial aspects of the operations of foreign firms in that country. Since such effects are both direct and indirect, one must examine the impact of the foreign firms' operations in terms of: (a) their absorption of the host country's factor inputs in the production process; (b) the proportions of their output sold in the host country's market and abroad and; (c) the distribution of the value of their output between the host economy's factor inputs, the host government in the form of tax revenue and their retained share.

Any initial capital inflow will be followed by 'the continuing outflow of dividends, royalties, and interest and administrative charges to the parent company. Another important issue is that of transfer pricing, which in turn is related to the role of tax havens and exchange speculation'.[13] The gains and losses extend much further than this. While this aspect of FDI is very important and complicated, this thesis will only focus on its impact on foreign trade in the host countries.

'The impact of foreign investment on levels of imports and exports is also significant, both in relation to the balance of payments and to economic growth' (Hood and Young, 1979, pp.179). These effects on the balance of payments can be classified into the broad categories of the export effect, the import substitution effect, the import effect and the remissions effect (Hood and Young, 1979, p.19). The first two lead to an improvement in the balance of payments, while the remaining two contribute to an overall deterioration. To obtain the net effect it is also necessary to take account of the raw materials and intermediate inputs which MNCs may import. Alternative import-substituting types of FDI may have positive balance of payments effects in releasing valuable foreign exchange, but the net impact depends on the import propensity of MNCs in the host country. The integration of operation of the JVs with indigenous economic activity also generates effects going far beyond the growth of the host country's economic potential and the direct benefits of import substitution. Evidence shows that FIEs are more able to sell in international markets than local firms, as MNCs are more familiar with marketing techniques in developed countries as compared with their local counterparts.

The total impact of the operations of foreign firms on the balance of payments of the host country is, therefore, the sum of the individual effects, which can only be established on empirical grounds for a specific country. The empirical evidence seems to indicate that the effects of inward investment on the balance of payments of developed nations are likely to be beneficial, not only because of import substitution (or export promotion) and lower import content, but also because of the ability of such host countries to keep for themselves a large share of the value of the output of MNCs.[14] On the other hand, the balance of payments of developing countries seem to benefit from FDI specifically in extractive industries, though by no means in all such investments, rather than in manufacturing, mainly because of the high import content of such investment and the mechanism of transfer pricing of MNCs. The high import content of the output of MNCs is explained not only by the nature of such firms, but also because of the unavailability of locally produced goods, materials, components, the uncompetitiveness of local prices and inferior quality in developing countries (Reuber, G. et al, 1973, p.163).

Vernon (1971) has tried to evaluate the impact of US FDI on the balance of payments of developing countries in the early 1960s and concluded that in the free choice model[15] FDI generated positive contributions to the balance of payments in Latin American countries and a slightly larger positive contribution in other developing countries. Under the defensive investment model, the effects on the balance of payments were negative in Latin America, implying a loss of foreign exchange for the host countries, and positive in other developing countries, representing a gain in foreign exchange. Hall and Streeten (1977) attempted to assess 159 FIEs in 6 developing countries in terms of overall balance of payments effects, and found that for all countries except Kenya the net impact was negative. Very few individual firms recorded positive balance of payments effects. 'On the whole the sample foreign firms do seem to be taking out more than they are putting in during the period studied'.[16] Nevertheless, these estimates cannot be accepted as conclusive or complete because of the different assumptions on which they are based.

Theoretically, a country should be able to borrow abroad for as long as the rate of growth of its foreign-exchange receipts equals or exceeds the average interest rate on its external debt. This condition should be met if the borrowed funds are invested in projects which promote the growth of output and exports, thereby strengthening the current-account balance. However, if a country simply borrows to sustain consumption and/or to postpone adjustment to changed external circumstances, its debt burden will increase, interest payments will rise and the current account will deteriorate.[17]

The effects of FDI on productivity

As compared with domestic firms, foreign subsidiaries with much higher capital intensity seem to generate a higher net output per head. In the case where the inward investment is export promoting, the products of the subsidiary are destined for the large world markets. The marketing policies and organisation of the parent company, as well as the size of the market will allow the installation of plants designed to achieve full economies of scale. Under these circumstances, it is likely that productivity will rise and unit costs will be reduced. On the other hand, where the FDI is import substituting, the size of the local market may be too small to permit the installation of the optimum size plant to capture the full economies of scale. Productive efficiency, therefore may not be attained in this case.

Productivity, however, is likely to be affected by the full utilisation of the firm's resources, the quality of existing manpower, and the climate of industrial relations.[18] It seems that foreign subsidiaries in the UK economy have managed to attain higher productivity than local firms (Steuer, M. et al, 1973, pp.80-1). However, one must treat these results cautiously because of the difficulty of comparability between foreign subsidiaries and local firms. 'Changes in productivity are notoriously difficult to measure and compare even under the best circumstances; and measuring the effects of FDI on productivity has proven more difficult still' (Reuber, G. et al, 1973, p.177). If this is the case with countries where the relevant information is available, the problem of trying to evaluate the impact of FDI on productivity in developing countries may become almost impossible because of a lack of reliable data.

FDI and technology

The interaction between FDI and technology is considered to be of paramount importance both for the investing and host countries. The particular issue in this respect is how foreign technology is transferred to and absorbed by the host country and how it affects the local economy.

By adopting established technologies, host countries can by-pass the risky invention and innovation stages and thereby make a significant leap forward. The introduction of new technology could be cost-saving, reducing the cost of inputs necessary to obtain a given amount of output. But the advantages to be gained by the host country will depend upon the suitability of the technology and associated products transferred. The choice of techniques used in various places and at different times depends essentially on the prices prevailing, particularly factor prices. Generally, the emphasis of the R & D effort in developed countries has been to devise labour-saving techniques; countries with surplus labour will have an incentive to choose technologies that make use of more unskilled labour, which would be appropriate to their environments. However, the problem of choosing the appropriate technology is not an easy one.

The transfer of knowledge is a crucial element of the FDI process and can confer advantages to both the developers and users of such a technology. This can take the form of selling, licensing or exploiting it directly in production. However, whether or not the transferred technology is adapted to local condition is ultimately connected with the ability of the host economy to absorb the new technical knowledge. A narrow range of industrial capability, a necessarily small scale of production for domestic markets, and a dearth of the technical and managerial skills necessary to adapt and absorb modern techniques impose additional obstacles to technological transplantation. The effect of these obstacles has been to increase manufacturing costs in LDCs above those in advanced ones.[19]

FDI and training/management

Another main role of FDI is to transplant superior production technology through the training of labour and management, and the introduction of marketing skills, from advanced industrial countries to LDCs. Foreign investors, much as they dislike to spend money on the training of locals, realise that such expenditures may be crucial to the success of their investment. While it is true that foreign affiliates can rely on expatriate personnel with most MNCs rotating and training promising young personnel from the headquarters in various affiliates around the world, they nevertheless have a strong incentive to employ more local employees in their labour force and management, as soon as practically feasible. This is due partly to cost considerations, as the remuneration of an expatriate is higher than that of a national, once the latter has been trained appropriately, and partly to political pressures and local regulations in the host country prioritising the employment of indigenous labour.

The training of local manpower is firstly undertaken within the firm and is of a technical nature, involving tuition at all levels of local employees in technical and engineering aspects as well as corporate systems of quality control and marketing. To the extent that the foreign subsidiary has strong interindustry linkages with other firms in the host country, the process of training may be extended to include the subsidiary's suppliers, as a way of guaranteeing a reliable flow of components. The final stage of local manpower training involves distributors and dealers, since the successful launching of the subsidiary products requires an effective distribution network. Whether the subsidiary is using an existing distribution network or decides to create an independent one, there is still a need to train distributors and dealers. The importance of after sales servicing facilities can be vital for the success of the entire JV, since it helps to build up and consolidate brand loyalty.[20]

FDI has a gradual spill-over effect on a given industry and related ones in the host country through the training of workers, engineers, and managers, and will make possible the establishment of competitive firms with local capital, ultimately improving the production function of an entire industry and making it more competitive in international markets. When this process is completed, it can be said that the new technology has been effectively transferred and established in the host country.

The provision of managerial skills may also produce important benefits for the host country: local personnel who are trained to occupy managerial, financial and technical posts in the MNC's affiliate may later leave the firm and help to stimulate indigenous entrepreneurship. Similarly there may be beneficial demonstration effects on local suppliers and competitors. On the other hand, there would be few positive results if management and highly skilled jobs in MNCs were mostly reserved for expatriate personnel; and adverse effects if local producers were choked off by the competition of foreign-owned subsidiaries. It has also been argued that the gains from training local personnel may not produce external benefits in LDCs, since these practices may have little relevance to the normal methods of business operation. The practices of large, complex MNCs may not be appropriate for small indigenous companies manufacturing fairly basic products and perhaps relying heavily on personal contacts. Moreover, the macroeconomic influences occurring from training of local manpower and the improved management skills are difficult to quantify; and the influences of FDI in widening the skills and capabilities of the local labour force may be rather limited (Reuber G.L.

et al, 1973, p.203).

Conclusion

Except the above impacts, MNCs operate within oligopolistic market structures and possess greater economic power than indigenous competitors. FDI is likely to affect the structure of the industries it is directed to, and may be responsible for improving the competitive forces or conversely for worsening monopolistic or oligopolistic elements in the host economy.[21] FDI can provide a significant widening of competition in the host market. Only MNCs can compete effectively with local oligopolist and break the latter's stranglehold on the domestic market. Therefore, FDI can improve the allocation of resources in the host country and increase their productivity by reducing monopolistic/oligopolistic distortions.[22]

This section has assessed the theoretical literature on a wide variety of potential gains and losses associated with foreign investment in host countries, with particular a focus on the impact of MNCs on LDCs. Many of the issues are highly controversial and admit to varying interpretation. No clear-cut conclusion could be reached on the issue of whether or not FDI brings positive net benefits to host states. There are costs as well as benefits associated with inward direct investment. The limited empirical work suggests that the overall impact is usually positive on national income, jobs and government revenues. Major doubts have been raised about the impact of FDI on the balance of payments, derived particularly from the payment of royalties, interest charges and dividends and from the uncertain effects of transfer pricing. The key feature of direct investment would seem to be that it provides the recipient nation with a 'package' of knowledge, capital and entrepreneurship which may make a positive contribution to economic growth and development in host countries.

The impact of foreign investment on the Hungarian economy

The Hungarian government has regarded inward direct investment as a means of fostering economic development by increasing the country's capital stock, or through a more efficient utilisation of existing resources in cases where foreign investors take-over domestic firms. Foreign capital, it is argued, has contributed in a considerable measure to an accelerating expansion of the value-generating process and a dynamic growth in trade. It is also frequently alleged that foreign firms in Hungary earn 'excessively high' or above average profits, as foreign investors have introduced superior technology and efficiency into a highly protected environment.[23] FDI's contribution to capital

196

formation and the balance of payments is viewed as having been less important than its role in economic development and structural transformation. In the case of capital formation in Hungary, net FDI inflows have rarely represented a significant proportion of gross domestic capital formation. However, the issue of technology transfer is becoming more important in the context of the current transformation process.

Provision of capital

The relative importance of FDI to Hungary may first of all be assessed by examining its contribution to domestic capital formation. Foreign capital primarily provided a very powerful supplement to limited domestic capital supplies, and met the enormous need for catching up and structural change.

Total foreign investment in Hungary was estimated at US$3.2 billion at the end of 1991, US$5.9 billion by the end of 1992, and US$6.1 billion by the end of 1993. The growth rate of foreign inward capital (100 per cent in 1989 and 1990; 50-70 per cent in 1991 and 1992) exceeded both that of GDP and of foreign trade.

In terms of capital formation, the contribution of FDI remains very limited, especially in cases of projects where the foreign partner only finances the remuneration of the work-force in the period prior to the initial start of production, or where financing comes from local financial institutions or the indigenous partner. FDI as a capital supplement, however, was especially important because the foreign capital was increasingly provided in hard currency, which compensated for the deteriorating trade balance, due to import liberalisation and FDI in kind. According to the National Bank of Hungary, a total of FDI in 1990 of US$800 million consisted of US$340-360 million in cash and US$440-460 million in kind. In the first ten months of 1991 there was US$1,270 million of foreign investment, of which US$1,070 million was in cash and US$200 million in kind. The reduction of contributions in kind within total FDI and the increase of cash contributions indicates a significant qualitative change. Though FDI flows were only a tiny fraction of gross domestic investment and remained relatively insignificant, its importance will grow in the future as Hungary continues to attract foreign capital.

Foreign investment in Hungary was also seen as particularly important in the context of privatisation. The Hungarian government recognised that the purchasing power of the population and its willingness to become shareholders was rather limited, and domestic savings could cover only a small part of the value of assets to be privatised (Hunya, 1992, p.507). Moreover, a number of factors reduced the potential demand for buying state property: (1) although the nominal value of indigenous savings increased from Ft217 billion in 1980 to Ft870 billion in 1992, their real value actually dropped from Ft217 billion to Ft194 billion, and the total sum of private savings did not even reach 10 per cent of the state property then on the books; (2) for most people, the savings were burdened by sizable credit sums, so a significant part of private savings was not intended for investment; (3) the embryonic state of the money market, as well as the high risk of investment, also made the purchase of property relatively inaccessible for most people, or discouraged them from investing in state property shares up for sale; (4) the Czech experience of voucher privatisation indicated that the distribution or sale of vouchers might represent an alternative approach to privatisation, but would hardly generate a real capital market. The involvement of Western capital would facilitate the participation of the population in privatised enterprises, as foreign managerial know-how would be seen as a very important asset in the privatisation process. The Hungarian government did not want to wait until domestic capital accumulation increased significantly and expected that privatisation would rely extensively on foreign capital, with foreign investment supporting the transformation process.[24]

In 1991, approximately 85 per cent of the SPA's revenues consisted of foreign currency, with US$1 billion worth of foreign capital invested in newly transformed and privatised companies in the form of direct purchases and capital additions. This corresponded to more than 60 per cent of new foreign capital inflows during 1991 (Hunya, 1992, p.506). About two thirds of privatisation receipts were accounted for by sales to foreign investors, although this share is liable to decrease in the future. Over 17 per cent of all Hungarian enterprises have a foreign capital component. The weight of the companies with foreign participation in the national economy is indicated by the fact that a successful solicitation of US$4.9 billion FDI commitment mostly within 3 years surpassed 5 per cent of the annual GDP in 1991. This growth rate was much higher than the average 1 per cent level in OECD countries and approached the corresponding figure of other rapidly industrialising countries,[25] not characteristic for other Eastern European countries.[26] However, it is estimated that the share of foreign capital stock in total national capital only increased from approximately 1.1 per cent in 1989 to 8.1 per cent in 1991 and 8.5 per cent in 1992,[27] and remains much lower than the average in countries, such as Austria, Belgium, Denmark, with an approximately similar size to Hungary.[28] Foreign investment in Hungary totalled US$446 per capita, compared with US$104 in Poland and US$64 in the Czech Republic and Slovakia.[29]

However, foreign equity capital provided instruments for the changeover to the market economy. In general, progress has not been as rapid, nor has the outcome been as successful, as either foreign investors or Hungarian officials had hoped.

Capital-intensive investment by foreign investors often leads to a high rate of increase in production in relation to inputs. Improvements in productivity, a transfer of high technology, and the construction of new facilities as a result of foreign investment usually lead to a growth in production and services.

Given the small overall value of investment projects prior to 1990, the role of FDI in Hungarian production was of course comparatively modest. Although FIEs in Hungary were still a small proportion of the massive domestic industry, the steep rise in foreign investment since 1990 has made their presence increasingly noticeable on the Hungarian market, especially in the hotel business, fruit processing, soft drinks, computer production and maintenance, building materials, sports equipment, electric turbines, light bulbs, pharmaceuticals, TV production and the car industry. In all these sections foreign investors usually manage in their own interests to improve capacity utilisation rates. By the end of 1990, the stake of foreign companies amounted to only some 2 per cent of Hungarian industry, compared with 20-40 per cent in smaller Western European countries such as Austria, Ireland and Portugal. FIEs accounted for 10.7 per cent of total sales in 1990, and almost 20 per cent in 1991. This was a remarkable achievement in a two-year period (Young, D.G., 1993, p.119).

It was reported that the average rate of profit achieved in 1988-89 was 10-13 per cent, which could be described as satisfactory for the early period of JVs. It is interesting to note that about 34 per cent and 40 per cent of those FIEs in operation showed a deficit in 1989 and 1990 respectively. The GDP produced by FIEs in 1990 was as much as Ft114.2 billion, or about 9.2 per cent of the national GDP reflecting an increase of 4.7 per cent compared with 1989. FIEs were more profitable than SOEs since their profits went up in 1990 by Ft15 billion while other companies registered a fall. At the same time, only 56 per cent of FIEs reported a profit, while 40 per cent showed a loss. The overall turnover of FIEs was Ft677.5 billion (accounting for 10.7 per cent of national turnover); 12 per cent of this was realised in hard currency exports and 4 per cent in the rouble sphere.[30] Ft20.4 billion (US$265 million) of JV profits in 1990 went into the state coffers, leaving a remaining profit of about 60 per cent. The savings due to tax breaks for foreign investors came to about Ft10 billion (US$130 million). Foreign investors earned a total of Ft12.4 billion (US$185 million), of which Ft4.2 billion (US$62.6 million) was remitted to the foreign home countries. Bank records showed that the money transferred to foreign banks, in total, was worth Ft2.3 billion (US$34.3 million). This suggests that much of the profit was recycled into the Hungarian economy.[31]

About 55.6 per cent of the 5,693 FIEs in operation produced profits in the first half of 1991, while only 44.4 per cent (2,280 JVs) were operating profitable in the fiscal year 1990. At the end of 1992 more than 13,000 of the registered 15,000 FIEs were in operation, and 85-90 per cent FIEs produced profits. The industrial output of FIEs in 1991 and 1992 accounted for about 10 and 11 per cent of GDP respectively.[32] But by the middle of 1993, 'the overall performance of FIEs has been poor, with net profits in the latest year down two-thirds from the previous year', according to the Economic Commission for Europe. 'This reflected generally difficult trading conditions in Hungary. Local companies without foreign investment suffered an even sharper decline. Most of the losses were in manufacturing, which accounts for 55 per cent of all overseas investment in Hungary, concentrated in the food and tobacco, textile and clothing industries.'[33] Moreover, the relative contributions of MNCs to local economic development may be assessed from the differences in the quality of goods and services they produce, compared with those of their local counterparts.

The growth of output as a result of foreign investment plays a crucial multiplier role, which stimulates a growth of activities in other branches of the economy. FIEs, such as Tungsram, normally require a larger number of indigenous sub-contractors. This contributes to the expansion of the market for the latter's products by a specific modernisation multiplier mechanism. Foreign firms have more exacting requirements and compel suppliers to pay more attention to quality and precision, strict delivery schedules, and technological progress. This inter-industry effect will certainly force local firms to change their attitudes towards product quality and management. FIEs will, therefore, serve as a 'model of behaviour' for many SOEs by acting as modulators, simulators and helpers.

It can be concluded that while the overall contribution of JVs and foreign capital to economic growth has been relatively very small so far, the value of their sales in certain specific segments of the economy has not been negligible, especially in pharmaceuticals, cosmetics and tourism. FDI represents one of the dynamic elements that serves to stabilise the Hungarian economy and integrate it with the world economy.[34] Further inflows of FDI and large-scale privatisation will become the main driving forces of economic growth in Hungary in the next decade.

Effect on employment

At the end of 1989 there were about 18-22,000 people employed in FIEs.[35] By 1990, the number had doubled. As Young (1993) indicates while most Hungarian companies have been making workers redundant (unemployment stood at 8.3 per cent at the end of 1991), FIEs doubled the number of employees to 0.5 per cent of the workforce at the end of 1990 (Young, D.G.,

1993, p.119). Between 1989 and 1992 FIEs more than doubled their work force in Hungary. By the end of May 1993 the number of FIE employees had increased by a further 18 per cent amounting to 250,000 - 300,000 or nearly 1.5 per cent of the country's total industrial labour force.[36] At the same time the overall number of employees had fallen by 15 per cent from 1990 to 1991 in the whole economy. As the activities of FIEs, especially those in export-oriented manufacturing, expanded rapidly, large numbers of local employees were increasingly hired, and the skill level of FIEs' employees are higher than the average for the national firms (Mihaly, Simai, 1990, pp.33-4). Foreign-owned businesses are therefore providing more job opportunities.

FIEs are also better at conserving manpower and paying their employees than SOEs. Empirical results suggest that foreign investors in Hungary pay higher wages than domestic companies in the same industry and have a much higher output per worker. 'Wages were 35 per cent higher for white-collar workers and 11 per cent higher for blue-collar workers' (Young, D.G., 1993, 119), but the difference is probably much greater because FIEs often pay their employees extra bonuses.

Individual localities in Hungary clearly want foreign investment, because it creates 'new jobs' and many top multinationals have increasingly recruited more manufacturing, sales and marketing employees locally. We should emphasize, however, that where FIEs have created totally new plants, they have tended to draw skilled manpower from existing SOEs, rather than reducing unemployment.

On the other hand, faced with a deteriorating economic situation, a large number of FIEs have shed labour to increase productivity and minimize cost. Evidence suggests that both large- and medium-sized FIEs and small-size JVs have pursued a reconstruction strategy by updating technology and reducing surplus labour by trimming their work force through early retirement schemes or buy-outs. A high employee turnover has enabled General Electric/Tungsram to cut its staff by 40 per cent and increase production by 30 per cent by adopting such strategies accompanied by a series of plans to help people find alternative jobs or retraining in order to soften the blow of redundancy.[37] In 1992, GE-Tungsram suffered losses of US$104 million, its third consecutive year of losses. GE, therefore, announced a further 900 job cuts after having already trimmed the workforce from 18,600 to 10,000 since acquiring the former state company in 1990, when it attributed poor results to a 90 per cent drop in sales to traditional Comecom customers and stagnant sales in Hungary. The labour force of Ganz-Hunslet, a FIE manufacturing railway rolling stock in Budapest, was cut down from an initial figure of 1,300 in 1989 to 500 in 1992. Ganz Meter Kft, a JV with participation by Schlumberger Ltd. from the Netherlands manufacturing and marketing electricity, gas and water meters for both the Hungarian market and export worldwide, also implemented a redundancy policy by cutting the number of employees from 1,800 in 1990 to 1,100 in 1992. Evidence from Petohaza & Kaposvar Sugar Plant, funded by Agrana International from Austria, also shows a large reduction in labour force within 2 years, from 1,900 in 1990 to 1,200 in 1992.[38]

Amongst medium-sized FIEs, for instance, Gfv-Otis Felvono Kft, a Hungarian-Austrian JV producing elevators, cut the labour force from 520 in 1990 to 460 in 1992. General Atlantic Kft, a FIE from Britain also cut its labour force from 70 in 1987 to 50 in 1992. Other smaller FIEs, such as Cutf Kft with participation from Cleco Ltd. in Britain, also cut its labour force by 15 per cent from 66 in 1988 to 56 in 1992. Morgan Materials Hungary Ltd, with investment from Morgan Crucible Company PLC also reduced the number of its employees from 20 in 1989 to 16 in 1992.

The general impression concerning the effects of FDI on employment in Hungary at this early stage seems to be negative. Most FIEs in Hungary did not create jobs for Hungarians in fact they reduced the number of available jobs as a result of the adaption of modern technology and increased productivity.

The argument is complicated, however, by the fact that most SOEs in Hungary were previously confronted with the problem of 'unemployment on the job' or overstaffing. According to one estimate made by the KSH, the Hungarian Central Statistical Office, the average real working time per worker per day in former Hungarian SOEs was only little more than three hours instead of the presumed six hours.[39] Some estimates place the amount of excess personnel in typical SOEs at 30 per cent of the total - a figure that applied both to management and shop-floor staff (Cooper, Sharyn, 1993, p.1).

The total employment effect of FDI is more modest than might be expected. But the evidence suggest that labour productivity and management has undoubtedly been enhanced by their association with foreign firms, and the spill-over effects, in terms of inter-firm labour movements and the internal dissemination of managerial skills and technologies, will certainly be increasing over time.

The balance of payments effect of FDI

Hungary became one of the most indebted countries in the world by the end of the 1980s. Though the rate of debt servicing (the ratio of interest on credit plus the part of debt due to the annual export income) dropped from 97 per cent in 1986, to 63 per cent in 1990 and 40 per cent in 1990, Hungary is still regarded as one of the most indebted nations on international money markets. Between 1989 and 1992, the annual sums spent on debt servicing ranged between US$3.7 billion and US$4.6 billion. It was revealed that Hungary's net debt servicing in 1994 amounted to US$3.72 billion, about US$100 million less than in 1993 and US$620 million less than in 1992, but this still constituted around 8.5-8.9 per cent of GDP. In the years to come Hungary will have to make annual foreign debt service payments of between US$3.5 billion to US$4 billion, representing 13-15 per cent of GDP in 1989 prices. Out of this sum, the interest alone amounts to around US$1.6 billion, or 6 per cent of the GDP in 1989. If Hungary wants to avoid insolvency and the need to reschedule its debt servicing, exports must exceed imports, otherwise it will have to borrow more loans and credit to bridge the gap. However, although Hungarian exports have doubled since 1975, their share of world trade has fallen constantly. The commodity structures of Hungary's exports increasingly consist of energy-intensive, low-value, mass-market products, while its technology-intensive products are increasingly squeezed out of export markets. Hungary has simply proved incapable of switching to producing the sorts of exports the world is willing to purchase in order to finance its borrowing (Swain, 1992, p.119). If Hungary borrows more from international money markets, then it will have to increase the stock of debts even further, placing nearly unsurmountable obstacles for economic development. The key question concerning macro-economic policy in the coming years will be whether Hungary can increase the proportion of FDI to an extent that this item will cover a major part of the country's foreign debt repayments. The inflow of foreign capital into Hungary is, therefore, a crucial factor that could ease external debt servicing without drawing away vital resources. It could also serve to improve the balance of payments and to stimulate economic growth in the coming years.

The net inflow of FDI in 1991-92 helped to neutralize the huge burden of foreign debt and improved the country's balance of payments. With increased inward foreign capital Hungary could finance debt interest payments without decreasing indigenous financial resources. In 1991, the net inflow of foreign capital in cash reached US$1.46 billion, with about US$10 million worth of cash invested each month, about the same level as the interest payments requirement on the foreign debt (the monthly interest payments were US$9-10 million, while the total monthly debt service amounted to approximately US$20 million).[40] The effect of FDI on improving the balance of payments in 1991 was almost five times greater than in 1990, and meant that Hungary had little difficulty in meeting its debt servicing obligation. Indeed, Hungary should not encounter any further problems in borrowing to service interest and principal repayments on its gross debt, which stood at US$21.6 billion at the end of February 1992.

Additional balance of payments difficulties, however, may arise from MNC remittances to pay shareholder dividends and royalties or rents to parent companies for the use of technology. If these remittances exceed incoming investment funds, then foreign payments will aggravate existing balance of payments difficulties (Hood and Young, 1979, Chapter 5), and act as a drain on the host country's growth-promoting capital. Moreover, in contrast to the positive assessment of MNCs in terms of taxes and royalties paid to host governments, many MNCs in Hungary have illegally extracted huge sums of funds from Hungary through transfer pricing - inflating the value of imports (materials, equipment and machinery as well as technology), and undervaluing their exports, and thereby offsetting their taxes liabilities. In the short run, the abolition of restrictions on the export of profits will create any major problems, as long as there are incentives to reinvest, and high profit rates will encourage most foreign enterprises to spend some of their earnings on new investment. Needless to say, some proportion of profits will inevitably be transferred abroad, particularly if the investment is really profitable, while interest on the bank credits obtained from foreign banks or bond issues to finance investment projects must be paid even if they yield no profit. But these payments are much smaller than the influx of new capital.

No assessment is made of the extent to which profits are repatriated from the Hungarian affiliates to foreign parent companies. However, what little evidence exists suggests that such financial flows were limited as the number of FIEs in operation was not large and most foreign firms reinvested profits in their local affiliates. According to some official sources, only US$50 million left the country in 1989 in the form of FIEs profits and capital repatriation.[41] Profit repatriation by foreign investors in Hungary amounted to US$20 million and US$24 million in 1990 and 1991 respectively, while the influx of foreign capital totalled US$500 million. By the end of 1991 the stock of foreign capital in cash accounted US$2.11 billion while net profit repatriation amounted to only US$32 million. The value of profit repatriation between January and November 1992 equalled US$42 million, while the current surplus account on the balance of payments reached US$704 million (Hamar, Judit, 1993, p.6). However, in the longer term, profit repatriation may exceed capital inflow and could generate difficulties if profits rates margins will eventually start to flatten out. If the level of new capital investment should begin to shrink, there would loom the painful problem of a profit drain from Hungary which is already struggling with acute debt service liabilities. This danger is certain to materialise.

As we have already discussed, the total impact of FDI on the balance of payments in Hungary depends on the combined effects of export promotion, imports and import substitution. The expectation of greater income from foreign trade has led Hungary to actively promote exports and FDI as a development policy, through export subsidies (lower tariffs on inputs for processing for re-export and lower taxes on profits from exports), an undervaluation of the exchange rate to make exports more attractive in foreign markets,[42] and the encouragement of export-oriented FDI. Through JVs Hungarian firms could better understand international marketing and promotion techniques for market penetration, and gain access to the established marketing networks of foreign partners,[43] thereby increasing Hungary's foreign exchange earning capacity and improving its trade balance through import substitution and export diversification. Many FIEs in Hungary are genuinely export-oriented, aiming at taking advantage of cheap labour and raw materials to manufacture for export and escape import tariffs on their products.

Scattered evidence suggests that FIES have already played an important, but not impressive, role in the recent increase in Hungarian manufactured exports.[44] In 1986, JV products only represented less than 1 per cent of total export volume, well below the export ratio of industrial cooperation projects (4-5 per cent of Hungary's total convertible currency exports at the same year). The contribution of foreign partners in the form of deliveries of machinery, equipment and raw materials, however, saves outlays of foreign hard-currency and reduces the import of finished goods. This effect was much stronger at the initial stage of FDI. The import of real cash, which is used to produce goods and expand import-substitution, may also save hard currency outlays on a considerable scale. However, no official data are available on an aggregated sectoral basis on the proportion of parts and materials sourced from home countries and/or the level of local content. So it is difficult to derive simple estimates of the effect of FDI on Hungary's trade balance.

It was estimated (see **Figure 6.1**) that FIEs in Hungary successfully balanced their imports and exports during 1988-90, but that imports were much higher than exports and during 1991-92 their balance of trade was, therefore, negative. This was mainly due to the high import content of investments, the mechanism of transfer pricing adopted by MNCs, the unavailability of locally-produced goods, materials, components, the non-competitiveness of local prices and the inferior quality of Hungarian intermediate products. The scattered statistics showed that FIEs' share in national imports doubled each year from 3.7 per cent in 1988 to around 27 per cent in 1991 , and 30 per cent in 1992, while their share in total national exports also increased from 6.5 per cent in 1988, to 14.7 per cent in 1991 and to 30 per cent in 1992.[45] This implies that in terms of foreign trade, the initial impact of FDI on the balance of payments at the end of 1992 was zero. So it came as no surprise that JVs had recorded a negative foreign trade balance in aggregate terms in the early stage of operation.

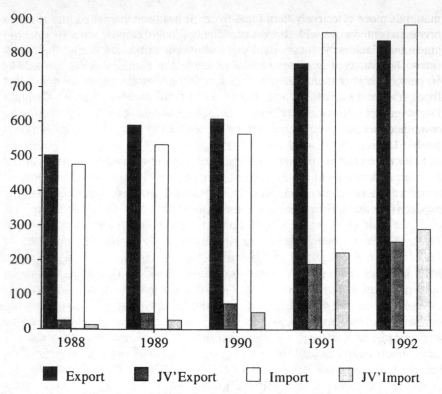

Figure 6.1   The role of FIEs in foreign trade in Hungary, 1988-92 (in billion Ft)

FDI's effect on productivity

While labour productivity in Hungarian industry is much lower than in the EC countries, the introduction of Western organisational methods in FIEs led to a rapid increase in labour productivity and higher rates of return. According to management reports, the productivity levels of Hungarian production workers were initially found to be 20-30 per cent of those of Western workers in comparable industries. However, after a period of work experience and closely supervised training, Hungarian workers achieved 70-80 per cent of this level. Significant increases in labour productivity are usually connected not only with more efficient organisation, but also an improved incentive reward system and certain additional investment outlays.

It is widely believed that FIEs are more profitable and efficient than their domestic counterparts, as most FIEs use more modern technologies, employ more modern management techniques, and utilise capital, labour, land, and materials more effectively than local firms. It has been estimated that if many privatised enterprises with foreign participation could employ western working hours and machinery, they would yield 40-90 per cent more output than local firms. The value of sales per employee in FIEs in Hungary were as much as 60 per cent higher than SOEs, and they paid higher average wages than local firms (Dobosiewicz, 1992, p.28). Per capita GDP and profit margins among JVs were also considerably higher than the national average. In 1990 the combined income of all companies was down by Ft7 billion (US$90 million), while FIEs registered a growth of Ft15 billion (US$185 million). Employees of FIEs were able to take home 20 per cent more money each month than the average and white-collar jobs paid as much as one third more. FIEs are, therefore, more efficient and productive than local firms due to higher labour productivity and a better investment structure.[46]

FDI and technology transfer

FIEs were an important source of new ideas about modern technology and mass production, and may also provide the competitive environment necessary to stimulate technology diffusion. Though it is difficult to quantify this transfer of knowledge, 'foreign investments don't merely inject money, they also transfer technology to Hungary. A lot of companies were not able to develop an effective and efficient management because, although they had the necessary funds, they lacked the proper technology, adequate professional expertise and the high standard of management required, moreover their operations were insufficiently integrated'.[47]

Others argue that 'the overall impact of technology transfer on the national economy in the 1980s seemed as yet to be negligible because they had limited or no spillover. The nature of the technology transferred was in most cases not up to date, compared to the competitive international levels. However, technology levels were higher than those already available in the Hungarian economy'.[48] In the 1990s, however, there is a considerable evidence that foreign firms generally introduced new products and production processes, employed more advanced production technologies than local firms, utilised local factor inputs more efficiently; and drew upon the R & D programmes of their parent companies thus expanding the flow of information available to Hungary. Though R & D activities were naturally kept in-house and by senior management, global firms started voluntarily to undertake some local R&D in order to adapt their products to local market requirements. The extent to which product characteristics were modified depended on the technological/scientific infrastructure of the host country.

Hungarian companies expected to obtain first-hand exposure to modern management practices and production processes, and gain insight into quality control techniques and product design. However, it has been argued that many transferred production techniques were typically outdated and standardised, with new products and processes only introduced in the home country. Indeed, the centralisation of R&D programmes by foreign firms might lead to the closure of Hungarian research facilities.[49] It is also argued that Hungarian firms may have paid too high a price for some technologies, especially for the right to use brand names.[50] On the other hand, the appearance of FIEs has obvious spin-offs for the modernisation of the Hungarian economy because they supply better and more attractive products, but this also causes some difficulties. For example, the sudden appearance of strong foreign competition drove many domestic producers out of business, or forced them to withdraw from the lucrative markets and set up new lines of production. In some industries, such as food-processing, automobiles, and electronics, FIEs hold dominant, monopolist positions.

It may be true that foreign investors invariably installed much newer technologies than the ones normally employed in national industry. However, the inflow of modern technology into Hungary had been modest, as foreign partners frequently transferred outdated equipment and kept capital stocks artificially low. A large proportion of foreign capital was also involved in various services industries[51] without introducing modern advanced technology. However, the benefits of JV activities were obvious in some areas, like food processing, pharmaceuticals, glass manufacturing, and bio-technology, where the transferred technologies were the same as those in the investor's parent company, and a range of new products was certainly introduced to the Hungarian consumer. The greater potential for technology transfer probably lies in JVs initiatives between the larger and more innovative foreign firms and leading Hungarian manufacturers.

Foreign investment in large assembling firms also has externalities and spin-off effects through sub-contracting with generally smaller supplier firms providing a wide range of specialist components. These sub-contracting networks are particularly important in the automotive, food-processing and soft drinks industries, in which the final manufacturing process consists largely of the assembly of components, and in which specialisation dictates that it is more economic to subcontract component production than to engage in extensive in-house manufacture. Although technology transfer was less than expected, in some cases it was quite substantial. Very strong vertical inter-firm linkages exist between assemblers and suppliers, with the former providing important technical and other resources to the latter, thereby reinforcing the role of sub-contracting as a effective means of technology transfer and diffusion.

Increased foreign direct investment by up-to-date manufacturing enterprises will therefore continue to provide the acquisition of concrete know-how and technology.

FDI and management/training

To bring a new management system into a Hungarian enterprise was also a
very important precondition for modernisation, but this was not always easy.
Confrontation between Hungarian and foreign participants in FIEs was
common, and even intense, especially during the early stages of individual
ventures. Many Hungarian workers and managerial staff were used to the old
system under state ownership and had difficulties getting accustomed to
stricter work discipline and productivity demands. Foreign executives, on the
other hand, were often unprepared to understand the historical and cultural
background of their local colleagues, and this sometimes provoked traditional
anti-foreign sentiment among the Hungarian workers. In most cases, however,
the initial misgivings gave way to mutual understanding. The majority of
Hungarian workers and managers at FIEs began to learn management know-
how from their foreign partners as soon as they saw the real benefits. Through
their efforts in improving work morale and teaching people the value of
performance, the presence of foreign investors exercises a beneficial influence
on employees and suppliers. Indeed, foreign investment can even influence the
legal structure within which the industry operates, as new owners lobby on
legislative and regulative issues. These benefits of FDI are impossible to
translate into figures, but no one doubts the significance of these indirect
effects of foreign capital involvement in Hungary.

The high productivity of FIEs resulted from higher wages, the recruitment
of more skilled labour, and internal training programmes. The experience of
many FIEs shows that persistent efforts to train local technical and managerial
staff has been one of secrets for success. Most FIEs in Hungary found it
necessary to provide basic technical training in order to adopt Western
managerial practices. Accordingly, many FIEs established regular on-the-job
training or intensive short-term training programmes, allowing a number of
their employees, in rotation, to receive free training related to their jobs. Our
survey in 1992 suggested that most FIEs provide a range of training
programmes. For upper and middle management, this training often took the
form of special courses conducted by local institutions, or at company
headquarters and institutions in the home countries. For production workers,
it consisted mainly of on-the-job instruction, but there was substantial training
outside the factory at supervisor level. The US motor giant Ford has invested
heavily in its new Hungarian workforce and introduced a series of extensive
training/re-training courses both in-plant and at GM locations elsewhere in
Europe. According to the Hungarian sales manager of the General Motors,
'our Hungarian workforce spends 480-600 hours a year on training courses

209

and I'm certain that will bring results'.[52] Foreign investors may provide training in managerial skills, which cannot be replicated in domestic firms or purchased from abroad. As a result, employees not only improve their productive performance, but also develop a loyalty to the enterprise. It also appears that FIEs provide considerable more training than comparable domestic firms, and labour turnover is much lower than in SOEs.

FIEs manufacturing high-tech products or using high technology in production often sent their employees abroad to receive more advanced technical and managerial training. Our survey conducted in 1992 shows that 62.5 per cent of the 90 surveyed firms had selected a small number of Hungarian employees for training abroad during the previous three years, for periods of normally less than six months. This had positive results in terms of technical training, particularly during their early stage of operation.[53]

Many Western firms increasingly employ local executives when they are qualified. Initially, FIEs usually found it necessary to hire technical and managerial staff from their home countries to fill key management positions or to solve technical problems, and training was provided for local technicians and managers who were normally unfamiliar with Western business and technical management. Once qualified local staff were available, they replaced the foreign expatriates. Our 1992 survey found that once local staff demonstrated sufficient ability, foreign expatriates would be kept to minimal levels. By 1992, most small- and medium-size FIEs had only one full-time expatriate employed in Hungary, if that only when some urgent technical or managerial problems emerged, which local staff could not solve them, would a foreign expert be called in. The reasons behind such a policy were as follows: the costs of hiring a local person were much lower than hiring a foreign national and local technical and managerial staff were much more familiar with the economic, business and political environment.

Evidence also indicates that a new group of managers and entrepreneurs directly 'trained' in FIEs has now emerged. They have become familiar with 'international standards of business management'. These Western-minded entrepreneurs will inevitably have an important impact on Hungary's current economic transformation and reconstruction.

FIEs, therefore, have not only brought with them additional resources and new technologies, expert management and a high standard of professionalism, but they have also introduced into Hungary new attitudes to business which have helped to transform the entire economic environment.

Summary

Foreign capital not only injects money into the Hungarian economy, but it also has a favourable influence on the infrastructure, the technological level, and export capacity.[54] It helps to raise domestic product quality and assists in spreading internationally competitive quality levels throughout the economy, and finally promotes the modernisation and integration of Hungary into the world economy.

Foreign investment in Hungary has also helped to some extent ease the shortage of foreign currency, stabilise the economy, promote international integration, improve competitiveness, and to increase employment. However, many of Hungary's objectives have not been realised, particularly in terms of the more limited role of foreign investment in for improving the balance of trade/payments, boosting economic growth and incorporating the national economy in the world economic system. More specifically, capital-deepening foreign technology may destroy jobs in existing industries, accentuated unemployment problems. The importation of foreign technology is usually accompanied by a host of agreements and arrangements that result in increased imports of equipment and materials, which tends to worsen the balance of payments. Therefore, the benefits of FDI to the host country may not be obvious, and may be either negligible or even negative.

The impact of foreign capital on economic development in China

This section looks at some aspects in which FDI is believed to have most directly benefits on the host country discussed in 6.1 by comparing with the Chinese experience over the past 16 years or so.

Provision of capital

FDI as a capital supplement was especially important for the rapid development in China over the past 16 years. By the end of 1990 China had approved 29,000 FIEs with US$40 billion FDI as pledged and US$19 billion actually utilized. The number of FIEs, and the amount of pledged and actually utilised FDI increased from 40,000, US$50 billion, and US$20 billion respectively at the end of 1991 to 84,300, US$60 billion and US$23 billion at the end of 1992.[55] A successful solicitation of US$94.69 billion foreign capital commitment between 1979-92 provided a powerful supplement to the short domestic capital supply. China actually utilised US$26 billion and US$33.8 billion foreign capital in 1993 and in 1994.

The most direct measure of FDI's impact on the recipient country's economy is its contribution to capital formation. We find that foreign investment in China was large in absolute amount but remained relatively small in terms of GDP and gross investment (GI) during the 1980s, but significantly increased in the 1990s.

211

Table 6.1 shows the relative share of foreign investment in total fixed asset formation in China during 1985-90. The high share shown for 1990 was likely to reflect the effect of the major RMB depreciation (by 22 per cent) against the U.S. dollar in December 1989. By contrast, the estimated share for 1988 probably understated the contribution of foreign investment to domestic capital formation: the RMB exchange rate, had, after all, not been readjusted since the 17 per cent devaluation of summer 1986. The average contribution of foreign investment to capital formation during 1985-90, as shown in Table 6.1, may well be understated. Although the regional distribution of foreign investment remained highly unequal, nevertheless, China's utilized FDI made up 2.22 per cent of the national gross investment of fixed assets during 1981-86. This figure further reached 3.8 per cent during 1988-91,[56] close to 9 per cent for FDI and capital borrowing combined for 1985-90, or 11 per cent for 1990 alone, 8 per cent in 1992 and 13 per cent in 1993. Foreign investment can hardly be discarded as being of only marginal significance.

A regional breakdown suggests FDI has a particularly significant financial role in the coastal regions or SEZs. As most FDI was invested in the SEZs and other Open-Coastal Cities (OCCs) or Open-Coastal Provinces (OCPs), not surprisingly, it was the SEZs that enjoyed the highest foreign investment shares in total fixed asset creation: 24 per cent of FDI, or 39 per cent of FDI and capital borrowing combined during 1985-90. By 31 September 1991, 15 coastal cities and 5 SEZs approved 11,335 FIEs, with US$45.97 billion accumulated pledged FDI.[57] However, the difference in the relative contribution of foreign investment to capital formation between pioneer OCPs (for example, Guangdong, Fujian and Hainan) and other OCPs, or even OCCs, remained quite striking. Coastal provinces such as Guangdong, Fujian and Zhejiang benefited enormously from massive inflows of investment. In Guangdong Province, about 15-21 per cent of its gross local investment infixed assets in 1980-90 was drawn from FDI sources (by the end of 1991 Guangdong utilised US$15 billion FDI). Accordingly, about 8.6 per cent of Fujian's gross investment in fixed assets in 1985-90 came from foreign investment. By the end of September 1993, Fujian Province approved 9,620 FIEs (4,036 in operation), with contracted foreign investment US$14.03 billion, in which US$3.76 billion were utilized.[58] Zhejiang Province utilised US$7 billion FDI between 1984-90 and FDI's proportion in gross local investment in fixed assets increased from 2 per cent in 1984 to 13 per cent in 1990.[59] By the end of 1991 and 1992, FIEs in Shanghai accumulated 1,227 and 4,848, with US$3.33 billion and US$10 billion pledged FDI, respectively.[60] By the end of 1994, FIE projects in Shanghai accumulated 11,800, in which 30 per cent were classified as large-size enterprises with US$10 million per project, and 6,000 FIEs were in operation. FDI's proportion in gross local investment in fixed assets increased from about 4.2

212

per cent in 1990 to 1/3 in 1994 in this city.[61]

The inland provinces, which were aware of the fact that the massive influxof foreign money had fuelled industrial growth in southern coastal regions, are determined to catch up. They increasingly demanded the similar privileges granted to the coastal regions or SEZs. They have sought to boost local economic growth and tax revenues so that they could, for example, finance much-needed improvements in infrastructure.

Table 6.1 further shows that the growth of foreign capital intake in the SEZs during 1985-90 was seen to have been consistently many times higher than the rate of domestic capital formation in all the economic-open coastal areas, including Beijing. Foreign capital was increasingly sought as a substitute for local resources. As for each dollar of foreign capital received, an average for 3 RMB must be spent as complementary domestic investment (this does not include the Chinese capital contribution to Sino-foreign JVs),[62] initial foreign-induced capital growth subsequently helped promote local investment. So the rapid growth of foreign capital was in most cases accompanied by a remarkable implied expansion of domestic capital.

FDI as a capital contributor was also especially significant in certain sectors. The main sector that absorbed a large proportion of FDI in the 1980s was the tourist industry, mainly through the construction of deluxe hotels in metropolitan cities. Between 1979 and 1988, over US$4 billion FDI was believed to be actually invested in big hotels and other tourism-related facilities in the metropolitan cities. The high concentration of FDI in this sector caused much controversy. Many questioned the desirability of having so much spent on luxury accommodation and also about allowing foreigners to operate a large part of the industry that generates foreign exchange relatively easily. It could also be argued that the rapid growth of China's tourist industry contributed significantly to the national economy in the decade, and such growth would not have been possible without the substantial participation of FDI. Moreover, the building of hotels can be a net gain to China, as many of the projects actually cost the Chinese partner little cash during the construction, and most hotels would become entirely Chinese property after operation duration (normally 15 years). The contribution of FDI to the industrial manufacturing sector was less prominent than that to tourism sector during the first decade. Nevertheless, FDI in this sector grew rather rapidly in the later years and its impact grew accordingly. In 1988 and 1992, for instance, over 80 per cent and 90 per cent of the FDI projects approved were reportedly related to manufacturing activities respectively. Chemical industry, for example, signed 900 projects participating with foreign investors, with actually utilised foreign capital US$1.72 billion by the mid-1992, each project averaging at least US$5 million investment.[63]

Table 6.1

Relative contribution of foreign capital to total fixed asset investment in China, 1985-90 (%)

	FDI only				Foreign Capital (FDI and capital borrowing)			
	1985	1988	1990	1985-90	1985	1988	1990	1985-90
SEZs	16.01	15.56	33.72	23.66	25.79	32.72	49.30	38.66
Shenzhen	18.37	25.53	34.68	30.53	31.27	37.82	46.11	43.42
Zhuhai	16.14	14.26	34.56	19.43	27.49	65.47	54.16	46.68
Shantou	4.76	4.66	49.21	11.45	10.77	10.35	62.99	22.37
Xiamen	18.31	14.44	19.76	22.83	21.49	49.40	47.03	40.37
OCCs	3.08	3.93	6.61	4.84	4.10	9.46	12.23	9.85
Dalian	1.91	7.15	33.44	10.12	1.98	20.38	65.49	24.84
Tianjin	1.42	2.56	1.99	2.63	3.03	14.41	5.32	10.21
Qingdao	0.63	1.75	7.69	4.66	5.18	5.66	12.61	10.35
Shanghai	2.65	3.28	3.72	4.17	2.68	6.20	6.75	6.80
Guangzhou	7.95	6.41	9.53	7.01	10.43	10.50	15.72	11.27
OCPs	2.90	3.76	6.77	4.30	4.33	7.16	10.12	7.17
	(2.66)	(3.10)	(2.96)	(3.50)	(3.89)	(7.03)	(9.14)	(6.94)
Liaoning	0.52	1.81	4.72	2.10	0.88	4.06	13.33	5.33

Hebei	0.21	0.30	1.17	0.52	0.27	0.44	2.56	1.00
Shandong	0.52	1.12	2.65	1.41	0.94	1.43	3.28	1.92
Jiangsu	0.65	1.24	1.77	1.20	1.00	1.54	3.27	1.82
Zhejiang	0.74	0.71	0.91	0.80	1.72	2.11	2.36	2.14
Fujian	6.32	5.88	14.06	8.60	9.11	11.88	18.77	12.85
Guangdong	9.99	13.57	18.56	14.14	14.59	27.32	23.65	23.17
Hainan	6.64	21.45	12.54	11.94	7.32	22.38	14.24	12.67
Guangxi	2.14	1.00	2.48	2.33	3.13	3.20	4.36	3.83
Beijing	2.75	11.49	6.98	6.64	3.60	13.33	11.93	8.73
PRC Total	2.26	3.09	4.03	3.11	5.14	8.44	11.04	8.72

Notes: FDI and capital borrowing in US dollar are converted into RMB (based on official annual average of exchange rate) to be related to the total fixed assets investment figures (all undeflated) for the years concerned. The Open Coastal Provinces (OCPs) total (in parenthesis) covers all the 11 OCPs, including Tianjin and Shanghai.

Sources: Kueh, Y.Y. (1992), Table 5 in 'Foreign Investment and Economic Change in China', *The China Quarterly* (*Special Issue: The Chinese Economy in the 1990s*), September 1992, Vol.132, p.656.

By the end of 1995, China is expected to attract US$100 billionaccumulated FDI with 100,000 FIEs.[64] Though the proportion of foreign capital in domestic capital formation is expected to slow down in the next years, and will be surprisingly high compared with many other developing countries, but will still lag behind neighbouring booming Asian countries. As Grub and Lin (1991) found that foreign equity investment in Singapore between 1980 and 1989 accounted for about 15 per cent of GDP and financed more than one-third of Singapore's total capital expansion. The same ratios for China were only 0.7 and 1.8 per cent, respectively. Even when compared with Malaysia, Thailand, and Indonesia, the ratios for China were extremely low (Grub and Lin, 1991, pp.96-97).

Effect on output

FIEs covered most industrial sectors except for that of military production and have become one of the most important factors for China's stable and sustained economic growth. The ratio of FIEs' output among the national industrial output increased from 1 per cent in 1989, 3 per cent (around RMB70 billion) in 1990 to 4.9 per cent (around RMB123.7 billion) in 1991, 7.5 per cent in 1992 (RMB205.2 billion), and 11 per cent in 1993 (RMB300 billion, increasing 46.2 per cent over 1992).[65] The increasing weight of FDI in China's national production was in part a result of generally good performance of FDI. Although FIEs were still a relatively small proportion of the massive domestic industry, their impact was increasingly noticeable during the 1990s.

In some regions and provinces where FDI participation was most active, its weight in the local economy was particularly visible. Gross production in the four SEZs (Shenzhen, Xiamen, Zhuhai and Shantuo) increased from RMB1.3 billion in 1980, to RMB4.8 billion in 1985, RMB6.78 billion in 1986, RMB10 billion in 1987, RMB21.44 billion in 1989 and RMB28.6 billion in 1990 (growing 5.8 folds than 1985). GDP growth rate in the four SEZs increased by leaps and bounds from 25 per cent to 35 per cent. **Table 6.2** shows that the utilized FDI increased from US$0.866 billion in 1984 to US$4.861 billion in 1990 in the 4 SEZs. The biggest SEZ - Hainan Province - utilized US$0.8 billion FDI over 1987-90, industrial output grew 70 per cent. At the end of 1991, manufacturing products exports in the 5 SEZs amounted to 60 per cent of their gross industrial products.[66]

For the SEZs as a whole, the average growth rate of FIE industrial output during 1985-90 -averaging 33 per cent per annum - was extremely high.[67] During the first six months of 1988, FIEs in the 14 coastal cities and 4 SEZs produced RMB5.6 billion industrial goods, about 4 per cent of the total industrial output of these regions of that period. The average annual increase in industrial output in Shenzhen was 56.4 per cent between 1979 and 1983, with about half of that figure contributed by FIEs. From 1987 to 1990, the average growth rate of FIE industrial output in coastal region was 50 per cent. Moreover, FIE industrial output in the 4 SEZs was RMB10.4 billion and RMB15.5 billion in 1990 and 1991, accounting more than 57.6 per cent of their total industrial output value of that period (in Xiamen and Shenzhen alone, FIEs' industrial output accounted about 54.8 per cent and 70 per cent of their total industrial output during the same year).

Table 6.2
Comparison of SEZs economic development in China

	GDP (RMB10 m)		GNP (RMB10 m)		Exports (US$10 m)		No of FIEs		Utilized FDI (US$10 m)	
	1980	1990	1980	1990	1981	1991	1984	1990	1984	1990
Shenzhen	2.7	135.86	2.21	69.72	0.17	59.90	130	643	5.89	26.44
Zhuhai	2.4	41.18	-	19.12	2.22	11.10	93	237	2.2	7.32
Shantuo	2.2	111.43	17.8	25.03	2.72	8.20	15	287	0.09	783
Xiamen	6.4	50.58	5.86	36.53	1.41	12.70	93	288	0.48	7.02

Sources: China State Statistic Bureau, *People's Daily,* 17 February 1992.

In Guangdong Province, the industrial output value of FIEs accounted for about 10 per cent of their total industrial output value in 1987, and 27 per cent in 1990.[68] From 1978 to 1992, 10 per cent of GDP and 22 per cent of industrial output in Fujian Province were generated by FIEs. By the end of 1992, FIEs' output amounted RMB21 billion, 32.8 per cent of total industrial output in this province. FIEs industrial output in the total industrial output in Shanghai increased from 5.5 per cent in 1990 to 7.9 per cent in 1991,[69] 11 per cent in 1993 (amounting to RMB55.3 billion in 1993, increasing 83.3 per cent over 1992), and 20.5 per cent in 1994 (amounting to RMB86 billion).[70] FIEs' productivity achieved RMB84,000/worker in 1993, four times as the averaged level of this city during the same period.[71] FIEs output accounted 9 per cent of Beijing's total industrial output in 1990. Its output, sales income, and profits in 1992 amounted RMB10.53 billion, RMB11.95 billion and RMB0.616 billion respectively.[72] By the end of November 1991, sales incomes of 235 FIEs in operation in Tianjin amounted RMB2.93 billion, averaged sale profit rate was 10.5 per cent, higher than 5.7 per cent in 1990. Productivity per capita amounted RMB100,000 and exports US$0.1 billion.

It can be concluded that foreign capital inflows made a considerable contribution to the rapid economic growth in China during 1978-92.

Effect on employment

We have already discussed above that FDI does not simply substitute new employment opportunities for old ones, but may also help to create new employment. However, evidence suggested that the effect of FDI on employment in China was minimal over the past 16 years or so.

As the activities of FIEs, especially those in export-oriented manufacturing, expanded rapidly, large numbers of local employees were increasingly employed by FIEs in China. According to one preliminary estimate, some 0.3-0.5 million Chinese employees were employed by 6,000 FIEs in operation in China by early 1988.[73] The number of workers involved FIEs would be between 1.5 and 2 million by the end of 1991, if one includes offshore processing and assembling activities. By the end of May 1992, about 3 million local employees were employed by more than 20,000 FIEs in operation, amounting to 1.4 per cent of the country's total industrial workforce.[74] By the end of 1993, 50,000 FIEs in operation employed 10 million Chinese.[75] We can conclude that the importance of FDI in the overall national employment picture was relatively minimal: FIE employees made up no more than 3 per cent of the country's total industrial labour force.

The importance of FDI in job creation was most evident in Guangdong Province, where about 1 million people, or one third of its total industrial labour force, were employed in all FDI activities by the end of 1987.[76] FIEs in Fujian Province employed 530,000 and 2.1 million workers by the end of 1992 and 1993 respectively.[77] About 2.6 per cent of Dalian's total labour force was working for 287 FIEs in operation at the end of 1990.[78]

It can be argued that the effects of FDI were visible not only in terms of how many jobs were created but also how much the quality of the jobs was improved.

One assertion in the literature is that foreign firms contribute little to employment creation, because they allegedly employ highly capital-intensive production technologies (Petrochilos, 1989, pp.29-32). Another is that foreign firms exacerbate problems of unemployment and underemployment, because they displace labour-intensive firms in traditional industries. The impact of FDI on local employment is, therefore, a complex matter. Where FIEs have created new plants, they have tended to draw high qualified and skilled manpower from existing SOEs, simply substituted new employment opportunities for old ones. Some examples exist about how local human resources were successfully mobilized and used by FDI when the strategy was well targeted. In other cases, where FIEs were formed in conjunction with

218

existing enterprises, the adaption of modern technology and increased productivity led to a reduction in the number of available jobs. Some FIEs simply push those surplus labour to labour market, which added a financial burden on the state subsidies.

The reason for redundancy in FIEs is that most SOEs were confronted with the problem of 'unemployment on the job' or overstaffing. In most cases FIEs were established on the base of previously SOEs, FIEs usually implemented structural and technical reform to get rid of the surplus labour. We can argue that the real problem lay in the fact that the country lacked an effective mechanism that would help transfer the 'surplus' workers from one sector to another in order to achieve maximum efficiency. In this sense, heavy redundance resulting from JV formation only exacerbate rather than create a social and economic problem that actually had existed all along.

The balance of payments effect of FDI

The Chinese government's goal of maximizing foreign exchange earnings is to finance its priority programme. Accordingly, the most important criterion for judging FDI's performance in China is the FIEs' ability to balance their foreign exchange requirements.

Open trade and export-led growth have been at the heart of China's post-Maoist economic reforms. China had gradually dismantled its restrictive trade regulations, allowed a substantial depreciation of the exchange rate, and encouraged foreign investors and private investors to participate China's development process. China's trade record has been astonishing: export volumes grew at an average rate of 12 per cent a year between 1980 and 1992 and its share of world trade doubled in a decade, making China the world's eleventh largest exporter in 1992, up from 26th place in 1980. Merchandise trade as a ratio of GNP increased from 12.8 per cent in 1980 to 38 per cent in 1992.

FDI activities clearly spurred both imports and exports in China over the past 16 years or so. The impact of FDI on China's total foreign trade remained relatively small up to the end of last decade but it has grown very rapidly after 1990. FIE's total imports and exports in 1993 and 1994 reached US$67.1 billion and US$87.65 billion. Its share among the national trade increased from 25 per cent in 1992 to 35.8 per cent in 1993 and 37 per cent in 1994.[79] Even though some FIEs were able to balance their foreign exchange accounts in 1992, its effects on the net foreign exchange balance, however, remained limited or most likely negative.[80] It is argued that a trade deficit caused by the rapid expansion of imports generated by foreign investors is not necessarily a bad thing, if it is accounted for by an influx of capital-goods imports which will yield greater exports in the future. However, a high

219

and rising level of non-essential consumer-goods imports caused by FDI may point to an over-expansion of domestic demand which is likely to prove unsustainable in the medium term (Solberg, 1993, ed., p.35).

Data on FIE exports are more easily available than data on its imports. Evidence shows that FIEs are leading the way in generating exports, in line with the government's foreign investment strategy aimed at using foreign funds to build a strong exporting base. **Table 6.3** shows the dramatic increase of FIE exports in China over the past decade. Between 1984 and 1992, FIE exports almost doubled every year, rising from US$115 million in 1984 to US$25.24 billion in 1993 (increased 45.4 per cent over 1992),[81] and US$34.71 billion in 1994.[82] FIEs accumulatively generated US$105.5 billion foreign exchange between 1986-94, and became one of the most important sources of foreign exchange for both central and local governments.

Table 6.3
Exports by FIEs in China, 1984-94

Year	Exports by FIEs ($bn) (1)	Total National Exports ($bn) (2)	National Manufacturing Exports ($bn) (3)	(1)/(2)	(1)/(3)
1984	0.115	26.14	14.42	0.42	0.82
1985	0.320	27.35	13.52	1.22	2.42
1986	0.480	30.94	19.67	1.62	2.42
1987	1.20	39.44	26.20	2.52	3.81
1988	2.40	47.54	33.11	5.02	7.22
1989	4.92	51.86	37.46	8.30	13.13
1990	7.81	61.27	46.21	12.60	16.90
1991	12.00	72.85	--	16.70	--
1992	21.25	85.00	--	25.00	--
1993	25.24	91.77	--	27.50	--
1994	34.71	121.00	--	28.70	--

Source: FIEs' exports figures provided by MOFERT and Customs Bureau, national export and national manufacturing export figures from *China Statistical Yearbook,* 1991-94, State Statistics Bureau, Beijing.

Their share of the country's total exports increased steadily as well. In 1984, FIE exports made up less than half of one per cent of the total national exports. They increased to over 5 per cent in 1988, 8.3 per cent in 1989, 12.6 per cent in 1990, 16.7 per cent in 1991, 25 per cent in 1992, 27.5 per cent in 1993, and 28.7 per cent in 1994,[83] a figure that matches the correspondent share in Taiwan in the 1970s.

The implication of FIEs export share is clear. If the new coastal frontiers can effectively emulate the success stories of the SEZs, Guangdong or Fujian, assuming that the current scale of imports is translated into exports in accordance with the export-orientated foreign investment strategy, FIEs share in national exports may be expected to increase to more than 30 per cent by the end of 1995.

The effect of FDI on China's manufacturing exports calls for special attention since the trend of China's exports after the 1986 oil price crisis moved away from exporting fuels and raw materials towards exporting manufacturing products where China's long-term comparative advantages lay. FIEs are believed to have contributed to such a shift, as most FIE exports were manufacturing goods, mainly comprising of electronics, textiles and light manufacturing goods, clothes and shoes, toys and suitcases, seafood and other foodstuffs, which amounted to a large proportion in the national exports of these products. For example, FIE electronic exports amounted to 28.8 per cent of national electronic exports, 16.6 per cent of textiles and clothing exports, and 50 per cent of shoes exports in 1991.[84] Table 6.3 shows that FIE exports in 1984 made up only 0.8 per cent of the total exports of manufacturing products, the figure increased to 7.2 per cent in 1988, and 16.9 per cent in 1990. The share of FIE manufacturing exports among FIE total exports rose from 46.5 per cent in 1978 to 80 per cent in 1992, and to 93 per cent in 1993.[85]

A proper assessment of FIE trade performance requires an examination of their foreign currency balances of exports and imports. Table 6.4 presents comprehensive data showing the shares of FIEs in total exports and imports of the economically opened coastal areas (EOCAs) between 1988 and 1991, based on U.S. dollar accounts.

The export data in **Table 6.4** reveal that FIE share in total exports in the EOCAs increased steadily during 1988-91. For China as a whole, FIE share in total exports rose from 5 per cent in 1988 to about 17 per cent in 1991. There was, however, significant variation between different regions: from a high of 46 per cent for the SEZs to 41 per cent (Fujian), 29 per cent (Guangdong) and a low of 11 per cent in both Shanghai and Beijing in 1991.

The impact of FDI on exports was most prominent in Guangdong Province which is best known for using FDI primarily to develop its export industries. FIE exports multiplied by almost seven times during 1984-86, increasing from

Table 6.4

Percentage share of FIEs in total export and import in the coastal areas in China, 1988-91

	Exports				Imports			
	1988	1989	1990	1991	1988	1989	1990	1991
SEZs	22.47	33.31	40.50	45.80	28.91	33.33	54.01	52.74
Shenzhen	26.38	36.99	43.96	50.52	30.67	33.00	51.66	57.24
Zhuhai	15.36	32.53	41.75	44.73	25.85	38.39	90.87	48.52
Shantou	11.56	18.49	23.63	28.38	14.89	2.18	26.57	31.51
Xiamen	18.36	28.02	37.37	41.70	42.83	42.95	56.73	58.50
OCCs	3.11 (5.99)	7.86 (8.05)	11.51 (11.71)	18.87 (18.78)	19.06 (20.00)	26.34 (26.51)	35.35 (36.70)	42.74 (50.35)
Dalian	6.73	18.70	24.10	40.43	60.77	36.77	50.23	61.64
Tianjin	2.29	3.94	6.00	10.41	13.17	20.91	28.65	33.71
Qingdao	1.39	5.23	7.54	13.07	29.58	37.63	30.83	37.41
Shanghai	1.71	4.65	6.38	10.82	15.81	22.93	29.74	43.87
Guangzhou	7.92	17.61	24.44	33.76	18.64	33.86	46.23	55.26
OCPs	7.61 (6.56)	12.99 (11.60)	17.19 (15.57)	21.97 (20.43)	19.76 (19.05)	25.69 (25.13)	38.35 (37.13)	37.12 (37.58)
Liaoning	0.99	2.97	4.24	9.26	24.32	17.67	28.89	37.90
Hebei	0.25	0.65	1.25	3.42	37.57	25.79	42.56	33.86
Shandong	0.60	2.34	3.62	6.00	9.72	17.27	25.69	33.89

Jiangsu	2.03	4.37	6.43	12.06	12.25	18.81	36.38	44.53
Zhejiang	2.52	3.73	6.11	9.02	9.52	13.07	19.32	25.24
Fujian	16.97	27.17	36.85	40.95	43.23	47.82	60.59	63.23
Guangdong	12.48	19.56	24.77	29.41	18.56	26.10	38.14	34.82
Hainan	2.10	7.55	7.10	8.48	12.79	17.64	34.89	29.05
Guangxi	1.64	3.40	4.82	7.50	14.72	21.66	26.29	24.50
Beijing	2.68	4.88	7.64	11.47	51.58	65.57	52.87	52.44
Provincial total	5.51	9.62	13.32	17.59	26.05	30.06	36.07	35.61
PRC Total	5.15	9.23	12.58	16.76	14.34	19.65	23.56	26.55

Notes:
Figures in brackets are sum total for all the 15 OCCs and 11 OCPs including Tianjin and Shanghai. There is a striking discrepancy in the FIEs share in imports between the provincial and PRC totals, compared with the very marginal difference in the FIEs share in exports. The implied percentage shares of total PRC imports conducted at the central level for the four years amounted to 46.2 (1988), 42.3 (1989), 34.70 (1990), and 29.9 (1991), and that for exports only 6.5, 4.2, 5.5 and 4.7 respectively. These figures may understate the real magnitude of centralised control, because in many instances both exports and imports as undertaken by the 'provincial-level trading firms' are still subject to various non-tariff restrictions, including export/import licensing, quotas and foreign exchange allocation. Nevertheless, the discrepancy shows that despite the trade decentralisation drive imports have remained subject to much greater central control than exports. The situation is thus basically the same as that in the mid-1980s, although the degree of central control over imports has tended to decline in recent years.

Sources: Kueh, Y.Y. (1992), op.cit., p.668, Table 9.

223

Table 6.5
Trade balance of FIEs in coastal areas in China, 1988-91

	As share of exports (%)				Trade balance (exports minus imports, in $100m)			
	1988	1989	1990	1991	1988	1989	1990	1991
SEZs	-4.01	0.74	-7.63	-6.07	-32.47	3.33	-23.73	-14.11
Shenzhen	-1.88	2.63	-1.70	-3.18	-19.46	15.81	-7.41	-10.08
Zhuhai	-1.11	-0.93	-4.82	-0.98	-130.59	-44.29	-137.32	-19.25
Shantou	-0.18	-0.14	-0.12	-0.57	-20.22	-9.15	-5.29	-16.76
Xiamen	-0.84	-0.82	-0.99	-1.34	-88.42	-41.62	-28.78	-25.28
OCCs	-9.23 (-7.64)	-12.72 (-13.26)	-11.55 (-12.28)	-12.97 (-14.88)	-340.59 (-137.91)	-173.53 (-158.61)	-93.83 (-86.05)	-55.76 (-56.11)
Dalian	-1.87	-0.39	-0.61	-0.82	-623.33	-36.79	-35.47	-19.11
Tianjin	-0.71	-1.39	-1.04	-1.20	-182.05	-207.46	-97.20	-65.93
Qingdao	-0.30	-0.69	-0.36	-0.44	-1000.00	-460.00	-128.57	-69.84
Shanghai	-4.23	-7.43	-6.90	-7.00	-503.57	-318.88	-197.14	-106.22
Guangzhou	-2.11	-2.83	-2.65	-3.51	-181.90	-90.71	-46.01	-35.35
OCPs	-20.57 (-25.52)	-18.06 (-26.88)	-28.96 (-36.89)	-20.51 (-28.67)	-91.59 (-107.68)	-40.43 (-56.59)	-40.49 (-48.48)	-18.97 (-24.59)

Liaoning	-2.21	-0.91	-1.10	-1.23	-566.67	-71.09	-49.55	-23.61
Hebei	-1.36	-0.91	-1.32	-0.59	-3400.00	-758.33	-550.00	-85.51
Shandong	-0.68	-1.12	-0.98	-1.39	-400.00	-157.75	-79.03	-61.78
Jiangsu	-0.77	-1.34	-2.45	-4.22	-157.14	-120.12	-129.63	-102.18
Zhejiang	-0.09	-0.13	0.21	0.25	-23.68	-18.57	15.67	9.54
Fujian	-3.71	-2.61	-2.43	-3.55	-154.17	-52.52	-26.91	-27.54
Guangdong	-10.95	-9.69	-19.57	-8.05	-59.38	-27.43	-35.71	-10.16
Hainan	-0.37	-0.87	-1.14	-1.57	-616.67	-348.00	-300.00	-296.23
Guangxi	-0.42	-0.46	-0.20	-0.16	-466.67	-209.09	-51.28	-27.59
Beijing	-4.72	-5.89	-4.44	-5.37	-1815.38	-1178.00	-516.28	-358.00
Provincial total	-54.76	-67.71	-47.55	-38.82	-223.69	-139.69	-60.68	-32.21
PRC Total	-77.51	-66.00	87.40	81.19	-	-	-	-

Notes: Figures in brackets refer respectively to the sum total of all 15 OCCs and 11 OCPs including Tianjin and Shanghai.

Sources: Kueh, Y.Y. (1992), op.cit, p.670, Table 10.

225

US$115 million in 1984 to US$750 million in 1986, while its total exports doubled from US$2.2 billion to US$4.2 billion during the same period. FIE share of the provincial exports thus jumped from 5.3 per cent in 1984 to nearly 18 per cent in 1986, 12.5 per cent in 1988, 29.41 per cent in 1991 and 35 per cent in 1992.[86] FIEs in Fujian Province contributed 16.97 per cent of the total provincial exports in 1988, 27.17 per cent in 1989, 36.85 per cent in 1990 and 40.95 per cent in 1991.[87] In other provinces, such as Zhejiang, Hainan, Guangxi, Shandong, Liaoning and Hebei, FIE exports among total provincial exports varied from as 3.42 per cent in Hebei to 9.02 per cent in Zhejiang in 1991, though enjoying significant growth rates from 1988 to 1991 in most cases. It was estimated that FIE exports in the 11 coastal provinces amounted to US$11.65 billion in 1991, accounting 20.43 per cent of these provinces' total exports and 96.7 per cent of national FIEs' exports.[88] Table 6.4 also suggests that the proportion of FIE exports increased from 3.11 per cent in 1988, to 18.78 per cent in total export volumes in those five open coastal cities (Dalian, Tianjin, Qingdao, Shanghai, and Guangzhou).

It is clear enough that FIEs not only brought China scarce capital, but also provided it with the export potentials and marketing skills needed for integrating with international markets. FIEs also encouraged domestic export producers and trading firms to improve their operational efficiency through a competition mechanism.

Evidence in **Table 6.4** shows that FIE imports increased more rapidly compared with its exports. FIE share in the four SEZs (Shenzhen, Zhuhai, Shantou and Xiamen) total import volumes increased from 28.91 per cent in 1988, to 33.33 per cent in 1989, 54.01 per cent in 1990 and 52.74 per cent in 1991. FIE share in the 15 OCCs total import volumes grew rapidly from 20 per cent in 1988 to 26.51 per cent in 1989, 36.70 per cent in 1990 and 50.35 per cent in 1991. The share of FIEs in all the 11 OCPs in their total import volumes also grew from 19.05 per cent in 1988 to 37.58 per cent in 1991. Taking the nation as a whole, FIE shares in the national total imports increased from 14.34 per cent in 1988 to 19.65 per cent in 1989, 23.56 per cent in 1990 and 26.55 per cent in 1991. This happened mainly because many FIEs had contracts calling for importing machinery, equipment and essential raw materials. Although specific data on machinery imports attributable to FIE operation in the 1980s are not available, a local survey taken in Guangdong Province may be indicative of overall trends. It is estimated that about US$ 1.78 bn was spent by FIEs on 1,551 packages of importing production equipment and assembly lines from 1979 to 1985. This was about half of the total expenditure (US$3.54 billion) on imports of the same categories of the province during the same period.[89]

The most striking finding to emerge from Table 6.5, which shows FIE trade balance, is that throughout 1988-91 virtually no coastal area succeeded inbalancing its foreign exchange requirements. Guangdong and Fujian provinces, as well as the SEZs all continued to exhibit substantial negative FIEs trade balances during 1988-91.[90] However, the foreign exchange balances of FIEs vary between different industrial destinations of foreign investment. Foreign exchange surpluses have generally characterised FIEs in hotels and recreational services, as well as in primary sector activities, especially the extraction of mineral ores, coal and oil for sale in world markets. It suggests that the imbalances suffered by manufacturing and processing FIEs are significantly greater than the net balance estimates as **Table 6.5** suggests. However, we found that the trade deficits of FIEs tended to decline as a proportion of their own exports during 1988-91. This suggests that as investment generates increased volumes of output and exports, most FIEs in coastal areas might be able to meet the requirements for foreign exchange balance in the years to come.

Taking the nation as a whole, the import figures for FIEs were much higher than their exports during 1990-94.[91] Total FIE imports increased from US$12.29 billion in 1990 to US$16.9 billion in 1991, US$26.35 billion in 1992,[92] US$41.83 billion in 1993 (58.6 per cent higher than 1992, and amounting to 40.2 per cent of national total imports in 1993), and US$52.9 billion in 1994, much higher than their total exports US$7.81 billion, US$12 billion, US$21.25 billion, US$25.24 billion, and US$34.71 billion in the same period respectively. FIE import and export deficits were US$4.88 billion in 1990, US$4.9 billion in 1991, US$5.1 billion in 1992, US$10.33 billion in 1993 and US$18.23 billion in 1994 respectively, showing a rapid growing trend.[93] FIE imports of machinery and equipment as a means of equity contribution became one of the main reasons of FIE trade deficit.

These figures suggest that FIEs in China are more dependent on imported raw materials than local firms in manufacturing industries. According to official statistics, about 70-80 per cent of FIEs in the electronics industry depended on imports for all or most of their supply of parts and components.[94]

By the end of 1994 the national aggregate foreign exchange balance of FIEs on current account was still negative, though some provinces or cities may have already balanced their current account of foreign exchange, or even produced a surplus. However, arguments were made that many FIEs, especially those in high-tech projects, were established to make products that China originally had to import. The availability of their products in the domestic market helped reduce the country's import needs. More and more FIEs, such as Tianjin Otis Elevator, Shanghai Schindler Elevator, Shanghai Volkswagen, Changchun Audi, Guangzhou Peugout, and Shanghai-Pilkington Floating Glass, not only produced high quality of products to replace the original imports in an effective way, but also exported to a third country. The impact of FDI on China's foreign trade should, therefore, include this indirect import-substitution effect on the current account.[95]

Arguments can be made, therefore, that in the long run FDI may have a positive trade balance by improving its export competitiveness. This is because FIEs provided domestic industries with better equipment and instruments, which in turn increased local firms' product quality and production capacity and thereby improving their export potentials. A large number of FIEs were established in the fields of energy, transportation, and other infrastructural industries that would help improving China's exporting production capacity and products quality.

It can also be argued that the significance of FDI in promoting host country's exports would depend on the country's resource endowment, predominant production technology, level of development, and governmental policy. FDI's contribution to manufacturing exports and economic growth depends very much on the level of the country's development.

FDI and technology transfer

Many famous MNCs have invested in a large number of high-tech projects into the country during 1979-92, and brought in advanced technology, equipment and management techniques which led some Chinese industries made great technological progress and produced many famous-brand products. There are numerous examples of how FIE high-tech products contributed to China's economy in the recent years. Shanghai CASCO Signal Company Ltd., a Sino-American JV manufacturing modern railway signal apparatus, made a notable contribution to modernizing the country's rail transportation system since 1986. The new signal system helped shorten the time needed for dispatching each train for departure from ten to six minutes, thus greatly enhancing the effective usage of existing rail-tracks. The installation of infrared devices not only replaced the previous manual operation which was time-consuming but also dramatically increased railways transportation safety. Beijing Jeep Corporation (BJC), Guangzhou Peugeot, Changchun Auti, Hubei Citroen and Shanghai Volkswagen all adapted advanced Western technology in making automobiles. Tianjin Otis and Shanghai Shilinder produced computerized high-speed elevators. Thereafter, China's elevator and car industries have ceased to rely heavily on imports as they did in the past, and have caught up the 1990s advanced standards of automobiles and elevators.

Absorbing foreign key advanced technology combined with maximizing inputs of China-made components was another strategy the Chinese government adopted to up-grade its technology. Shanghai Volkswagen is an good example of maximising inputs of Chinese-made components and parts up to world standards.[96] Its production capacity and local input reached

90,000 car/year and 95 per cent by the end of 1995. It has been recognized by the Volkswagen headquarters in Germany as the best overseas plant among 4 host countries where Volkswagen produced similar products.

The Daya Bay Nuclear Plant in Guangdong Province, aimed not only to solve the problem of electricity shortage in the southern China, but also to help the country to master large-capacity nuclear power technology and to consolidate the foundation for the country's nuclear power industry. The Pingshuo Coal Mine in Shaanxi Province, built in two years to achieve an annual production capacity of 15 million tons, was another attempt to gain experience in using world advanced technology and equipment to build modern giant coal mines in the country. Other prominent examples of advanced technology transfer included Shanghai Yaohua Pilkington Floating Glass Company which used highly automated production technology from Pilkington from Britain; Shanghai Bell Telephone Equipment Manufacturing Ltd., a JV between Shanghai Bureau of Post and Telecommunications with Belgian Alcatel Bell, designed to transfer some of the latest overseas standards and technologies to produce the advanced S1240 circuit telecommunications exchanges and switches. All these large foreign invested projects have significantly improved China's infrastructure, telecommunications, and energy facilities.

What made the technology transfer through FDI particularly appealing to China, was not only the way in which technology obtained, but also the way in which technology was transferred. Technology transfer through FDI was generally more effective because they were packaged with management know-how, which China badly needs. They also encouraged more dynamic and progressive technology transfer as compared with other forms of technology transfer, and tended to be pragmatic and to emphasize economic results.[97]

Compared with indigenous SOEs, FIEs were more conscious of economic results in deciding what technology was to be adopted and how. Most FIEs tried to adopt suitable technology to improve the quality and variety of their products while combining with the advantage of relatively cheap labour. In order to minimize the initial costs and maximize the economic results, many FIEs resorted to a staged development strategy, i.e., first invested a small amount of capital to build one or two production line using rather simple technology and equipment, put them into operation right away to generate new capital, and then used the newly generated capital to build more and better production lines. This strategy helped a number of small-sized FIEs to succeed in a short time.[98]

Because technology transfer is directly related to enterprise performance, foreign partners have greater incentives to continuously update the technology used by FIEs so as to maintain the competitiveness of their products. Many FIEs which concluded dynamic or progressive technology transfer agreements were able to follow closely the latest technical development abroad.[99]

Given that most foreign partners in FIEs are from Hong Kong, there is little doubt that these have mainly involved labour-intensive manufacturing activities, driven by soaring local land rentals and labour costs across the border to the Pearl River Delta and other congenial sites in China. The relevant FDI ventures, whether export-orientated or import-substitution undertaking, have for the most part involved products at the very end of the relevant product cycle. In other words, they have been internationally well-known products, embodying appreciate technological standards. Bearing in mind the predominant Hong Kong share in FDI ventures, many can probably be described as 'sunset' industries in terms of their marketability and technological level (Kueh, Y.Y., 1992, pp.656-7). The fact that most foreign partners had to base their technology selection on their own assessment of economic benefits made some of the Chinese government's efforts to encourage 'advanced' technology transfer unsuccessful. Despite the constant emphasis and extra incentive offered by the government, as of the end of 1987, only 287 out of over 4,000 FIEs operating throughout the country were officially recognized as 'advanced technology enterprises'. So FIEs' overall contribution to the technological transfer was quite weak.

On the other hand, among those 'advanced technology enterprises', many were facing serious problems ranging from foreign exchange deficits (mainly due to a reliance on imported inputs of machinery and equipments) to ineffective use of the imported equipment. In the cases of AMC (USA), Pilkington (UK) and Bell Telecommunications (Belgium), the level of technology transferred through the JVs were found much higher than actually needed. Consequently, the gap between the technology transferred by foreign partners and the ability of the JVs to absorb it effectively became wider. In such cases, foreign partners found it advantageous to provide unsophisticated technology for which components and parts could be found in China (Chen, Jinghan, 1993, p.181).

Much of the criticism of FDI in China focuses on technology choice - the higher capital intensity of foreign firms is symptomatic of their inefficient use of domestic resources, including excessively import-intensive operations and the production of 'inappropriate' products. Some cases did support the claim that foreign firms choose more inappropriate production techniques than their local counterparts in China. Some studies found that foreign firms to be significantly more capital-intensive than local firms, but could not make good use of labour-intensive process.[100]

The sub-contracting networks are widely used by FIEs in the automotive and appliance industries acting as a means of technology transfer. But the result of the government's sub-contracting policies is so far not very encouraging. Since the mid-1980s, several measures have been introduced which compel the assemblers not only to backward integrate, but also to procure from local firms rather than to engage in in-house manufacturing. Most assemblers have been sub-contracting only because of the government pressure. Moreover, in response to the mandatory deletion programme, they have preferred wherever possible to manufacture in-house; most subcontract has been confined to a few insignificant and non-essential items. Consequently, linkages - technical, managerial, and financial - between assemblers and sub-contractors have generally been weak. The result is hardly surprising, as many studies suggested that MNCs often have fewer links with the local economy than do domestic firms (Caves, 1982, pp.270-2). These weak links are the result of both 'policy' and 'commercial' factors. 'Policy' factors include the establishment of SEZs, technological development zones (TDZs) and export processing zones (EPZs), which discourage forward and backward linkages, and a cascading protective structure, which encourages overseas rather than domestic sourcing of components, so that inhibited internal economic integration. 'Commercial' factors include the introduction of new products, for which inputs are not locally available, and the fact that foreign firms are less familiar with the local business environment. There is considerable evidence on the high import intensity of foreign investors, another factor contributing to low linkages. Consequently, the technology spin-off through sub-contracting have been minimal, although they may develop over time.

It could be concluded that many foreign investors have transferred appropriate advanced technology to China. Few cases of JVs with the foreign partners supplying a high level of technology had proved to be successful, and there have been minimal forward or backward linkages with local domestic economy.

Enterprise management

The impact of FDI on enterprise management was, perhaps, the most valuable result of foreign capital in China. Adaptation of new management know-how in Sino-foreign JVs not only helped many Chinese enterprises succeed in transferring technology, but also helped raise the overall efficiency of the Chinese SOEs. Encouraged by the FDI policies, FIEs in China either entirely or partially adopted the management system introduced by the foreign partners, and they enjoyed more or less astomous power in JV decisions and daily operational management.[101] In FIEs redundant positions were eliminated, duties and responsibilities were clearly divided, labour disciplines were much better enforced, and rewards and punishments were more closely related to individual performance.[102]

The transfer of more modern and efficient techniques and exploitation of their technological advantages can be highly rewarding for FIEs in many fields of production and services. Lower taxes, low labour costs and high prices in the domestic market made FIEs more profitable than local SOEs. Some FIEs reaped additional profits from certain other sources. This implied that FIEs in China were more profitable than domestic firms: the former's net profit margin (net income to sales) remained two to three times higher than that of domestic firms. In China, gross profit rates in JVs were normally 30 per cent per annum, even more than 50 per cent.[103] As a result, most FIEs reported rather dramatic improvements in productivity and efficiency. It was commonplace that a job that would take three to five persons to perform in a SOE needed only one person to work in a FIE, or the same job that took several days to finish in a SOE required only a few hours in a FIE, even with the same technical equipment. Chinese managers of JVs often boasted, with real pride, that their labour productivity was two to three times that of indigenous SOEs in the same industry.

Numerous stories could be recounted of how FIEs succeeded in turning deficit-ridden SOEs into profit makers in a short time through technical and managerial transformation. BJC was a well-known case in the automobile industry in turning a deficit-maker into a profit-generator. Its predecessor, the Beijing Auto Manufacturing Plant (BAMP) was an inefficient SOE with 11,000 workers. In 1984, half of its property and 4,000 workers became part of BJC, the Sino-American JV. Mainly through management readjustment, technical renovation and introduction of a new wage and bonus system which reflected the responsibility, performance and contribution of the employees at all levels, BJC achieved an efficiency never seen in the BAMP history. In 1986, the second year of the JV operation, its annual production almost doubled that of BAMP in 1983, the year before the JV formed. Labour productivity, average profits and tax contribution per capita that year reached unprecedented levels and made BJC stand at the top in the automobile industry and one of the best FIEs in the country.[104]

Most FIEs in China found it necessary to provide basic technical training in order to adopt Western new production methods. Accordingly, they established regular training programmes, allowing a number of their employees, in rotation, to receive free training related to their jobs. As a result, employees not only improve their productive performance, but also develop a loyalty to the enterprises. These programmes entailed FIEs with extra costs, but they usually found the payback worthwhile.

FIEs making high-tech products or using high technology in production often sent their employees abroad to receive more advanced technical and managerial training. Shanghai Foxboro, for instance, sent about one third of its 380 employees to the United State for technical instruction.[105] BJC also sent several hundred Chinese technicians and managerial staff to Detroit for training during the first 3-4 years of its operation. This had positive results in terms of improving employees' knowledge and skill and increasing output and product quality.

Many FIEs in China show a willingness to substitute Chinese employees for foreign experts once they are qualified. Initially FIEs usually found it necessary to hire technical and managerial staff from their home countries to fill key management positions or to solve technical problems. Many foreign experts, however, were frequently asked to train local technicians and managers. Once qualified local staff were available, they replaced the 'foreign teachers'.[106]

FDI's contribution to Chinese management system must include that fact that foreign managers in FIEs helped train Chinese managers. Many Chinese managers in FIEs have learnt 'international standards of business management' through day-to-day practice and cooperation with their foreign counterparts. Many in China thus saw FIEs not only as factories producing high quality products but also as valuable business schools training high quality managerial personnel.[107]

One of the most important contribution of FDI was one not generally discussed in the literature - its policy realm: the intentional use of foreigners to reform recalcitrant sections of the economy, even the political system. FIEs have opened windows through which Chinese people can look outward more clearly and realistically. A new group of managers and entrepreneurs directly trained in FIEs has now emerged - a group that will unquestionably have an important impact on transforming the Chinese economy into a free market system in the near future.

Summary

It is clear enough that FIEs not only brought China scarce capital, much-needed technology and managerial know-how, as well as increased governmental revenue and productivity, but they also provided it with the export potentials and marketing skills needed for integration into international markets.

Conclusion

This chapter has provided an overview of the role and extent of FDI in LDCs and compared development in Hungary and China to it by integrating the scattered and limited information available from secondary sources on FDI.

Foreign investors introduce a package of highly productive resources into the host countries. These include managerial skills, production technology, continuing access to established R & D facilities, proprietary use of international brand names, and knowledge of and access to international product and capital markets.

JVs have largely contributed to technical and managerial modernisation, labour productivity and export performance. FIEs also accounted for substantial percentages of both net output and employment, and contributed towards the transformation and competitiveness of the local economies through the introduction of more efficient management practice, better industrial relations, and the transfer of technology. Investment inflows can, however, create balance of payments problems if the tradable sector as a whole becomes not more competitive by industrial restructuring and macroeconomic adjustment. Balance of payments problems and ensuing local currency devaluations can fuel inflationary expectations, contribute to a price-wage-price spiral and thereby destabilize the whole transformation process. From this perspective FDI is a necessary ingredient of systemic transformation but FDI inflows should be mobilized in a gradual and sustaining manner rather than in one major wave.

It is clear that for the time being that foreign capital is so far still not playing a decisive role in the Hungarian economy: foreign capital has not met Hungary's objectives serving as a major instrument to speed up privatisation, boost economic growth, and better incorporate the national economy into the world economic system to any marked extent. In the future, the drive to make more profits will lead more and more MNCs introduce new technology and develop higher quality products as well as management and marketing techniques that improve the living standard within Hungary. FDI's impact is, therefore, likely to grow, to deepen and to broaden in scope: will be of particular assistance in balancing Hungary's payments. FIEs will become the most dynamic sector of the national economy.

In the case of China, although the overall impact of FDI on the national economy was still limited at this stage, contribution by FDI appeared evident in the areas of capital supplement, technology transfer, foreign trade and enterprise management, which are strategically important in China's modernisation. FIEs have become a well-established and important part of Chinese economic activity. Within the SEZs, OCPs and OCCs, where FDI was more engaged in labour-intensive and export-oriented activities, the effects on employment and exports were becoming more positive and significant. On a nation-wide scale, however, the effects of FDI in these latter two areas was mixed, and, to some extent, they even caused some major concern about the effects upon balance of payments and labour redundance. What appears to be the most important contribution by FDI to the Chinese economy is its introduction into China of a new way of thinking, which emphasizes competition, efficiency and free market.

Notes

1.Lall, Sanjaya and Streeton, Paul (1977), *Foreign Investment, Transnational Corporations and Developing Countries*, MacMillan, London.

2.Reuber G. L., et al. (1973), *Private Foreign Investment in Development*, Clarendon Press, Oxford.

3.Ballance, R. H., Ansari, J. A., and Singer, H. W. (1982), *The International Economy and Industrial Development: The Impact of Trade and Investment on the Third World*, Osmun Publishers, Allanheld.

4.Additional empirical evidence regarding the influence of FDI on the economy of developing country which is particularly relevant to the employment issue is offered by a study on Thailand. This analysis attempted to evaluate the contribution of foreign firms to the host economy by reference to four criteria, viz., (a) the contribution to national income; (b) the creation to employment; (c) the utilisation of domestic resources and (d) earnings and foreign exchange savings. The empirical findings suggest that, despite the rapid increase of FDI in manufacturing such investment was unable to render a significant contribution to the host country, in terms of the criteria mentioned above, because of the high capital intensity and import dependency of most foreign firms. Such firms have shown a preference in securing imported materials from the home country and retaining a high proportion of imported personnel and skilled workers for a long time, thus impeding the stimulation of domestic investment and the upgrading of the skills of the local workforce.

The implications of the preceding analysis for policy considerations seem to be that: (a) there is a need for adaptation of production processes to meet the endowed factor proportions of host countries; (b) host countries need to develop new investment policies to encourage a better use of surplus factors, i. e. labour and (c) developing nations may need to regulate investors having a technological monopoly. Whether, of course, such policies could be pursued by most developing countries is a difficult question to answer. See, Tambunlertchai, S. (1976), *Foreign Direct Investment in Thailand's Manufacturing Industries*, PhD dissertation, Duke University.

5.See, for example, Areskoug, K. (1973), 'Foreign Capital Utilisation and Economic Policy in Developing Countries', *Review of Economics and Statistics*, Vol.55, No.2; Griffin, K. B. (1970), 'Foreign Capital, Domestic Savings and Development', *Bulletin of the Oxford University Institute of Economics and Statistics*, No.32; Left, N. H. (1969), 'Dependency Rates and Savings Rates', *American Economic Review*, Vol.59, No.5.

6.Inotai, Andras (1990), 'Experiences and Lessons of FDI in Developing Countries'. The World Bank and Ghana Investment Promotion Conference, State House, Accra, 26-28 February 1990.

7.See, for example, Chenery, H. B. and Strout, A. M. (1966), 'Foreign Assistance and Economic Development', *American Economic Review,* Vol.56, September 1966, pp.679-733.

8.Dunning, J. (1969), *The Role of American Investment in the British Economy,* PEP Broadsheet 507, p.142.

9.Sylos-Labini, P.(1969), *Oligopoly and Technical Progress,* Revised Edition, Harvard University Press, p.154.

10.Ibid., p.155.

11.Both Reuber and Vaitsos (1976) provide evidence to show that the capital/labour ratio of foreign subsidiaries is considerable and, as a rule, it exceeds the corresponding ratio of local enterprises. See, Vaitsos, C. (1976), 'Employment Problems and Transnational Enterprises in Developing Countries: Distortions and Inequality', International Labour Office, World Employment Programme Research, Working Paper II, memo; and also Reuber, G., et al. (1973), *Private Foreign Investment in Development,* Clarendon Press, London, p.168; Vaitsos, C. (1974), 'Employment Effects of Foreign Direct Investment in Developing Countries', in Edwards, E.O.(ed.), *Employment in Developing Nations,* Columbia University Press.

12.Chenery, H.B. (1961),'Comparative Advantage and Development Policy', *American Economic Review,* No.51, pp.18-51.

13.Hood, Neil and Young, Stephen (1979), *The Economics of Multinational Enterprise,* Longman, London & New York, p.179.

14.Steuer, M.D. et al (1973), *The Impact of Foreign Direct Investment on the United Kingdom,* Department of Trade and Industry, London, pp.16-35; and also Stubenitsky, G. (1967), *American Direct Investment in the Netherlands Industry: A Survey of the Year 1966,* PhD dissertation, California University.

15.Vernon (1971) utilised data from the US Treasury Department's study - *Overseas Manufacturing Investment and the Balance of Payment* by Hufbauger and Adler (1968) and their assumptions regarding FDI, and put forward: (a) the American investors has a free choice between investing abroad to produce the products with which to supply the foreign markets, and exporting them from the US and (b) the investment was defensive, in the sense that if the

American investor did not undertake it, someone else would have done so and the product would have been produced in the host country in any case. See, Vernon, Raymond (1971), *Sovereignty at Bay: The Multinational Spread of U.S. Enterprises,* New York, pp.170-5.

16.Hall, S. and Streeten, P. (1977), *Foreign Investment, Transnational and Developing Countries,* Macmillan, London, p.142.

17.Solberg, Ronald L. (1993), (ed.), *Country-Risk Analysis: A Handbook,* Routledge, London & New York, pp.37-38.

18.The fact that decision-making by foreign firms is taken at the overseas headquarters of the parent company, implies a degree of remoteness that may introduce elements of friction between management and work force, and increase economic conflict in a manner that might have been avoided by local firms. However, foreign firms operating in environments with a strongly unionist labour force have sought to influence and improve industrial relations and, therefore, achieve better labour utilisation. Accordingly, the workers agree to change certain working practices in return for higher pay or other benefits and this tends to lead to a more efficient production.

19.Baranson, J.(1966), 'Transfers of Technical Knowledge by International Corporations to Developing Countries', *American Economic Review,* Vol.56, pp.256-7.

20.Galbraith, J.K. (1969), *The New Industrial State,* Pelican, London, p.71.

21.Hymer, Stephen H. (1976), *The International Operations of National Firms: A Study of Direct Foreign Investment,* M.I.T. Monograph in Economics, 14 Cambridge, Mass; and Caves, Richard E. (1971), 'International Corporations: The Industrial Economics of Foreign Investment', *Economica,* N.S., Vol.38, London, pp.1-27.

22.Caves, R.E. (1974), 'Multinational Firms, Competition and Productivity in Host-Country Markets', *Economica,* Vol.41, pp.176-93; Dunning, J. (1974), 'Multinational Enterprises, Market Structure, Economic Power and Industrial Policy', *Journal of World Trade Law,* Vol.8, pp.575-613.

23.Hunya, Gabor (1992), 'Foreign Direct Investment and Privatisation in Central and Eastern Europe', *Communist Economics and Economic Transformation,* Vol.4, No.4, pp.501-10.

24.Dietz, Raimund (1991), 'The Role of Western Capital in the Transition to the Market - A Systems' Theoretical Perspective', in Csaba, Laszlo (1991) (ed.), *Systemic Change and Stabilisation in Eastern Europe*, Dartmouth Publishing Company, London, pp.115-6.

25.Kadar, Bela (1992), speech at the Seventh Anniversary of Joint Venture Association, 9 October 1992.

26.Csorba, Andras (1993), 'Joint Ventures in Hungary', *Hungarian Business Herald*, No. 1, 1993, p.7.

27.Hamar, Judit (1993), 'FDI & Privatisation in Hungary', paper presented at International Workshop on 'Privatisation Experiences in Eastern Europe' organised by Kopint-Datorg and UNCTAD on 21-22 May 1993, Budapest, p.7.

28.Gombocz, Zoltan (1993), 'The Situation and Future of Foreign Equity Capital in Hungary', Investment and Trade Promotion Agency, Ministry of International Economic Relations.

29.Kadas, Carolyn (1993), 'Hungary: Is the Boom Over', *Business Eastern Europe*, 14 April 1993.

30.Csaki, Gyorgy (1992), 'East-West Corporate Joint Ventures: Promises and Disappointments', working paper at Institute for World Economics, Hungarian Academy of Sciences, No.3, January 1992, pp.8-9.

31.*Invest in Hungary*, No.1, 1992, p.16.

32.Interview with an official at Hungarian Joint Ventures Association in May 1993.

33.*Financial Times*, 23 November 1993, p.6.

34.Kadar,Bela (1993), 'The Role of Foreign Investment in Hungary', *Hungarian Business Herald*, Hungarian Ministry of International Economic Relations, No.1, p.4.

35.Mihaly, Simai (1990), 'Foreign Direct Investment in the Hungarian Economy - 1990, manuscript, IWE-HAS, Budapest, p.26.

36.Interview with officials at Hungarian Ministry of International Economic Relations in May 1993.

37.Cooper, Sharyn (1993), 'Managing Lay-outs in An EE Acquisition', *Business Eastern Europe*, 22 February 1993, p.1.

38.Ibid., p.1.

39.Hungarian Central Statistical Office (1992), *Foreign Direct Investment and Foreign Joint Ventures in Hungary*, KSH, Budapest, p.7.

40.The Chairman of Hungarian National Bank stated that 'the sharp increase in FDI inflow was more important because it greatly facilitated the internal financing of the national economy. The foreign capital currently being invested came close to the monthly interest payable on foreign credit, about US$9-10 million. The principal to be repaid every month amounted to US$20 million'. See, *MTI*, 1423 Gmt, 4 August 1992, and *Hungarian Review*, No.31, 1992, p.5.

41.Kiss, Karoly (1991), 'Privatisation in Hungary', *Communist Economies and Economic Transformation*, Vol.1, 1991, pp.309-10.

42.Until recently, Hungary has been criticised for having an overvalued currency.

43.FIEs in Hungary are considered to be easier to expand exports than those indigenous SOEs because the quality, packaging, appearance, and prices of their products could more or less measure up to the international standards; and they could take advantage of their foreign partners' international marketing networks around the world. The latter is a decisive factor of export marketing of such goods as automobiles, tractors, machine tools, furniture, or electrical household appliances.

44.FIEs in Hungary had been recently criticised by economists for their allegedly poor export performance. The main explanation by FIEs was the unattractive commercial environment rather than the nationality of investors.

45.Hungarian Central Statistical Office (1993), *Foreign Direct Investment and Foreign Joint Ventures in Hungary*, SKH, Budapest, p.6.

46.Hungarian Central Statistical Office (1992), *Foreign Direct Investment and Foreign Joint Ventures in Hungary*, KSH, Budapest, pp.1-3.

47.Kadar, Bela (1993), 'The Role of Foreign Investment in Hungary', *Hungarian Business Herald*, No.1, 1993, p.5. The Minister of International Economic Relations also admitted that 'new modern technologies, marketing and management knowledge, improvement of quality, experience in plant organisation which are indispensable for the technical-structural modernisation of the Hungarian economy, are frequently attached to FDI'. See, Kadar, Bela (1992), Speech at the Seventh Anniversary of Joint Venture Association, 9 October 1992.

48. United Nations (1989), *Joint Ventures as a Form of International Economic Cooperation,* Taylor & Francis, New York, p.40.

49. We find that most of the FIEs had extremely limited research and development capacity. In some cases, modest laboratories had been established to conform with the government requirements or to ensure quality control.

50. Soos, Karoly Attila (1992), 'The Changing Role of Joint Ventures in the Central-East European Transition Process', *Russian and East European Finance and Trade,* Spring, pp.63-8.

51. Low capital requirement, suitable-generation technology and low risk, accompanied by unsatisfied or growing internal demand for the products in service sector motivated foreign investment decision.

52. Corporate Location (1993), 'Hungary Country Report', p.9.

53. Wang, Z.Q. (1993), 'Foreign Investment in Hungary: A Survey of Experience and Prospects', *Communist Economies and Economic Transformation,* Vol.5, No.2, p.249.

54. Koves A. and Oblath G. (1991), 'Stabilization and Foreign Economic Policy', *Acta Oeconomica,* No.43, 1991, p.12.

55. *People's Daily (Overseas Edition),* 31 December 1992.

56. Ibid., 16 December 1991.

57. Ibid., 31 October 1991.

58. Ibid., 25 September 1993, p.2.

59. Ibid., 18 April 1991.

60. Ibid., 31 May 1993.

61. Ibid., 4 May 1995, p.2.

62. Wu Zhenkun and Song Zihe (1991) (ed.), *A Comparative Study of the Development Strategies of Opening up the Economy*, Academy of Central Committee of the China Communist Party Press, Beijing, p.45. The estimate seems to cover both FDI and foreign borrowing.

63. Wang, Junshi (1993), 'On China's Foreign Capital Utilisation', *Intertrade*, Vol.133, No.1, pp.17-8.

64. *People's Daily*, 27 June 1992.

65. *People's Daily*, 7 August 1992, 5 April 1994, and 18 May 1994.

66. Ibid., 10 February 1992.

67. Kueh, Y.Y. (1992), 'Foreign Investment and Economic Change in China', *The China Quarterly*, September, Vol.132, p.661.

68. Guangdong and Fujian Reports to the October Central Meeting on FDI.

69. *People's Daily*, 16 January 1991.

70. *People's Daily*, 4 May 1995, p.2.

71. FIEs in Shanghai realised surplus of foreign exchange since 1989, reaching US$1.08 billion in 1993.

72. *People's Daily*, 19 March 1991 and 30 December 1992.

73. Xinhua News Agency, *People's Daily*, 5 February 1988, p.1.

74. *People's Daily*, 7 August 1992, p.1.

75. Walker, Tony (1993), 'Investment in China Set to Top US$100 billion', *Financial Times*, 8 November 1993, p.5.

76. 'Conspicuous Achievements of Coastal Opening', *Financial Times*, 11 March 1988, p.3.

77. *People's Daily*, 25 September 1993, p.2, and 5 April 1994.

78. Ibid., 2 August 1991.

79. *People's Daily*, 18 May 1994 and 18 January 1995.

80. According to Zhang Haoruo, by 1987, 42 per cent of the 3,000 FIEs in operation in China failed to balance their own foreign exchange accounts; and except in Shanghai, Beijing and Tianjin, FIEs as a whole saw deficit in their foreign exchange accounts in most provinces and cities in the country. Zhang's Report at the October Central Committee Meeting on FDI, 1987.

81. See, Chinese State Statistical Bureau, *China's Statistical Yearbook,* various volumes.

82. It is worthwhile to mention that FIEs export surge has been attributed partly to the unification on 1 January 1994 of the Chinese yuan resulting in an effective 50 per cent devaluation and partly to China's economic stabilisation programme introduced in July 1993 which squeezed opportunities at home, making external markets more attractive.

83. *People's Daily,* 9 December 1992 and 31 January 1993.

84. Ibid., 18 January 1992.

85. This could be partly explained by the fact that foreign firms have a greater knowledge of world demand and alternative sources of raw materials than local firms. They are more efficient for the economy that they choose the cheapest sources, whether foreign or local, and export the competitive products to international market. See, *People's Daily (Overseas Edition),* 31 May 1993 and 5 April 1994.

86. See *People's Daily (Overseas Edition),* 27 October 1992, p.12; Zhang, Le-yin (1994), 'Location-specific Advantages and Manufacturing Direct Foreign Investment in South China', *World Development,* Vol.22, No.1, p.47.

87. Fujian Report at the October Central Committee Meeting on FDI in 1987.

88. *People's Daily,* 18 January 1992.

89. Guangdong Report at the October Central Committee Meeting on FDI, 1987.

90. It is likely that a number of factors were involved, including illicit sales of imported FIEs machinery and equipment to domestic buyers, 'over-pricing' of import bills, and depressed export quotations for tax evasion purposes. This seems to be a real and widespread practice among FIEs, but it is impossible to estimate to what extent it accounts for the estimated FIEs deficit.

91. *People's Daily,* 13 October 1993, p.1.

92.Ibid., 31 May 1993.

93.Ibid., 16 November 1993, p.2.

94.Wu, Chao (1988), 'Overhaul or Just a Tune-up?', *Intertrade*, August 1988, p.13.

95.Fu, Lianfeng (1993), 'FIEs' Export: A Recorded High', *Intertrade*, Vol.6, 1993, pp.21-22.

96.This FIE only introduced some key advanced technologies in engine, spray and welding by its German partner, but encouraged local delivery enterprises to supply more local parts and components which should meet German standards by updating their technology. Since 126 local sub-contracted enterprises/institutions undertook a series of technological up-gradation, local-made content rose from 40 per cent in the initial phase to 75 per cent at the end of 1992. The production output increased from 35,000 car/year, 180 car/day in 1991 to 65,000 car/year, 250 car/day in 1992, with annual productivity per capita 65 car/person.

97.FDI, which usually carried technology transfer with management know-how, personnel training and on-the-spot cooperation between foreign experts and indigenous staff members, naturally proved to be superior to other methods of obtaining complicated technology.

98.Interview with Furi Television Manufacturing Ltd in Fuzhou, Fujian Province, and Guangzhou Floating Glass Manufacturing Ltd in Guangdong Province during my fieldwork collaborated with Development Research Centre of the State Council conducted in 1987.

99.The Beijing Jeep Corporation was a good instance of progressive technology transfer through FDI cooperation. When negotiating the JV, the Chinese partner insisted on a contract with the American partner for continuous technology transfer which would enable the JV to update its products in line with new developments in the auto industry abroad. This contract proved to be very helpful to the development of the JV.

100.The World Bank (1986), *China: External Trade and Capital*, China Finance & Economics Press, Beijing, pp.45-50.

101.Xin, Huiji (1991), 'Will China Become One of the Hottest Destination for Foreign Investment', *Economic Bulletin*, Hong Kong, Vol.2201, No.2, pp.90-91.

102. In FIEs, workers and staff members of FIEs were often reminded of the principle that 'time is money and efficiency is life'

103. Quoted by Grub and Lin (1991), *Foreign Direct Investment in China*, Quorum, New York & London, p.102.

104. Aiello, Paul (1991), 'Building a JV in China: The Case of Chrysler and the Beijing Jeep Corporation', *Journal of General Management*, Vol.17, No.2, pp.47-64.

105. McClenahen, John S. (1988), 'Playing the China Card', *Industry Week*, 21 March, p.76.

106. There were several obvious reasons for this phenomenon. First, as in most LDCs, the costs of hiring a local person were much lower than hiring a foreign national. Second, Chinese technical and managerial staff in FIEs were usually chosen from the best group in the country, so normally they learnt and adapted quickly to the new system. Third, due to the rather immobile nature of labour in the Chinese economic system and the large technical gap between FIEs and local enterprises, FIEs had little fear of losing the individual after having trained them.

107. Li Kefu (1988), 'FIEs Are Also Schools', *People's Daily*, 19 May 1988, p.1.

7 FDI and economic growth in Hungary and China: Time-series approach

This chapter provides an empirical analysis regarding whether foreign capital inflow stimulates economic growth during 1978-92 within the framework of a neoclassical model of growth. We regressed its relationship to domestic investment, savings, foreign investment, labour, and exports. The chapter is organized as follows: Section 7.1 profiles the hypotheses and previous empirical studies. Section 7.2 contains the one-equation model and hypotheses, with a view to identifying the various output factors and their relative importance in determining growth performance within the context of classic economic growth model. This is supplemented in Section 7.3 by a formal empirical test of the relative importance of these factor and presenting the estimation results whether a favourable foreign capital inflows exerts a positive influence on economic growth by using time-series data from Hungary and China during 1978-92. The previous empirical evidence on FDI's contribution to economic growth, the data sources and the method of data compilation are described in the Appendix 7.1 - 7.5.

Theory and hypotheses on foreign capital's contribution to LDCs' growth

Harrod-Domar Model

There have been two waves of quantitative growth theorists who test the effect of growth factors. The first, led by Robert Solow of MIT, stressed the role of capital: output resulted from a 'production function' of capital, labour and technical progress. Technical progress was thought to be fairly steady and automatic, labour similarly steadily growing for demographic reasons, leaving capital accumulation as the key source of growth. The second wave of theorists has come in the last decade: noticing that the technical progress residual was actually accounting for the major variations in countries' growth, Robert Lucas and Paul Romer of the University of Chicago came up with an explanation of this residual mainly in terms of human skill and knowledge.[1]

It is generally agreed that capital formation takes the top priority in the strategy of economic development and that 'the process of economic growth and capital accumulation are closely interconnected whether there is abundant labour or not'.[2] Investment increases output, and output in turn increases capital formation. The saving ratio is regarded as an important variable in the growth equation, while the savings-investment gap forms one corner of the triangular accounting identity, thus: savings less investment equals export less imports, equals income less expenditure. It is generally accepted that the growth rate of output is correlated to the investment rate as follows:

$$G = s*n \quad \text{(Harrod-Domar Model)} \quad (7.1)$$

where G = the growth rate of output; s = the saving rate, i.e. S/Y, which in a closed economy, at equilibrium, is equal to the investment rate, I/Y; n = the output capital ratio, i.e. the multiplier which relates the investment rate to growth.

Given an investment rate and the output-capital ratio, the resultant growth rate can be generated from this formulation. Should the existing rate of saving be inadequate to achieve the desired growth rate, then additional investment has to be made available from an outside source, e.g., foreign savings. FDI and borrowing may seem like an attractive alternative to supplement domestic savings. This is the basic orthodox view of the contribution of foreign investment to growth, is expressed as follows:

$$G = n (s + FCI/Y) \quad (7.2)$$

where s = S/Y, domestic saving rate; FCI/Y = foreign capital inflow as a proportion of output.

With the inflow of foreign capital, the investment rate becomes:

$$s + FCI/Y = (S + FCI)/Y$$

Clearly, with positive inflows,

$$(S + FCI)/Y > S/Y$$

implying that the investment rate achievable with FCI is higher than that achievable without FCI.

Given the assumption of similar and unchanged capital output ratio for the two sources of funds, the contribution of FCI to LDCs growth can never be other than positive. The increased income achieved partially by foreign capital inflows is expected to increase the domestic savings rate, based on the usual expectation that the marginal savings rate is higher than the average rate. Should the positive direct effects via augmenting investment and positive indirect effects on savings and exports emphasized by the orthodox analysis by the only import effects, then the effect of FCI on the growth performance of the recipient economies cannot be other than positive.

Empirical testing of FDI's contribution to growth has usually been carried out in the context of a production function, where aggregate output is a function of the factors of production: labour, capital and technology. The rate of growth of output can thus be expressed in terms of increments in the various factor inputs, the unexplained part being usually attributed to productivity changes or 'technological improvements' (See Dension, Solow and Kendrick).[3] From these assumptions, the growth rate can be specified as a function of the investment rate, the rate of growth of the labour force, and technology.

$$\text{Growth} = a + b\ I/Y + c\ L'/L \qquad (7.3)$$

where I/Y = the investment rate, used as a proxy for increments in the capital stock; L'/L = the rate of growth of the labour force; a = the rate of 'technological change'; b = the partial elasticity of output with respect to increments in the capital stock; c = the partial elasticity of output with respect to increases in labour input.

The effect of FCI on growth can be tested by noting the theoretical identity: $I/Y = S/Y + FCI/Y$, where S/Y is the domestic savings rate and FCI/Y is foreign capital inflows, expressed as a proportion of GDP.

Substituting for I/Y in the production function derived equation:

$$\text{Growth} = a + b^*S/Y + b'^*FCI/Y + c^*L'/L \qquad (7.4)$$

This basic formulation can clearly be extended by disaggregating FCI into its components or by including other variables which may have effects on the growth rate, as additional explanatory variables. Under the orthodox expectations, the coefficients of the FCI variable should be positive and significant.

Many empirical studies have tested the FCI's contribution to the local economic growth in various developing countries, and these have confirmed that foreign investment has different impact on individual LDCs (see, **Appendix 7.1**).

Most found that investment was the most important determinant of growth, with growth of labour force playing a smaller role,[4] and FCI positively related with economic growth. The studies by Cohen (1968), Papanek (1973), and Stoneman (1976),[5] using cross-section data from the 1950s and early 1960s, show that growth is positively and significantly related to both domestic savings and foreign capital inflows. Similar results were found by Dowling and Heimenz (1983) using data from the 1970s, and San'tans (1983)[6] using Brazilian data from 1964-74. Kraska and Taira (1974)[7] also found a positive relationship between growth and FDI, and suggested a positive contribution over and above FDI's contributions via augmenting investment. Other studies, however, did not support the orthodox hypotheses: Griffin and Enos (1970), Voivodas (1973), El Shibly (1980),[8] Mosley, Hudson and Horrell (1987),[9] Mosley (1987)[10] and Karikari (1992)[11] either found an insignificant relationship or even a significant negative relationship.[12]

We note that domestic savings and exports contribute to growth by allowing a higher level of investment. In most cases domestic savings produced a strong positive relationship with economic growth. The same holds true for exports in the regressions which include this explanative variable [see, Cohen (1968), El Shibly (1980), Mosley and Hudson (1987) and Mosley (1987)]. If FCI is free of any undesirable side effects, then its contribution to economic growth should be comparable to, if not better than, that of savings and exports. Thus like these, FCI's contributions should also be consistently positive. The evidence, however, shows that for most components of FCI, there is often a non-significant or even a significant negative relationship, which indicates that FCI may suffer from serious side effects which reduce or negate its contribution to the recipient economy.

Evidence of undesirable side effects was found by some of the studies: Griffin and Enos (1970) believed that the negative relationships between FCI and economic growth was caused by FCI's indirect negative effects on the recipients' domestic savings behaviour and on the efficiency of capital. Mosley, Hundson and Horell (1987), Gupts and Islam (1983) gave some empirical evidence in support of such a hypothesis.[13]

Some studies also provide some evidence on the existence of undesirable indirect affects via the balance of payment position. Stoneman (1976) shows that while the effect of FCI to growth was positive, the effect of stock of foreign assets in the country was negative. This effect was later attributed by Bornschier et al (1978)[14] as resulting from large outflows of profits, interests, royalties and other payments having a negative influence on capital formation in the host country, such factor payments being a positive function of the stock of foreign capital existing in the host country.

The evidence examined above indicated that foreign capital inflows often perform more poorly than either savings or exports. We note that not all studies explicitly used the production function as a starting point. Many simply regressed FCI or FCI and other components of investment against growth, and may suffer from bias due to the omission of other important explanatory variables. We believe that these undesirable effects provide strong prima facie evidence on the existence of negative indirect effects as emphasised by authors more critical of FCI.

'Direct' contribution of foreign capital inflows to the growth in Hungary and China, 1978-92

The preceding discussion has presented the basic growth equation and a number of previous empirical studies on FCI's contribution to LDCs' economic growth. This section attempts to undertake such an econometric evaluation of FDI's direct contributions to the growth in Hungary and China in the period between 1978 and 1992.

Hypotheses and model specification

Turning to the empirical evidence regarding the contribution of various production factors to the growth rate, a number of alternative hypotheses were specified and tested by multiple regression analysis in the cases of those LDCs in Latin America, Africa and Asia. Even though the reality is rather more complex, an equation can be derived by using the multiplicative form of the production function as a starting point, which indicates that the growth rate of output is related to the investment rate and the rate of growth of the labour force. Some authors suggest that the effect of investment may be lagged (Mosley, et al., 1987).

In a classic developing country, agriculture is normally the largest sector of the economy, providing the main source of income, employment and exports. The manufacturing sector is likely to be small, geared mainly to the domestic market and heavily protected from external competition. Rapid economic development is frequently synonymous with a fast-growing manufacturing sector. In some cases, this sector may have become sufficiently large to warrant classifying the country as a newly industrialized economy

249

(Solberg, ed., 1993, p.30). Many studies, therefore, included a proxy for resource shifts from less productive to more productive sectors as an additional explanatory variable, to take into account the economic 'duality' that exist in LDCs. The hypothesis is that such shifts, by increasing the relative size of the more productive sector, have positive effects on the growth rate.

Other researchers include export as an explanatory variable in the growth equation, as exports is 'an engine of growth'.[15] Given the importance of export for stimulation of the economic growth in Hungary and China,[16] we include export as an explanatory variable in our simple model. So the basic growth equation can thus be re-specified as follows:

$$\text{Growth} = a + b\,I/Y + c\,L'/L + d\,RT + e\,X/Y \qquad (7.5)$$

where: I/Y is the investment rate; L'/L is the rate of growth of the labour force proxied by the rate of change in the number of people employed; RT is the 'resource shift' variable proxied by the relative size of the non-agricultural sector as a proportion of total GDP.

In order to test FCI/Y's contribution to the economic growth rate in Hungary and China, we have adopted the usual procedure of substituting the investment rate, I/Y, with its theoretical identity, S/Y plus FCI/Y, so that the basic growth equation yields the following testable relationship:

$$\text{Growth} = a + b1\,S/Y + b2\,FCI/Y + c\,L'/L + d\,RT + e\,X/Y \qquad (7.6)$$

The hypothesis is that both b1 and b2 are positive and significant. Those previous empirical studies which included labour force as an explanatory variable (for example, Kraska and Taira ,1974; Gupta and Islam, 1983) found that the rate of growth of the labour force in the cases of Latin American, Asian, African countries in the 1950s-70s played a significant positive role in the local economic growth.

The FCI variable in equation (7.6) can be disaggregated into its components, FDI/Y and Debt/Y to test any difference in their contribution to economic growth. Also, any lags in the effects of I/Y may involve lag structures in its constitutions, i.e. S/Y and the FCI/Y variables (including FDI/Y and Debt/Y).

We must stress that since domestic capital formation, exports, savings are themselves part of the national product, an autocorrelation is present; and a positive correlation of these variables is almost inevitable, whatever their true relationship to each other. In order to avoid over-simplification and mis-specification, the variables used to represent investment, export, savings must refer not to the absolute level but to the proportion of gross domestic product.[17] In this study, the investment, savings, exports, foreign capital inflows are represented by their proportions of GDP.

Comparison of the data for evaluation of FCI's contribution to growth in Hungary and China

The data-base for empirical analysis of FDI's impact on economic growth is presented in **Appendix 7.2 - 7.5**, along with an explanation of the sources and definitions of the specific variables. **Tables 7.1 and 7.2** report the correlation coefficients between all variables used in the subsequent regression analysis. In view of the fairly small correlation between the independent variables, we should not expect any serious multicollinearity problems to arise. The means, standard deviations, maximums and minimums of the main data for estimating the FCI's contribution to local economic growth in Hungary and China for the period covered are shown in **Table 7.3**.

Table 7.1

Correlation among savings, investment, growth and foreign capital inflows in Hungary, 1977-92

	Growth	I/Y	L'/L	RT	FCI/Y	S/Y	X/Y
Growth	1.00	0.66	0.09	0.43	-0.33	-0.01	0.81
I/Y		1.00	0.12	0.81	-0.39	0.30	0.47
L'/L			1.00	0.19	-0.26	0.05	-0.06
RT				1.00	-0.37	0.18	0.33
FCI/Y					1.00	-0.41	-0.33
S/Y						1.00	-0.15
X/Y							1.00

Comparing the above data for both Hungary and China, an interest picture emerges. First, China enjoys faster economic growth than Hungary during the period covered. Second, the averaged investment rate in Hungary was 28.5 per cent, higher than that of 25.73 per cent in China. Third, the rate of growth of the labour force in Hungary showed a decreasing trend (with the averaged decreasing rate of 0.05 per cent per cent, while it showed a increasing trend, with averaged rate of 2.99 per cent in China. Fourth, it shows that the averaged savings rate in Hungary (28.36 per cent) was much

251

lower than China (33.10 per cent). Fifth, the remaining variables show that Hungary was a more advanced and opening economy than China: the averaged level of the 'resource shift' variable in Hungary (82.16 per cent), proxied by the relative size of the non-agricultural sector as a proportion of total GDP, was much higher than that of China (70.45 per cent); though the export

Table 7.2
Correlation among savings, investment, growth and foreign capital inflows in China, 1977-92

	Growth	I/Y	L'/L	RT	FCI/Y	S/Y	X/Y
Growth	1.00	0.14	0.50	-0.03	-0.04	0.18	-0.10
I/Y		1.00	0.04	-0.27	-0.53	-0.15	-0.55
L'/L			1.00	0.07	0.24	-0.26	0.35
RT				1.00	0.84	0.75	0.73
FCI/Y					1.00	0.25	0.91
S/Y						1.00	0.32
X/Y							1.00

Table 7.3
Mean, S.D., maximum and minimum of used data for estimating FCI's contribution in Hungary and China, 1977-92

Series	Mean		Standard Deviation		Maximum		Minimum	
	Hungary	China	Hungary	China	Hungary	China	Hungary	China
Growth (%)	0.65	9.26	4.16	3.21	7.60	14.60	-10.20	3.60
I/Y (%)	28.50	25.71	6.28	2.67	43.93	31.20	21.64	23.10
L'/L (%)	-0.05	2.99	1.16	0.78	4.20	4.90	-0.76	1.83
RT (%)	82.16	70.45	1.60	3.01	86.00	76.10	79.90	66.00
FCI/Y (%)	2.76	1.80	2.60	1.04	5.03	3.70	1.85	0.58
S/Y (%)	28.36	33.10	1.21	2,50	29.90	36.50	25.50	28.30
X/Y (%)	38.02	10.74	4.72	4.71	45.20	19.75	27.10	4.67

rates in China during 1978-92 increased rapidly from 4.67 per cent in 1978 to 19.75 per cent in 1992, the averaged export rate (10.74 per cent) was much lower than Hungary (38.02 per cent). The data for Hungary also showed that the higher the export rate, the higher the growth rate. Last but not least, the averaged foreign capital inflow as a proportion of GDP in Hungary in 1977-92 (2.76 per cent) was also much higher than China (1.8 per cent) in 1978-92.

Empirical results and interpretation

Time-series data for the period of 1978-92 for both Hungary and China were fitted into the basic growth equation specified as above. We then use the method of Ordinary Least Square (OLS) to derive estimates of the coefficients of the production factors, including the investment rate, the rate of growth of the labour force, resource shift, FCI/Y and export rate, as well as their contribution to the dependent variable - growth rate in both Hungary and China.

Multiple regression results and their interpretation in Hungary

Preliminary exercises We first try to obtain a satisfactory growth equation in which FCI's contribution to economic growth in Hungary can be tested. Regressing growth against its explanatory variables suggested by equation (7.1) yielded a poor fit as follows:

$$\text{Growth} = 50.01 + 0.602 \ I/Y + 0.142 \ L'/L - 0.809 \ RT$$
$$\phantom{\text{Growth} = }(0.689) \quad (2.520) \qquad (0.185) \qquad (-0.853)$$

$$\bar{R}^2 = 0.337 \quad \text{D-W} = 1.267 \quad \text{SE} = 3.384 \quad F = 3.539 \quad N = 16$$

where: Growth = the real growth rate of GDP; I/Y = the investment rate, i.e. gross capital formation scaled against GDP; L'/L = growth rate of actual numbers employed proxying for the growth rate of the labour force; RT = the resource transfer proxy by the value of the non-agricultural sector as a proportion of total GDP.

The results reveals that Hungarian growth rate is positively related to investment rate and labour change, but negatively related to the resource transfer variable. Only the investment rate is statistically significant, while the contribution of labour growth to output growth is small as the rate of population growth is very slow in Hungary.[18] So we can conclude that in the case of Hungary, the contribution of investment is greater than that of labour force. This is probably because labour was undervalued in comparison with capital.

The fit became more poor when one year straight lag structures were applied to I/Y, which produced the following results:

Growth = 69.585 + 0.438 I/Y + 0.190 I/Y$_{t-1}$ + 0.185 L'/L - 1.06 RT
  (0.753)   (1.168)   (0.533)   (0.223)   (-0.869)

$\overline{R}^2$ = 0.105   D-W = 1.251   SE = 3.641   F = 1.411   N = 15

The results show that only the un-lagged I/Y variable is near statistical significance suggesting that an un-lagged specification will be adequate.

If exports are included as an explanatory variable in the growth equation, we will find that the growth equation is more appropriate, as certain general observation become immediately apparent and the equation performs significantly: coefficients of determination, adjusted for degrees of freedom are quite high; the estimated F-ratio is well above the tabulated values; and D-W test is quite higher than those estimation above.

Growth = 18.71 + 0.352 I/Y + 0.379 L'/L - 0.604 RT + 0.566 X/Y
  (0.38)   (2.05)   (0.73)   (-0.95)   (3.98)

$\overline{R}^2$ = 0.705   D-W = 2.21   SE = 2.26   F = 9.90   N = 16

The fit also becomes less plausible when one-year distributed lagged structure is applied to I/Y in our re-specified growth equation.[19] This further confirmed our above finding that the un-lagged I/Y specification will be adequate.

Growth = 11.12 + 0.414 I/Y - 0.07 I/Y$_{t-1}$ + 0.367 L'/L - 0.52 RT + 0.586 X/Y
  (0.17)   (1.62)   (-0.29)   (0.65)   (-0.61)   (3.54)

$\overline{R}^2$ = 0.58   D-W = 2.19   SE = 2.48   F = 4.93   N = 15

The best fit growth equation, therefore, is the basic growth equation including export variable without any lagged variable. The positive signs of the regression coefficients for the investment rate, labour growth rate, and export variables agree with the underlying economic theory, while only the 'resource shift' variable shows a negative sign. As non-agricultural output as a proportion of GDP in Hungary decreased from 84 per cent in 1977 to 81.4 per cent in 1992, this is still consistent with the hypothesis (the decreasing proportion of the more productive sector among GDP is expected to have negative effect on the growth rate), though the variable shows negative sign.

Regarding the significance of these coefficients, we can see that the export and investment rates play significant roles in the economic growth in Hungary during 1978-92, while the coefficients of the growth rate of the labour force and the growth rate of 'resource shift' variables were not statistically significant, meaning that they are weakly related with economic growth in Hungary in 1978-92. Our regression, therefore, shows that each 1 per cent increase in the export rate contribute to a 0.57 per cent increase in the growth rate, each 1 per cent increase of the investment rate contributes 0.35 per cent increase in the growth rate in Hungary.

Our findings confirm the result of previous studies (Emery, 1967; Maizels, 1968, pp.41-49; Kravis, 1970; Addington,[20] 1992): the rate of growth of the labour force proved to be statistically insignificant, and exports make a larger contribution to economic growth than other variables.[21]

It should be noted that this specification 'explain' 70 per cent of the variation in the data, the estimated F-ratio ($F = 9.9$) is well above the tabulated value (Tabulated $F = 3.2$), and D-W test ratio 2.21 is above the tabulated value (Tabulated D-W $= 1.97$), This specification is therefore quite satisfactory.

Evidence regarding the 'direct' contribution of FCI to growth in Hungary The investment rate variable in our basic growth equation, I/Y, is substituted by its theoretical constituents, S/Y and FCI/Y, to enable us to obtain some ideas on their separate contributions to Hungarian economic growth during the period covered.

Regressing growth against its explanatory variables in the forms of L'/L, RT, FCI/Y, S/Y and X/Y yielded a reasonable and acceptable fit as follows:

$$\text{Growth} = -70.76 + 0.425 \, L'/L + 0.389 \, RT + 0.025 \, FCI/Y + 0.382 \, S/Y$$
$$\quad\quad (-1.57) \quad (0.65) \quad\quad (0.77) \quad\quad (0.34) \quad\quad\quad (0.55)$$
$$\quad\quad + 0.714 \, X/Y$$
$$\quad\quad\quad (3.96)$$

$$\bar{R}^2 = 0.56 \quad \text{D-W} = 2.02 \quad \text{SE} = 2.75 \quad F = 4.86 \quad N = 16$$

where: Growth = the real growth rate of GDP; L'/L = growth rate of actual numbers employed proxying for the growth rate of the labour force; RT = the resource transfer poxy namely the value of the non-agricultural sector as a proportion of total GDP; FCI/Y = relative size of FCI as a proportion of GDP; S/Y = the savings rate; X/Y = export rate.

All variables in the equation with non-lagged structures applied to FCI/Y and S/Y agree with the underlying economic theory as they show positive signs, but only the export rates shows significant correlation with economic growth, while the rest, including foreign capital inflows, were all not statistically significant. This suggests that Hungary's 'export-led growth' strategy was favourable to economic growth over the past years. The insignificant FCI/Y variable reveals that those projects, where foreign funds have been used, may not be able to generate sufficient return to service the debt.

Our regression shows that each 1 per cent increase in the export rate contributes to a 0.714 per cent increase in the growth rate, each 1 per cent increase of the FCI/Y contributes 0.025 per cent (very weak contribution) increase in the growth rate.

The fit became poor when one year straight lag structures were applied to FCI/Y and S/Y, which produced the following results:

$$\text{Growth} = -37.25 + 0.289 \, L'/L + 0.32 \, RT - 0.08 \, FCI/Y + 0.07 \, FCI/Y_{t-1} +$$
$$\phantom{\text{Growth} = } (-0.51) \quad (0.39) \qquad\quad (0.44) \qquad (-0.50) \qquad\qquad (0.47)$$
$$0.22 \, S/Y - 0.63 \, S/Y \; + 0.64 \, X/Y_{t-1}$$
$$(0.19) \qquad (-0.67) \qquad (2.29)$$
$$\bar{R}^2 = 0.37 \quad \text{D-W} = 2.19 \quad \text{SE} = 3.06 \quad F = 2.17 \quad N = 15$$

No further significant results emerge in this equation, i.e. with the exception of export, all variables are not, on their own, of any significance. It may be argued that there are statistical problems interfering the meaning of these results through mixing source-data. The results produced when one year distributed lag procedure was applied to FCI/Y and S/Y also show a lagged FCI/Y and non-lagged S/Y specification will be adequate.

If we condense our basic growth equation by dropping other insignificant variables and regressing the growth rate with the S/Y, FCI/Y by lagged one year and X/Y, the coefficients of FCI/Y and S/Y variables still remain statistically insignificant and the export rate plays the dominant positive role in the economic growth in Hungary during the period covered.

$$\text{Growth} = -42.74 + 0.04 \, FCI/Y_{t-1} \; + 0.44 \, S/Y + 0.75 \, X/Y$$
$$\phantom{\text{Growth} = } (-1.50) \quad (0.54) \qquad\qquad (0.59) \qquad\;\; (3.55)$$
$$\bar{R}^2 = 0.51 \quad \text{D-W} = 1.80 \quad \text{SE} = 2.71 \quad F = 5.76 \quad N = 15$$

If we further condense the equation by dropping all the domestic variables and just regress the growth rate with the external variables, i.e. FCI/Y by lagged one year and X/Y, we will see that the coefficient of FCI/Y by lagged one year still remains statistically insignificant while the export rate still shows the significant positive sign in the growth equation in Hungary during the period covered.

256

$$\text{Growth} = -26.80 + 0.019 \, \text{FCI/Y}_{t-1} + 0.69 \, \text{X/Y}$$
$$\quad\quad\quad (-3.01) \quad\quad (0.30) \quad\quad\quad\quad (3.90)$$

$$\bar{R}^2 = 0.53 \quad \text{D-W} = 1.78 \quad \text{SE} = 2.63 \quad \text{F} = 8.95 \quad \text{N} = 15$$

It should be noted that these two specifications can 'explain' about 51 per cent and 53 per cent of the variation of the growth rate, the estimated F-ratios (F = 5.76 and 8.95) are well above the tabulated value (Tabulated F = 3.2), and D-W test ratios are lower than the tabulated value (Tabulated D-W = 1.97), These specifications are not so satisfactory but are acceptable, given the limitation and quality of the data and the consequent restriction on the possibilities for analysis.

We can conclude that foreign capital is found to be positively related to Hungarian economic growth, but with insignificant correlationship. Why did foreign capital inflows not contribute significantly to the economic growth in Hungary, although FCI/Y's coefficient shows positive sign? The possible explanation may be that over the past decade, foreign loans dominated a lion's share of the inflows of foreign capital and it is only till the recent three year that foreign direct investment flowed increasing into Hungary. Moreover, FCI was mainly used for consumption purposes and maintaining the living standards, or caused other 'indirect' problems for Hungary, such as the high debt service rate and deteriorated its problems of balance of payment, this variable is therefore statistically insignificant.

Summary Most variables in our extended or condensed specification carried the expected sign in all the alternative specifications, which support the theories that all production factors exert positive effects on the local economy. The best fit equation is that one substituting I/Y with non-lagged FCI/Y and S/Y, together with other explanatory variables, i.e. L'/L, RT, X/Y. These findings, although not free of statistical problems are plausible and can be partially reconciled with our initial theoretical expectations.

The results obtained by our simple model suggest that the contribution of the export rate is superior to that of other explanatory variables applied, such as labour growth rate, investment rate and 'resource shift' rate, both in terms of the size of the coefficients as well as in terms of their statistical significance; FCI's 'direct' contribution to economic growth has been positive in the period covered but not quite significantly. It suggests that FCI was in fact mainly used for consumption purposes to maintain the living standards, or caused other 'indirect' problems for Hungary, such as the high debt service rate and deteriorated its problems of balance of payment. Our findings have not confirmed some of the previous studies concerning LDCs in Latin America, Africa or Asia, where the savings rate variable shown significant

257

positive role in LDCs' economic growth, but agreed with Cohen's (1968) findings that the regression coefficient for exports is larger than for foreign investment.[22]

It is apparent that, as is generally the case, the equations in the case of Hungary fail to meet the significance level as determinants of Hungary's economic growth, suggesting much of the explanation for the dependent variable lies outside these specifications.

Multiple regression results and their interpretation in the case of China

Preliminary exercises Similar to the regression analysis for Hungary, we firstly try to obtain a proper growth equation in which FCI's contribution to the Chinese economic growth can be tested. Regressing growth against its explanatory variables suggested by equation (7.1) yielded a quite satisfactory fit as follows:

$$\text{Growth} = -15.13 + 0.92 \, I/Y + 1.26 \, L'/L - 0.04 \, RT$$
$$\qquad\qquad (-1.38) \quad (5.52) \qquad (2.21) \qquad (-0.30)$$

$$\bar{R}^2 = 0.748 \quad D\text{-}W = 1.526 \quad SE = 1.613 \quad F = 14.847 \quad N = 15$$

where: Growth = the real growth rate of GDP; I/Y = the investment rate, i.e. gross capital formation scaled against GDP; L'/L = growth rate of actual numbers employed proxying for the growth rate of the labour force; RT = the resource transfer proxy namely the value of the non-agricultural sector as a proportion of total GDP in the case of China.

The fit became slightly improved when one year straight lag structures were applied to I/Y, which produced the following results:

$$\text{Growth} = -21.26 + 0.90 \, I/Y + 0.17 \, I/Y_{t-1} + 1.32 \, L'/L - 0.015 \, RT$$
$$\qquad\qquad (-1.69) \quad (5.38) \qquad (0.99) \qquad\quad (2.29) \qquad (-0.10)$$

$$\bar{R}^2 = 0.748 \quad D\text{-}W = 1.709 \quad SE = 1.613 \quad F = 11.375 \quad N = 15$$

The results show that the lagged I/Y variable plays insignificant role in the economic growth in China.

If exports are included as an explanatory variable in the basic growth equation, we will find that certain general observation become slightly different: coefficients of determination, adjusted for degree of freedom, the estimated F-ratio become lower than those estimation without the export variable; the 'explanatory power' decreases slightly as well. The most striking result is the negative sign of exports variable. This may suggest that the impact of a rapid rise in exports on overall GDP growth can be quite different, depending on the structure of an economy and its degree of openness. In an open economy the potential for export-led growth is likely to be much higher, given the smooth reallocation of resources between the tradeable and non-tradable-goods sectors, indicating a higher degree of structural flexibility. A country with a growing share of manufactured goods in its exports will be much less susceptible to price fluctuations on world markets and should enjoy more stable demand conditions. The impact of export on economic growth depends on a country's exports in absolute terms, export-commodity concentrations, the geographical concentration of export markets, and the prospects for export growth (Solberg, 1993, p.34).It may also be argued that there are statistical problems interfering with this conclusion, as it begs the question of how the negative influence of export variable on growth rates arose.

$$Growth = -15.93 + 0.89\ I/Y + 1.13\ L'/L - 0.004\ RT - 0.056\ X/Y$$
$$\quad\quad\quad (-1.02)\quad (4.49)\quad\quad (1.66)\quad\quad (-0.02)\quad\quad (-0.31)$$

$$\bar{R}^2 = 0.71 \quad D\text{-}W = 1.1.63 \quad SE = 1.69 \quad F = 10.13 \quad N = 15$$

The fit becomes a little bit improved when one year distributed lag structure was applied to I/Y in our re-specified growth equation, as the explanatory power and strongly significant coefficients for all explanatory variables became slightly improved. This confirmed that the lagged I/Y specification will be adequate in the case of China.

$$Growth = -20.76 + 0.91\ I/Y + 0.18\ I/Y_{t-1} + 1.30\ L'/L - 0.03\ RT + 0.01\ X/Y$$
$$\quad\quad\quad (-1.28)\quad (4.54)\quad\quad (0.90)\quad\quad\quad (1.76)\quad\quad (-0.10)\quad\quad (0.05)$$

$$\bar{R}^2 = 0.719 \quad D\text{-}W = 1.717 \quad SE = 1.701 \quad F = 8.193 \quad N = 15$$

All the growth equation regression results, therefore, suggest that the regression coefficients for the labour growth rate and the investment rate variables agree with the underlying economic theory,[23] while other variables, i.e. the 'resource shift' rate carries the 'wrong' signs, which can not support the growth hypothesis. No certain pattern appears to the export rate as its coefficient in the non-lagged specification shows 'wrong' sign, while in the lagged one shows positive sign.

We should emphasize that as manufacturing exports were found to contribute more than do primary exports to economic growth in LDCs and primary exports might not make an independent contribution to the export-output nexus,[24] the dominance of exports of raw materials and low value-added intermediate products in China over the past 15 years may be the main explanatory reason why this variables yielded an uncertain contribution to the

259

economic growth. This finding seems to be contrary to the popular view that a 'rapid growth of exports accelerates economic growth' (Michaely, M., 1977, p.49), but agrees with another viewpoint that among low-income LDCs, there is often a negative relationship between export and income growth.[25] We may conclude that although a positive association of growth with export expansion has been established, such a relationship holds only once the countries achieve some minimum level of development (see, Michaely, 1977; Tyler, 1981).

The labour growth rate and the investment rate are significantly different from zero at the 95 per cent confidence level, which suggest that they make a significant contribution to the economic growth in China during 1978-92. The growth rate of 'resource shift' and the export rate variables appear to have either 'wrong' or uncertain signs and show statistically insignificant coefficients. We also find that the contribution of labour input is greater than the capital input in China during the sample period covered, which confirm Zhang's (1988) finding by using the data between 1949 and 1986.[26]

Our regression of the re-specified equation including the export variable with lagged structure applied to I/Y, therefore, shows that each 1 per cent increase in the labour growth rate contributes to a 1.3 per cent increase in the growth rate, each 1 per cent increase of the investment rate in last year and the same year contribute 0.18 per cent and 0.91 per cent increases in the growth rate respectively, and each 1 per cent increase in the export rate contributes 0.01 per cent increase in the economic growth in China during the period covered.

It should be noted that this specification 'explains' 71 per cent of the variation, the estimated F-ratio (F = 8.19) is well above the tabulated value (Tabulated F = 3.2), and D-W test ratio 1.72 is quite high. This specification can, therefore, be considered satisfactory.

FDI's direct contribution to economic growth in China The investment rate I/Y is then substituted by its theoretical constituents, S/Y and FCI/Y, which enable us to obtain some ideas on their separate contributions to the economic growth in China during the period covered. In addition, FCI/Y was further disaggregated into FDI/Y and Debt/Y (the ratio of debt volume and GDP), to test for the differences in their contributions.

Regressing growth against its explanatory variables in the forms of L'/L, RT, FCI/Y, S/Y and X/Y yielded a reasonable fit as follows:

Growth = 7.36 + 3.65 L'/L - 0.66 RT + 0.39 FCI/Y + 1.20 S/Y - 0.25 X/Y
$\quad\quad\quad$ (0.25) (3.84)$\quad\quad$ (-1.20)$\quad\quad$ (0.19)$\quad\quad\quad$ (2.50)$\quad\quad$ (-0.65)

$\bar{R}^2$ = 0.66   D-W = 1.81   SE = 2.35   F = 3.44   N = 15 where: Growth = the real growth rate of GDP; L'/L = growth rate of actual numbers employed proxying for the growth rate of the labour force; RT = the resource transfer proxy namely the value of the non-agricultural sector as a proportion of total GDP; FCI/Y = relative size of FCI as a proportion of GDP; S/Y = the savings rate; X/Y = export rate.

Further disaggregating FCI/Y into FDI/Y and Debt/Y, we could generate the following result:

Growth = 6.98 + 3.26 L'/L - 0.54 RT + 0.42 FDI/Y + 0.09 Debt/Y + 1.20 S/Y - 0.21 X/Y
　　　　　(0.34)　(3.56)　　(-1.12)　　(0.56)　　　　(0.21)　　　　(2.60)　　(-1.12)

$\bar{R}^2$ = 0.61　D-W = 1.70　SE = 2.14　F= 3.11　N = 15

We find that FDI fails to meet the significance level as a determinant of China's economic growth. This is not too surprising, given that within the confines of our own present study and relatively limited FDI with the tremendous Chinese market.

The fit became more improved when one year straight lag structures were applied to FDI/Y and S/Y, which produced the following results:

Growth = 　11.89 + 4.63 L'/L - 0.60 RT - 1.29 FDI/Y + 0.35 FDI/Y$_{t-1}$ +
　　　　　(0.55)　(4.62)　　　(-1.32)　　(-0.76)　　　　(2.00)

　　　　　1.49 S/Y - 0.65 S/Y - 0.50 X/Y
　　　　　(4.16)　　(-2.36)　　(-1.70)

$\bar{R}^2$ = 0.73　D-W = 2.47　SE = 1.67　F = 6.42　N = 15

The results show that the lagged FDI/Y variable is near statistical significance, which suggest that an lagged FDI/Y specification will be adequate.

The best fit growth equation is, therefore, the growth equation substituting I/Y with FDI/Y and S/Y variables with lagged structures. The signs of the regression coefficients for most of the explanatory variables, i.e. the labour growth rate, lagged foreign capital inflows rate as well as FDI, and non-lagged savings rate variables, agree with the underlying economic theory. The remaining variables, including the 'resource shift' and the export rate show 'wrong' signs suggesting that the quantitative evidence can not support the relevant hypotheses in which these two variables are expected to play positive contributions to the economic growth.

Regarding the significance of these coefficients, we can see that the labour growth rate, foreign direct investment lagged by one year and the savings rate are significantly different from zero at the 99 per cent confidence level, which mean that they played significant contributions in the economic growth in China during 1978-92. The evidence also confirms that the contributions of domestic savings and the labour growth rate are superior to that of FDI in the case of China, both in terms of the size of the coefficients as well as in terms of their statistical significance. This is clearly supportive to our theoretical expectations. On the other hand, not only is the coefficient of the FDI/Y in the same year statistically insignificant, it also carries the 'wrong' sign. The savings rate lagged by one year is statistically significant, but it carries a 'wrong' sign.

Our regression, therefore, shows that each 1 per cent increase in the labour growth rate contributes to a 4.63 per cent increase in the growth rate, each 1 per cent increase of the FDI/Y lagged by one year contributes 3.5 per cent increase in the growth rate, and each 1 per cent increase of the domestic savings rate contributes 1.49 per cent increase in the growth rate in China during the period covered.

Regressing the best fit equation using a log-linear specification could result with much improved explanatory powers as well as improvement in the significance of the most of the explanatory variables: coefficients of determination, adjusted for degree of freedom and F-ratio are quite higher than linear formulation, while the standard error of the regression is much lower by using the log-linear specification.

$$\text{Log(Growth)} = \underset{(0.89)}{10.01} + \underset{(5.48)}{1.82\,\text{Log(L'/L)}} - \underset{(-1.18)}{3.97\,\text{Log(RT)}} - \underset{(-0.89)}{0.25\,\text{Log(FDI/Y)}}$$

$$+ \underset{(-2.26)}{0.71\,\text{Log(FDI/Y)}_{t-1}} + \underset{(-1.98)}{4.91\,\text{Log(S/Y)}} - \underset{(2.56)}{2.41\,\text{Log(S/Y)}_{t-1}} - \underset{(3.62)}{0.78\,\text{Log(X/Y)}}$$

$$\bar{R}^2 = 0.76 \quad \text{D-W} = 2.40 \quad \text{SE} = 0.19 \quad F = 7.47 \quad N = 15$$

These results further confirm that the labour growth rate, the domestic savings rate and the FDI/Y lagged by one year are significantly related with the economic growth rate in China, and the first two variables are superior to that of FDI/Y lagged by one year both in terms of the size of the coefficients as well as in terms of their statistical significance. The coefficients of the 'resource shift' rate and the export rate still carry negative signs though statistically significant. This finding seems to agree with one previous conclusion that there is, at best, a very weak, and perhaps even a negative relationship between export performance and output growth.[27]

It should be noted that the log-linear specification can 'explain' about 76 per cent of the variation in the data, the estimated F-ratios ($F = 7.47$) is well above the tabulated value (Tabulated $F = 3.2$), and D-W test ratio (D-W = 2.40) is higher than the tabulated value (Tabulated D-W = 1.97). The standard error of the regression is very low. This log-linear specification is, therefore, satisfactorily acceptable, given the limitation and quality of the data and the consequent restriction on the possibilities for analysis.

Summary We found that the investment rate, the labour growth rate agree with the hypothesis, while the 'resource shift' and the export rate variables seem to be contrary to the theoretical expectation. Domestic investment, labour and saving had the strongest influence on economic growth. The labour growth rate seems to be superior to that of the investment rate in terms of the size of the coefficients. The 'immediate contribution' of the investment rate is greater than that of lagged by one year in the case of China.

After substituting the theoretical substituent of S/Y, FCI/Y and its disaggregated FDI/Y and Debt/Y variables without lagged structures with the investment rate variable, the evidence indicates that the 'resource shift' and the export rate variables still carry negative signs. The labour growth rate, domestic savings rate and foreign capital inflows rate as well as FDI show positive signs, and the first two variables were significantly different from zero at the 95 per cent confidence level. Our findings at this stage further confirm that the contribution of the labour growth rate is superior to that of other explanatory variables applied, i.e. the domestic savings rate, foreign capital inflows rate and FDI rate, both in terms of the coefficients as well as in terms of the statistical significance.

The results obtained by introducing lagged structures applied to the FCI/Y and S/Y variables, however, seem to suggest that the contribution of the FCI/Y rate lagged by one year begins to show increasingly significant contribution to the economic growth in China during 1978-92, both in terms of the size of the coefficient as well as in terms of its statistical significance, while the labour growth rate and the domestic savings rate still contribute significantly to the economic growth rates in China at the 95 per cent confidence level. The coefficient of the labour input rate was still superior to that of the savings rate and FCI/Y variables in terms of the size of coefficient and statistical significance.

When the log-linear formulation of the growth equation with lagged structures applied to the model, certain general observations become immediately apparent. The 'explanatory powers', the D-W test, the F-ratio and the standard error of the regression are all much improved. The labour growth rate, the domestic savings rate and the lagged FDI/Y contribute significantly and positive to the economic growth in China, while their coefficients and significance are varying.

All evidence provided by the regressions of different specifications shown above indicates that the 'direct' contribution of FDI to Chinese economic growth has generally been positive in the period covered, and in some specifications, the coefficient of FCI's 'direct' contribution to the growth rate shows a significant positive sign.

These findings, although not free of statistical problems are plausible and partially reconciled with our initial theoretical expectations.

Summary and implications

Our one-equation model is highly aggregated and simple in structure due to the complexity of this issue and the availability of database. Nevertheless, the present analysis reveals that most production factors, including investment, savings, FCI/FDI, and labour indicated positive contributions to the economic growth rate, even though showing us a different picture of FDI's 'direct' contribution to the economic growth between Hungary and China during 1978-92: the equations generate a larger number of statistically significant results for China than Hungary, which may suggest the omission of significant variables may occur in the Hungarian model.

All variables applied for production factors in the case of Hungary are supportive to the expectations as all coefficients show the right signs, while in the case of China, the investment rate, the labour growth rate agree with the hypothesis and expectation, but the 'resource shift' and the export rate variables seem to be contrary to the theoretical expectation, which is completely unexpected. The labour growth rate seems to be superior to that of the investment rate in terms of the size of the coefficients. In sum, all evidence for both cases indicate that the investment rate and labour growth rate contributed positively to the economic growth performances in both Hungary and China in the sample period.

After substituting the theoretical substituent of S/Y, FCI/Y and FCI's disaggregated FDI/Y and Debt/Y variables without lagged structures with the investment rate variable in both cases, the evidence indicates that in the case of China, the 'resource shift' and the export rate variables still carry negative signs, which seem to be contrary to the hypothesis; the labour growth rate, domestic savings rate, foreign capital inflows rate and FDI rate show positive signs, and the first two variables were significantly different from zero at the 95 per cent confidence level. Our findings at this stage further confirm that the contribution of the labour growth rate is superior to that of other explanatory variables applied, i.e. the domestic savings rate, and foreign capital inflows rate and FDI rate, both in terms of the coefficients as well as in terms of the statistical significance. In the case of Hungary, all variables applied at this stage supported the hypotheses and expectations, but the coefficients of all variables, except the export rate, show statistically insignificant contribution to the economic growth performance. The export rate was found to be not only superior to that of other explanatory variables applied, such as labour growth rate, investment rate and 'resource shift' rate, but also the only main determinant of the economic growth performance both in terms of the size of the coefficients as well as in terms of their statistical significance in the case of Hungary.

Our findings seem to indicate that the low-income transforming economy with large proportion of exports of primary products does not seem to benefit much from an improved export performance, while the correlation between export and output growth is much higher for those higher-income transforming economy. 'Perhaps one can conclude that a high export share favours capital accumulation and this in turn promote economic growth.'[28] When the income per capita remains at a certain low level, the capacity of the export sector to affect growth of the whole economy is very limited, even negative. With much high income levels, the export variable increases its contribution to growth of the whole economy. Higher than 'normal' export shares have a stimulating impact at least on capital accumulation, thus improving the conditions for economic growth. One recent study found that the estimated regression coefficient between export performance and output growth is, in the case of high-income developing countries, about four to five times that of the low-income and middle-income developing countries by regressing GDP growth on growth in export of 70 LDCs according to income groups during 1960-81.[29] We could also reach another important conclusion that unless greater exports are associated with a freer economic system, there is little reason for an economy to experience positive growth as a result of such exports (Ahiakpor, 1991, p.72).

The evidence shows that the 'direct' contribution of FCI/FDI to the economic growth has in general been positive in both cases in the period under study. But the degree of its contribution to the economic growth in both sample countries varied in terms of the size of coefficient and statistical significance: FDI contributed statistically significantly to the rapid economic growth rate in China, but was insignificant in Hungary. We may conclude that the rate of foreign capital inflows/FDI is of greater importance for GDP growth in the rapidly growing transforming countries than slowly growing ones. Although foreign capital was not a very important component of total gross domestic capital formation in any of the two sample countries, there is no doubt that foreign capital has indeed promoted economic growth in both Hungary and China to some extent degree, as the results of the model show that foreign capital and economic growth are positively related.

The statistical analysis probably under-estimates the full impact of FDI because it ignores any productivity differentials between FIEs and other local firms; because is takes no account of technology transfers, balance of payment, future trends towards greater local souring by FIEs due to lack of data; and because it makes no further quantitative assessment of the indirect benefits which accrue from the internationalisation of local industry and the

265

integration with the world economy.

Notes

1.Minford, Patrick (1993), 'The Magic of Capitalism', *Quarterly Economic Bulletin*, Liverpool Macroeconomic Research Group, Vol.14, No.3, October, 1993, p.27.

2.Cairncross, A. K. (1963), 'Capital Formation in Take-off', in Rostow, W.W. (ed.), *The Economics of Take-off into Sustained Growth*, St. Martin Press, New York, pp.240-60.

3.Denison, E. F. (1962), *The Sources of Economic Growth in the U.S. and the Alternatives before U.S.*, Committee for Economic Development, New York; *Accounting for the Economic Growth in the U. S. 1929-1969*, Brooking Institution, New York, 1974; Solow, R. M. (1957), 'Technical Change and the Aggregate Production Function', *Review of Economics and Statistics*, August; Kendrick, J. (1961), *Productivity Trends in the U. S.*, Princeton University Press, New York.

4.See, for example, Hagen and Hawrylyshyn (1969), 'Analysis of World Income and Growth, 1955-65', *Economic Development and Cultural Change*, Vol.17, October 1969, pp.81-96.

5.Stoneman, C.(1976), 'Foreign Capital and Economic Growth', *World Development*, Vol.3, January, pp.11-26.

6.San'tana, J. A. (1983), 'The Role of Foreign Capital in Recent Brazilian Development', in Kirkpatrick, C. H. and Nixson, F. I. (ed.), *The Industrialisation of Less Developed Countries*, Manchester University Press, Manchester, pp.172-95.

7.Kraska, M. and Taira, K. (1974), 'Foreign Capital, Aid and Growth in Latin America', *The Developing Economies*, Vol.12, September, pp.214-28.

8.El Shibly M. (1980), *Capital Formation, Inflation and Economic Growth: The Experience of Sudan 1960/61 - 1974/75*, PhD Thesis, University of Kent at Canterbury.

9.Mosley, P., Hudson, J. and Horrell, S. (1987), *Aid, the Public Sector and the Market in Less Developed Countries*, Discussion Papers, No.9, IDPM: University of Manchester.

10.Mosley, P. (1987), *Overseas Aid: Its Defence and Reform*, Wheatsheaf Books, Brighton, Sussex.

11.Karikari, J. A. (1992), 'Causality between DFI and Economic Output in Ghana', *Journal of Economic Development*, Vol.17, No.1, June, pp.7-15.

12.For example, Ahmed, Quazi Mesbahuddin (1992) finds that foreign aid and economic growth are inversely related while domestic savings seem to have been supplemented by foreign aid.

13.Gupta, K. L. and Islam M. A. (1983), *Foreign Capital, Savings and Growth: An International Cross-section Study*, D Reidel Publishing Company, Dordrecht.

14.Bornschier, V., Chase-Dunn, C. and Rubinson, R. (1978), 'Cross-national Evidence of the Effects of Foreign Investment and Aid on Economic Growth and Inequality: A Survey of Findings and a Reanalysis', *American Journal of Sociology*, Vol.84, pp.651-83.

15.See, for example, Cohen (1968); Kim, Seung Hee (1963), pp.48-49; and Voivodas (1975).

16.The export variable is included in the growth equation for at least reasons: First, export enable transforming countries to specialise in the production of commodities in which they have a comparative advantage; resources which are saved in this way can then be used for investment. Second, trade provides a vent for surplus commodities which bring otherwise unemployed resources into use. Third, trade can expand production possibilities through its effect on such factors as competition, access to new knowledge, technology and ideas; these are the so-called dynamic gains from trade. Fourth, trade enable transforming countries to purchase goods from abroad.

17.See, for example, Michaely, M. (1977), 'Exports and Growth - An Empirical Investigation', *Journal of Developing Economics*, Vol.4, No.1, p.50.

18.The experience of the developed Western countries shows that since the rate of population growth is low and as a result, the contribution of labour growth to output growth is small. See Chen, E.K.Y. (1977), 'Factor Inputs, Total Factor Productivity, and Economic Growth: The Asian Case', *The Developing Economies*, Vol.XV, No.1, 1977, p.137.

19.The insignificance of the lagged variable suggests that in the case of Hungary, the impact of an increase in the investment rate in accelerating the rate of output growth can be adequately modelled by employing the simplifying assumption that such accelerating effect occurs 'immediately', within the first year.

20.Addington, C. (1992), 'Are Primary Exports Really Unimportant to the Export-output Relationship', *Journal of Economic Development,* Vol.17, No.1, June, p.39.

21.See, Syron, R. and Walsh, B. (1968), 'The Relation of Exports and Economic Growth', *Kyklos,* Vol.21, No.3, pp.541-7.

22.Cohen found that export rate plays a more positive and significant role than FCI in the growth in his sample countries for 27 LDCs and 41 LDCs respectively during the period of 1955-60 and 1960-65.

23.In the cases of those rich labour countries, most empirical studies reveals that the rate of growth of capital and labour are important determinants of the rate of growth of GDP. Furthermore, the growth rate of labour is a much more important determinant of the rate of growth. See, for example, Chen E. K. Y. (1977), op. cit., pp.131-2.

24.Fosu, A. (1990), 'Export Composition and the Impact of Exports on Economic Growth of Developing Countries', *Economic Letters,* Vol.34, No.1, pp.66-71.

25.For example, employing dummies to capture the difference between middle- and low-income LDCs, Ram (1985) obtains negative coefficients for low-income countries. He thus concludes, exports have 'a much smaller impact .. on economic growth in the low-income LDCs'(p.420).

26.Zhang, Fengbao (1988), 'Chapter 5: Labour Input and Economic Growth', in *China: Macroeconomic Structure and Policy,* China Financial and Economic Press, Beijing.

27.Ballance, R. H., Ansari, J. A. and Singer, H. W. (1982), *The International Economy and Industrial Development: The Impact of Trade and Investment in the Third World,* Wheatsheaf Books, Brighton, Sussex, pp.152-4.

28.Heitger, Bernhard (1987), 'Import Protection and Export Performance - Their Impact on Economic Growth', *Weltwirtschaftliches Archiv (Review of World Economics),* Vol.123, p.255.

29.Goncalves, R. and Richtering, J. (1987), 'Inter-country Comparison of Export Performance and Output Growth', *The Developing Economics*, Vol. XXV, No.1, March, pp.11-13.

8 Foreign capital inflows and external trade in Hungary and China

As was already discussed in Chapter 7, foreign capital had a favourable effect on growth in both Hungary and China during 1979-92. Our survey of the literature, however, reveals that foreign capital inflows may contribute positively to the foreign exchange situation of the recipient country, or may exert indirect, usually negative and perhaps more long-term influences on the balance of payments and foreign exchange situation. Some empirical studies show that foreign capital plays a positive and important role in balance-of-payments stabilisation, while others stress the contradiction and otherwise perverse effects of foreign capital inflows.

This chapter is to provide some fresh evidence on the effect of foreign capital on imports and exports, by testing a model of import and export determination. Our empirical regression analysis reveals that foreign capital inflows contributed significantly to the growth of imports in both sample countries, while it reduced exports in the case of Hungary but promoted exports in the case of China.

Theoretical models of foreign capital and external trade

In order to import a certain level of capital and intermediate goods to carry out their productive activities, LDCs need foreign exchange whether earned from export or otherwise obtained. There is thus a close relationship between exports and growth. A number of previous empirical studies identified export's economic role as that of an earner of foreign exchange and as a contributor to the exporting country's 'capacity to import'.[1] We examine here some of the theories which established the link between foreign capital and external trade.

Using LDCs' import dependency for capital and intermediate goods as a starting point, Linder (1967)[2] argues that LDCs are generally faced with what he terms an 'import minimum', if the capacity to import is below the minimum level required then part of domestic potential savings will be frustrated because of the non-availability of required import inputs to match domestically available resources. The LDCs affected will thus not be able to achieve their full growth potential. LDCs therefore have to earn or receive enough foreign exchange in order to meet their respective 'import minimums', the cost of not meeting this requirement being a frustration of their growth potential or even a retrogression in their economic situation.

Linder illustrates the binding nature of such a constraint by fitting his ideas into the context of external and internal equilibrium analysis. Having assumed for simplicity that the trade balance is the balance of payment (there are no capital flows), he defines 'external equilibrium' as being when exports equal imports. There is also 'internal equilibrium' when the domestic economy is operating at 'full employment' in the Keynesian sense of full capacity utilisation in an environment of stable prices thus indicating that there is no unused capacity as well as no excess demand. Of the two equilibriums, the external balance was thought to be more highly binding because a country cannot continue indefinitely with a balance of payments deficit without finally triggering a crisis as its reserves are drained away.[3] Internal disequilibrium on the other hand may lead to political problems and economic inefficiency, but a country can theoretically struggle along indefinitely with such a handicap.

Thus, when faced with a conflict between the two requirements, Linder argues that LCDs will be forced to accept external balance at the expense of internal imbalance. The balance of payments constraint can therefore cause the economy to operate at below full potential because of an inadequate level of input import. In the case of inadequate export earning, however, actual import will be less than the level of import necessary to realise the potential level of investment, because of the constraint that in order to maintain external equilibrium import earning must be equal to export earning.

Linder's arguments summarised above can easily incorporate the effect of capital flows by redefining the capacity to import as the sum of export and net capital inflows less factor payments abroad. A foreign exchange constraint will be forced when export earnings and net FCI fall below the minimum import requirement.

Hicks and McNicoll (1971)[4] emphasise that for LDCs the savings constraint is, in a way, subordinate to the foreign exchange constraint. This is because the relationship between non-consumption (i.e. savings) and investment is not a direct one due to their inability to produce their own capital goods. LDCs therefore have to export their surplus to earn foreign exchange and use the proceeds to import needed capital goods before investment can take place. Growth is, therefore, likely to be constrained by the ability to 'transfer' savings abroad, as by the inability to save as such. FCI may directly and indirectly affect the foreign exchange situation and the domestic savings rate of the recipient economy.

Thirlwall and his associates found that the foreign exchange constraint on growth is binding for both LDCs and developed countries (DCs).[5] They introduced the concept of the 'balance of payments equilibrium growth rate', the maximum rate of growth that can be sustained without causing a deficit in the balance of payment. Thirlwall (1979)[6] showed that, on the simplifying assumption that there are no capital flows, this theoretical rate can be approximated by the ratio of the rate of export growth and the income elasticity of demand for imports.

$$Y = x/x'$$

where: Y = the balance of payments equilibrium growth rate; x = the rate of export growth, x' = the income elasticity of demand for import.

Since capital inflows represents an important element in the balance of payments, the balance of payments equilibrium growth rate could be given by the following expression.

$$Y = \{ E/R(x) + F/R(f-p)\}/x'$$

where: E/R = share of export in proportion to 'total receipts' $(E+F)$; F/R = share of FCI in 'total receipt'; f = rate of growth of FCI; p = rate of growth of domestic prices.

In both formulations, Y, the balance of payments equilibrium growth rate can be interpreted as the upper limit of growth that can not exceeded without upsetting the balance of payments equilibrium defined with or without the inclusion of FCI.

By using the data in 15 mostly developed countries and 20 LDCs, Thirlwall further found that the actual growth rate achieved generally did not exceed the balance of payments constrained growth rate. The balance of payments position exercises an affective limit on growth which applies to both LDCs and developed countries.

These theories reveal, then, that there is a close link between the balance of payment position and a country's ability to grow. We should next consider the trade effect of FDI.

The net trade effects of FDI on recipient country

The net trade effect means that the balance of the effects that FDI may have on the import and export propensities of the capital importing country. If FDI causes exports to increase and imports to reduce or, if export growth is larger than import growth, then we have a positive net trade effect. If FDI induces imports by more than it induces exports or, if it actually depresses exports, then we have a negative net trade effect.

Underlying theoretical influences

Early studies usually believed that the net trade effects of FDI were likely to be positive (trade-surplus-creating). McDougall (1960) found that profits and interests flight abroad incurred as a result of FDI may be offset or more than offset by favourable effects on the balance of payments resulting from extra production, induced by the capital inflows which were import-saving or export-creating in nature. The expectation is, therefore, that the positive trade effects may help host countries pay for the factor costs of funds borrowed or investments received from abroad.[7]

Later theoretical and empirical studies provided much less optimistic view on FDI's net trade effects. Loo (1977)[8] finds that FDI has a negative rather than a positive net effect on the trade position of host country: (a) in a 'two country' world (e.g. a capital exporting country versus a host country, normally LDC), if both countries are at below full employment, FDI will increase the spending power and thus induce it to spend more on imports in the host country. The opposite effect will occur in the home country, whose imports will decline. The net trade effect of FDI can be, therefore, expected to be negative, as FDI cause imports to increase and exports to decrease; (b) if both countries are at full employment, FDI will have the effect of increasing liquidity and cause price levels to rise in the host country. The opposite effect will occur in the capital leading country. The net effect is that prices in the host country will rise relative to the price levels in the home country. As a result, exports in the host country will become relatively more expensive while imports from home country becomes relatively cheap. The host country will depress exports but boost its import, resulting in negative net trade effect. In both types of situation, therefore, the expected net trade effect of FDI is negative.

The above expectations merely refer to the general underlying effects of FDI on trade. The nature of the trade effects of FDI may depend on the sectors in which foreign invested projects are undertaken. As Polak (1943)[9] argued that if FDI was used for investment in the tradeable sector, i.e. producing goods for export or import substitution, then the entire additional

273

value added produced represented net foreign savings or earnings. He further argued that the export value added or import value saved, which together form the 'export surplus', represented an increase of income of equal magnitude. Since import is a function of income, this increase will, however, induce increases in the demand for imports. This will negate only part of the 'export surplus' effects. Thus overall investment in the tradeable sector can be expected to lead to favourable net trade effects. If FDI is used for investment in the non-tradeable sector, such investment will not yield any positive effects on exports or any savings on imports. They can be expected to produce negative impacts on the trade balance equivalent to their import content. In addition, such investments increase income, thus inducing further imports, via the positive relationship between import and income. The net trade effects produced by such investments can, therefore, be expected to reinforce the underlying negative influences described by Loo (1977).

Import and export generating effects

Import generating effect refers to the additional importing of finished goods, components, raw materials and capital equipment from the investing country induced by the existence of affiliates of its MNCs in the host country. This includes direct export from parents or other subsidiaries to the affiliates, or export from other suppliers resulting from the trade links fostered between the home and host countries. Second generation imports may occur as competitors in the host country begin to emulate the practices and mode of production of MNCs affiliates in the country and buy their supplies and equipment from abroad.

Export generating effects occur when the MNCs subsidiaries in the host country begin to export components and finished goods back to the home market, or to third country markets.

A strong positive correlation can, therefore, be expected to exist between MNC investments and imports of host countries. But the export generating effect, on the other hand, only occur at the last stage of the international product cycle, or not at all. MNCs were found to establish subsidiaries in the more advanced Latin American countries, then cater for the local market and/or to export to the surrounding less favoured countries mainly because of closer proximity, or even to export to the home market if they are efficient enough or if factor costs are effectively cheap enough.[10] We should point out that FDI policies in host countries can significantly influence the types and trade impacts of foreign direct investment.

Foreign capital inflows were therefore criticised because initial inflows of foreign capital would lead to future outflow of factor payments and capital repayments. The long-term net financial contributions may thus be negative.

FDI may exert positive and negative indirect effects on the recipient country's import and export propensities, on the terms of trade, and on the capital flights behaviour based on different situations.

All these indirect effects will filter through into the balance of payments position of the recipient country and thus affect the availability of foreign exchange and the recipient's ability to import. FDI's effects on the balance of payments, both direct and indirect, will therefore influence its effect on the growth rate of the recipient country.

Empirical evidence regarding the trade effects of FDI

Most empirical studies found a negative net trade effect of FDI. Based on the experience of 11 Latin American countries between 1955-66, Massell, et al.(1972)[11] found that the import propensity attached to foreign exchange obtained via FCI, was much higher than that for foreign exchange earned from exports. The relationship was found as follows:

$$M = 0.495 + 0.296\ X + 0.333\ X(t\text{-}1) + 0.968\ G - 0.213\ G(t\text{-}1)$$
$$\quad (3.16) \quad (4.69) \quad\quad (4.01) \quad\quad\quad\quad (3.96) \quad\quad (\text{-}0.44)$$
$$\quad + 0.749\ P + 0.213\ P(t\text{-}1)$$
$$\quad\quad (10.35) \quad\quad (3.71)$$

$$\bar{R}^2 = 0.732$$

where: M = imports, X = exports, G = public capital inflows, P = private capital inflows.

This regression indicates that there is a positive relationship between import and foreign capital inflows (public and private investment). The impact coefficients are very high in both cases (0.97 and 0.75 respectively). The lagged coefficient is, however, negative but insignificant with regard to public inflows, but positive and significant with regard to private inflows. It implies that in the long term, public induced inflows may have been import-saving, while private foreign investment may be negative.

Massell et al 1972) did not investigate the impact of such FDI on export propensity, thus we can not compare FDI's net trade effects. Chenery and Syrquin (1975),[12] however, found the following relationship between exports, imports and FDI:

1. $Ep/Y = 0.359 - 0.008 \ln y - 0.002 (\ln y)^2 - 0.056 \ln N + 0.03 (\ln N)^2$
   (3.86) (-0.18)   (-0.92)   (-6.96)   (2.22)
   $- 0.983$ FCI
   (-23.23)

$\bar{R}^2 = 0.67$

2. $Em/Y = 0.05 - 0.05 \ln y + 0.007 (\ln y)^2 + 0.026 \ln N - 0.005 (\ln N)^2$
   (0.49) (-1.3)   (2.51)   (3.01)   (-3.36)

       $+ 0.06$ FCI
       (1.33)

$\bar{R}^2 = 0.31$

3. $M/Y = 0.123 + 0.05 \ln y - 0.002 (\ln y)^2 - 0.032 \ln N - 0.004 (\ln N)^2$
   (1.39)   (1.55)   (-0.74)   (-3.85)   (-2.25)
         $+ 0.532$ FCI
         (12.13)

$\bar{R}^2 = 0.34$

Where: Ep = exports of primary products, Em = exports of manufacturing products, M = imports, Y = GDP, N = population size, y = GNP per capita.

The first regression shows a very significant negative relationship between exports of primary products and FDI. The second regression shows that manufacturing export is positively related to FDI. The coefficient is, however, not very significant. Regression 3 shows that import is very significantly related to FDI and the coefficient is also quite large. The study is based on a world-wide cross-country sample of LDCs, thus we can conclude that net trade effects of FDI on FDI recipients is generally negative.

In summary, Pizer and Cutler (1965),[13] Natke and Newfarmer (1985)[14] and Loo (1977) and Mainardi (1986) all found that FDI has negative net trade effects on recipient countries, as MNCs affiliates in host countries import more than their exports.

The terms of trade represent the rate at which a country changes its exports for its import and is conventionally defined as the ratio of indices of export and import prices. If export prices increase relative to import prices, then the terms of trade are said to be turning in a country's favour. If import prices increase relative to export prices or export prices decline relative to import prices, then the country is said to be suffering from a deterioration in its terms of trade. Clearly a country's export earnings and its import costs will be affected by the movements in the terms of trade.

Our literature survey reveals that foreign capital inflows causes a deterioration in the terms of trade of the recipient countries in the long run. It is claimed that increased production of exportable commodities by MNCs reduces their exchange value relative to the value of imports. This argument is buttressed by the fact that the world price elasticity of demand for most major exports from LDCs is usually less than unity. It is, therefore, suggested that worsening terms of trade from increased exports reduce the income (well-being) of affected LDCs.[15]

The empirical test of FDI's net trade effects in Hungary and China

This section we tests the FDI's net trade effect in Hungary and China for the period 1978-1992. The test will be performed by inserting FDI as an additional explanatory variable in the simplified export, import and terms of trade equations. One advantage of this simplified equations is that the these equations are no longer simultaneous, and so can be estimated by ordinary least squares method without fear of simultaneous-equation bias. The sign and significance of the FDI variable in the equations specified will be taken as indicative of the direction and significance of the effect that FDI has on the explained variable under consideration. These effects will, therefore, indicate to use the overall net trade effects of FDI with regard to our sample countries in the period studied.

Equations for the empirical testing of FDI's net trade effects

The export equation Under given external demand conditions, relative export success of individual countries depends on domestic supply conditions. Exports are usually specified as a function of domestic price, prices of export competing goods and the world demand situation, which can be used to capture the net effect of supply-side and demand-side factors on export performance.[16] This can be specified by combining the influences of the domestic and foreign prices in a single terms of trade measure and hypothesising that export earnings are a positive function of improvements in the terms of trade. The export formula can be expressed as follows:

$$X = f\,(TT', WD) \qquad (8.1)$$

Where: $TT' = TT - TT(t-1)$ and the terms of trade itself is defined as $TT =$ export price index/import price index; $WD =$ world demand (export market potential) for traditional exports is measured in terms of a weighted-average index of imports by either Eastern European countries (except Hungary) or OECD countries.

In addition, the ability to export can be hypothesised to increase with the level of development, a variable which is proxied by either the level of income or GDP per capita.[17] Other studies have simply posited the ability to export growth with time.[18] Taking these into account, equation 8.1 can be extended as follows:

$$X = f\,(TT', WD, y, t) \qquad (8.1a)$$

Where: $y =$ per capita income, used as a proxy for the level of development, $t =$ time trend.

Where all the explanatory variables are expected to show positive relationships with export earnings. It is noted that development and the progress of time trend may both be capturing the same effects, thus y and t should perhaps be used alternatively rather than together.

In order to test the effects of FDI on export, the function can be extended to include FDI as an additional explanatory variable, giving the following testable relationships:

$$X = f\,[TT', WD, y \text{ or } t, FDI, X(t-1)] \qquad (8.1b)$$

A positive coefficient for FCI will indicate that foreign capital has indeed helped the country to increase exports. A negative coefficient on the other hand will indicate that the converse is true.

The models discussed so far have assumed that exports are homogeneous in terms of their responsiveness to foreign import demand growth, relative prices, and time trend/development process.

The import equation Voivodas (1973) showed that consumption imports and inputs imports (i.e. imports of capital and intermediate goods) exert different

278

and opposing influences on growth. The two types of imports will therefore be kept separate in the study to allow for this.

Following the normal Keynessian hypothesis, consumption import is posited as a positive function of income and a negative function of import prices.[19] Hypothesising further that consumer spending behaviour responds slowly to changing circumstances, we hypothesise that consumption import responds not only to current income, but also to the previous pattern of expenditure. The previous level of consumption import may therefore also be a significant explanatory variable. The consumption import function is therefore specified as follows:

$$MC = f [y, pm, MC(t-1)] \qquad (8.2)$$

Where: MC = consumption import; y = GDP per capita; pm = import price index.

In order to capture any import effects of capital inflows, FCI can simply be introduced as an additional explanatory variable in the equation specified. The consumption import equation now becomes:

$$MC = f [y, pm, MC(t-1), FCI] \qquad (8.2a)$$

While the input import function remains as the equation (8.2a) because it contains FCI as an explanatory variable.

If the estimated coefficient of the FDI variable in the consumption import function is significantly positive, then it indicates that FDI exerts a positive effect on the propensity to consume imported goods. A significant negative coefficient on the other hand indicates that FDI has helped the country to substitute away from such imports. With regard to the input import function, the coefficient is expected to be positive, in line with theoretical expectation that FDI contributes to the 'capacity to import' such goods.

According to Linder theory and the dual-gap theory, we expect import of capital and intermediate goods to be basically a function of the 'capacity to import', i.e.

$$MKI = f ('capacity to import') \qquad (8.3)$$

For LDCs, the capacity of import' is clearly related to foreign exchange availability and this is made up of export earnings, the balance of foreign capital inflows and outflows. In addition, foreign exchange which is used simply to beef up reserves will reduce the amount presently available to finance imports. The input import function is therefore be specified as follows:

$$MKI = f [X, FDI, CF, IR, MKI(t-1)] \qquad (8.3a)$$

Where: X = export earnings, FDI = foreign direct investment, CF = 'capital flight', IR = foreign exchange reserve position.

Factor services encompass profits and dividends, and interest receipts and payments. Most LDCs incur a net outflow on profits and dividends which may be large, depending upon the stock of foreign investment in the country. Interest payments are potentially one of the largest and most volatile items in the current account and need close attention. Hungary used to run persistent current-account deficits in the past and borrowed abroad to finance them. The lagged endogenous variable $MKI(t-1)$ is added to take into account the usual observation that investment behaviour in time t is usually affected by the previous period's investment because of the long term nature of the implementation process with most investment projects.

The term of trade equation   Under transfer theory, the terms of trade are expected to improve when FDI is received and to decline when capital flows out, whether in the form of capital flight or factor payments abroad, i.e.

$$TT = f (Z, CF, FDI) \qquad (8.4)$$

Where: Z = factor payment abroad, CF = capital flight out, FCI = foreign capital inflows.

Singer (1950), Prebisch (1950),[20] and Thirlwall (1983), among others hypothesised that LDCs terms of trade is suffering from a secular declining trend, while studies such as Wijnbergen (1985)[21] pointed to the fact that the economic situation in OECD countries has strong influence on the terms of trade in LDCs.
   Equation (8.4) can therefore be extended to include these other influences as follows:

$$TT = f (Z, CF, FDI, t, UOECD) \qquad (8.4a)$$

Where: UOECD = OECD-wide unemployment rate used as a cyclical indicator.

Overall, FDI and the factor payments outflows caused by it, are expected to have a long term negative influence on the recipient LDC's terms of trade.

The effects of FCI on exports The basic export equation tested was as follows:

$$X/Y = f [TT', WD, y \text{ or } t, X/Y(t-1)]$$

It should be noted that in this and subsequent regressions all variables are in the form of levels have been scaled against GDP to preclude the possibility of heteroscedasticity.

The world demand variable WD may be proxied alternatively or together by any of the following: WDEE - The import volume of Eastern European countries and Soviet Union (WDEE) is used as a proxy for the external demand situation; or WDOECD - The growth rates of import volume of OECD countries.

Both of the alternative world demand variables have been proxied for the case of Hungary, but only the WDOECD is used for the case of China, because the WDEE does not best reflect the actual external demand situation with regard to China.[22]

The results obtained when the basic export equation was run confirm that y and t capture quite different type of effects on export:

$$X/Y = 59.03 - 0.085 \text{ TT'} + 0.03 \text{ WDEE} - 0.008 \text{ y} - 0.168 \text{ X/Y(t-1)}$$
$$(7.16) \quad (-1.11) \quad\quad (1.98) \quad\quad (-7.57) \quad (-1.09)$$

$$R^2 = 0.96 \quad \text{D-W} = 1.48 \quad \text{SE} = 0.86 \quad F = 77.64 \quad N = 15$$

This result surprisingly indicates that Hungary has been actually reducing its export level with the increasing of GDP per capita and the deteriorating of the terms of trade. Previous year's export seems negatively related with the export performance in current year. Only the import volumes of other Eastern European countries and Soviet Union were positively contributed to the export rate in Hungary during 1978-92.

Substituting the time trend t with y, we then got a poor regression equation as follows:

$$X/Y = 11.25 - 0.082 \text{ TT'} + 0.046 \text{ WDEE} - 0.53 \text{ t} + 0.60 \text{ X/Y(t-1)}$$
$$(0.95) \quad (-0.45) \quad\quad (0.78) \quad\quad (-1.37) \quad (2.35)$$

$$R^2 = 0.75 \quad \text{D-W} = 1.27 \quad \text{SE} = 2.04 \quad F = 11.63 \quad N = 15$$

If we use both t and y together to proxy the passing of time/development, we will get an improved regression equation:

281

$$X/Y = 67.99 - 0.079\ TT' - 0.011\ WDEE - 0.01\ y + 0.42\ t - 0.20\ X/Y$$
$$\quad (8.87)\quad (-1.27)\qquad (-0.54)\qquad\qquad (-8.71)\quad (2.44)\quad (-1.56)$$

$$\overline{R}^2 = 0.97 \quad D\text{-}W = 2.44 \quad SE = 0.70 \quad F = 94.19 \quad N = 15$$

The result reveals that most explanatory variables, except the time trend t, are negatively related with the export rate in Hungary. This appears to be contrary to theoretical expectations until it is revealed that Hungary's exports from 1977-92 remained at US$8-10 billion levels and the growth rate is very small.

When testing the trade effects of FCI, the equation yielded the following results:

$$X/Y = 55.89 - 0.15\ TT' - 0.009\ y + 0.59\ t + 0.008\ WDEE + 0.057\ X/Y(t\text{-}1)$$
$$\quad (5.50)\quad (-2.09)\quad (-7.91)\quad (3.13)\quad (0.34)\qquad\qquad (0.29)$$
$$\quad - 0.079\ FCI/Y$$
$$\quad (-1.65)$$

$$\overline{R}^2 = 0.98 \quad D\text{-}W = 2.41 \quad SE = 0.64 \quad F = 93.91 \quad N = 15$$

The initial testing results show that FCI does not have a positive effect on the export rate. Hungary's empirical evidence does not support the hypothesis - FDI favours host country's exports.

We assume that the export rate is not only affected by current FCI, but also by the previous inflow of foreign capital. So we insert FCI(t-1) variable to test its continues effect on export as follows:

$$X/Y = 56.16 - 0.15\ TT' - 0.009\ y + 0.56\ t - 0.001\ WDEE + 0.063\ X/Y(t\text{-}1)$$
$$\quad (5.54)\quad (-2.08)\quad (-7.14)\quad (2.93)\quad (-0.04)\qquad\qquad (0.33)$$
$$\quad - 0.043\ FCI/Y - 0.032\ FCI/Y(t\text{-}1)$$
$$\quad (-0.73)\qquad\quad (-1.02)$$

$$\overline{R}^2 = 0.98 \quad D\text{-}W = 2.80 \quad SE = 0.64 \quad F = 81.08 \quad N = 15$$

This suggests that previous foreign capital inflows affect the export rate more significantly than current FCI.

At this stage, we introduce a new variable, i.e. world demand proxied by the growth rate of import volume in OECD countries, we then obtain the following result:

$$X/Y = 53.98 - 0.13\ TT' - 0.008\ y + 0.40\ t - 0.00001\ WDEE + 0.074\ X/Y(t\text{-}1)$$
$$\quad (5.39)\quad (-1.82)\quad (-5.03)\quad (1.72)\quad (-0.00045)\qquad\qquad (0.39)$$
$$\quad - 0.017\ FCI/Y - 0.076\ FCI/Y(t\text{-}1) + 0.076\ WDOECD$$
$$\quad (-0.28)\qquad\quad (-1.57)\qquad\qquad (1.20)$$

$\overline{R}^2 = 0.98$ D-W = 3.21 SE = 0.62 F = 75.47 N = 15

The coefficients of WDEE, X/Y(t-1) and FCI/Y are however not significant at all. Deleting these variables, we found that there is virtually no information loss as a consequence of the deletion.

X/Y = 56.98 - 0.11 TT' - 0.008 y + 0.33 t + 0.08 WDOECD - 0.062 FCI/Y(t-1)
       (53.50) (-2.38)   (-11.86)   (3.64)   (1.78)   (-3.54)

$\overline{R}^2 = 0.89$ D-W = 3.15 SE = 0.52 F = 174.99 N = 15

The regression results of these exercises, together with relevant test statistics, are summarised in **Table 8.1**.

All the regressions pass the F-test for overall statistical significance. And in all regressions, the overall degree of multiple correlation (R) is higher relative to the degree of multiple correlation among the explanatory variables suggesting that the OLS method can meaningfully disentangle the separate effects of each of the explanatory variables on the dependent variable.[23]

The results in **Table 8.1** shows that there are few strong results for Hungary, and indeed the equations do not attain general significance. It indicates that the terms of trade and GDP per capita carried significant but negative coefficients effects on export at 10 percent level of confidence. Only the time trend variable carried significant and positive coefficients in most of the regression equations. Other explanatory variables shown insignificant results. All coefficients of foreign capital inflows variable in both non-lagged and lagged forms concerned shown negative contribution to export, most of them are statistically insignificant. Thus, the results suggest that, overall, foreign capital is not an important determinant of export performance in Hungary.

We found that equation 7 produces the best fit result, since the standard error of regression is the lowest one, the D-W test is quite high, and the estimated F-ratios are well above the tabulated value, and finally, the 'explanatory power' is very high, as it could explain 98 per cent of the variation of the export rates in the data. Equation 7 therefore could be considered to be satisfactorily accepted.

283

Table 8.1
OLS estimates of the contribution of FCI to exports in Hungary, 1978-92

(t-test in parentheses, n=15)

No	Constant	TT'	y	t	FCI/Y	FCI/Y(t-1)	X/Y(t-1)	WDEE	WDOECD	R^2	D-W	Estim. F	Tabul F (0.95)	SE
1	59.03 (7.16)	-0.085 (-1.11)	-0.008* (-7.57)				-0.168 (-1.09)	0.029*** (1.98)		0.96	1.48	77.64	3.33	0.86
2	11.25 (0.95)	-0.082 (-0.45)		-0.53*** (-1.37)			0.599*** (2.35)	0.046 (0.78)		0.75	1.27	11.63	3.33	2.04
3	67.99 (8.86)	-0.079 (-1.27)	-0.01* (-8.70)	0.42** (2.44)			-0.20*** (-1.56)	-0.011 (-0.54)		0.97	2.43	94.19	3.37	0.70
4	55.89 (5.49)	-0.15** (-2.09)	-0.009* (-7.91)	0.59* (3.13)	-0.08*** (-1.65)		0.057 (0.29)	0.008 (0.343)		0.98	2.41	93.91	3.50	0.64
5	56.16 (5.54)	-0.15** (-2.08)	-0.009* (-7.14)	0.56** (2.93)	-0.043 (-0.73)	-0.032 (-1.02)	0.063 (0.33)	-0.001 (-0.04)		0.98	2.80	81.07	3.73	0.64
6	53.98 (5.39)	-0.13*** (-1.82)	-0.008* (-5.04)	0.399*** (1.73)	-0.017 (-0.28)	-0.06*** (-1.57)	0.073 (0.39)	-0.00001 (-0.0004)	0.076 (1.20)	0.98	3.21	75.47	4.10	0.62
7	56.98 (53.50)	-0.113** (-2.38)	-0.008* (-11.86)	0.33* (3.64)		-0.06* (-3.54)			0.08*** (1.78)	0.98	3.15	174.99	3.37	0.52
8	59.36 (36.02)	-0.135** (-2.52)	-0.01* (-13.67)	0.596* (4.54)	-0.066** (-2.66)					0.98	2.47	172.91	3.33	0.58
9	58.84 (34.92)	-0.14** (-2.59)	-0.009* (-11.60)	0.525* (3.67)	-0.035 (-0.98)	-0.03 (-1.15)				0.98	2.70	142.99	3.37	0.57

Notes:

*   Coefficient significant at the 1 per cent level of confidence
**   Coefficient significant at the 5 per cent level of confidence
***   Coefficient significant at the 10 per cent level of confidence

Explaining equation 7, we found that the estimated coefficient of the FCI variable lagged by one year in the export equation function is significantly negative, as well as the terms of trade and the GDP per capita variable. This meant that both FCI, terms of trade and GDP per capita exert significant negative effects on the export rate in Hungary during 1978-92. Only the time trend and the world demand proxied by the import growth rate in OECD countries have positive effect on the export rate in Hungary during the period studied.

The strong negative effect for FCI on the export rate can be partly explained by noting that much of foreign capital inflows had been used by the Hungarian government for investment in the non-trade sector, such as social, infrastructure and rural development projects, in import substitution activities or in consumption, even for service old debt. Such expenditure, by switching expenditure away from export related activities, reduces exports. Its combined effect is thus a drastic reduction in the export rate.

The effects of FCI on consumption imports On the basis of equation (8.2) specified earlier, we tested the following consumption import function:

$$MC/Y = f[y, pm, Mc/Y(t-1)]$$

Where MC had, following our normal practice, been scaled against GDP to avoid heteroscedasticity and to put it line with other variables.

Regressing the basic equation alone, we obtained the following relationship:

$$MC/Y = 7.43 + 0.004 \ y - 0.11 \ pm + 0.34 \ MC/Y(t-1)$$
$$(2.63) \quad (3.27) \quad (-3.62) \quad (1.82)$$

$$\bar{R}^2 = 0.70, \ D\text{-}W = 2.29 \quad SE = 0.90 \quad F = 12.08 \quad N = 15$$

Inserting the time trend t to capture for the influence, we found the following:

$$MC/Y = 7.15 + 0.004 \ y - 0.07 \ t - 0.10 \ pm + 0.32 \ MC/Y(t-1)$$
$$(2.30) \quad (3.14) \quad (-0.28) \ (-2.10) \quad (1.53)$$

$$\bar{R}^2 = 0.68 \ D\text{-}W = 2.21 \quad SE = 0.94 \ F = 8.32 \quad N = 15$$

The time trend variable carries the 'wrong' sign and is insignificant. Deleting this variable and inserting FCI/Y variable to test the contribution of FCI on consumption imports, produced the following version of equation:

$$MC/Y = 11.71 + 0.003 \, y - 0.09 \, pm + 0.12 \, MC/Y(t-1) - 0.058 \, FCI/Y$$
$$(3.41) \quad (2.98) \quad (-2.99) \quad (0.56) \quad (-1.86)$$

$$\bar{R}^2 = 0.76 \quad D\text{-}W = 2.36 \quad SE = 0.81 \quad F = 11.94 \quad N = 15$$

The FCI variable was found to carry the negative sign and the coefficient was statistically significant, thus indicating that in the case of Hungary, FCI had significantly negative effect on the rate of import of consumption goods. This means that the increasing of foreign loans and debt posed Hungarian government to reduce import of consumption goods over 1978-92.

Since the import rate lagged one year shows insignificant coefficient, we deleted this variable and produced the improved results:

$$MC/Y = 13.53 + 0.003 \, y - 0.09 \, pm - 0.07 \, FCI/Y$$
$$(13.49) \quad (3.03) \quad (-3.15) \quad (-2.77)$$

$$\bar{R}^2 = 0.77 \quad D\text{-}W = 2.24 \quad SE = 0.79 \quad F = 16.87 \quad N = 15$$

In order to test the contribution of world supply to the consumption import rate in Hungary proxing by the OECD export growth rate during 1978-92, we obtained the following relationship:

$$MC/Y = 13.65 + 0.003 \, y - 0.09 \, pm - 0.09 \, EXOECD - 0.06 \, FCI/Y$$
$$(14.21) \quad (3.08) \quad (-3.24) \quad (-1.45) \quad (-2.53)$$

$$\bar{R}^2 = 0.79 \quad D\text{-}W = 2.68 \quad SE = 0.75 \quad F = 14.43 \quad N = 15$$

Where: EXOECD = export growth rate in OECD countries, 1978-92.

Both import price index and export growth rates in OECD countries are negatively related with Hungary's consumption import variable, only the GDP per capita inserted a positive contribution to the consumption import rates in Hungary during 1978-92. It interestingly indicates that FCI has exerted significantly negative effects on consumption imports, suggesting that such foreign capital may have been import substituting, old debt servicing and investing in non-trade sector in nature.

The effect of FCI on input imports One of the main arguments put forward by critics of FDI is that local manufacturing affiliates are typically little more than assembly operations which source most of their inputs of parts, etc. from overseas. Furthermore, it is often alleged that it is only the more standard, unsophisticated parts which are sourced locally, whereas the more complex components are brought in from the parent companies at home. For their part, many foreign firms point out a number of practical difficulties associated with increasing local content. Though the long-established firms tend to buy more from local sources, most of the products manufactured by FIEs were based primarily on parent company's specifications and it was therefore not surprising that many of the parts could only be supplied from specific home sources. It is thus necessary to analyze FDI's import effect in the Hungarian economy.

We early posited input imports as a function of the 'capacity to import' as well as of their own past level. We also noted that the capacity to import is enhanced by export earnings and FCI and is reduced by 'capital flight'.

The relationship tested was therefore as follows:

$$MKI = f [X/Y, FCI/Y, CF/Y, MKI/Y(t-1)\}$$

Where: input imports were defined as the import of intermediate and capital goods, CF refers to factor payments abroad.

The estimated equation is as follows:

$$MKI/Y = -10.28 + 0.66 \, X/Y + 0.48 \, MKI/Y(t-1) - 0.45 \, CF/Y + 0.047 \, FCI/Y$$
$$\quad\quad\;\; (-1.02) \quad (2.37) \quad\quad (1.78) \quad\quad\quad\quad (-0.32) \quad\quad (0.45)$$

$$\bar{R}^2 = 0.80 \quad D\text{-}W = 1.63 \quad SE = 2.36 \quad F = 11.96 \quad N = 15$$

All explanatory variables carry the expected signs, but the capital flight and capital inflows variables arc statistically insignificant. The regression confirms that FCI/Y has a positive influence on the import of investment goods. The coefficient and its significance is, however, quite small, which indicating that a large part of foreign capital was not in fact spent on input imports but was either spent on locally produced investment goods, consumed or simply serviced old debt. A large part of foreign capital was used by Hungarian government to finance social, infrastructure or rural development construction project using local labour and material input, only a small proportion used to import machinery. The purchase of locally produced capital goods does not require the use of foreign exchange.

The effect of FCI on imports in the aggregate Having seen the effect of FCI on consumption and input imports taken separately, we feel that it may be interesting to test FCI's effects on import in the aggregate.

The aggregate import equation was initially posited as a simple linear combination of the consumption and input import functions specified earlier, such that:

$$M/Y = f [y, t, X/Y, FCI/Y, CF/Y, M/Y(t-1)]$$

Testing this relationship produced the following poor-fit estimated equation:

$$M/Y = 32.94 - 0.0003 \, y - 1.19 \, t + 0.29 \, X/Y + 0.15 \, FCI/Y - 0.72 \, CF/Y$$
$$\quad (0.66) \quad (-0.04) \quad (-1.93) \quad (0.33) \quad (1.62) \quad (-0.68)$$

$\bar{R}^2 = 0.89$ D-W = 1.05 SE = 1.97 F = 22.80 N = 15

If lagged structure and one development variable are used alternatively, we will obtain more improved equation:

$$M/Y = 3.85 + 0.58 \, M/Y(t-1) - 0.08 \, FCI/Y(t-1) + 0.41 \, X/Y(t-1) - 0.0007 \, y(t-1)$$
$$\quad (0.09) \quad (2.43) \quad (-1.71) \quad (0.68) \quad (-0.01)$$

$\bar{R}^2 = 0.93$ D-W = 2.03 SE = 1.59 F = 44.51 N = 15

and

$$M/Y = 3.01 + 0.59 \, M/Y(t-1) + 0.42 \, X/Y(t-1) - 0.08 \, FCI/Y(t-1) + 0.02 \, t$$
$$\quad (0.25) \quad (2.17) \quad (1.90) \quad (-1.30) \quad (0.04)$$

$\bar{R}^2 = 0.93$ D-W = 2.05 SE = 1.59 F = 44.52 N = 15

Since both time trend and GDP per capita are statistically insignificant in terms of coefficient and significance, we deleted these variables and obtained the restricted equation as follows:

$$M/Y = 3.39 + 0.58 \, M/Y(t-1) - 0.08 \, FCI/Y(t-1) + 0.42 \, X/Y(t-1)$$
$$\quad (0.62) \quad (4.20) \quad (-2.16) \quad (2.00)$$

$\bar{R}^2 = 0.93$ D-W = 2.03 SE = 1.52 F = 65.29 N = 15

All coefficients of explanatory variables lagged one year are significant at well above the 1 per cent level of confidence. The result thus indicates that both export rates and import rates lagged one year exerted strong positive effects on aggregate imports while FCI played a significant negative contribution on aggregate imports.

The net trade effects of FCI Lagged FCI's coefficient in the export equation is - 0.062, indicating that each 1 per cent increase in lagged FCI reduces the export rate by around 0.06 per cent. FCI's coefficient in the lagged import equation is -0.08, indicating each 1 per cent increase in lagged FCI reduces the import rate by around 0.08 per cent. The net trade effect of FCI is therefore shown to be strongly negative.

The trade effects of FCI in China, 1978-92

The effects of FDI on exports On the basis of equation (8.1b), the basic export equation tested was as follows:

$$X/Y = f [TT', WD, y \text{ or } t, X/Y(t-1)]$$

It should be noted that in this and subsequent regressions all variables are in the form of levels have been scaled against GDP to preclude the possibility of heteroscedasticity.

The world demand variable WD may be proxied by WDOECD - the growth rates of import volume of OCED countries.

The results obtained when the basic export equation was run found that y and t capture quite same type of effects on export:

$$X/Y = 1.43 + 0.042 \text{ TT'} - 0.03 \text{ WDOECD} + 0.005 \text{ y} + 0.53 \text{ X/Y(t-1)}$$
$$\quad\quad (1.89)\quad (3.02)\quad\quad (-0.46)\quad\quad\quad\quad (2.24)\quad\quad (2.18)$$
$$\bar{R}^2 = 0.97 \quad \text{D-W} = 1.32 \quad \text{SE} = 0.82 \quad \text{F} = 112.6 \quad \text{N} = 15$$

This result indicates that China has been actually increased its export level with the increasing of GDP per capita and improvement of the terms of trade. Previous year's export is strongly related with the export performance in current year. Only the import growth rates of OECD were negatively but insignificantly contributed to the export rate in China during 1978-92.

Substituting the time trend t with y, we then got a poor regression equation as follows, which suggests that China's exports are significantly and positively related with the time trend:

$$X/Y = 0.65 + 0.044 \text{ TT'} - 0.023 \text{ WDOECD} + 0.35 \text{ t} + 0.73 \text{ X/Y(t-1)}$$
$$\quad\quad (1.03)\quad (2.94)\quad\quad (-0.37)\quad\quad\quad\quad (1.81)\quad (3.69)$$
$$\bar{R}^2 = 0.97 \quad \text{D-W} = 1.40 \quad \text{SE} = 0.87 \quad \text{F} = 99.19 \quad \text{N} = 15$$

If we use both t and y together to proxy the passing of time/development, we will get an improved regression equation:

$$X/Y = 1.38 + 0.039 \text{ TT'} - 0.039 \text{ WDOECD} + 0.0035 \text{ y} + 0.21 \text{ t} + 0.45 \text{ X/Y(t-1)}$$
$$\quad\quad (1.82)\quad (2.71)\quad\quad (-0.64)\quad\quad\quad\quad (1.55)\quad\quad (1.03)\quad (1.78)$$

289

$$\overline{R}^2 = 0.94 \quad \text{D-W} = 1.42 \quad \text{SE} = 0.82 \quad F = 90.83 \quad N = 15$$

The result reveals that most explanatory variables, except the world demand proxying by the import growth rate of the whole OECD countries, are positively related with the export rate in China. These results agree with the normal expectations.

In order to test the trade effects of FDI on the equation, foreign capital inflows variable was added and yielded the following results:

$$X/Y = 1.414 + 0.038 \text{ TT'} + 0.003 \text{ y} + 0.202 \text{ t} - 0.042 \text{ WDOECD} + 0.439 \text{ X/Y(t-1)}$$
$$\quad (1.742) \quad (2.364) \qquad (1.409) \quad (0.936) \quad (-0.649) \qquad\qquad (1.593)$$
$$\qquad + 0.149 \text{ FDI/Y}$$
$$\qquad\quad (0.244)$$

$$\overline{R}^2 = 0.96 \quad \text{D-W} = 1.41 \quad \text{SE} = 0.86 \quad F = 67.79 \quad N = 15$$

The initial testing results show that FDI has a positive effect on the export rate in China during the period covered.

Since the t and WDOECD variables are statistically insignificant, we delete them. We assume that the export rate is not only affected by current year's FDI, but also by the previous inflow of foreign capital. So we insert FDI/Y(t-1) variable to test its continues effect on export as follows:

$$X/Y = 1.382 + 0.045 \text{ TT'} + 0.005 \text{ y} + 0.612 \text{ X/Y(t-1)} + 0.824 \text{ FDI/Y}$$
$$\quad (2.77) \quad (4.83) \qquad (3.31) \qquad (3.62) \qquad\qquad (1.94)$$
$$\qquad - 1.494 \text{ FDI/Y(t-1)}$$
$$\qquad\quad (-3.59)$$

$$\overline{R}^2 = 0.91 \quad \text{D-W} = 2.64 \quad \text{SE} = 0.56 \quad F = 196.69 \quad N = 15$$

This suggests that the foreign capital inflows variable starts to affect the export rate significantly. The results of these exercises are summarised in **Table 8.2**.

All the regressions pass the F-test for overall statistical significance. The results in **Table 8.2** indicate that the terms of trade, GDP per capita and X/Y(t-1) is statistically significant coefficients at 10 percent level of confidence or better with the expected positive sign for all equations. Other explanatory variables shown insignificant results. The coefficients of foreign capital inflows variable in non-lagged form shown significant contribution to export at 5 per cent level of confidence. There is, thus, ample support for the hypothesis that, while other variables, including world demand do influence

Table 8.2
OLS estimates of the contribution of FDI to export in China, 1978-92

(t-test in parentheses, n = 15)

No	Constant	TT'	y	t	FDI/Y	FDI/Y(t-1)	X/Y(t-1)	WDOECD	$\bar{R}^2$	D-W	Estim. F	Tabul. F (0.95)	SE
1	1.43 (1.89)	0.042* (3.02)	0.005** (2.24)				0.53** (2.18)		0.97	1.32	112.59	3.33	0.82
2	0.65 (1.03)	0.044* (2.94)		0.35** (1.81)			0.73* (3.69)		0.97	1.40	99.19	3.33	0.87
3	1.38 (1.82)	0.039* (2.71)	0.004*** (1.55)	0.21 (1.03)			0.45*** (1.78)		0.97	1.42	90.83	3.37	0.82
4	1.41 (1.74)	0.038* (2.36)	0.003*** (1.41)	0.20 (0.94)	0.15 (0.24)		0.44*** (1.59)	-0.042 (-0.65)	0.97	1.41	67.79	3.50	0.86
5	1.38 (2.77)	0.045* (4.83)	0.005* (3.31)		0.824** (1.94)	-1.49* (-3.59)	0.612* (3.62)		0.99	2.64	196.69	3.73	0.56

Notes: *   Coefficient significant at the 1 per cent level of confidence
           **   Coefficient significant at the 5 per cent level of confidence
           *** Coefficient significant at the 10 per cent level of confidence

export levels in general, countries can still achieve superior export performance through active FDI policy to promote exports.

We found that equation 5 produces the best fit result, since the standard error of regression is the lowest one, the D-W test is quite high, and the estimated F-ratios are well above the tabulated value. Finally, it could explain 99 per cent of the variation of the export rates in the data. Equation 5 therefore could be considered to be satisfactorily accepted.

Explaining equation 5, we found that only the estimated coefficient of the FDI variable lagged by one year in the export equation function is significantly negative. Other variables, such as FDI/Y, terms of trade, GDP per capita, X/Y(t-1) exert significant positive effects on the export rate in China during 1978-92.

The strong positive effect for FDI on the export rate can be partly explained by noting that much of foreign capital inflows had been used by the Chinese government for the improvement and development of essential industries, including the power, transportation, and communication industries, and particularly in the export-oriented manufacturing sector. These projects have significantly improved China's ability to promote a functional, balanced development among the various basic industries and increased China's export capacity.[24]

The effects of FCI on consumption imports: On the basis of equation (8.2) specified earlier, we tested the following consumption import function:

$$MC/Y = f[y, pm, MC/Y(t-1)]$$

Where MC had, following our normal practice, been scaled against GDP to avoid heteroscedasticity and to put it line with other variables.

Regressing the basic equation alone, we obtained the following relationship:

$$MC/Y = 2.08 - 0.002 \, y + 0.013 \, pm - 0.068 \, MC/Y(t-1)$$
$$(3.53) \quad (-1.85) \quad (2.85) \quad (-0.25)$$

$\bar{R}^2 = 0.75$, D-W = 1.68 F = 14.92 SE = 0.37 N = 15

Inserting the time trend t to capture for the influence, we found the following:

$$MC/Y = 0.025 - 0.00005 \, y + 0.002 \, t + 0.0001 \, pm - 0.31 \, MC/Y(t-1)$$
$$(4.67) \quad (-3.09) \quad (2.25) \quad (4.01) \quad (-1.23)$$

$\bar{R}^2 = 0.82$ D-W = 1.82 F = 16.57 SE = 0.003 N = 15

Inserting FDI/Y variable to test the contribution of FDI on consumption imports, produced the following version of equation:

$$MC/Y = 0.025 - 0.00005 \ y + 0.0002 \ pm - 0.257 \ MC/Y(t\text{-}1) + 0.002 \ t - 0.0025 \ FDI/Y$$
$$\quad (4.72) \ (-3.12) \qquad (4.18) \qquad (-0.95) \qquad\qquad (2.45) \ (-1.10)$$

$$\overline{R}^2 = 0.82 \quad D\text{-}W = 2.00 \quad SE = 0.003 \quad F = 13.78 \quad N = 15$$

The FDI variable was found to carry the negative sign, thus indicating that in the case of China, FDI has negative effect on the rate of import of consumption goods. This means that the increasing of foreign capital posed Chinese government to reduce import of consumption goods, or to substitute consumption imports over 1978-92.

In order to test FDI/Y's long term effect on the rate of import of consumption goods, we insert lagged FDI/Y variable and obtain the following result:

$$MC/Y = 0.029 - 0.00005 \ y + 0.0002 \ pm + 0.003 \ t - 0.24 \ MC/Y(t\text{-}1)$$
$$\quad (4.49) \quad (-2.65) \qquad (3.57) \qquad (2.37) \quad (-0.90)$$
$$\quad - \ 0.004 \ FDI/Y + 0.002 \ FDI/Y(t\text{-}1)$$
$$\quad (-1.20) \qquad\qquad (0.63)$$

$$\overline{R}^2 = 0.81 \quad D\text{-}W = 1.97 \quad SE = 0.003 \quad F = 10.78 \quad N = 15$$

We find that foreign capital inflows variable is negatively related with the import of consumption goods in the short term, but will induce China to increase the import of consumption goods in the long term, since the coefficient of lagged FDI/Y show positive sign.

The result indicates that FDI has exerted significantly negative effects on consumption imports, suggesting that such foreign capital may have been import substituting. Only import price index, time trend and lagged FDI/Y are positively related with China's consumption import. Other variables, such as the GDP per capita, lagged MC/Y and FDI/Y insert negative contribution to the consumption import rates in China during 1978-92.

The effect of FDI on input imports We earlier pointed out that the input imports is a function of the 'capacity to import' as well as of their own past level. We also noted that the capacity to import is enhanced by export earnings and FDI and is reduced by 'capital flight'.

The relationship tested was therefore as follows:

$$MKI = f \ [X/Y, \ FDI/Y, \ CF/Y, \ MKI/Y(t\text{-}1)]$$

Where input imports were defined as the import of intermediate and capital goods, CF refers to factor payments abroad.

The estimated equation is as follows:

$$MKI/Y = 0.008 + 0.006 \; X/Y + 0.78 \; MKI/Y(t\text{-}1) - 0.85 \; CF/Y + 0.015 \; FDI/Y$$
$$(2.65) \quad (2.00) \qquad\qquad (1.49) \qquad\qquad (\text{-}0.48) \qquad\quad (1.50)$$

$$\overline{R}^{2} = 0.72 \quad D\text{-}W = 1.51 \quad SE = 0.02 \quad F = 9.87 \quad N = 15$$

All explanatory variables carry the expected signs, but the capital flight variable is statistically insignificant. The regression confirms that FDI/Y has a positive influence on the import of investment goods. FDI/Y's coefficient and its significance is, however, quite small, which indicates that a large part of foreign capital was used by the Chinese government to finance social, infrastructural or rural development construction project using local labour and material input, and only a small proportion was used to import machinery. The purchase of locally produced capital goods does not require the use of foreign exchange.

The effect of FDI on imports in the aggregate As with the Hungarian data, we feel it might be interesting to test FDI's effects on import in the aggregate, so that our findings can be more directly compared with that of Hungary.

The aggregate import equation was initially posited as a simple linear combination of the consumption and input import functions specified earlier, such that:

$$M/Y = f\,[\; y,\; t,\; X/Y,\; FDI/Y,\; or\; CF/Y,\; M/Y(t\text{-}1)\;]$$

Testing this relationship produced the following good fit estimated equation:

$$M/Y = 0.05 - 0.0005 \; y + 0.01 \; t - 0.002 \; X/Y + 0.05 \; FDI/Y - 0.53 \; M/Y(t\text{-}1)$$
$$(2.31) \;\; (\text{-}1.11) \qquad (2.22) \quad\; (0.53) \qquad\quad (2.14) \qquad\quad (\text{-}1.01)$$

$$\overline{R}^{2} = 0.90 \quad D\text{-}W = 1.66 \quad SE = 0.014 \quad F = 25.92 \quad N = 15$$

Inserting the capital flight variable, we obtain an improved equation:

$$M/Y = 0.079 + 0.0002 \; y + 0.002 \; t + 0.002 \; X/Y + 0.03 \; FDI/Y - 0.41 \; CF/Y$$
$$(2.39) \quad (0.36) \qquad (0.25) \qquad (0.32) \qquad\quad (1.23) \qquad\quad (\text{-}1.21)$$
$$- 0.26 \; M/Y(t\text{-}1)$$
$$(\text{-}0.47)$$

$\overline{R}^2$ = 0.90 D-W = 1.69   SE = 0.01   F = 22.96   N = 15

Deleting those statistically insignificant variables, and regressing export rate, foreign capital inflows and capital flight variable, we obtain the restricted equation as follows:

$$M/Y = 0.062 - 0.39\ CF/Y + 0.025\ FDI/Y + 0.005\ X/Y$$
$$(4.22)\quad (-2.65)\qquad\quad (2.78)\qquad\qquad (2.55)$$

$\overline{R}^2$ = 0.92 D-W = 1.82   SE = 0.01   F = 53.09   N = 15

All coefficients of explanatory variables are significant at well above the 95 per cent level of confidence. The result thus indicates that both export rates and foreign capital inflows rates exerted strong positive effects on aggregate imports while capital flight rates played a significant negative contribution on aggregate imports.

The net trade effects of FDI FDI's coefficient in the export equation is 0.824, indicating that each 1 per cent increase in FCI increases the export rate by around 0.82 per cent. FDI's coefficient in the import equation is 0.025, indicating each 1 per cent increase of FDI increases the import rate by around 0.03 per cent. The net trade effect of FDI is therefore shown to be strongly positive.

Concluding remarks

In this chapter we have examined the relative importance of foreign capital inflows for external trade performance within the context of external demand conditions and internal supply factors, drawing upon the experience of Hungary and China over the period of 1978-92.

The results run parallel to the conventional view that foreign capital inflows in LDCs increase imports because they need supply input intermediate goods from other subsidiaries but can also promote exports of final products. As regards import of consumption goods, our analysis of the comparative export performance clearly demonstrates that foreign capital is able to promote export in transformation process, provided these countries pursue appropriate domestic policies. It is true that foreign investment in manufacturing has been overwhelmingly import substituting in nature (although foreign firms generally have a higher export propensity than domestic counterparts). As both countries have not well-developed capital goods industries and imports of machinery and equipment usually account for a large share of total imports, it is not surprising that foreign direct investment contributed largely on import of industrial goods in both cases. This seems to suggest that these two countries have a high propensity to import at the early stages of FDI development.

This analysis only focuses on the trade effects of FDI rested upon the assumptions regarding the level of import penetration in the absence of FDI, and upon the different propensities of foreign firms to export from their Chinese/Hungarian base and to source their inputs from within the Chinese/Hungarian economies. A more comprehensive analysis should take account of differences in productivity, differences in pricing, and any multiplier effects upon the rest of the Chinese/Hungarian economies.

Notes

1. See, for example, Maizels, A. (1968), *Exports and Economic Growth of Developing Countries*, Cambridge University Press, Cambridge, p.58 and p.101; Sachs, I.(1965), *Foreign Trade and Economic Development of Underdeveloped Countries*, Asia Publishing House, London, p.69; Macbean, A.I.(1966), *Export Instability and Economic Development*, George Allen & Unwin Ltd, London.

2. Linder, S. B. (1967), *Trade and Trade Policy for Development*, Pall Mall Press, London.

3. Krugman, P. (1979), 'A Model of Balance-of-Payments Crises', *Journal of Money, Credits and Banking*, Vol.11, No.3, August, pp.311-25.

4. Hicks, G. L. and McNicoll, G. (1971), *Trade and Growth in the Philippines: An Open Dual Economy*, Cornell University Press, Ithaca and London.

5. Thirlwall, A. P. (1983), *Growth and Development*, 3rd Edition, Macmillan, London; (1985), 'International Borrowing, Debt and Development', *Estudos de Economia*, Abr-Jun, pp.251-75; Thirlwall, and Hussain, M. N. (1982), 'The Balance of Payments Constraint, Capital Flows and Growth Differences between Developing Countries', *Oxford Economic Papers*, Vol. 34, pp.498-509.

6. Thirlwall, A. P. (1979), 'The Balance of Payments Constraint as an Explanation of International Growth Rate Differences', *Banca Nazionale del Lavaro Quarterly Review*, Vol.32, pp.45-53.

7.McDougall, G. D. A. (1960), 'The Benefits and Costs of Private Investment from Abroad: A Theoretical Approach', *Bulletin of Oxford University Institute of Statistics,* Vol.22, August, pp.189-211.

8.Loo, Van (1977), 'The Effect of Foreign Direct Investment on Investment in Canada', *The Review of Economics and Statistics,* Vol.59, pp.474-81.

9.Polak, J. J. (1943), 'Balance of Payments Problems of Countries Reconstructuring with the Help of Foreign Loans', *Quarterly Journal of Economics,* Vol.57, pp.208-40.

10.Mainardi, S. (1986), 'Market Orientation of Multinational Enterprises in Chile: An Econometric Analysis', *Savings and Development,* No.3, pp.293-317.

11.Massell, B. F., Pearson, S. R. and Fitch, J. B. (1972), 'Foreign Exchange and Economic Development: An Empirical Study of Selected Latin American Countries', *The Review of Economics and Statistics,* Vol.54, May, pp.208-12.

12.Chenery, H. B. and Syrquin, M. (1975), *Patterns of Development 1950-1970,* Oxford University Press for the World Bank, Washington, D.C.

13.Pizer, S. and Cutler, F. (1965), 'US Exports to Foreign Affiliates of US Firms', *Survey of Current Business,* US Department of Commerce, Vol.45, December, pp.208-40.

14.Natke, P. and Newfarmer, R. S. (1985), 'Transnational Corporations, Trade Propensities and Transfer Pricing', in *Transnational Corporations and International Trade: Selected Issues,* UNCTC, New York, pp.16-43.

15.A problem with this argument is that it is founded more on a priori reasoning, albeit incomplete, than on empirical evidence. Terms of trade could fall and yet more income may be earned from exports. Furthermore, the price elasticity of demand facing an exporting country is roughly equal to the coefficient of world demand elasticity divided by the share of the country's export in total world supply, thus the elasticity is usually greater than unity.

16.A similar equation was used by Thirlwall (1979).

17.Nwanna, G. I. (1986), 'Foreign Investment and Capital Formation in Nigeria', *Savings and Development,* No.3, pp.265-76; and Semudram, M. (1982), 'A Macro-model of the Malaysian Economy: 1959-77', *The Developing Economies,* Vol.20, pp.154-72 include GDP as an explanatory variable in their export equations, both finding it to be significant, while

Chenery and Syrquin (1975) included per capita income to proxy for the degree of economic development, with similarly satisfactory results.

18. One typical assumption of development model is that exports are assumed to increase over time. Perhaps one reason for this optimistic assumption is that exports might serve as 'the engine of the economic growth' in developing countries. See, for example, Adelman and Chenery (1966); Bos, et al., (1974); Kim, Seung Hee (1970), pp.14-15.

19. Adelman and Chenery (1966), op. cit.; and Thirlwall (1979), op. cit.

20. Prebisch, R. (1950), *The Economic Development of Latin America and Its Principle Problems,* ECLA, United Nations Department of Economic Affairs, New York.

21. Wijnbergen, S. V. (1985), 'Interdependence Revisited: A Developing Countries Perspective on Macroeconomic Management and Trade Policy in the Industrial World', *Economic Policy,* November, pp.82-137.

22. Over the past 15 years or so, China's main trade partners were OECD countries, while Hungary's main trade partners before 1989 were those Central and Eastern centralised countries.

23. Madddala, G.S. (1988), *Introduction to Econometrics,* New York, pp.224-7.

24. Dong, Shizhong, Zhang, Danian and Larson, M.R. (1992), *Trade and Investment Opportunities in China: The Current Commercial and Legal Framework,* Quorum Books, Connecticut and London, p.148.

9 Conclusion

This chapter summarizes the substantive conclusions on the determinants and impact of FDI in Hungary and China over the period of 1978-92 drawn from the preceding chapters. In addition, it explores the prospects of foreign investment in Hungary and China, and points out some directions for further research.

Summary of the principal findings

Since the late 1970s, foreign investment has been rushing into those economies that for decades operated under communism. The rapid increase of foreign direct investment in Eastern Europe and China represents a salient new feature on the international economic scene. After 1989, Hungary and China have been considered as the biggest magnets within post-socialist economies in attracting foreign capital. There exists, therefore, a pressing need for an empirical analysis of foreign investment in these two transforming economies.

The objective of this research has been to gain some understanding of the determinants and effects of foreign direct investment on the process of economic development and systemic transformation in Hungary and China during 1978-92. Our findings support the view that FDI has tended to serve as a vehicle for economic development and international integration in both Hungary and China.

FDI has become, and will continue to be, an increasingly important element in the world economy: contemporary FDI inflows towards those emerging markets in China and Central and Eastern Europe are likely to increase further through the 1990s. The first part of this book has, therefore, addressed such issues as the legislative framework of FDI policy, its impact on foreign investment, and whether there are any special characteristics in the sectoral distribution and national origins of these investments in Hungary and China. This served as a background for an assessment of the causes and consequences of FDI on the Hungarian and Chinese economies.

Dynamic economic reform and increasing integration in terms of international policies have been the major contributory factors to the rapid inflow of FDI in both countries. As we discussed in Chapter 2, Hungary and China share an overriding economic goal - the increase of national income through a rapid development and structural transformation. In achieving this end, they both regard an increased inflow of foreign capital as an important element, and have been pioneers at finding ways to create incentives for capital investment by private firms, especially foreign ones. To this end, since 1972 and 1978 respectively, both countries have adopted a range of legislative and institutional reforms to improve their locational attractiveness for foreign investors and thereby to attract foreign firms. Competition among LDCs, especially emerging Eastern European and Chinese markets, for FDI appears to have resulted in ever more generous concessions being offered over time: corporate tax reductions or holidays, accelerated depreciation allowances, investment allowances and investment subsidies. A positive attitude to direct inward investment is the norm and this, combined with relatively low wages and expanding domestic markets, makes both countries attractive locations to MNCs. The political and economic uncertainty in both countries does not present a barrier to the growth of inward investment. Future codification of investment laws is expected to provide a more stable framework for investment in both countries.

Chapter 3 examined the industrial content and geographical spread of FDI in the context of historical developments over the past 15 years or so. Even with the negative impact of continuing Communist control in Hungary and the events of June 1989 in China, both countries have been successful in attracting FDI in critical industries such as hotels, chemicals, electrical engineering, motor vehicles and information-based technologies. Germany, Austria and the United States are major sources of this investment capital for Hungary, while Hong Kong/Macao, Taiwan, Japan and the United States are the major sources for China. Geographical proximity still matters, as there is a cluster of countries in which inward flows of FDI are dominated by companies from neighbouring regions. Foreign investment in China has been considerably larger than in Hungary in aggregate terms, but FDI per capita has been rather smaller than in Hungary.

Although there is no single explanation for FDI, our statistical study of factors influencing FDI in Hungary and China based on regression analysis in Chapter 4 suggests that the size of domestic markets (measured by the level of GDP), economic growth performance, political stability, and cost-of-capital are much more influential in attracting FDI than other variables. More

300

specifically, market-size and inexpensive labour costs exert a positive influence on the FDI decision-making process, while political instability and capital cost variables play negative role in FDI flows. This finding further confirmed Lim's (1983) and Balasubramanyam's (1984) findings that market-size, resource endowments, and growth performance in LDCs are more influential than tax concessions. Our findings also indicate that countries pursuing a strategy of import-substituting industrialisation are likely to attract less FDI. Tariff protection is found to either carry a 'wrong' sign or be statistically insignificant in both cases. This might imply that tariff protection should be designed to induce foreign firms to adopt suitable or relatively appropriate capital-intensive technologies, as well as to take advantage of the low wages and labour endowments of these two countries. The complementary questionnaire survey concerning the motives of foreign investors, which was analyzed in Chapter 5, found that foreign investors regard market size, growth potential, political stability, and the availability of relatively cheap labour to be much more important in their investment decisions than other variables (such as tax concessions), which is consistent with some earlier studies.[1] Currently, MNCs are unlikely to treat their Hungarian/Chinese affiliates as stand-alone ventures, but as a part of their global marketing and production strategies. Western European MNCs, in particular, view Eastern Europe as offering an enlarged market for their products, thus better enabling them to spread increasing overhead costs of R&D and marketing, and to compete more effectively with Japanese and US MNCs.

If private foreign investment is to play an active role in the process of development, to the advantage of investors and hosts alike, a better understanding of its effects upon all aspects of development is essential. Chapter 6 analyzed empirically the impact of inflows of FDI on the competitiveness of the host country's industry, economic development, employment, exports and industrial structure. It has shown that FDI has a mixed impact upon output, trade and employment across the national economies. The effects on employment are analogous, although it may be negative in some cases in the short term. The overall impact of FDI is shown to be beneficial to both countries in terms of industrial structure and economic growth. Critical sectors, such as the tourist-related industries, chemical industries, electrical engineering, motor vehicles and those based on information technology, are heavily dependent on foreign investment. FDI contributes to a restructuring of the host country's industry in a direct way, which tends to enhance both Hungary and China's international competitive position. Foreign investment seems to play a negative role in the balance of payments in both countries, as FIEs' imports were much higher than their exports, although FIEs accelerated both import and export growth during the period under study. However, FDI certainly serves as a means for the transfer of needed capital, technological and managerial resources in both Hungary and China. FDI, on the whole, is beneficial to the host countries. There is no compelling reason to believe that FDI will bring more harm than good. While FDI appears to stimulate economic development, it also affects all aspects of the host countries' environment: social, economic, and political. However, over-reliance on FDI may also result in inappropriate industrial development, in cultural, technological and perhaps political dependence, and in some loss of control over basic social and economic policy in relation to long-term development. Given the economic growth potential and continuous political stability, in the future, the potential benefits of such increased FDI are likely to grow substantially in both countries.

The impact of FDI on economic growth and the trade balance were monitored in Chapters 7 and 8. Our study finds that foreign capital inflows have generally favoured economic growth and exports in both countries, but remained insignificant. The gross benefits of FDI are offset by substantial costs relating, in particular, to the propensity of foreign firms to import high proportions of their parts and components from abroad thus causing a deterioration in the balance of payments: the national aggregate foreign exchange balance of FIEs in the current account in both Hungary and China was still negative, though some regions or cities may have already balanced their current account of foreign exchange, or even produced a surplus. However, arguments were made that many FIEs, especially those in high-tech fields, were established to manufacture products that Hungary and China originally had to import. The availability of these products in the domestic market helped reduce these countries' import needs. The impact of FDI on foreign trade should, therefore, include this indirect import-substitution effect on the current account. It could be argued that the significance of foreign direct investment in promoting host country exports would depend on the country's resource endowment, predominant production technology, level of development, and government policy. FDI's contribution to manufacturing exports and economic growth depends very much on the level of the host country's development.

However, from a macroeconomic viewpoint, the short-term costs of FDI are of minor importance compared to the potential long-term benefits of greater market integration, as FDI might help both Hungary and China to have a positive trade balance by improving its export competitiveness. This is because FIEs provided domestic industries with better equipment and instruments, which in turn increased local firms' product quality and production capacity and thereby their potential for increasing exports. A large number of FIEs were established in the fields of energy, transportation, and other basic industries which have helped improve the general capacity of the host country's production and the quality of its export products.

302

We would surmise that foreign investment can contribute to the structural transformation of the Chinese and Hungarian economies by raising productivities and efficiency in such a way as to create a basis for the future integration of their productive capacity in the international economy. Given the importance of FDI for economic development and for structural reform, a more liberalised policy towards FDI and an improvement of the investment climate may not only be desirable, but essential if in the future both countries are to remain viable in an increasingly competitive international economy.

All these findings, however, do not necessarily lead one to a final conclusion that FDI is a net positive force in development. But if the free-market system and capitalist industrialisation are accepted as development goals in both countries, then FDI can be seen as accelerating the changes necessary to achieve these ends. Given a proper framework of regulation, agreements allowing the participation of foreign enterprises should be attainable, which provide for both a net positive contribution to indigenously determined development goals and a reasonable return to the foreign investors.

The future trends of FDI in Hungary and China will depend not only on whether both countries can provide MNCs with a stable, profitable and low-risk environment with a very high rate of return, as well as investment opportunities and infrastructural conditions, but also on the world-wide availability of capital funds and existence of alternative destinations. Both Hungary and China have started to compete for FDI with developing countries and some industrial nations. The rapid unification of Germany in 1990 served to concentrate West German investors' attentions on Eastern Germany and away from Eastern Europe and China.[2] However, continuing price and currency stability, progress in establishing property rights, patent protection, along with general economic growth, and a great desire for Western products and lifestyles is likely to carry Hungary and China ahead of other Eastern European countries and other LDCs in attracting FDI. The high level of education and well-developed technical skills of the population in Hungary, and the cheap labour force in China will offer foreign investors further comparative advantages in terms of human resources.[3]

Prospects of FDI in Hungary and China

Foreign direct investment will flow sufficiently and abundantly only if the investors are confident enough that the host countries are going to have prosperous market economies with a satisfactory performance and a stable government with reasonable policies that are friendly to foreign investment. From the demand side of FDI, there is no doubt that these host governments are willing and able to accept FDI, but how to absorb FDI efficiently remains a problem. From the supply side of FDI, the prospects in Hungary and China will depend largely on whether MNCs are willing and able to undertake it.[4]

Despite the increasing interest in establishing JVs in Eastern Europe, 'it is by no means clear that the risk-benefit ratio of investing in Eastern Europe compares favourably with Latin America or the Asian Pacific region'.[5] The potential for attracting FDI in both Hungary and China will vary and depend on a number of factors: market-size, the speed and extent of systemic changes, the location of specific advantages, infrastructural capacities, the development of human capital, and the potential for political and economic stability. In terms of economic efficiency, the prospects for foreign investment in Hungary and China depend largely on the direction and spread of free-market transformation.

Hungary

The rapid growth in FDI in recent years lends credence to the thesis that Hungary's threshold for investment expanded significantly during the period 1989-92 (the FDI growth rate in 1989 and 1990 was 100 per cent and in 1991 was 50-70 per cent). However, this does not mean that we should expect similar exceptional rates of growth in the coming years. The rapid increase in FDI took place against a background of negligible foreign investment in the period prior to 1989. Now that reasonable investment levels have been achieved, it will be much more difficult for Hungary to reach the exceptionally high annual growth rates achieved during 1989-90. Yet modest growth should be possible, and the key will be the privatisation process and the improvement of the investment incentive framework.

Theoretically, in the short to medium term, several large foreign investment projects enjoying the patronage of the current political leadership could be implemented in Hungary, in order to explore the new possibilities which Hungary offers, particularly as a location from which to supply the large Russian market. The inflow of foreign portfolio investment will probably exceed that of FDI in the coming years, as equity in Hungary and other emerging Eastern European markets looks fundamentally more attractive than it did. The recognition by the European Union of Hungary's associate membership may attract a large number of non-EC countries, such as USA, Japan, and South Korea, to invest in Hungary and to set up export bases to service the Single European Market with the aim of reducing production costs and avoiding market protection. The inflow of capital from small- and medium-sized enterprises is likely to be more closely linked to Hungary's economic recovery and its political stability.

Practically, Hungary, once the lustrous pioneer in attracting Western investment to Eastern Europe, is losing its glamour as a result of the ambivalent policies of a coalition government led by former Communists elected since 1994. The favourable trend in economic growth of 2-3 per cent in 1995 might encourage foreign investment,[6] but in the short run, it would be unrealistic to expect a major inflow of FDI into Hungary.

The pace of privatisation and systemic change will, to a large extent, determine the future growth of FDI, particularly export-oriented FDI. Thus the government will need to make companies undergoing privatisation more attractive by easing the negotiation process and finding creative solutions to the company debt situation. The authorities should also consider implementing additional investment incentives - from tax concessions to outright grants - in order to maintain the country's lead as the primary destination of FDI in the region and to compete successfully with other developing markets worldwide. If it can do this, Hungary should be able to maintain and even increase current investment levels.

In the long term, however, the real question for Hungary is whether this rate of growth will continue, or whether there are limits to Western demand and Hungary's ability to absorb foreign capital.

Foreign demand to invest in Hungary is naturally difficult to measure. In 1991 Western MNCs, independent investment funds and international financial institutions, were all actively searching for investment opportunities throughout the country. Although concrete data do not exist, anecdotal information gained from discussions with frustrated potential investors indicates that demand to invest in Hungary exceeded the country's absorptive abilities. This is not surprising. Hungary's economic underdevelopment and the practical policy-related problems surrounding privatisation have placed constraints on inbound investment. Hungary's obstacles to foreign investment have been discussed at length in many publications, but, in brief, include her poor infrastructure, the slow company registration process, the Hungarians' lack of experience in dealing with foreign investors and an inefficient banking system, as well as insufficient domestic capital. More importantly, foreign investment is discouraged by political instability and civil war in some of its neighbouring states, its deteriorating economy, and a potential external debt crisis (around US$20 billion, as high as US$2,000 per capita), and unfavourable external economic growth in the main capital-exporting countries. Perhaps just as discouraging for the foreign investor was the relatively slow pace of privatisation of SOEs. Many are deeply in debt, inefficient and uncompetitive in Western markets, which also helps to explain the difficulties of privatisation and the reluctance of foreign investors to invest. From the point of view of potential foreign investors, the attractiveness of the opening-up of new investment opportunities is tempered by many uncertainties surrounding the prospects for political and economic stability, by

305

the difficulty of assessing prospective rates of return over the medium-term, by unfamiliarity with operating and legislative conditions, and by doubts about the security of assets and the repatriation of profits. Nor should it be forgotten that potential investors will always compare prospects and conditions in alternative destinations (e.g. in Western Europe, Asia, or Latin America) before committing their capital to any one project or country. The combination of such uncertainties accounts for the caution which has so far characterized the response of foreign investors. It might be concluded that though, in the long term, Eastern Europe and the former Soviet Union may become one of the very powerful competitors for foreign investment, in the coming few years, these countries (including Hungary) will not able to change the current direction of international foreign capital flows, or attract large-scale foreign direct investment. Foreign capital which will be channelled into this area is likely to be limited mainly to foreign loans, and private foreign investment will not witness any great leap forward.

Thus it can be argued that these factors, inter alia, place limits on the amount of FDI that can be absorbed by the country. It is also argued that Hungary has lost its competitive edge in attracting international investors partly because of its increasingly critical debt ratio and balance of payment constraints. 'Most Hungarian consumer goods companies attractive to multinationals have been sold and foreign economic penetration has come close to its political limits. Increasingly foreign investors are looking to Poland which has four times the population of Hungary, or the Czech Republic.'[7] However, as market mechanisms gain in strength, and provided stabilization measures succeed, viable opportunities for foreign investment will be abundant and should become increasingly attractive. It is expected that this will result in significant capital inflows and foreign capital in Hungary will enjoy a moderate growth in the future.

China

Any attempt to forecast FDI trends in China during the rest of the 1990s must confront two closely related issues: the availability of foreign capital and the likely rate of return on investment in China relative to that available elsewhere. Both issues should be viewed against the international perspective of global economic interdependence and the economic evolution of the Asia-Pacific Region. Political upheaval in South-East Asia may cause a reassessment of regional investment risks which favours China. Above all, the domestic political situation will remain a critical determinant of outside perceptions of China's credit-worthiness and thereby the scale of FDI there.

The Chinese government realised that the collapse of the Soviet bloc might precipitate a reallocation of international capital away from China, as these countries have been enthusiastically opening their markets and industries to foreign investors, permitting 100 per cent ownership of foreign invested enterprises, and, therefore, providing an attractive alternative for foreign investors. The government also understood that maintaining the open-door policy and opening the Chinese market further to foreign investors was essential if future investment inflows were to be attracted. So the challenge for the Chinese leadership is to develop long-term strategies designed to move ahead with economic reform, while at the same time preventing social unrest and inflation from bringing chaos. Assuming that China's political and economic situation remains stable in the medium term, China's potential for attracting FDI will in principle depend on the government's success in putting the brakes on the current overheating in the economy, in introducing effective macro-economic policy (especially fiscal and monetary policies) and setting up a market system. It is essential for the Chinese government to avoid the sharp stop-go cycle which has been plagued China's economy since the reforms began. 'As the economy has developed, the step-by-step approach to reform has become much harder'.[8] The Third Plenary Session of the 14th Central Committee of the Communist Party of China, held in Beijing between 11 and 14 November 1993, took a revolutionary step by publishing 'Decision on issues concerning the establishment of a socialist market economic structure', which made it clear that the Chinese government 'is determined to push ahead with further reforms and open-door policies to create a market economy in the next few years'.[9]

In the long run, assuming a decisive breakthrough in market-oriented reform in China, it is probable that the 'comparative' advantages of market-size and high economic growth rates will play decisive role in foreign investment decisions. Even though the prospective political shake-ups will slow down China's current 9 per cent growth to 6 per cent by the late 1990s, China will continue to be a major force in determining world economic growth in the future, as total imports and exports are predicted to amount to US$400 billion by the end of 2000. Its total GNP will be the same as America's, but smaller than that of the 13-member European Community, its GNP per capita will be 20 per cent that of America and 13 per cent of Japan by 2025.[10]

Faster economic development will further provide a powerful stimulus to FDI growth. Recent evidence shows that since the beginning of the 1990s more and more famous MNCs realise that it is high time to penetrate the Chinese market.[11] Japanese firms, for example, have changed their cautious investment strategies and increased their investment commitment in high-technology, large-scale and export-oriented projects in China (especially in the north of China). It is expected that foreign investment will continue flowing into China at an average annual rate of US$15 billion a year to the end of this century. China can therefore remain the top FDI recipient, far ahead of other leading LDCs and Eastern European countries by the year of 2000.

Prospects for both countries

More and more Western companies are realising that it is shortsighted not to pay attention to the economic transformation and development of China and Eastern Europe, and not to grasp existing opportunities to participate actively the transformation process. Whether it is acknowledged widely or not, economic transformation and potential growth in both China and Eastern Europe have already played an important role in the world. China and Hungary have already become important areas of the global economy. Their full integration will provide tremendous investment and cooperation opportunities for foreign investors.

The prospects for FDI in these two countries will depend crucially upon the policies which they pursue in relation to their own internal goals and changing external circumstances. Sound macro-economic policies could be expected to be aimed at such broad long-term policy goals as sustainable economic growth with low inflation, the modernisation of domestic savings, a business climate conducive to foreign investment and a viable balance-of-payments position. The instruments available to attain these goals are fiscal and monetary policies (which promote demand management and capital flows), exchange-rate policy, and supplementary trade and exchange controls for balance-of-payments management.

The future of FDI in Hungary and China will depend to a large degree on what happens politically and economically during the second half of the 1990s. It remains to be seen whether Hungary and China will be able to honour the foreign debt obligations which become due in the near future. Hungary and China have a firm commitment to their modernisation programmes, to their open-door policies, to FDI, and to other international economic cooperation programmes. Based on these facts, Hungary and China seem likely to go forward with their present economic policies and to further expand the role of foreign investment in economic development. FDI seems certain to rise considerably through the 1990s.

The increased flow of FDI will achieve a deeper local market penetration. Our expectation is that as Hungary becomes fully integrated into the EC, and China makes a decisive breakthrough in market-oriented reforms, the inflow of FDI will increase and this will increase its impact on both countries' economic development and industrialisation. What matters most in the development of an efficient economy in both countries is a competitive business environment, a strong and supportive government, and ready access to foreign skills, technology, and markets. The human and natural resources of Hungary and China are impressive. What is lacking at present is an appropriate institutional structure, and also the managerial and marketing expertise, effective entrepreneurship, organisational capacities and monetary incentives to efficiently utilise and upgrade these resources. Hungary and China should make good use of their market and labour advantages to attract both large and small MNCs, and to provide initiatives for economic growth. This is not simply a question of a further liberalisation of investment policies or of offering foreign investors generous fiscal incentives. It is more important to create and sustain a favourable economic and social environment in which both domestic and foreign firms can compete effectively, and to foster supportive attitudes in labour and management alike towards productivity improvements and global competition.

Given the above preconditions, the long-term future for FDI in Hungary and China is indeed highly promising. The next decade or so is likely to be a particularly taxing time for both foreign investors and the governments of both host countries. Nevertheless, it is expected that by the year 2000 foreign capital will rise from its current US$3-4 billion to around US$20 billion in Hungary and from its current US$100 billion to around US$200 billion in China.

Suggestions for further research

This book brings together the current theoretical knowledge of international investment with a close empirical examination of both the determinants and the impact of FDI in Hungary and China, and indicates avenues of approach which may usefully be followed up. The model used is highly aggregated and simple in structure, so there are some aspects which require further investigation or which will benefit from extensions. It seems appropriate to emphasize several limitations in studies such as the present one in the hope that it will encourage further research.

The model that has been advanced here is not entirely free of econometric problems. Individual equations need further investigation, particularly the determinants of FDI, and the net trade equation. In defence of the model, however, we suggest that, despite problems in the individual specification, its overall performance is satisfactory. The model provides a theoretical interpretation of FDI in 1978-92 in Hungary and China.

The experience gained in our studies has indicated, however, that we cannot rely on obtaining an adequate basis for economic decision-making simply by studying the determinants and effects of FDI based on a simplified model or small-scale survey. Single-equation models suffer from the problem of simultaneity, because they ignore interdependence between the dependent and independent variables involved. Instead of relying on single equation techniques, a high priority is to develop simultaneous equation models of foreign direct investment and its impact on the host country's economy and to decompose the aggregate foreign capital into three elements, namely, foreign aid, foreign private investment, and other capital inflows in the case of Hungary, which would provide useful and illuminating insights and results for policy purposes. Such models avoid a major deficiency of previous studies by more clearly distinguishing exogenous from endogenous variables, and they may provide essential clues for a more comprehensive analysis of the foreign investment phenomena in such countries. Since there are persistent and serious data deficiencies in relation to FDI, it is imperative that more complete time-series data are collected and compiled by both government and international organisations.

Major changes in a host-country's political, economic, social, and financial conditions frequently have a major impact on the profitability and success of foreign investment. It would be extremely interesting to analyze risk involved in both direct and indirect investment in these two countries. The opening up of the communist world for foreign investment will necessitate careful assessment of the types of non-economic risks that may arise. This includes the eruption of deep-seated ethnic, religious, and nationalist conflicts that have long been suppressed under dictatorial rule. The democratic revolutions in Eastern Europe have been, and will continue to be, followed by the painful and long process of building democratic institutions where none had previously existed, or at least not since the inter-war period. Systemic changes has raised expectations among many foreign investors for a more optimistic future in the 1990s. But they need to reassess the future investment climate in China, as its political future remains very much in doubt, and will be a source of continual uncertainty for the international business community. Further research, utilizing political-risk analysis, should also include the external debt risk, expropriation risk, foreign exchange transfer risk and sovereign risk, as well as the potential for civil war, radical political change, and general strikes in international businesses. Various research methods, such as empirical studies, case studies, comparative analysis, quantitative and qualitative methods, can be applied to gain particular information that may be highly important for explaining, assessing or predicting the future political and business environment in the host country. The macro-political risk variables should include those actions and policies that are directed against all foreign business in a host country; while developments that affect only selected businesses or specific sectors are defined as micro-risk variables. There are also societal risk and government-related risk, each of which can have macro and micro-components. The nature of political conflicts is such that today's optimism can be shattered by tomorrow's unexpected events. It will therefore be important for MNCs to continue to take political risk into account as they ponder their direct investment, and for analysts to assess political risk in these countries.

Given Hungary's and other Eastern European countries' determination to successfully implement their transformation into market economies, the long-term strategic views of Western firms and general optimism concerning the prospects offered by Eastern European markets, JVs will play a significant economic role for both the East and the West. Thus, further research into factors facilitating further foreign investment and JV activities in Hungary and other Eastern European markets would be of great significance. Because of the exploratory nature of the research and the complex and sensitive issues involved, the questionnaire approach might be a very useful alternative way, but extensive field-work and in-depth interviews are expensive and time-consuming.

A call for improved data is worth very little unless it recognises the practical problems. Most official data reach the economist in a secondary manner, that is the researcher often uses data in a way for which it was not designed. It is thus very important to establish an effective relationship with local officials among relevant authorities which collect data from firms, often on a universal basis, in order to ensure that more appropriate and reliable information is gathered. The important point is that essential data are collected. Both academic and business circles can join forces to explore this challenging field and to offer recommendations for the benefit of both business and academics, both West and East.

From the viewpoint of an econometric study, it is worth analyzing quantitatively the determinants of inward foreign investment, such as the relationship between the economic growth rate or market size in the host country and the inflow of foreign investment, by using multiple regression analysis, as well as linear and log-linear econometric techniques. Moreover, further efforts could be focused on the effects of FDI on output, employment, balance of payments, productivity, technology, training of labour and management, inter-industry linkages and effects on structural changes in the economic and industrial organisation of host countries.

Foreign investment is not a purely economic phenomenon, but rather an integrated social and political phenomenon, whose origins and repercussions cover the entire social life of the investing nation and the nation in which the investment is made. Our study focuses only on its economic effects, 'while accepting that there are other potentially important political, social and cultural influences'.[12] The effects of FDI reach well beyond the economic and technical. It appears reasonable to expect it to exert a relatively greater influence in creating a 'modernized' social structure and to affect the process of social modernisation in accordance with Western principles in managerial

311

style and philosophy. As Thorelli (1966) stated: 'directly or indirectly, MNCs will also be a transplanter of organisational know-how and a transformer of attitudes towards economic behaviour in general and business in particular'.[13] In the long run, these may well be its most important functions, as an agent of cross-cultural transfer of the essential elements of industrialisation, technology, and management from Western countries to these transforming economies. This can happen in several ways: through a transfer of specific aspects of industrialisation, such as technology and management, a transfer of institutions and formal organisations, and the assimilation of Western industrial culture in the host country's socio-economic system.

Thus, it will be very useful to analyze the relationship between FDI and social change, and between social modernisation and industrialisation in economies undergoing rapid transformation. It appears reasonable to view FDI as a vehicle for the extension of the international market system in host country economies and to recognise it as an agent of social and political change.

This book with its limited assumptions has attempted to fill only a small corner of the canvas which needs to be painted. It will, I hope, contribute to the research agenda necessary to reveal the whole picture.

Notes

1.See, Frank, I. (1980), *Foreign Enterprises in Developing Countries,* Baltimore; Hughes and Seng (1969), *Foreign Investment and Industrialisation in Singapore,* Canberra.

2.McMillan, C.H. (1991), 'Foreign Direct Investment to the Soviet Union and Eastern Europe: Nature, Magnitude and International Implications', *Journal of Development Planning,* No.20.

3.See *Columbia Journal of World Business,* Vol.XXVI, No.1, Spring, 1991, p.19.

4.Elhassan, Mazen Darwiche rightly stresses that FDI takes place not only because firms are able and willing to undertake it but also because host governments are able and willing to accept it. It should be fully recognized that there are two sides: the supply side of FDI and the demand side of FDI. See Elhassan, Mazen Darwiche (1992), *Theoretical and Empirical Research on Foreign Direct Investment: Survey, Review and New Directions,* unpublished PhD thesis at Syracuse University.

5.Turner, Ian D. (1991), 'Strategy and Organisation', *Manager Update,* Vol.2, No.4, Summer 1991, p.1.

6.*The New York Times,* 15 February 1995.

7.*Financial Times,* 1 November 1993, p.17.

8.*Financial Times China Survey,* 18 November 1993, p.3.

9.'China Speeds on to Market', *The Economist,* 20 November 1993, p.85.

10.*The Economist,* 12-19 September 1993, pp.15-21.

11.*Daily of Wall Street,* 'China Survey', 10 December 1993.

12.Young, Stephen; Hood, Neil and Hamill, James (1988), *Foreign Multinationals and the British Economy: Impact and Policy,* Croom Helm, London, New York and Sydney, p.63.

13.Thorelli, Hans B. (1966), 'The Multinational Corporations as a Change Agent', *The Southern Journal of Business,* Vol.3, July, p.3.

Appendices

Appendix 2.1
Preferential policies in Pudong New Development Area

Preferential policies for foreign investment in Pudong New Development Area could be concluded as follows:

1. Enterprises funded by domestic and foreign investors could get preferential treatment and exemption from customs duties and the consolidated industrial and commercial tax if they import the following goods: machinery, equipment, vehicles, building materials used in the construction of enterprises; equipment and spare parts, vehicles, components, raw and auxiliary materials and office appliances for the enterprise own use; household goods and vehicles for domestic residences for foreign businessmen; transit goods in the free trade zone and export goods produced and manufactured by enterprises in the free trade zone; goods transported into the free trade zone from other areas shall be treated as exports, enterprises can apply for the return of product tax and value-added tax assessed in production, the imported materials contained in the export products can be exempted from tax. The products manufactured by FIEs must be primarily for export. Products exported by FIEs in compliance with state regulations are exempt from both export duties and the consolidated industrial and commercial tax. However, upon approved by the relevant governmental authorities, a certain portion of their products may be sold on the domestic market as import substitutes, provided that customs duties and the consolidated industrial and commercial tax is paid on such products.

314

2.	The consolidated industrial and commercial tax was to be reduced for the following FIEs: foreign banks or branches, join Sino-foreign investment banks and financial companies and other financial organisations. They were now to pay the consolidated industrial and commercial tax at the rate of 3 per cent on loan business and 5 per cent on other financial business.

3.	Exemption and reduction of income tax was extended. First, foreign investment in ports, airports, railways, highways, power stations and other energy or transportation construction projects were to pay for the enterprise income tax at the rate of 15 per cent. For those enterprises operating over 15 years, an exemption from enterprise income tax for five consecutive years starting from the first profit-making year was to be granted and a 50 per cent reduction allowed from the sixth to tenth years. Secondly, foreign investment in industrial production was to pay enterprise income tax at a rate of 15 per cent. For those enterprises operating over 10 years, an exemption from enterprise income tax for two consecutive years starting from the first profit-making year was to be granted and a 50 per cent reduction allowed from the third to fifth years. Technologically advanced enterprises were to pay the enterprise income tax at a reduced rate of 10 per cent for another three years, when the period of enterprise income tax exemption and reduction expires. Thirdly, wholly foreign-owned banks, joint Sino-foreign investment banks and financial companies were to be exempt from tax in the first year, and benefit from a tax reduction of 50 per cent in the second to third years. Those with paid-up capital totalling over US$10 million and with an operating period exceeding 10 years were to pay the enterprise income tax at the reduced rate of 15 per cent.

4.	Special policies for the free trade zone. Foreign investors were allowed to set up trade organisations in the free trade zone to engage in entrepot trade or act as import agents for enterprises within the zone. Industrial production enterprises were granted the right to import and export; with official approval, FIEs in the zone could undertake basic processing in warehouses, enterprises could commission out-of-zone enterprises to undertake manufacturing; imported goods for self-use, goods in bond and manufactured products of enterprises and organisations in the free trade zone could be transferred and sold to other enterprises in the zone or used for other purposes without prior approval from the customs; for imported materials and spare parts used for exports production by zone enterprises, simplified account books

315

were replaced the 'register handbook'. The following goods were to be exempt from import and export licence: machinery, equipment, construction materials, commercial use vehicles, office appliance imported into China and used in the free trade zone; imported raw materials, spare parts, components, fuel and packing materials used for manufacturing export products; imported entre-pot goods stored in the zone; products that are manufactured in the zone and shipped out of China.

A series of special policies were also implemented for the management of foreign currencies:

(1)　Enterprises in the zone could retain foreign exchange for circulation and did not need to settle foreign exchange balance or draw extra dividends at the end of a year if there was no surplus; they could open accounts and normal business expenditures no longer needed approval by foreign exchange administrative departments but could be handled by banks; they could buy and sell foreign exchange in the foreign exchange transaction centre according to existing regulations, and both RMB and foreign exchange could be transferred into and out of the zone according to business needs.

(2)　For enterprises in the zone engaged in production, storage and foreign trade business, all dealings of goods in bond were to be priced in foreign exchange and settled through banks; payments not included in this regulation were to be priced and settled in RMB.

(3)　Goods in bond supervised by the customs were to be priced and settled in foreign exchange entering and leaving the free trade zone; and goods not in bond were to be priced and settled in RMB.

(4)　Foreign exchange profit and other foreign exchange income of foreign investors of in zone enterprises were to be remitted by bank according to tax certificates and decisions could be made concerning their contribution by the board of directors.

(5)　Foreign investors in zone enterprises could transfer foreign investment and foreign capital remittances from legal liquidation proceedings after approval by the National Foreign Exchange Administrative Shanghai Branch.

316

(6)   Foreign capital borrowed by zone enterprises from abroad was to be supervised and controlled according to foreign-debt management regulations by the State government. Enterprises were to be able to borrow foreign exchange or demand guarantees from local financial institutions within the territory of China.

5.   Preference for profit remittance and reinvestment. Foreign investors remitting the share of profit earned from the enterprise out of the territory of China were to be exempt from income tax. Foreign investors who reinvested their profit shares in their enterprises, or other FIEs for a period of no less than five years were to be refunded 40% of the enterprise income tax paid on the reinvested amount; while those who reinvested their profits to set up or extend export enterprises or technologically advanced enterprises for no less than five years were to be granted a full refund of enterprise income tax paid on the reinvested amount.

Appendix 4.1

Wage ratios between Hungary and the United States

Year	Monthly wage in Ft	Monthly wage in US$	Working hours per month	Wage (US$)/hour	US wage per hour (US$)	Hungary's wage/US wage (%)
1977	3248	79.29	172.0	0.46	5.25	8.8
1978	3515	92.72	169.0	0.54	5.69	9.5
1979	3718	104.50	168.0	0.62	6.70	9.3
1980	3941	121.14	167.0	0.73	7.27	10.0
1981	4212	122.75	159.3	0.77	7.99	9.6
1982	4478	122.25	153.9	0.79	8.49	9.3
1983	4694	110.00	151.7	0.73	8.83	8.3
1984	5286	110.20	148.1	0.74	9.19	8.1
1985	5972	119.16	146.8	0.81	9.54	8.5
1986	6260	136.59	145.1	0.94	9.73	9.7
1987	6840	145.62	147.4	0.99	9.91	9.9
1988	8832	175.19	144.7	1.21	10.19	11.9
1989	10461	177.10	143.9	1.23	10.49	11.7
1990	13092	207.13	141.2	1.23	10.84	13.9
1991	14200	190.00	140.1	1.35	10.98	12.3
1992	16500	214.81	139.0	1.55	11.05	14.0

Notes: Hungarian average wage was converted into US dollar by official exchange rate between Forint and US dollar. The exchange rates came from *International Financial Statistic Yearbook (1991),* pp.396-7, International Monetary Fund, New York.

Sources: Hungarian average wages by month, working hour per month and US wage per hour come from *Yearbook of Labour Statistics,* various volumes from 1977 to 1992, International Labour Office, Vienna.

Appendix 4.2

Wage ratios between China and the United States

Year	Monthly wages in RMB	Monthly wages in US$	Working hours per month	Wage/hour (US$)	US wage/hour (US$)	China's wage/US wage (%)
1977	50.40	27.13	192	0.140	5.25	3.20
1978	52.90	33.54	192	0.175	5.69	3.25
1979	57.58	38.48	192	0.200	6.70	2.90
1980	65.33	42.70	192	0.222	7.27	3.67
1981	65.67	37.62	192	0.196	7.99	3.36
1982	66.83	35.28	190	0.185	8.49	2.6
1983	68.25	34.65	190	0.183	8.83	2.45
1984	82.33	35.79	190	0.188	9.19	2.41
1985	92.58	31.52	190	0.165	9.54	2.07
1986	106.42	30.85	180	0.173	9.73	1.98
1987	118.08	31.72	180	0.176	9.91	2.00
1988	145.58	39.11	176	0.222	10.19	2.20
1989	164.08	43.58	176	0.248	10.49	2.20
1990	181.33	37.94	176	0.216	10.84	2.10
1991	210.71	39.76	176	0.226	10.98	2.20
1992	250.40	46.37	176	0.264	11.05	2.40

Notes: China's average wage was converted into US dollar by official exchange rate between Renminbi (RMB) and US dollar. The exchange rates came from *International Financial Statistic Yearbook (1991)*, pp.396-7, International Monetary Fund, New York.

Sources: China's average wages by month, working hours per month and US wage per hour come from *Yearbook of Labour Statistics,* various volumes from 1977 to 1992, International Labour Office, Vienna.

Appendix 4.3

Data used for estimating the determinants of foreign inward capital in Hungary, 1977-92

Year	FDI	GDP	GDPA	GR	TARIFF	DISCOUNT	BOND	WAGE	EXRT	IMP	GROECD	DUMMY
1978	0.0002	16.61	3.70	4.40	35.45	9.00	8.41	9.50	35.58	8.46	4.00	1.00
1979	0.0005	19.18	2.57	2.70	34.22	9.00	9.44	9.30	35.58	8.68	3.60	1.00
1980	0.0010	22.16	2.95	0.20	34.23	9.00	11.46	10.00	32.21	9.31	1.20	1.00
1981	0.0040	22.72	0.56	2.90	32.47	11.00	13.91	9.60	34.43	9.13	1.60	1.00
1982	0.0050	23.14	0.42	2.80	31.05	14.00	13.00	9.30	39.61	8.20	0.50	1.00
1983	0.0120	21.00	-2.14	0.70	30.67	13.00	11.11	8.30	45.19	8.08	2.70	1.00
1984	0.0150	20.36	-0.64	2.60	29.45	13.00	12.52	8.10	51.20	7.63	4.40	1.00
1985	0.0190	20.62	-0.95	-0.30	24.67	10.50	10.62	8.50	47.35	8.66	3.50	1.00
1986	0.0210	23.75	2.28	1.50	23.68	9.50	7.68	9.70	45.93	9.57	2.80	1.00
1987	0.0500	26.10	0.36	4.10	22.33	10.00	8.38	9.90	46.39	9.98	3.20	1.00

1988	0.1500	27.90	-1.60	-0.10	20.78	10.50	8.85	11.90	52.54	8.99	4.60	1.00
1989	0.3000	28.88	-3.91	-0.20	19.02	14.00	8.50	11.70	62.54	8.29	3.70	0.00
1990	0.9000	32.90	-1.62	-4.30	15.60	20.00	8.55	13.90	61.45	8.87	3.30	0.00
1991	1.6500	34.78	1.88	-10.20	12.33	19.00	7.86	12.30	75.62	7.47	2.00	0.00
1992	1.8000	35.23	0.45	-4.00	10.32	21.00	8.50	14.00	85.45	6.94	1.20	0.00

Sources: The inflows of foreign capital in Hungary were taken from Hungarian Central Statistics Office, various issues; *The EIU Country Profile: Hungary*, various issues, The Economic Intelligence Unit; *International Financial Statistics Yearbook (1992*, pp.396-9, IMF, 1992. The Hungarian GDP series were taken from *International Financial Statistics Yearbook (1992)* and *International Financial Statistics*, Vol.1, 1993, and were converted into US dollar at the current official exchange rate to ensure comparability with the rest of the data. The Hungarian tariff rates, discount rate, the US government long-term bond yield, and the official exchange rate were all taken from the *International Financial Statistics Yearbook (1992)*, *UN National Account Statistics*, and *IMF Government Financial Statistics*, various issues 1977-92, United Nations, New York. The data of the real GDP growth rate in OECD countries came from *OECD Economic Outlook*, Vol.52, December 1992, pp.201-2, and Vol.53, March 1993, pp.201-2, OECD Publication, Paris.

321

Appendix 4.4

Data used for estimating the determinants of foreign inward capital in China, 1977-92

Year	FDI	GDP	GDPA	TARIFF	DISCOUNT	BOND	WAGE	EXRT	IMP	GROECD	PRDTVY	DUMMY
1977	0.060	264.40	3.60	36.00	4.06	7.42	3.20	1.86	13.28	3.80	6.10	1.00
1978	0.540	358.81	12.30	34.67	5.04	8.41	3.25	1.68	18.74	4.00	10.50	0.00
1979	2.520	399.80	7.00	34.57	5.04	9.44	2.90	1.56	24.29	3.60	4.80	0.00
1980	2.597	447.00	6.40	33.60	5.04	11.46	3.67	1.50	29.88	1.20	3.60	0.00
1981	4.370	477.51	4.90	32.23	5.04	13.91	3.36	1.71	36.77	1.60	1.60	0.00
1982	5.299	518.23	8.20	31.69	5.04	13.00	2.60	1.89	35.75	0.50	4.60	0.00
1983	3.910	578.70	10.00	31.34	7.20	11.11	2.45	1.98	42.18	2.70	6.70	0.00
1984	6.280	692.82	13.60	30.67	7.20	12.52	2.41	2.32	62.05	4.40	10.10	0.00
1985	13.650	852.74	13.50	30.74	7.20	10.62	2.07	2.94	125.78	3.50	9.50	0.00

1986	25.060	968.76	7.70	29.34	7.74	7.68	1.98	3.45	149.83	2.80	4.40	1.00
1987	31.460	1130.71	10.20	28.33	7.92	8.38	2.00	3.72	161.42	3.20	7.10	1.00
1988	38.060	1402.42	11.30	27.25	7.92	8.85	2.20	3.72	205.53	4.60	7.90	0.00
1989	37.870	1592.06	3.60	26.68	8.28	8.50	2.20	3.77	219.99	3.70	1.30	1.00
1990	49.210	1767.11	4.80	26.35	11.15	8.55	2.10	4.78	257.43	3.30	2.60	0.00
1991	56.800	2089.28	7.70	25.90	10.00	7.86	2.20	5.32	339.57	2.00	4.50	0.00
1992	86.670	2340.96	12.80	22.00	11.50	8.50	2.40	5.55	443.47	1.20	3.70	0.00

Source: The inflows of foreign capital, GDP, IMP, EXRT, PRDTVY were taken from the *China Statistics Yearbook (1992)*, China Statistical Information and Consultancy Office, Beijing, 1992. Data for the central bank's discount rate, the US government long-term bond yield came from *International Financial Statistics Yearbook (1992)*, and *IMF Government Financial Statistics*, various issues 1977-92, United Nations, New York. The data of the real GDP growth rate in OECD countries came from *OECD Economic Outlook*, Vol.52, December 1992, pp.201-2, and Vol.53, March 1993, pp.201-2, OECD Publication, Paris.

Appendix 7.1

Effect of FCI on growth: summary of previous studies

1. Cohen (1968):

   a. 27 LDCs, cross-section (1955-60):

   $$\text{Growth} = 0.194 + 0.621 \; X'/Y + 0.13 \; F/Y$$
   $$\phantom{\text{Growth} = 0.194 + } (9.27) (4.69) (5.37)$$

   $$\bar{R}^2 = 0.627 \qquad F \, (2,24) = 22.81$$

   b. 41 LDCs, cross-section (1960-65):

   $$\text{Growth} = 0.243 + 0.215 \; X'/Y + 0.101 \; F/Y$$
   $$\phantom{\text{Growth} = 0.243} (8.77) (2.15) (3.47)$$

   $$\bar{R}^2 = 0.250 \qquad F \, (2,38) = 7.68$$

2. Griffin and Enos (1970):

   a. African and Asian LDCs, n=15 (1962-64):

   $$Y = 4.8 + 0.18 \; A/Y \qquad \bar{R}^2 = 0.33$$
   $$ (0.69)$$

   where: Y = average rate of growth of GNP; A/Y = ratio of foreign aid to GNP

   b. Latin America, sample n=12 (1957-64):

   $$Q(t+1) = 12.5 - 0.047 \; A(t) \qquad \bar{R}^2 = 0.62$$

   where: Q = percentage change in GNP per capita
   A = percentage change of foreign aid

3. Voivodas (1973), OLS, 22 LDCs using country dummies:

$$\text{Growth} = a - 0.013 \text{ F/Y} \qquad \bar{R}^2 = 0.182$$
$$(-0.201)$$

$$\text{Output-capital Ratio} = a + 5.552 \text{ F/Y} \qquad \bar{R}^2 = 0.221$$
$$(5.219)$$

4. Papanek (1973), cross-section (1950s, 1960s):

a. Total Sample:

$$\text{Growth} = 1.5 + 0.20 \text{ S/Y} + 0.39 \text{ AID/Y} + 0.17 \text{ FPI/Y}$$
$$(2.5) \quad (6.0) \qquad (5.8) \qquad\qquad (2.5)$$
$$+ 0.19 \text{ Other FCI/Y}$$
$$(2.1)$$

$$\bar{R}^2 = 0.37 \quad F = 13.50$$

b. Asian Sample, n=31:

$$\text{Growth} = 1.5 + 0.21 \text{ S/Y} + 0.46 \text{ AID/Y} + 0.35 \text{ FPI/Y}$$
$$(1.5) \quad (4.2) \qquad (4.4) \qquad\qquad (1.7)$$
$$+ 0.13 \text{ Other FCI/Y}$$
$$(0.8)$$

$$\bar{R}^2 = 0.46 \quad F = 7.7$$

c. Central and Latin American Sample, n=37:

$$\text{Growth} = 2.5 + 0.11 \text{ S/Y} + 0.29 \text{ AID/Y} + 0.19 \text{ FPI/Y}$$
$$(2.7) \quad (2.0) \qquad (1.7) \qquad\qquad (1.4)$$
$$- 0.06 \text{ Other FCI/Y}$$
$$(-0.3)$$

$$\bar{R}^2 = 0.11 \quad F = 2.4$$

5. Stoneman (1976), cross-section, 1960s:

$$\text{Growth} = 1.088 + 0.252 \text{ S/Y} + 0.318 \text{ AID/Y} + 0.076 \text{ Pte FCI/Y}$$
$$(2.29) \quad (9.27) \qquad (8.57) \qquad\qquad (1.37)$$

$$- 0.029 \text{ FCI Stock/Y}$$
$$(-3.41)$$

$$\overline{R}^2 = 0.369$$

6. Kraska and Taira (1974), 13 Latin American countries (1950- 68):

$$\text{Growth} = -1.35 + 0.156 \text{ I/Y} + 0.872 \text{ FDI/Y} + 0.551 \text{ L'/L}$$
$$(2.73) \qquad (2.52) \qquad (2.21)$$
$$- 0.74 \text{ CDRR}$$
$$(-3.87)$$

$$\overline{R}^2 = 0.9161$$

where: CDRR is reduction in the crude death rate

7. Gulati (1978):

a. Model I countries, i.e. countries whose development is hampered by lack of sufficient investment funds (mostly Asian):

$$\text{Growth} = -0.09 + 0.32 \text{ F/Y} + 0.35 \text{ S/Y}$$
$$(2.20) \qquad (2.36)$$

$$\overline{R}^2 = 0.29$$

b. Model II countries, i.e. countries whose development is hampered by other factors, such as 'lack of a minimum cultural base' (Africa) or 'lack of development oriental social structure (Latin America)

$$\text{Growth} = 3.35 + 0.06 \text{ F/Y} + 0.11 \text{ S/Y}$$
$$(0.46) \qquad (0.89)$$

$$\overline{R}^2 = 0.08$$

8. El Shibly (1980), time-series, Sudan (1960s - 70s):

$$\text{Growth} = 0.0811 + 0.2886 \text{ X'/X} - 1.1188 \text{ Fo/Y} - 0.095 \text{ Fp/Y}$$
$$(1.84) \qquad (1.95) \qquad (-1.06) \qquad (-0.04)$$

$$\overline{R}^2 = 0.583 \quad \text{D-W} = 1.986$$

9. Dowling and Heimenz (1983): cross-section, Asian region 1968-79, pooled time series and cross-section:

$$\text{Growth} = 0.47 + 0.46 \text{ AID/Y} + 0.72 \text{ Pte FCI/Y} + 0.24 \text{ S/Y}$$
$$ (2.46) (2.72) (4.50)$$

$$\bar{R}^2 = 0.43 \quad \text{D-W} = 1.96$$

10. Gupta and Islam (1983), cross-section (1965-73):

a. Total Sample (2SLS estimation):

$$\text{Growth} = 0.0075 + 0.2 \text{ S/Y} + 0.256 \text{ AID/Y} + 0.156 \text{ FPI/Y}$$
$$ (0.435) (2.36) (1.78) (1.35)$$
$$ + 0.382 \text{ RFI/Y} + 0.039 \text{ L'/L}$$
$$ (2.54) (1.99)$$

$$\bar{R}^2 = 0.43$$

b. Asian Sample (OLS estimation):

$$\text{Growth} = -0.036 + 0.35 \text{ S/Y} + 1.034 \text{ AID/Y} + 0.60 \text{ FPI/Y}$$
$$ (-2.03) (6.06) (3.78) (1.40)$$
$$ +0.356 \text{ RFI/Y} + 0.073 \text{ L'/L}$$
$$ (1.89) (2.25)$$

$$\bar{R}^2 = 0.71$$

c. African Sample (OLS estimation):

$$\text{Growth} = -0.006 + 0.304 \text{ S/Y} + 0.138 \text{ AID/Y} + 0.038 \text{ FPI/Y}$$
$$ (-0.55) (5.39) (0.41) (0.116)$$
$$ + 0.543 \text{ RFI/Y} + 0.0254 \text{ L'/L}$$
$$ (1.86) (0.99)$$

$$\bar{R}^2 = 0.88$$

d. Latin American Sample (OLS estimation):

$$\text{Growth} = 0.027 + 0.03 \text{ S/Y} + 0.134 \text{ AID/Y} + 0.13 \text{ FPI/Y}$$
$$ (1.28) (0.25) (0.77) (0.98)$$

$$+ \ 0.2796 \ \text{RFI/Y} \ + \ 0.0572 \ \text{L'/L}$$
$$(1.20) \qquad\qquad (1.52)$$

$$\bar{R}^2 = 0.12$$

11. Sant'ana (1983), Brazilian data 1964-74:

$$\text{Growth} = -10.26 + 2.32 \ \text{S/Y} + 5.16 \ \text{F/Y} - 5.25 \ \text{MK/Y}$$
$$(-0.61) \quad (1.93) \qquad (3.30) \qquad (-2.75)$$

$$\bar{R}^2 = 0.71 \quad \text{D-W} = 3.05$$

$$\text{Growth} = 1.63 \ \text{S/Y} + 5.23 \ \text{F/Y} - 5.19 \ \text{MK/Y}$$
$$(4.13) \qquad (3.52) \qquad (-2.86)$$

$$\bar{R}^2 = 0.71$$

where: MK/Y = import of capital and intermediate goods, as a percentage of GDP.

12. Mosley, Hundson, Horrell (1987), cross-section 80 LDCs (3SLS):

$$\text{Growth} = 1.85 + 0.084 \ \text{AID/Y} - 0.077 \ \text{Other FCI/Y} + 0.13 \ \text{S/Y}$$
$$(1.85) \quad (0.70) \qquad\qquad (-1.62) \qquad\qquad\qquad (2.72)$$
$$- \ 0.017 \ \text{L'*} + 0.22 \ \text{X'/X}$$
$$(-0.47) \qquad (4.64)$$
$$\text{SE} = 2.19$$

where: L* = growth in literacy rate used as a proxy for growth in labour force in qualitative terms.

13. Mosley (1987), 67 LDCs cross-section:

1960-70:

$$\text{Growth} = 3.31 - 0.04 \ \text{AID/Y} - 0.01 \ \text{Pte FCI/Y} + 0.03 \ \text{S/Y}$$
$$(4.78) \ (-1.72) \qquad\qquad (-0.67) \qquad\qquad (0.97)$$
$$+ \ 0.15 \ \text{X'/X} + 0.08 \ \text{L}$$
$$(3.67) \qquad (2.11)$$

$$\bar{R}^2 = 0.30$$

1970-80:

$$\text{Growth} = 2.45 + 0.024 \text{ AID/Y} - 0.082 \text{ Pte FCI/Y} + 0.09 \text{ S/Y}$$
$$(0.21) \qquad (-1.60) \qquad (2.11)$$
$$+ 0.23 \text{ X'/X} + + 0.006 \text{ L}$$
$$(4.87) \qquad (0.16)$$

$$\bar{R}^2 = 0.36$$

where: L = percentage annual rate of growth of literacy.

14. Karikari J A (1992), Ghana data 1961-88:

$$\text{GDP} = 1.204 + 0.789 \text{ GDP(t-1)} - 22.86 \text{ FDI(t-1)}$$
$$(0.151) \quad (0.0001) \qquad (-0.454)$$

$$\bar{R}^2 = 0.77$$

Notes on variable names:

Growth	=	annual rate of increase in GDP, i.e. Y'/Y
GDP	=	Gross Domestic Product
S	=	domestic savings
F	=	foreign capital inflows of all kinds
Y	=	GDP
Fo	=	Official capital inflows, comparable to AID below
Fp	=	private capital inflows, comparable to FPI below
AID	=	net transfers received by governments plus official long-term borrowing
FPI	=	private long-term borrowing plus private direct investment
Other FCI	=	net private transfers, net short-term borrowing, errors and omissions
FDI	=	foreign direct investment
RFI	=	residual inflows, comprising mostly private aid
L'/L	=	growth rate of labour force
X'/X	=	growth rate of exports
X/Y	=	exports as a proportion of GDP, i.e. the export rate

Appendix 7.2

Primary data used for estimating the FCI's contribution to growth in Hungary, 1977-92

Year	GDP (bn Ft)	GDP Growth Rate(%)	Exchange Rate (Ft/$)	Gross Capital Formation (bn Ft)	Labour Force (000s)	Foreign Capital Inflows (bn US$)	Export (bn Ft)
1977	580.585	7.60	40.600	216.032	5075.0	8.020	238.542
1978	628.336	4.40	35.578	259.568	5074.9	7.890	241.359
1979	680.873	2.70	35.578	233.378	5077.3	7.490	279.771
1980	721.031	0.20	32.213	220.692	5044.1	10.314	278.809
1981	779.912	2.90	34.430	231.342	5256.0	10.023	308.221
1982	847.871	2.80	39.610	241.806	5223.4	8.989	321.809
1983	896.367	0.70	45.193	237.155	5183.6	9.624	360.713
1984	978.456	2.60	51.199	251.775	5147.3	10.104	401.961
1985	1033.660	-0.30	47.347	258.423	5121.0	13.008	436.180

Year	GDP	GDP Growth Rate	Gross Capital Formation	Exports	Labour Force	Foreign Exchange Rates	Foreign Capital Inflows
1986	1088.800	1.50	45.927	292.739	5111.2	16.907	431.585
1987	1226.370	4.10	46.387	327.484	5092.8	19.584	464.391
1988	1435.190	-0.10	52.537	358.947	5069.7	19.602	530.395
1989	1710.760	-0.20	62.543	446.028	5051.8	20.390	620.857
1990	2089.540	-4.30	61.449	499.205	5048.5	21.316	668.979
1991	2600.000	-10.20	75.620	569.112	5046.2	22.500	754.000
1992	2706.000	-4.0	75.750	653.625	5042.1	23.500	733.326

Sources: GDP, GDP Growth Rate, Gross Capital Formation, Exports were taken from *Statistic Yearbook 1992*, Budapest:Central Statistic Office, pp.16-26; supplemented by *UN National Account Statistics, various volumes, and The EIU Country Profile: Hungary 1992*; Labour Force was taken from *Yearbook of Labour Statistics*, various volumes from 1977 to 1992, International Labour Office, Vienna. Foreign Exchange Rates came from *International Financial Statistics Yearbook 1992*, IMF; p.397; Foreign Capital Inflows were taken from *World Debt Tables, 1984-85*, pp.284-5, 1991-92, pp.182-183 and *Balance of Payments Statistics*, 1984, pp.257-61 and 1992, pp.310-5.

Appendix 7.3

Converted data used for estimating the FCI's contribution to growth in Hungary, 1977-92

Year	GDP Growth Rate (%)	I/Y (%)	L'/L (%)	RT (%)	FCI/Y (%)	S/Y (%)	X/Y (%)
1977	7.60	41.240	-2.40	84.00	2.17	29.90	45.20
1978	4.40	43.93	-2.00	85.00	2.56	29.60	38.60
1979	2.70	34.20	4.70	86.00	3.10	28.10	41.30
1980	0.20	30.99	-6.54	82.50	2.55	28.50	39.10
1981	2.90	29.57	4.200	82.60	4.12	2860	38.60
1982	2.80	26.38	-6.20	79.90	3.85	29.30	37.90
1983	0.70	24.99	-7.62	81.10	2.21	28.40	41.40
1984	2.60	24.16	-7.00	81.60	3.34	28.90	42.10

1985	-0.30	26.47	-5.10	81.40	2.68	27.10	41.10
1986	1.50	26.84	-1.91	81.10	3.19	25.50	41.40
1987	4.10	27.05	-3.59	82.30	5.03	26.20	38.60
1988	-0.10	24.49	-4.54	81.00	3.26	28.20	36.80
1989	-0.20	24.69	-3.53	81.50	2.60	29.50	35.70
1990	-4.30	24.69	-6.50	82.10	4.79	28.10	34.40
1991	-10.20	21.64	-4.60	81.10	4.74	29.30	29.00
1992	-4.00	24.74	-8.10	81.40	3.38	28.50	27.10

Notes: All of our primary explanatory data in Appendix 7.3 were scaled against GDP as 'levels' in order to obviate any problems relating to heteroscedasticity. Such scaled data, as well as data specified in terms of rates of growth, are converted to percentage terms by multiplying by 100.

Appendix 7.4

Primary data used for estimating the FCI's contribution to growth in China, 1978-92

Year	GDP (bn RMB)	GDP Growth Rate(%)	Exchange Rate (RMB/$)	Investment /GDP (%)	Labour Force (00,000s)	Foreign Capital Inflows (bn RMB)	Exports (bn RMB)
1978	358.81	12.03	1.5771	31.20	40152	3.540	16.76
1979	399.80	7.60	1.4962	23.40	41024	2.520	21.17
1980	447.00	8.40	1.5303	30.40	42361	2.597	27.12
1981	477.51	5.20	1.7455	28.90	43725	4.370	36.76
1982	518.23	8.70	1.9227	27.40	45295	5.299	41.38
1983	578.70	10.30	1.9809	24.60	46436	3.910	43.83
1984	692.82	14.60	2.7957	23.60	48197	6.280	58.05
1985	852.74	12.70	3.2015	31.20	49837	13.650	80.89
1986	968.76	8.30	3.7221	23.80	51282	25.060	108.21
1987	1130.71	11.00	3.7221	23.40	52783	31.460	147.00

1988	1402.42	10.90	3.7221	23.10	54334	38.060	176.67
1989	1592.06	3.60	4.7221	23.50	55329	37.870	195.60
1990	1767.11	4.80	5.2221	23.60	56740	49.210	298.58
1991	2089.28	7.70	5.4342	24.00	58397	56.800	390.45
1992	2340.96	12.80	5.5673	23.80	61258	86.670	463.68

Sources: GDP, GDP growth rate, investment rates, exports were taken from *Statistic Yearbook 1991*, State Statistical Bureau, Beijing, p.31, p.41, and p.615, supplemented by *UN National Account Statistics*, various volumes; labour force was taken from *China Statistics Yearbook 1991*, p.95, and *Yearbook of Labour Statistics*, various volumes from 1977 1992, International Labour Office, Vienna. Foreign exchange rates came from *International Financial Statistics Yearbook 1992*, IMF; p.279; foreign capital inflows were taken from *Balance of Payments Statistics*, 1984, p.131, 1987, p.74-76 and 1992, p.146-150. Those figures related to 1991 and 1992 were taken from *People's Daily (Overseas Edition)*, 1992 and 1993, mainly, 7 August, 23 October, 24 November and 9 December 1992; 9 February, 18 March and 20 March 1993.

Appendix 7.5

Converted data used for estimating the FCI's contribution to growth in China, 1978-92

Year	GDP Growth Rate (%)	I/Y (%)	L'/L (%)	RT (%)	FCI/Y (%)	S/Y (%)	X/Y (%)
1978	12.30	31.20	1.968	71.60	0.987	36.50	4.671
1979	7.60	24.60	2.170	68.50	0.630	34.60	5.295
1980	8.40	24.70	3.259	69.60	0.581	31.50	6.067
1981	5.20	23.40	3.220	67.30	0.915	28.30	7.698
1982	8.70	23.60	3.591	66.00	1.023	28.80	7.985
1983	10.30	27.40	2.519	66.10	0.676	29.70	7.574
1984	14.60	30.40	3.792	66.90	0.906	31.50	8.379
1985	12.70	27.10	3.477	70.20	1.601	35.00	9.486

1986	8.30	23.80	2.825	71.40	2.587	34.70	11.170
1987	11.00	25.21	2.927	71.70	2.782	34.10	13.001
1988	10.90	25.30	2.939	72.70	2.714	34.50	12.598
1989	3.60	23.10	1.831	73.40	2.379	34.30	12.286
1990	4.80	23.40	2.550	71.60	2.785	34.10	16.897
1991	7.70	23.60	2.920	73.70	2.719	34.40	18.307
1992	12.80	28.90	4.900	76.10	3.702	34.50	19.753

Note: All of these primary explanatory data in absolute amount for 1977-92 in Table 7.5 were scaled against GDP as 'levels' in order to obviate any problems relating to heteroscedasticity. Such scaled data, as well as data specified in terms of rates of growth, are converted to percentage terms by multiplying by 100.

Selected bibliography

Abramson, Robert J.(1989), 'Strategic Alliances with the East', *The Magazine for Magazine Management*, Folio, Vol. 18, No. 2, pp.143-7.

Agarwal, Jamuna P. (1980), 'Determinants of Foreign Direct Investment: A Survey', *Weltwirtschaftliches Archiv*, Kiel, Vol.116, pp.739-44.

Aharoni, Yair. (1966), *The Foreign Investment Decision Process*, Harvard University Press, Boston.

Ahiakpor, James, C.W. (1990), *Multinationals and Economic Development: An Integration of Competing Theories*, Routledge, London & New York.

Ahmed, Quazi Mesbahuddin (1992), *Foreign Aid, Domestic Savings and Economic Growth: the Experience of Bangladesh, 1972-91*, unpublished PhD dissertation at University of Illinois at Urbana Champaign.

Ahmed, Ahmed Abdelrahman (1975), *The Determinants of Direct Investment with Special Reference to Developing Countries*, unpublished PhD thesis, University of Pennsylvania, Philadelphia.

Ahmed, Masood and Gooptu, Sudarshan (1993), 'Portfolio Investment Flows to Developing Countries', *Finance & Development*, No.1, Vol.XXX, March, pp.9-12.

Aiello, Paul (1991), 'Building a Joint Venture in China: The Case of Chrysler and the Beijing Jeep Corporation', *Journal of General Management*, Vol.17, No.2, pp.47-64.

Alexander, S. and Murphy J.C. (1975), *Exchange Rates and Direct International Investment*, Department of Economics, Southern Methodist University, Dallas, Working Paper, No.7, February.

Aliber, Robert Zelwin (1970), 'A Theory of Direct Foreign Investment', in Kindleberger C.P. (ed.), *The International Firm*, MIT Press, Cambridge, pp.17-34.

Aliber, Robert Zelwin (1978), *Exchange Risk and Corporate International Finance*, Macmillan, London.

Allen & Overy (1993), *Key Legal Facts for the Foreign Investor in Hungary*, Allen & Overy, London.

Andrews, M. (1972), *American Investment in Irish industry*, unpublished Senior Honours Thesis, Harvard University, Cambridge, Mass.

Artisien, Patrick, F.R. (1985), *Joint Ventures in Yugoslav Industry*, Gower Publishing Co. Ltd, Hants.

Artisien, Patrick, Matija Rojec and Marjan Svetlicic (1993), *Foreign Investment in Central and Eastern Europe*, St.Martin's Press, New York.

Athukorala, Premachandra (1991), 'An Analysis of Demand and Supply Factors in Agricultural Exports from Developing Asian Countries', *Review of World Economics*, Vol.127, No.4, pp.764-92.

Balassa, B. (1966), 'American Direct Investment in the Common Market', *Banca Nazionale del Lavoro Quarterly Review*, pp. 121-46.

Balasubramanyam, V.N.(1984), 'Incentives and Disincentives for Foreign Direct Investment in Less Developed Countries', *Weltwirtschaftliches Archiv*, Kiel, Vol.120, pp.720-33.

Baldwin, Robert E. (1979), 'Determinants of Trade and Foreign Investment: Further Evidence', *The Review of Economics and Statistics*, Vol.61, pp.40-48.

Ballance, R. H., Ansari, J. A., and Singer, H. W. (1982), *The International Economy and Industrial Development: The Impact of Trade and Investment on the Third World*, Osmun Publishers, Allanheld.

Bandera, Vladimir N. and White, J.T. (1968), 'U.S. Direct Investments and Domestic Markets in Europe', *Economia Internazionale*, Geneva, Vol. 21, pp.117-33.

Bandera, Vladimir N. and Lucken J.A. (1972), 'Has U.S. Capital Differentiated between EEC and EFTA?', *Kyklos*, Basel, Vol.25, pp.306-14.

Basi, Raghbir.S. (1963), *Determinants of United States Private Direct Investment in Foreign Countries*, Kent State University Press, Kent, Ohio.

Bass, B. M., McGregor, D. W. and Walters, J. (1977), 'Selecting Foreign Plant Sites: Economic, Social and Political Consideration', *Academy of Management Journal*, Vol.4, No.20.

Behrman, Jack. N. (1962), 'Foreign Associates and Their Financing', in Mikessel, Raymond Frech (ed.), *U.S. Private and Government Investment Abroad*, National Foreign Trade Council, Eugene, pp.77-113.

Bennett, Peter T. and Robert. T. Green (1972), 'Political Instability as a Determinant of Direct Investment in Marketing', *Journal of Marketing Research,* Vol.9, pp.182-6.

Bergsten, C.F., Horst, T. and Moran, T.H. (1978), *American Multinationals and American Interests,* Brookings Institute, Washington, D.C.

Blais, Jeffrey P.(1972), *A Theoretical and Empirical Investigation of Canadian and British Direct Foreign Investment in Manufacturing in the United States,* unpublished PhD thesis, University of Pittsburgh.

Boatwright, B.D. and Renton G. A. (1975), 'Analysis of United Kingdom Inflows and Outflows of Direct Foreign Investment', *The Review of Economics and Statistics,* Cambridge, Mass, Vol.57, pp.478-86.

Bornschier, V., Chase-Dunn, C. and Rubinson R. (1978), 'Cross-national Evidence of the Effects of Foreign Investment and Aid on Economic Growth and Inequality: A Survey of Findings and A Reanalysis', *American Journal of Sociology,* Vol.84, pp.651-83.

Bos, H.C.,Sanders, M. and Seechi, C. (1974), *Private Foreign Investment in Developing Countries,* D. Reidel, Boston.

Brash, Donald.T.(1966), *American Investment in Australian Industry,* Cambridge University Press, Cambridge & Canberra.

Buckley, Peter J. and Casson, Mark C. (1976), *The Future of the Multinational Enterprise,* Macmillan, London.

Buckley, Peter J. and Casson, Mark C. (1985), *The Economic Theory of the Multinational Enterprise,* Macmillan, London.

Buckley, Peter J. and Artisien Patrick (1987), *North-South Direct Investment in the European Communities: the Employment Impact of Direct Investment by British, French and German Multinationals in Greece, Portugal and Spain,* Macmillan Press, London.

Buckley, P. J. Newbould G. D. and Thurwell, J. C. (1987), *Foreign Direct Investment by Smaller UK Firms: the Success and Failure of Investors Abroad,* (2nd ed.), Macmillan, London.

Buckley, P. J.(1990) (ed.), *International Investment,* Edward Elgar Publishing Ltd, Hants.

Bulcke, Van Den; Martens, Bonddewyn and Klemmer (1979), *Investment and Divestment Policies of Multinational Corporations in Europe,* Saxon House, Hampshire.

Business International & Creditanstalt (1992), *1992 East European Investment Survey,* October, Vienna.

Business Eastern Europe, 24 October 1988, pp.337-8; 5 February 1990, p.43; 14 January 1991, p.12; Vol. XX, No.1, 1991.

Cassidy, Henry J. (1981), *Using Econometrics: A Beginner's Guide,* Reston Publishing Company, Inc., Reston, Virginia.

Casson, Mark (1979), *Alternatives to the Multinational Enterprise,* Macmillan, London.

Casson, Mark (1985), 'The Theory of Foreign Direct Investment', in Buckley, P.J. and Casson, M.(ed.), *The Economic Theory of the Multinational Enterprise,* Macmillan, London, pp.113-43.

Casson, Mark (1987), *The Firm and the Market,* Basil Blackwell, Oxford.

Casson, Mark and Zheng, Jurong (1991), 'Western Joint Ventures in China', *Journal of International Development,* Vol.3, No.3, pp.293-323.

Caves, Richard E. (1971), 'International Corporations: The Industrial Economics of Foreign Investment', *Economica,* Vol.38, pp.1-27.

Chambers, Robert Lloyd (1993), *An LDC Model of Growth and Trade Involving Foreign Investment and Human Capital,* unpublished PhD dissertation at University of Houston.

Chan, Raissa and Hoy, Michael (1991), 'East-West Joint Ventures and Buyback Contracts', *Journal of International Economics,* Netherlands, Vol.30, No.3-4, pp.331-43.

Chase, Carmen D. and Kuhle, James L. (1988), 'The Relevance of Political Risk in Direct Foreign Investment', *Management International Review,* Vol. 28, No. 3, pp.31-38.

Chen, Jinghai (1993), 'The Environment for Foreign Direct Investment and the Characteristics of Joint Ventures in China', *Development Policy Review,* Vol.11, No.2, pp.167-183.

Chenery H.B. and Syrquin, M. (1975), *Patterns of Development 1950-70,* Oxford University Press for the World Bank, Washington.

China Statistical Information and Consultancy Office (1991), *China Statistics Yearbook 1991,* China Statistical Information and Consultancy Office, Beijing.

Clager, Christopher and Rausser, Gordon C. (1992) (ed.), *The Emergence of Market Economies in Eastern Europe,* Blackwell, London.

Clegg, Jeremy (1987), *Multinational Enterprise and World Competition: A Comparative Study of the USA, Japan, the UK, Sweden and West Germany,* Macmillan Press, London.

Cohen, B. I. (1968), 'Relative Effects of Foreign Capital and Larger Exports on Economic Development', *The Review of Economics and Statistics,* Vol.50, pp.281-4.

Connor, J. M.(1977), *The Market Power of Multinational: A Quantitative Analysis of U.S. Corporations in Brazil and Mexico,* Praeger Publishers, New York and London.

Csaba, Laszlo (1991) (ed.), *Systematic Change and Stabilisation in Eastern Europe,* Dartmouth Publishing Co.

Cushman, David.O. (1985), 'Real Exchange Risk, Expectations, and the Level of Direct Investment', *The Review of Economics and Statistics,* Vol.67,

341

pp.297-308.

Cushman, David O. (1988), 'Exchange-Rate Uncertainty and Foreign Direct Investment in the United States', *Weltwirtschaftliches Archiv*, Kiel, Vol.124, pp.322-35.

Deane, Roderick.S.(1970), *Foreign Investment in New Zealand Manufacturing*, Praeger, Wellington.

Dobosiewicz, Zbigniew (1992), *Foreign Investment in Eastern Europe* Routledge, London.

Dong, Shizhong, et al (1993), *Trade and Investment Opportunities in China: The Current Commercial and Legal Framework*, Quorum Books, Greenwood Publishing Group, London.

Dowling, J. M. and Heimenz, U. (1983), 'Aid, Savings and Growth in the Asian Region', *The Developing Economies*, Vol.21, March, pp.3-31.

Duesenberry, J., Kuh E., Fromm, G., and Klein, L.(1965), (ed.), *The Brookings Quarterly Econometric Model of the United States*, Rand-McNally.

Dunning, John H. (1973), 'The Determinants of International Production', *Oxford Economic Papers*, Vol.25, pp.289-336.

Dunning, John H. (1977), 'Trade, Location of Economic Activity and MNE: A Search for an Eclectic Approach', in Berti Ohlin, Per O. Hesselborn, Per M. Wijkman (ed.), *The International Allocation of Economic Activity: Proceedings of a Nobel Symposium Held at Stockholm on 8-11 June*, Holmes & Meier, London & New York.

Dunning, John H. (1979), 'Explaining Changing Patterns of International Production: In Defence of the Eclectic Theory', *Oxford Bulletin of Economics and Statistics*, Oxford, Vol.41, pp.269-96.

Dunning, John H. (1981), *International Production and The Multinational Enterprise*, Allen & Unwin, London.

Dunning, John H. (1993), 'The Prospects for Foreign Direct Investment in Eastern Europe', in Artisien, Patrick, et al (ed.), *Foreign Investment in Central & Eastern Europe*, St Martin's Press, London, pp.109-22.

ECE (1991), *Reforms in Foreign Economic Relations of Eastern Europe and Soviet Union*, UN, New York.

ECE (1988), *East-West Joint Ventures: Economic, Business, Financial and Legal Aspects*, UN, New York.

ECE (1989), *East-West Joint Venture Contracts*, UN, New York.

Economic Intelligence Unit, *The EIU Country Profile: Hungary*, Various issues (1989-1993), The Economic Intelligence Unit, London.

Edwards A. (1964), *Investment in the European Economic Community*, New York.

EI, Shibly M. (1980), *Capital Formation, Inflation and Economic Growth: The Experience of Sudan 1960/61 - 1974/75*, unpublished PhD thesis,

University of Kent at Canterbury.

Elhassan, Mazen Darwiche (1992), *Theoretical and Empirical Research on Foreign Direct Investment: Survey, Critical Review and New Directions,* unpublished PhD dissertation at Syracuse University.

Emery, R.F.(1967), 'The Relation of Exports and Economic Growth', *Kyklos,* Vol.20, pp.470-84.

Emmott, Bill (1993), 'Multinationals', *The Economist,* 27 March 1993, pp.1-28.

Euromonitor Plc (1992), *European Marketing Data and Statistics* (27th edition), London.

Faber, Mike (1993), 'Governance and the Foreign Direct Investor', *IDS Bulletin,* Vol.24, No.1, pp.51-57.

Fan, Qimiao and Schaffer, Mark E. (1991), 'Enterprise Reforms in Chinese and Polish State-Owned Industries', The Development Economic Research Programme, STICERD, London School of Economics, *China Programme,* No.13.

Fatehi-Sedeh, K. and Safizadeh, M. H. (1989), 'The Association Between Political Instability and Flow of Foreign Direct Investment', *Management International Review,* Vol. 29, No. 4, pp.5-13.

Ferber, R. (ed.) (1967), *Determinants of Investment Behaviour,* National Bureau of Economic Research, Washington, D.C.

Feuchtwang, Stephan, Hussain, Athar, and Pairault T. (ed.) (1983), *The Chinese Economic Reforms,* St.Martin's Press, New York.

Feuchtwang, Stephan, Hussain, Athar, and Pairault T. (1988), *Transforming China's Economy in the Eighties,* Volume II, Boulder, Westview Press, Colorado.

Financial Times (1992), *Eastern European Market,* 26 June, Vol.12, No.13.

Forsyth, David J.C. (1972), *U.S. Investment in Scotland,* Praeger Special Studies in International Economics and Development, New York.

Frank, I. (1980), *Foreign Enterprise in Developing Countries,* Baltimore.

Fritsch, Winston and Franco, Gustavo (1991), *Foreign Direct Investment in Brazil: Its Impact on Industrial Restructuring,* OECD Publication, Paris.

Giddy, Ian H. and Young, Stephen (1982), 'Conventional Theory and Unconventional Multinationals: Do New Forms of Multinational Enterprise Require New Theories?' in Rugman, A. M. (ed.), *New Theories of the Multinational Enterprise,* Croom Helm, London and Canberra.

Goldberg, M.A. (1972), 'Determinants of U.S. Direct Investment in the EEC: Comment', *The American Economic Review,* Vol.62, pp.692-9.

Gorden, Warner M.,(1974), 'The Theory of International Trade', in Dunning J.H. (ed.), *Economic Analysis of the Multinational Enterprise,*

Macmillan, London, pp.184-210.

Graham, Edward M. and Krugman, Paul R. (1989), *Foreign Direct Investment in the United States*, Institute for International Economics, Washington.

Green, Robert T. and Cunningham, William H. (1975), 'The Determinants of US Foreign Investment: An Empirical Examination', *Management International Review*, Vol.15, pp.113-20.

Griffin, K. B. and Enos, J. (1970), 'Foreign Assistance: Objectives and Consequences', *Economic Development and Culture Change*, Vol.18, April, pp.313-27.

Group of Thirty (1984), *Foreign Direct Investment, 1973-83*, New York.

Grub, Phillip Donald and Lin, Jian Hai (1991), *Foreign Direct Investment in China*, Quorum, New York and London.

Gupta, Kanhaya L. and Anisul, Islam M. (1983), *Foreign Capital, Savings and Growth: An International Cross-Section Study*, D.Reidel Publishing Co., Dordrecht, Boston and London

Hagen and Hawrylyshyn (1969), 'Analysis of World Income and Growth, 1955-65', *Economic Development and Cultural Change*, Vol.17, October, pp.81-96.

Haign, Robert W. (1989), *Investment Strategies and the Plant Location Decisions*, Praeger Publisher, London.

Hare, Paul and Grosfeld, Irena (1991), *Privatisation in Hungary, Poland and Czechoslovakia*, Discussion Paper Series No. 544, Centre for Economic Policy Research, April 1991, London.

Harrigan, K. R.(1985), *Strategies for Joint Ventures*, Lexington Books, Lexington, Mass & Toronto.

Harrigan, K. R. (1986), *Managing for Joint Venture Success*, Lexington Books, Massachusetts & Toronto.

Helleiner, G.K. (1988), 'Direct Foreign Investment and Manufacturing for Exports in Developing Countries: An Review of the Issues', in Sidney Dell (ed.), *Policies for Development*, Macmillan, New York.

Helleiner, G.K. (1979), 'Manufacturing Exports from Less Developed Countries', in Cline W.R. (ed.), *Policy Alternatives for a New International Economic Order*, Praeger, New York.

Hicks, G.L. and McNicoll, G. (1971), *Trade and Growth in the Philippines: An Open Dual Economy*, Cornell University Press, Ithac and London.

Hill, H. and Johns, B. (1985), 'The Role of Direct Foreign Investment in Developing East Asian Countries', *Weltwirtschaftliches Archiv*, Vol.121, pp.355-81.

Hill, Hal (1988), *Foreign Investment and Industrialisation in Indonesia*, Oxford University Press, Singapore.

Hillman, A. L. (1990), 'Macroeconomic Policy in Hungary and Its

344

Microeconomic Implications', *European Economy*, Vol.53, May.

Hinson, Steven Yates (1993), *Exchange Rate Fluctuations, Direction of Trade and Foreign Investment in the U.S.*, unpublished PhD dissertation at University of Kentucky.

Ho, Samuel P.S. and Huenemann, Ralph W. (1984), *China's Open Door Policy*, University of British Columbia Press, Vancouver.

Ho, Alfred K. (1991), *Joint Ventures in the People's Republic of China*, Praeger, London.

Hoberg, B. and Wahlbin, C. (1984), 'East-West Industrial Cooperation: The Swedish Case', *Journal of International Business Study*, Spring/Summer.

Hood, Neil and Young, Stephen (1979), *The Economies of Multinational Enterprise*, Longman, London and New York.

Hornell, Erik and Vahlne, Jan-Erik (1986), *Multinationals: the Swedish Case*, Croom Helm, London and Sydney.

Horst, Thomas (1972a), 'The Industrial Composition of U.S. Exports and Subsidiary Sales to the Canadian Market', *The American Economic Review*, Vol.62, pp.37-45.

Horst, Thomas (1972b), 'Firm and Industry Determinants of the Decision to Invest Abroad: An Empirical Study', *The Review of Economics and Statistics*, Vol.54, pp.258-66.

Horton, Thomas R. and Oleinik, Igor S. (1991), 'Can We Fulfil the Promise of East-West Ventures?', *Management Review*, Vol.80, No.9, pp.46-49.

Howe, C.(1978), *China's Economy*, Paul Elek, London.

Howell, Jude (1993), *China Opens Its Doors: The Politics of Economic Transition*, Harvester Wheatsheaf, Brighton.

Huang, Gene (1992), *Comparative Analysis of US and Japanese Overseas Direct Investment*, unpublished PhD thesis at University of Pennsylvania, Pennsylvania.

Hufbauer, G.C. (1975), 'The Multinational Corporation and Direct Investment', in Peter B. K (ed.), *International Trade and Finance*, Cambridge University Press, Cambridge, pp.253-319.

Hughes, H. and Seng, Y.P. (1969), *Foreign Investment and Industrialisation in Singapore*, Canberra.

Hungarian Central Statistics Office, *Economic and Social Development Annual Report*, various issues, Central Statistics Office, Budapest.

Hungarian Scientific Council for World Economy (1990), *Foreign Direct Investment and Joint Ventures in Hungary: Experience and Prospects*, Institute of World Economy, Hungarian Academy of Sciences, Budapest.

Hungarian Scientific Council for World Economy (1991), *Foreign Direct*

Investment and Joint Ventures in Hungary: Experience and Prospects, Hungarian Scientific Council for World Economy, Budapest.

Hunya, G. (1992), 'Foreign Direct Investment and Privatisation in Central and Eastern Europe', paper presented at the 2nd EACES Conference, 24-26 September 1992, Groningen, the Netherlands.

Hutabarat, Pos Marodjahan (1992), *The Role of International Trade in Economic Growth in Developing Countries: the Case of Indonesia,* unpublished PhD dissertation at Michigan State University.

Hymer, Stephen H. (1976), *The International Operations of National Firms: A Study of Direct Investment,* MIT Monographs in Economics, No.14, Cambridge, Mass.

IMF (1992), *International Financial Statistics Yearbook 1992,* New York, pp.396-9.

IMF, *Government Financial Statistics,* various issues 1977-92.

Industrial Policy Group (1970), *The Case for Overseas Direct Investment,* Industrial Policy Group, London, Paper Number 4.

Jeon, Yoong-Deok (1992), 'The Determinants of Korean Foreign Direct Investment in Manufacturing Industries', *Weltwirtschaftliches Archiv,* Vol. 128, No.3, pp.527-41.

Jorgenson, Dale W.(1963), 'Capital Theory and Investment Behaviour', *American Economic Review,* Vol.53, 1963, pp.247-59.

Jorgenson, Dale W.(1965), 'Anticipations and Investment Behaviour', in Duesenberry J., Kuh E., Fromm G. and Klein L. (ed.), *The Brookings Quarterly Econometric Model of the United States,* Rand-McNally, Chicago, pp.35-94.

Jorgenson, Dale W.(1967), 'The Theory of Investment Behaviour', in Ferber R.(ed.), *Determinants of Investment Behaviour,* National Bureau of Economic Research, Washington, pp.129-55.

Juhl, Paulgeorg (1979), 'On the Sectoral Patterns of West german Manufacturing Investment in Less Developing Countries: The Impact of Firm Size, Factor Intensities and Protection', *Weltwirtschaftliches Archiv,* Vol.115, pp.508-21.

Julius, Deanne (1990), *Global Companies and Public Policy: The Growing Challenge of Foreign Direct Investment,* Chatham House Papers, Pinter, London.

Kamath, Shyam J. (1990), 'Foreign Direct Investment in a Centrally Planned Developing Economy: The Chinese Case', *Economic Development and Cultural Change,* Chicago, No.2, pp.107-30.

Kelly, M.W. (1981), *Foreign Investment Evaluation Practice of U.S. Multinational Corporations,* UMI Research Press, Ann Arbor.

Kennedy, C. and Thirlwall, A. P. (1971), 'Foreign Capital, Domestic Savings and Economic Development: A Comment', *Bulletin of the Oxford*

346

Institute of Economics and Statistics, Vol.33, May, pp.135-8.

Kenneth, F.A.(1992), 'Foreign Direct Investment in Eastern Europe: Some Economic Consideration', paper prepared for the conference 'Transition in Eastern Europe', 26-29 February 1992, Cambridge, Massachusetts.

Kim, Seung Hee (1970), *Foreign Capital for Economic Development: A Korean Case Study,* Praeger special studies in international economics and development, New York.

Klein, Michael, and Rosengren, Eric (1991), 'Determinants of Foreign Direct Investment in the United States', Tufts University, Medford, Mass, memo.

Kobrin, Stephen Jay. (1976), 'The Environmental Determinants of Foreign Direct Manufacturing Investment: An Ex Post Empirical Analysis', *Journal of International Business Studies,* Vol.7, No.2, Newwark, pp.29-42.

Kobrin, Stephen Jay (1977), *Foreign Direct Investment, Industrialisation and Social Changes,* Jai Press, Connecticut.

Kohlhagen, Steven W. (1977), 'Exchange Rate Changes, Profitability, and Direct Foreign Investment', *The Southern Economic Journal,* Vol.44, Chapel Hill, pp.43-52.

Kojima, Kiyoshi (1978), *Direct Foreign Investment: A Japanese Model of Multinational Business Operation,* Croom Helm, London.

Kolde, E.J.(1968), *International Business Enterprise,* Prentice-Hall, Englewood Cliffs (N.J.).

Kraska, M. and Taira, K. (1974), 'Foreign Capital, Aid and Growth in Latin America', *The Developing Economies,* Vol.12, September, pp.214-28.

Kravis, I.B.(1970), 'Trade as a Handmaiden of Growth: Similarities between the Nineteenth and Twentieth Centuries', *Economic Journal,* Vol.80, pp.870-2.

Kueh, Y.Y. and Howe, Christopher (1982), "China's International Trade: Policy and Organisational Change and Their Place in the 'Economic Readjustment'", *The China Quarterly,* Vol.100, pp.811-48.

Kueh, Y.Y. (1992), 'Foreign Investment and Economic Change in China', in Special Issue: The Chinese Economy in the 1990s, *The China Quarterly,* September, Vol.132, pp.637-90.

Kwak, Sung Y. (1972), 'A Model of US Direct Investment Abroad: A Neoclassical Approach', *Western Economic Journal,* Vol.10, pp.376-83.

Lall, Sanjaya and Streeton, Paul (1977), *Foreign Investment, Transnational Corporations and Developing Countries,* MacMillan, London.

Lardy, Nicholas R. (1988), *China's Entry into the World Economy: Implications for Northeast Asia and the United States,* University Press

347

of America, New York and London.

Lebkowski, M. and Monkiewicz, J. (1986), 'Western Direct Investment in Centrally Planned Economies', *Journal of World Trade Law*, Vol.XX, No.6, November-December.

Leung, H.M., Thoburn, John T., Chau, Esther and Tang, S.H. (1991), 'Contractual Relations, Foreign Direct Investment, and Technology Transfer: The Case of China', *Journal of International Development*, Vol.3, No.3, pp.277-91.

Levcik, F. and Stankovsky, F. (1979), *Industrial Cooperation between East and West*, M. E. Sharpe, New York.

Levis, Mario. (1979), 'Does Political Instability in Developing Countries Affect Foreign Investment Flow: An Empirical Examination', *Management International Review*, Vol.19, No.3, pp.59-68.

Lim, D.(1983), 'Fiscal Incentives and Direct Foreign Investment in Less Developed Countries', *The Journal of Development Studies*, Vol.19, pp.207-12.

Linder, S.B. (1967), *Trade and Trade Policy for Development*, Pall Mall Press, London.

Lin, Lianlian (1992), *Risk Analysis of International Business with and within China*, unpublished PhD dissertation at the University of Texas at Austin.

Liu, Yuelun (1993), *China's Policy-making in the Context of the Reform (1976-1990): with a Focus on the Establishment of Economic Development Zones*, unpublished PhD dissertation at the University of Liverpool.

Lizondo, J.S. (1991), 'Foreign Direct Investment', in *Determinants and Systemic Consequences of International Capital Flows*, IMF Occasional Paper, Washington, D.C. No.77, pp.68-82.

Lo, T. W. C. (1989), *New Developments in China: Trade, International Cooperation with the West*, unpublished PhD thesis, City University.

Logue, Dennis E. and Willet, Thomas D. (1977), 'The Effects of Exchange Rate Adjustment on International Investment', in Peter B. Clark, Dennis E. Logue, Richard J. Sweeney (ed.), *The Effects of Exchange Rate Adjustments*, Federal Reserve Bank, Washington, pp.137-50.

Lorinczi, G.G.(1982), 'U.S. - Hungarian Joint Ventures', *International Business Lawyer*, Vol.10, No. 4, pp.113-9.

MacDougall, G.D.A. (1960), 'The Benefits and Costs of Private Investment from Abroad: A Theoretical Approach', *Economic Record*, Vol.36, pp.13-35.

Maizels, A.(1968), *Exports and Economic Growth of Developing Countries*, Cambridge University Press, Cambridge.

Majumdar, B.A. (1980), 'A Case Study of Industrial Organisation Theory of

Direct Foreign Investment', *Weltwirtschaftliches Archiv,* Vol.116, pp.353-64.

Marer, Paul (1987), *Can Joint Ventures in Hungary Serve as a 'Bridge' to the CMEA Market,* European University Institute, Italy.

Marie, Lavigne (1992) (ed.), *The Soviet Union and Eastern Europe in the Global Economy,* Cambridge University Press, Cambridge.

Marrese, Michael (1992), 'Hungary Emphasizes Foreign Partners', *RFE/RL Research Report,* Vol.1, No.17, 24 April 1992, pp.25-38.

Marsh, D. (1992), 'Political Worries Fail to Deter Western Investors', *Financial Times,* 12 October 1992, p.3.

McMillan, C. H. and Charles, D. P. St. (1973), *Joint Ventures in Eastern Europe: A Three-Country Comparison,* Canadian Economic Policy Committee and Howe Research Institute.

McMillan, C.H. (1991), 'Foreign Direct Investment Flows to the Soviet Union and Eastern Europe: Nature, Magnitude and International Implications', *Journal of Development Planning,* No.20.

Meier, G.M.(1989), *Leading Issues in Economic Development* (5th ed.), Oxford University Press, New York.

Michaely, M.(1977), 'Exports and Growth: An Investigation', *Journal of Development Economics,* Vol.4, No.1, pp.49-53.

Mihaly, Simai (1990), 'Foreign Direct Investment in the Hungarian Economy in 1990', Institute for World Economics, Hungarian Academy of Sciences, manuscript.

Miller, Robert R. (1993), 'Determinants of US Manufacturing Investment Abroad', *Finance and Development,* Vol. XXX, No.1, March, pp.16-18.

Mirza, Hafiz (1986), *Multinationals and the Growth of the Singapore Economy,* Croom Helm, London and Sydney.

Moore, Michael O. (1993), 'Determinants of German Manufacturing Direct Investment: 1980-1988', *Weltwirtschaftliches Archiv,* Vol.129, No.1, pp.120-37.

Moose, J. (1968), *U.S. Direct Investment Abroad in Manufacturing and Petroleum: A Recursive Model,* unpublished PhD thesis, Harvard University, Cambridge, Mass.

Morley, S.A.(1966), *American Corporate Investment Abroad since 1919,* unpublished PhD thesis, University of California, Berkeley.

Mosley, P., Hudson, J. and Horrell, S. (1987), *Aid, the Public Sector and the Market in Less Developed Countries,* Discussion Papers, No.9, IDPM: University of Manchester.

Mosley, P.(1987), *Overseas Aid: Its Defence and Reform,* Wheatsheaf Books, Brighton, Sussex.

Nelson-Horchler, Joani (1990), 'Hungary: Bridge Between East and West',

Industry Week, Vol.239, No.3, pp.40-42.

Newbery, David M.G.(1993), 'Transformation in Mature versus Emerging Economies: Why Has Hungary Been Less Successful than China?', paper presented at the International Symposium on the theoretical and Practical Issues of the Transition towards the Market Economy in China, held in China (Hainan) Institute of Reform and Development in Haikou, Hainan, China from 1-3 July 1993.

Newbould, G., Buckley, P. J. and Thurwell, J.(1978), *Going International, the Experience of Smaller Companies Overseas,* Associated Business Press, London.

Nigh, D.(1985), 'The Effect of Political Events on United States Direct Foreign Investment: A Pooled Time-Series Cross-Sectional Analysis', *Journal of International Business Studies,* Vol.16, pp.1-17.

O'Sullivan, Patrick J.(1993), 'An Assessment of Ireland's Export-Led Growth Strategy via Foreign Direct Investment: 1960-80', *Weltwirtschaftliches Archiv,* Vol.129, No. 1, pp.139-57.

OECD (1983), *Investment Incentives and Disincentives, and the International Investment Process,* OECD Publications, Paris.

OECD (1990), *How the OECD Sees JV Financing,* OECD Publication, Paris.

OECD (1992a), *OECD Economic Surveys Hungary 1991,* OECD Publication, Paris.

OECD (1992b), *International Financial Market,* OCED Publication, Paris, Vol.2.

OECD (1992, 1993), *OECD Economic Outlook,* Vol.52, December 1992, pp.201-2; and Vol.53, March 1993, pp.201-2, OECD Publications, Paris.

Ogata, Shijuro (1991), 'Role of Financial Institutions in East-West Joint Projects', *Management Japan,* Vol.24, No.1, pp.8-10.

Orr, Dale (1975), 'Foreign Control and Foreign Penetration in the Canadian Manufacturing Industries', unpublished paper, July 1975.

Papanek, G. F. (1972), 'The Effect of Aid and Other Resource Transfers on Savings and Growth in Less Developed Countries', *The Economic Journal,* Vol.82, September, pp.934-50.

Pearson, Lester B., et al.(1969), *Partners in Development: Report of the Commission on International Development,* Praeger, New York.

Pearson, Margaret M. (1991), *Joint Ventures in the People's Republic of China: The Control of Foreign Direct Investment under Socialism,* Princeton University Press, Princeton.

Petrochilos, George. A. (1989), *Foreign Direct Investment and the Development Process: The Case of Greece,* Avebury Publishing Company Ltd, Aldershot, Hong Kong and Singapore.

Piper, James R.(1971), 'How U.S. Firms Evaluate Foreign Investment

Opportunities', *MSU Business Topics,* Vol.19, East Lansing, pp.11-20.

Polk, Judd, Irene W. Meister and Lawrence A.Veit (1966), *U.S. Production Abroad and the Balance of Payments: A Survey of Corporate Investment Experience,* National Industrial Conference Board, Special Study, New York.

Pomfret, R. (1991), *Investing in China: Ten Years of the 'Open Door' Policy,* Harvester Wheatssheaf, Brighton.

Popkin, J. (1965), *Inter-firm Differences in Direct Investment Behaviour of U.S. Manufactures,* unpublished PhD thesis, University of Pennsylvania.

Price Waterhouse (1990), *Doing Business in Hungary,* Price Waterhouse, Budapest.

Ram, R.(1987), 'Exports and Economic Growth in Developing Countries: Evidence from Time-Series and Cross-Section Data', *Economic Development and Cultural Change,* Vol.36, No.1, pp.51-72.

Ravasz, K. (1974), 'Penetration of Foreign Markets through Cooperation and Joint Ventures', ESOMAR Congress.

Razvigorova, Evka and Gottfried Wolf-Laudon (1991) (ed.), *East-West Joint Ventures: the New Business Environment,* Blackwell, London.

Reuber, Grant L., H.Crokellel, M.Emersen and G.Gallias-Hamono (1973), *Private Foreign Investment in Development,* Clarendon Press, London.

Richman, B.(1976), 'Multinational Corporations and the Communist Nations', *Management International Review,* No.3.

Riedel, James (1975), 'The Nature and Determinants of Export-oriented Direct Foreign Investment in a Developing Country: A Case Study of Taiwan', *Weltwirtschaftliches Archiv,* Vol.111, pp.505-28.

Riley, Jonathan (1992), 'Eastern Europe and the Former Soviet Union: Recent Developments and Prospects', *Liverpool Macroeconomic Research Bulletin,* Vol. 2, pp.25-29.

Robinson, Harry J.(1961), *The Motivation and Flow of Private Foreign Investment,* Stanford Research Institute, Menlo Park.

Rollo, J. M. C. et al.(1990), *The New Eastern Europe: Western Responses,* Pinter, London.

Root, Franklin. (1978), *International Trade and Investment* (4th ed.), Cincinnati.

Rosser, Marina Vcherashnaya (1990), 'East-West Joint Ventures in the USSR and China: A Comparative Study', *International Journal of Social Economics,* Vol.17, No.12, pp.22-33.

Rugman, Alan M.(1975), 'Motives for Foreign Investment: The Market Imperfections and Risk Diversification Hypothesis', *Journal of World Trade Law,* Vol.9, pp.567-73.

Rugman, Alan M.(1976), 'Risk Reduction by International Diversification',

Journal of International Business Studies, Vol.7, pp.75-80.

Rugman, Alan M. (1977a), 'Risk, Direct Investment and International Diversification', *Weltwirtschaftliches Archiv,* Vol.113, pp.487-500.

Rugman, Alan M. (1977b) 'International Diversification by Financial and Direct Investment', *Journal of Economics and Business,* Vol.30.

Rugman, Alan M. (1978), 'Review of the International Operations of National Firms: A Study of Direct Foreign Investment by Stephen Hymer', *Journal of International Business Studies,* Vol.9, pp.103-4.

Rugman, Alan M.(1979), *International Diversification and the Multinational Enterprise,* Farnborough, Lexington.

Rugman, Alan M. (1980), 'Internalisation as a General Theory of Foreign Direct Investment: A Re-Appraisal of the Literature', *Weltwirtschaftliches Archiv,* Vol.116, pp.365-79.

Rugman, Alan M. (1981), *Inside the Multinationals: the Economics of Internal Markets,* Croom Helm, London.

Rugman, Alan M.,(1982) (ed.), *New Theories of the Multinationals Enterprise,* Croom Helm, London.

Sabirin, R.A. (1977), *American Foreign Investment in the European Common Market: Determinants and Consequences of Direct Foreign Investment in Manufacturing by U.S.,* unpublished PhD thesis, Claremont Graduate School.

Sachchamarga, Sukrita (1978), *The Effect of Exchange Rate Changes on Direct International Investment,* unpublished PhD thesis, Southern Methodist University.

Scaperlanda, Anthony E.(1974), *Trends, Composition and Determinants of United States Direct Investment in Canada,* U.S. Department of Commerce, Office of Foreign Direct Investment, Washington.

Scaperlanda, Anthony E. and Mauer, L. (1969), 'The Determinants on US Direct Foreign Investment in the EEC', *American Economic Review,* Vol. 59, pp.558-68.

Schliemann, Peter Uwe (1981), *The Strategy of British and German Direct Investors in Brazil,* Gower Publishing Co. Ltd, Hants.

Schmieding, Holger (1993), 'From Plan to Market: On the Nature of the Transformation Crisis', *Weltwirtschaftliches Archiv,* Vol.129, No.2, pp.217-53.

Schmitz, Andrew and Bieri, Jurg (1972), 'EEC Tariffs and U.S. Direct Investment', *European Economic Review,* Amsterdam, Vol. 3, pp.259-70.

Schollhammer, H. and Nigh, D.(1984), 'The Effect of Political Events on Foreign Direct Investments by German Multinational Corporations', *Management International Review,* Vol. 28, No.1, pp.18-40.

Schwartz, Rebecca H. (1976), *The Determinants of U.S. Direct Investment*

Abroad, unpublished PhD thesis, Texas Technical University.

Scott, Norman (1992), 'The Implications of the Transition for Foreign Trade and Investment', in *Macroeconomics of Transition in Eastern Europe, Oxford Review of Economic Policy,* Vol.8, No.1, pp.44-53.

Severn, Alan K.(1972), 'Investment and Financial Behaviour of American Direct Investors in Manufacturing', in Fritz Machlup, Walter S. Salant, Lori Tarshis (ed.), *International Mobility and Movement of Capital,* National Bureau of Economic Research, New York, pp.367-96.

Shen, Xiaofang (1990), 'A Decade of Direct Foreign Investment in China', *Problems of Communism,* March-April, pp.61-74.

Siegel, M.H.(1983), *Foreign Exchange Risk and Direct Foreign Investment,* Ann Arbor Publisher, Michigan.

Simai, Mihaly (1990), *Foreign Direct Investment and Joint Ventures in Hungary: Experience and Prospects,* Hungarian Scientific Council for World Economy, Budapest.

Situmeang, Baginda J.(1978), *The Environmental Correlates of Foreign Direct Investment with Reference to Southeast Asia,* unpublished PhD thesis, University of Oregon.

Solberg, Ronald L.(1992) (ed.), *Country-Risk Analysis: A Handbook,* Routledge, London.

State Economic System Reform Commission (1988), *A Collection of Planning Works on China's Economic System Reform 1979-87,* Academy of Central Committee of the China Communist Party Press, Beijing.

Steuer, M.D. et al (1971), *The Impact of Foreign Direct Investment on the United Kingdom,* Department of Trade and Industry, London.

Stevens, Guy V.G.(1969), 'U.S. Direct Manufacturing Investment to Latin America: Some Economic and Political Determinants', *Federal Reserve Bank A.I.D. Research Paper,* Washington.

Stevens, Guy V.G. (1974), 'The Determinants of Investment', in Dunning, John (ed.), *Economic Analysis and The Multinational Enterprise,* Allen and Unwin, London.

Stoneman, C. (1976), 'Foreign Capital and Economic Growth', *World Development,* Vol.3, January, pp.11-26.

Strange, Roger (1993), *Japanese Manufacturing Investment in Europe:Its Impacts on the UK Economy,* Routledge, London and New York.

Street, Paul (1971), 'Foreign Investment in the LDCs', *Columbia Journal of World Business,* Vol.5, May-June, pp.31-39.

Strikker, Dirk W. (1968), *The Role of Private Enterprise in Investment and Promotion of Exports in Developing Countries,* UNCTD, New York.

Sugar, Tamus (1986)(ed.), *Joint Ventures in Hungary,* Hungarian Chamber of Commerce, Budapest.

353

Swain, Nigel (1992), *Hungary: The Rise and Fall of Feasible Socialism*, Verso, London and New York.

Swansbrough, Robert H. (1972), 'The American Investor's View of Latin American Economic Nationalism', *Inter-American Economic Affairs*, Vol.26, No.3, Washington, pp.61-82.

Szalkai, I.(1989), 'The Elements of Policy for Rapidly Redressing the Hungarian Balance of Payments', *European Economy*, May 1989.

Szekely, Istvan, P. and Newbery, David M.G. (1993), (ed.), *Hungary: An Economy in Transition*, Macmillan, London.

Takahashi, Akira (1975), *Some Short-run Aspects of Direct Foreign Investment*, unpublished PhD thesis, University of Pittsburgh.

The Hungarian Observer (1992), Vol.1, p.16; Vol.2, p.8.

The Economic Intelligence Unit, *EIU Country Profile: Hungary*, various issues.

The Economist (1992), *Survey China*, 28 November, pp.1-22.

The World Bank (1986), *China: External Trade and Capital*, World Bank, Washington, D.C.

Thomsen, Stephen and Nicollaides, Phedon (1991), *The Evolution of Japanese Direct Investment in Europe: Death of Transistor Salesman*, Harvester Wheatsheaf, New York and London.

Thorelli, Hans B. (1966), 'The Multinational Corporations as a Change Agent', *The Southern Journal of Business*, Vol.3, July, pp.1-9.

Tiusanen, Tauno Juhani (1990), *Western Direct Investments in European CMEA Countries in the 1970s and 1980s*, unpublished PhD thesis, Glasgow University.

Tsai, Pan-Long (1991), 'Determinants of Foreign Direct Investment in Taiwan: An Alternative Approach with Time-Series Data', *World Development*, Vol.19, pp.275-85.

Tyler, W.G. (1981), 'Growth and Export Expansion in Developing Countries', *Journal of Development Economics*, Vol.9, No.1, pp.121-30.

U.S. Department of Commerce (1954), *Factors Limiting U.S. Investment Abroad, Part 2: Business Views on the U.S. Government's Role*, Washington.

U.S. National Industrial Conference Board (1969), *Obstacles and Incentives to Private Investment, 1967-68, Vol.I: Obstacles, Studies in Business Policy*, No.130, New York.

United Nations, *National Account Statistics, Part I*, various issues 1977-92, New York.

United Nations (1989), *Joint Ventures as a Form of International Economic Cooperation*, Taylor & Francis, New York.

UNCTC (1989), *Foreign Direct Investment and Transnational Corporations*

354

in Services, UN, New York.

Voivodas, C. S. (1973), 'Exports, Foreign Capital Inflows and Economic Growth', *Journal of International Economics,* Vol.3, pp.337-49.

Walia, Tirlochan S.(1976), *An Empirical Evaluation of Selected Theories of Foreign Direct Investment by U.S. Based Multinational Corporations,* unpublished PhD thesis, Graduate School of Business Administration, New York University.

Wang, Hong (1993), *China's Exports Since 1979,* Macmillan, London.

Wang, Zhen Quan (1993), 'Foreign Investment in Hungary: A Survey of Experience and Prospects', *Communist Economies and Economic Transformation,* Vol.5, No.2, pp.245-54.

Wang, Zhen Quan and Swain, Nigel (1995a), 'The Determinants of FDI in Transforming Economies: Empirical Evidence from Hungary and China', *Weltwirtschaftliches Archiv,* Vol.131, No.2.

Wang, Zhen Quan and Swain, Nigel (1995b), 'Determinants of Foreign Capital Inflows in Hungary and China: A Time-Series Approach', *Journal of International Development,* Vol.7, No.3.

Wilczynski, J. (1976), *The Multinational and East-West Relations: Towards Trans-ideological Collaboration,* Macmillan, London.

Winter, David (1990), *Eastern Bloc Joint Ventures: A Collection of Papers Delivered at the International Bar Association Regional Conference, Warsaw, Poland, 22-24 April 1990,* International Bar Association, Butterworth.

Wu, Zhenkun and Song, Zihe (1991), *Development Strategies of Open up the Economy,* Academy of Central Committee of the China Communist Party Press, Beijing.

Xue, Muqiao (1981), *China's Socialist Economy,* Foreign Language Press, Beijing.

Young, A.S.(1978), 'Factors Affecting Flows of Direct Foreign Investment to Southeast Asian Economies', *Journal of Philippine Development,* Vol.5, pp.75-96.

Young, David G. (1993), 'Foreign Direct Investment in Hungary', in Artisien, Patrick, et al (ed.), *Foreign Investment in Central & Eastern Europe,* St Martin's Press, London, pp.109-122.

Young, Stephen; Hood, Neil and Hamill, James (1988), *Foreign Multinationals and the British Economy: Impact and Policy,* Croom Helm, London and New York.

Zhao, Haiying (1992), *The Impact of Economic Structure on Long-term Growth,* unpublished PhD dissertation at University of Maryland, College Park.

Zhang, Fengbao (1988), *China: Macroeconomic Structure and Policy,* China Financial and Economic Press, Beijing.